THE
INVENTION OF
INTERNATIONAL RELATIONS
THEORY

THE
INVENTION OF
INTERNATIONAL
RELATIONS
THEORY

*Realism, the Rockefeller Foundation, and
the 1954 Conference on Theory*

EDITED BY NICOLAS GUILHOT

Columbia University Press   *New York*

Columbia University Press
Publishers Since 1893
New York   Chichester, West Sussex
Copyright © 2011 Columbia University Press
All rights reserved

Library of Congress Cataloging-in-Publication Data
The invention of international relations theory : realism, the Rockefeller
Foundation, and the 1954 Conference on Theory / edited by Nicolas
Guilhot.
        p. cm.
    Includes bibliographical references and index.
    ISBN 978-0-231-15266-2 (cloth : alk. paper)—ISBN 978-0-231-15267-9
(pbk. : alk. paper)—ISBN 978-0-231-52644-9 (e-book)
    1. International relations—Philosophy—History—20th century.
2. International relations—Philosophy—Congresses—History—20th
century.   3. International relations—Study and teaching (Higher)—United
States—History—20th century.   4. Rockefeller Foundation.   5. Realism—
History—20th century.   I. Guilhot, Nicolas, 1970–   II. Title.
    JZ1307.I58 2011
    327.101—dc22   2010022746

Columbia University Press books are printed
on permanent and durable acid-free paper.

This book is printed on paper with recycled content.
Printed in the United States of America

c 10 9 8 7 6 5 4 3 2 1
p 10 9 8 7 6 5 4 3 2 1

References to Internet Web sites (URLs) were accurate at the time of writing.
Neither the author nor Columbia University Press is responsible for URLs
that may have expired or changed since the manuscript was prepared.

CONTENTS

ACKNOWLEDGMENTS

THIS BOOK would not exist without the goodwill of many people who turned the long process of its production into a truly enjoyable one. At the Rockefeller Archive Center, Erwin Levold and Tom Rosenbaum have provided me with their invaluable help and their extensive knowledge of the foundation archives from the day I first set foot there. I would never have found my way to the documents reprinted in this volume without their kind assistance, nor would I have learned so much about the Rockefeller Foundation without the numerous conversations I have had the pleasure to have with them. It is thanks to passionate scholars such as Tom and Erwin and to a terrific staff that the Rockefeller Archive Center is, much more than an archive, a true intellectual community. I am also greatly indebted to Darwin Stapleton, who, upon hearing my plea in favor of the publication of some of the material in his custody, enthusiastically authorized me to proceed, and to James Allen Smith, who fully supported this decision and helped me implement it. All of this, in turn, would not have been possible without the generous grant-in-aid I was awarded by the Rockefeller Archive Center in 2005. The center also awarded me a conference grant in 2007 that allowed me to assemble the group of scholars whose contributions are included here. I would have never been able to organize this event without the help of Norine Hochman, who turned a logistical nightmare into the most seamless and pleasant experience.

The organization of the workshop and the subsequent editing process were also made possible by the early and enduring support of Craig Calhoun and the Social Science Research Council. For two years, the council and the Institute for Public Knowledge at NYU provided me with a home where I was able to carry this project forward. I hope this volume finds its place within the traditional interest for the history of the social sciences that is represented by the SSRC. The final stages of the edition of this volume were completed while I was associated with the CNRS center at NYU. I wish to thank its directors, Emilienne Baneth-Nouailhetas and Christophe Goddard, for their kind support.

At Columbia University Press, Peter Dimock was the first to see the value of this project and helped me turn it into a book. I hope it lives up to his expectations. While academics are usually convinced that they know what books are and tend to consider editors as mere printers, I am only too aware of how much I still have to learn—or rather unlearn—about books from such a teacher. I am also immensely grateful to Anne Routon, who took over this project and saw it to completion, and to Robert Fellman for the amazing job he did on the manuscript. I would like to thank two anonymous reviewers for their comments on a previous version of this book. Wiley-Blackwell kindly gave me permission to reprint here "The Realist Gambit," originally published in *International Political Sociology*. Finally, I would like to thank the contributors for the exciting discussions we had in Tarrytown.

THE
INVENTION OF
INTERNATIONAL RELATIONS
THEORY

INTRODUCTION

ONE DISCIPLINE, MANY HISTORIES

NICOLAS GUILHOT

C AN THERE be a science of politics? The development of political science as an academic discipline can hardly be considered a practical answer to this question; rather, it has provided the institutional space in which the question itself was formulated and debated. In the late 1940s and early 1950s, the possibility of developing a science of politics constituted an important subject of debate within the discipline. This discussion took a special significance when it came to the study of international relations, where it raised further questions about the more or less rational nature of international politics. It is in this context of disciplinary anxiety that the need to develop a distinct *theory* of international relations initially took shape, thus laying the foundations for the discipline we know as "IR." Whether such an intellectual endeavor could be construed as "science" was, at the time, "the subject of impassioned debate within the discipline" (Wight 2002, 23). For many participants in this debate, the question was to decide what, exactly, would this science be a science of—or, in other words, to decide upon the meaning of "politics." Was politics an existential dimension of human activity, of which power was a manifestation ultimately impervious to complete rationalization—what is also called "the political"? Did it refer instead to the bureaucratic realm of governmental activity and its administrative rationality? Or did it designate the pluralist interplay of social interests in the arena of public institutions? Many theorists of international relations, and certainly those who adhered to some form of "realism," tended to opt for the first case. The recent collapse of attempts at building a rational world order through legal institutions and the harrowing experiences of refugee scholars seemed to be convincing evidence of the impossibility of containing the political within the limits of rationality. Thinkers as diverse as Morgenthau and Niebuhr did not hesitate to equate politics with the manifestations of a deep-seated will to power constitutive of the human condition, an anthropological substratum of which rationality was but one, almost Nietzschean expression.

Yet, by the same token, such views made the articulation of a scientific discourse on politics highly problematic. Although early realists often pretended to expound "objective" and "scientific" laws of politics, such claims were often qualified by an acute awareness of the incommensurability between scientific reason and political action: the latter realized itself through complex and transient historical situations that the former could not entirely rationalize and comprehend. As Morgenthau succinctly captured it, "politics must be understood through reason, yet it is not in reason that it finds its model" (1946, 10). Scientific rationalism reduced politics to an ends-means calculation, but politics was first and foremost the capacity to decide between incommensurables. In line with the lesson imparted by Carl Schmitt, Morgenthau championed a vision of politics essentially as a decision—something that science could not approximate despite all its subsequent talk about "rational choice" (Frei 2001; Koskenniemi 2002; Scheuerman 1999). In this view, politics takes place precisely when there is no common measure—it becomes instead an existential affair of amity and enmity. By the same token, if politics is amenable to a rational understanding, this understanding can only take the form of prudential maxims, not of scientific principles—or, as we would say today, of an ethical discourse. Contrary to a widespread reputation of cynicism, early IR theorists located the "moral dilemmas of politics" at the center of their field. These dilemmas, along with the conviction that they could not receive a scientific solution, gave IR its distinctive intellectual style and set it apart from mainstream political science, at least for a while.

This book explores this founding moment, and it looks closer both at the process of discipline formation that took place at the time and at the obstacles blocking the path to a "science" of politics. In doing so, however, it differs in some important respects from conventional intellectual histories of the field, including the so-called revisionist historiography that has developed in the past ten years or so and is now in full swing. Intellectual histories deal essentially with more or less canonical sets of texts. More often than not, they provide a rationalized reconstruction of ideological formations that seem to respond to or flow from one another. Although this approach to intellectual history has been discredited by the work of the Cambridge school, it still informs a number of introductions to the discipline or readers in international relations theory.[1] In fact, the academic context itself often works as an incentive for over-rationalizing selected ideational threads that, once put together, allow for the orderly presentation of "doctrines" that can be *taught*. An artificial coherence is thus manufactured and projected into quite diverse intellectual sources. This, as Ole Wæver argues in this volume, is one of the reasons for presenting the discipline as a series of "great debates": this format belongs to the social and intellectual structure of the discipline. Such categories as "idealism," "realism," "neorealism," "constructivism," and so on introduce a measure of order into a material that is hardly univocal and employs different meanings in different contexts. They also entail an implicit evaluation, as they magnify some aspects of the works under consideration that fit the larger category they are supposed to fall into while downplaying or overlooking others. They may be ideal types, but they are hardly legitimate historical categories. Needless to say, such a rendition of the historical development of the discipline of international relations begged to be challenged. A closer reading of the texts is generally sufficient to expose the inadequacy of existing categories and to point at the justificatory functions they fulfill in the maintenance of certain disciplinary hierarchies. And indeed, the new "revisionist" history of international relations did not encounter much resistance as it started its foray into a discipline largely deprived of a genuine interest in history. In the process, it contributed to renewing its self-understanding and some of its core assumptions (the current revival of realism is discussed more specifically in the next section).

But even such histories have their own blind spots and limitations. Depending on the point of view they adopt, they can of course challenge the disciplinary canon, for instance, by exhuming less-known authors and vindicating their ideas, by emphasizing the arbitrary nature of the criteria that generated a canon in the first place, or by suggesting that the canonical texts were originally successful authorial moves made in opposition to other texts over which they prevailed. They can usefully challenge the historical narratives retrospectively generated by dominant traditions—the so-called Whig histories.[2] Yet even in their revisionist incarnation, such histories often remain framed as a system of relations among texts or ideas or among actors occupying a self-evident disciplinary field. They rarely move beyond the hermeneutic horizon of the officially constituted field, even though they reshuffle or revolutionize its internal organization. And in doing so, they may actually reinforce it by restoring its "true" identity.

This is even more so in the case of IR, where the current revisionist historiography is often meshed with a realist tradition that is central to the discipline. It is somewhat surprising that nobody has yet pointed out that

the critique of "Whig" history, which is now the *figure obligée* of any revisionist study of the discipline, was inaugurated by a British historian, Herbert
Butterfield, who played a major role in the transatlantic conversation of the
1940s that led to the academic institutionalization of IR as a discipline.
Butterfield's thesis started as a methodological discussion of a bias in historiography that, to put it in a nutshell, "praise[s] revolutions provided they
have been successful." The practitioners of this history organize their material in terms of "roots," "antecedents," "precursors" of the present, and other
"seminal" moments, and they fail to understand it in terms of its location
within an open-ended context rich with alternatives (Butterfield 1959, v, 12).
The result is a history that ratifies the triumph of one principle, tradition,
or set of ideas whose relevance is an artifact of the historian's concern with
the present. This teleological illusion is then projected retroactively into
the past and provides the backbone of historical narration. But the context
in which Butterfield's critique was formulated was also related to the repudiation of the liberal conception of history as progress, an important theme
in the emergence of realist thought. A member of the Rockefeller-sponsored
British Committee on International Relations, Butterfield became an intellectual reference and an interlocutor for the scholars (Morgenthau and
Niebuhr *in primis*) who sought to deprive liberalism of its confident view
of history as they preached realism on American campuses after 1945. The
revisionist historiography of IR thus shares a crucial strand of intellectual
DNA with realism itself, and it should come as no surprise that the former
often serves the purpose of rediscovering the richness and complexity of
the latter. This should be taken as a reminder that revisionist histories operate as agents for redistributing authority within a field. As a contributor
to this volume has shown elsewhere in the case of the discipline of economics, the rewriting of Whig histories and the rediscovery of the founding fathers usually coincide with important shifts in both knowledge and policy
(Mirowski 2004, 43). But this redistribution of authority more often than
not takes the form of a restoration. Such histories often call for a "return
to" the original insights that are supposed to define the field but have been
lost or eroded over time. That such returns to the fundamentals are attempts
at consolidating a present authority is something that an old realist like
Machiavelli knew perfectly: *"a vòlere che una sètta o una republica viva
lungamente, è necessario ritirarla spesso verso il suo principio."*[3] In order to
situate this volume in the current effervescence of revisionist literature, it
is useful to understand what is really at stake in the current rediscovery of
realism by asking the old question: *cui bono?*

REALISM IS THE NEW IDEALISM

The remarkable surge in disciplinary history and the renewed interest in early realism cannot be disentangled from each other and must be analyzed jointly. If the present rewriting of disciplinary canons may be seen as part of a more general reflexive mood that has swept the social sciences of late, the rediscovery of classical realism must also be understood in the context of the crisis of the ideologies that have sustained recent U.S. foreign policy and the lack of an alternative vision. The recent wave of literature on Hans Morgenthau and on realism cannot be dissociated from an attempt at reviving a specific version of realism in order to emphasize its relevance for contemporary American politics.[4] The time seems ripe for this resurgence, because realism provides an effective language for criticizing the moral crusades of neoconservatives and the aggressive idealism of militarized democracy promotion (Williams 2007a). As these grandiose dreams of worldwide democratization ended up in the brutish and miserable cul-de-sac of besieged green zones, the stage was set for a rediscovery of the founding fathers of realism, whose wisdom about politics and suspicion vis-à-vis moral crusades seemed vindicated. Suddenly, it was hip again to read Niebuhr or Morgenthau.

Yet this new vogue of realism is not simply backtracking to some political or ideological *status quo ante* in the discipline. The realism that is being rediscovered has nothing to do with formalistic "neorealism" or with the rational-choice methodologies developed in security studies, and it certainly does not aim at ridding the field of moral considerations—on the contrary. It goes back to the philosophical, quasi-theological reflections of the immediate postwar years debated within a loose network of academics, diplomats, journalists, and denizens of the philanthropic foundations. As Robert Jervis observes in this volume, it was the product of an era "in which the academic division of labor had not gone as far as it has today." It is a "prescientific" or literary realism that is back in fashion today. What is the purpose, then, of the current exercises in rehabilitation?

For years if not decades, cohorts of students schooled in IR have been taught a cursory and highly stylized version of realism, through the lens of a discipline more concerned with the retrospective construction of a tradition of "great debates" between simplistic constructs fit for sophomoric consumption than with a historical understanding of its own roots.[5] Often reduced to abstract principles emphasizing the material dimensions of power and interest as well as the cold-blooded calculations of survival in the international arena, realism was widely considered as "the antithesis of ethical reflection," as Duncan Bell (2008b, 2) puts it, both within and outside the field of IR. This is precisely the narrative that is being revised in the current historiography, which tells quite another story: by reaching back to the early realism of the postwar years, it is able to suggest that realism is at heart a moral discourse.[6] It reads Morgenthau, Niebuhr, Wolfers, and many others as classical moralists, and in many ways it is justified in doing so. It catches the constant concern of these authors with the limits of reason and the need for ethical ratiocination or prudence. The recent publication of Morgenthau's New School lectures on Aristotle, for instance, very much belongs to this trend (Lang 2004). It also rediscovers the centrality of values in postwar intellectual debates, and in particular the Christian revival in some intellectual circles eager to find a rational ground for politics while moving away from value relativism. And in the context of a recent engagement of IR theory with religion, it should come as no surprise that the theological roots of realism are also coming to light.[7] In this new literature, realism is conflated to such an extent with its normative and ethical dimensions that it is now legitimate to ask whether Morgenthau, so concerned with morality, could really have been a "realist" (Scheuerman 2007).

Yet such a rendition of post-1945 realism reflects a lost strand of political theory as much as the ideological needs of the present time. The strong emphasis on the moral component of realist discourse should make us sensitive to the rehabilitative functions that the new historiography of IR may have, willingly or not, in the present context. Michael Williams is right to insist on the ambiguous nature of realism, especially in its current revival (Williams 2007a, 228). It is not yet clear whether the taunting of the moral dimension of realism serves the purpose of justifying it as an alternative to neoconservatism that is able to challenge the latter *also* on moral grounds, or whether it contributes instead to the emergence of a synthesis between the neoconservative emphasis on a moral foreign policy and the sober, realist assessment of its necessary limitations—a synthesis that seems to garner consent among the Washington establishment and in such ideological outlets as *The American Interest*. The born-again realists of today are, almost by definition, unrepentant idealists. In this respect, the emphasis laid by postwar realists on the ethical nature of prudence and on the moral dimension of the national interest, that is, on the necessarily imperfect effectuation of morality within the limits of power,[8] seems to provide a perfect justification for a policy of selective and limited interventionism that will not relinquish the moralistic tones of the past decades. Moreover, in the context of the "global war on terror," occupying the moral ground is part of the strategy, even from the most "realist" point of view. But as this strategy has failed, one may wonder whether today's reclaimed realism will become the official ideology of a declining empire, just as early realism provided a nascent one with its worldview. Maybe . . . but whatever the outcome of this transition, it is hard not to discern, in all this revisionist unrest, a new orthodoxy in the making.

These considerations are not meant to question the legitimacy or accuracy of current disciplinary history, which has generated a wealth of new and interesting insights into the development of IR, not a small feat in a discipline traditionally resistant to genuine historicization. But it is useful to keep in mind that historiography is no less situated within specific social and political contexts than its own subject matters. It is with this caveat that this volume intends to contribute to the current discussion of early realism, but in what is perhaps a more sober and, at times, more critical approach than most contemporary reassessments.

A DIFFERENT HISTORY OF IR THEORY

While the important contribution of revisionist historiography is acknowledged, the approach followed here differs in several respects. First, it is not so much concerned with the internal history of the discipline per se as with the set of upstream decisions, external resources, and processes of differentiation initiated in adjacent fields that created a space where IR could exist as a distinct disciplinary project. It is not trying to reinterpret the canon of IR theory or suggest that its composition should be revised; rather, it seeks to understand how certain texts came to be considered as forming a canon distinct from those of international law or political science. In other words, this approach does not consider the field of IR as given but tries instead to step back and trace some of its formative stages.

This slight difference in focus is accompanied by a difference in object: the contributions in this volume do not deal primarily with classical IR texts, although they obviously draw abundantly on them. They revolve instead around an altogether different historical material: the transcript of a meeting organized by the Rockefeller Foundation in May 1954, for the purpose of discussing "the possibility, nature and limits of theory in international relations" and the concrete steps that could encourage "theoretical scholarship in international politics." This meeting is to my knowledge the first that ever stemmed from an explicit *decision* to carve out a disciplinary space for IR by grounding it in an underlying theory, a theory at that point still undefined but clearly perceived as necessary if IR was to be autonomous from other disciplinary trends (in fact, the meeting was convened in order to flesh out this decision) and no longer what Waldermar Gurian once called a "hodgepodge" of disciplinary influences ranging from geography to economics and political science. All previous discussions of the field were surveys of work on international relations being done across a wide range of disciplines, such as the 1946 conferences organized by the Council on Foreign Relations, or prewar compendiums of research in international politics. But in 1953, the Rockefeller Foundation's official policy consisted in promoting the development of "theory" as a crucial component of its efforts to reshape the field. Of course, there was previously something like a "field" of IR, if one means that "international relations" was already considered to be a subfield of political science as early as 1904, with the founding of the American Political Science Association, or that the first chair in international relations was created at the University of Aberystwyth in 1919. But talking about a "field" in such cases only refers to a multifarious body of works loosely related to one another by a common theme or a focus on things international and often grounded in different traditions. This, in fact, is very much what the Rockefeller Foundation and the participants it convened for the 1954 conference were intent on changing. In the United States at least, but arguably elsewhere too, there was no coherent set of methods, no stable set of research institutions functioning as a coherent and relatively autonomous space organized around the development of common standards for the study of international affairs. A disciplinary field is very much a field in the sense that Pierre Bourdieu gave this notion: a relatively autonomous and distinct social (and, in this case, also intellectual) space, organized according to its own rules, recognizing specific resources as legitimate, and structured along differentiated institutional or individual positions (Bourdieu 1976, 1997). As long as the study of international affairs was divided between geography, diplomatic history, and international law, not to mention the ill-defined disciplinary commons known as "area studies," IR simply could not exist independently. Developing a distinct "theory" of IR was indeed the very first step in a deliberate effort to establish its autonomy vis-à-vis neighboring disciplines.

The 1954 conference and the long conversation that preceded it are the first instance in which IR is apprehended as potentially constituting a systematic field:[9] not only were the participants aware that a proprietary "theory" was necessary if they wanted to insulate themselves from the trends affecting political science in general and have control over a small swathe of the discipline, but during the previous years the Rockefeller Foundation had commissioned various reports and surveys that carefully mapped out the various institutional, bibliographic, financial, and educational resources that could contribute to the emergence of the new field. Under the leadership of Kenneth W. Thompson, lists of scholars were drawn, potential institutional bases were carefully selected, existing publishing outlets were reviewed, personnel needs were assessed, curriculum structures were discussed, and the scholarly literature deemed relevant was specified. Would the new theory build upon work done at Yale and Princeton or upon the vision developed at Chicago and Columbia? In fact, the various reports on these subjects amount to nothing less than a thorough empirical sociology of the field to be: oppositions between different groups of scholars were duly noted, such as the divide between "behavioralists" and those more oriented toward political theory; differences between institutions in terms of financial resources or access to policy institutions were duly analyzed. A Bourdieuian sociologist would have hardly done better!

Compared to previous efforts at portraying the state of the art in the study of IR, therefore, the 1954 conference was a wholly different kettle of fish, since it was organized by an institution whose business was precisely the creation of new disciplinary fields, through a combination of institutional and individual grants, the creation of "invisible colleges" of like-minded scholars, and the coupling of research and policy. Whether in industrial relations, economics, physics, or sociology, the Rockefeller Foundation had already an extensive record of scientific planning. By the time it convened a small and discrete gathering in Washington, the foundation had explicitly decided to promote the development of IR theory and to demarcate the field from the adjacent domains of law, history, and even political science, after extensive internal and external discussions.

The 1954 conference was also convened to think about the relevant strategies for institutionalizing the field beyond the initial impetus given by the foundation and a bunch of senior scholars. Partly, this was a legitimate concern in the perspective of building a more permanent field and a consequence of the perceived need for a better training of foreign-policy personnel. But there was also another reason, related to the exotic nature of IR theory in the postwar years. The issue of teaching and transmission was important, as it would ensure the routinization of the original Germanic charisma characterizing much social and political theory at the time.[10] Whether in international relations, law, or political theory, the foundation sought to acclimatize this intellectual strand to the academic conditions prevailing on U.S. soil. Despite all their prestige, the Morgenthaus, the Herzes, the Kelsens, and many others still remained institutionally isolated in the 1940s and 1950s. They were seen as interesting but idiosyncratic think-ers in a land where pragmatism and empiricism still bore sway. If nobody could adopt, extend, and apply their insights, this intellectual strand would eventually disappear—a loss all the more regrettable since this Teutonic wisdom, as we shall see, seemed to solve a number of cultural and political conundrums afflicting a liberal democracy trying to cope with the neces-sity of exercising global hegemony. It provided a quasi-ontological notion of sovereignty and of the state that removed a number of obstacles blocking the way to such hegemony. In some minds, it seemed to constitute the rite of passage for a country coming of age and ready to be revealed the ancient secrets of statecraft and power politics. Writing to Joseph Willits in May 1947, Arnold Toynbee, the Samuel Huntington of those times, ever so sen-sitive to the rise and fall of civilizations, warned that

> an awkward situation for all of us has been produced by the cumulative effect of the two World Wars, which have so accelerated the course of events that a transfer of power which might otherwise have taken as long as a century to work itself out has been telescoped into the short span of a single life-time. History has now brought responsibilities to America without having given her time to prepare herself for them psychologically. But it would be danger-ous if America's psychological unpreparedness to assume responsibilities, in combination with the obvious inability of Great Britain, France, Belgium and the Netherlands to continue to carry the whole of their previous responsi-bilities, were to produce a kind of political vacuum.[11]

A rapid process of *Bildung*, however, under the supervision of German pro-fessors, would remedy this and ensure an orderly transition ushering Amer-ica into its imperial age.

The thrust of the Rockefeller Foundation's efforts to develop a field of IR after 1945 was indeed the need to train policy personnel for the State De-partment and other policy institutions. In the short term, therefore, the con-ference was meant to unfold into a regular seminar on theory, the purpose of which was the "assistance to the growth of young men in the field."[12] The seminar would bring such young researchers in contact with "five or six major scholars," and the discussion thus generated "might serve to inspire the creation of a continuing committee in the theory of international poli-tics drawn perhaps from the younger men who might build on the work of the original group."[13]

What makes the 1954 conference on international politics remarkable is not only its agenda but also its attendees. Behind closed doors and without a public audience, Dean Rusk, then the president of the Rockefeller Foundation, and Kenneth W. Thompson, who had organized this event in his capacity as consultant for international relations within the foundation's Division for Social Science, presided over a most unusual gathering of intellectual and political luminaries. Hans J. Morgenthau, Reinhold Niebuhr, Paul Nitze, William T. R. Fox, Walter Lippmann, Arnold Wolfers, Dorothy Fosdick, James Reston, and Don K. Price sat for two days, hashing out their opinions about what IR theory should be and going over the practical minutiae of its academic institutionalization. George Kennan, Herbert Butterfield, and Raymond Aron were invited but unable to attend because of other commitments, although Kennan sent a paper addressing some of these issues. The transcript of this two-day session, as well as the short position papers on what IR theory should be, are reproduced in this volume and made public for the first time since they entered the carefully monitored vaults of the Rockefeller Archive Center several decades ago.

"LITTLE UNANIMITY ON POINTS OF DETAIL . . . "

Surely, such a gathering of eminent minds around such an agenda must have triggered a major theoretical breakthrough. No doubt the august words spoken back then explain the impressive career and the high status that the discipline achieved thereafter—or do they? Alas, the reader who is already leafing feverishly through the transcript in the hope of discovering the *ultima ratio* of IR theory is bound to remain very disappointed! For instead of a seminal statement setting the nascent discipline on a triumphal scientific course—or instead of an academic conspiracy masterminded by a bunch of conjurors with the help of well-connected philanthropists and a couple of State Department retirees—what there is instead is fifty pages of unfocused discussion, misunderstandings, equivocal notions, disagreements about fundamental concepts, and much soul searching that remains inconclusive down to the very end, notwithstanding the occasional witticism. *Sic transit scientia inter gentes rerum gestarum . . .*

But then, part of the frustration experienced by our reader longing to be revealed the true origin of IR may be imputed to the longing itself. The idea that history can unveil an absolute *incipit*, a fixed point from which a subsequent cascade of events would then flow, is certainly one of the most resilient illusions generated by the historical mode of inquiry itself. Genealogy, as Michel Foucault has shown, is not the elusive quest for an origin; it consists in tracing a process whereby a number of disparate elements gradually recombine to behave as a system and generate patterned effects (Foucault 2001 [1971]). And surely the field of IR is in many respects an eclectic assemblage of different traditions, interests, institutional languages, and, not least, individuals who, in the mid-1950s, converged into a single disciplinary project. There is no reason why this convergence should have taken place smoothly, on the basis of a clear, self-evident, and rational foundation easily translatable into a common language, and the 1954 conference certainly reflects these difficulties. Many notions that have since become part and parcel of a standardized disciplinary lexicon—"realism," "interest," "morality," and so on—were still in flux, ill defined, and contested. Also, there were no "IR scholars" yet and no curriculum to train them, but only jurists, political scientists, philosophers, theologians, journalists, and diplomats trying to carve out a common intellectual ground and a modicum of agreement. Not to mention the fact that many among these scholars were recent immigrants who attached different meanings to many important notions. Thus, a lot of what was said back in 1954 was lost in translation: building a *theory* of international relations may have meant doing "science" by trying to emulate physics for some participants, especially those, like Wolfers, somewhat attracted by the promises of behavioral methods, while others probably saw it as a more spiritual form of *Wissenschaft*, which is obviously not the same thing. The different understandings of politics and policy making also played a role in creating confusion. Is this enough to convince our reader that this document is worthy of attention? Probably not. Our reader may now wonder what he or she can possibly learn from such an inchoate discussion.

Well, once again, our reader may be looking in the wrong direction, as he or she searches in vain for some clear definition of what IR theory is or a statement of purpose of the new discipline. For if there is nothing of this kind in the document, the 1954 conference nevertheless remains the first instance in which IR is discussed as a distinct theoretical project—a meeting of separatists of sorts, opening the way for disciplinary independence. It therefore deserves full attention and scrutiny. And the first lesson we can draw from it is perhaps that it contains no clear statement of what IR theory is because there is *no such thing as IR theory, only an institutional decision to generate an autonomous disciplinary subspace inhabited by a specific group of scholars.* Here, the reaction of our reader has a real heuristic value: one can only take note of the intellectual paucity of the foundations upon which the discipline was erected and be flabbergasted by the triumphant course of its subsequent career.[14] As Morgenthau candidly observed in the course of the discussions, IR theory is not so much about theory as it is about the limits of theory.[15] What can we learn from that?

First, it suggests that the raison d'être of IR is not theoretical but primarily institutional and political. It is the academic conditions and in particular the strength of liberalism, scientific rationalism, and the normative approach to international law in the United States—not some intrinsic epistemological difference—that explain why realism did not find a space within existing disciplinary structures and had to develop along a separate path. While in other contexts, like Germany, realism developed as a conservative critique of liberal constitutionalism that still remained rooted in the field of jurisprudence (*vide* Carl Schmitt), it could not take roots within a U.S. legal profession wedded to Wilsonianism and rationalism, all the more since the latter was immune to the kind of German realism that had become so unfashionable after 1933. As a result, as Martti Koskenniemi observes, international lawyers "continuing to construct their normative systems through the thinnest sociological generalizations . . . have been compelled to witness the growth of a neighboring discipline—'international relations'—that has incorporated Schmittian insights as part of its professional identity" (2002, 423–424). And for many scholars of international law from Central Europe coming to the United States, not only did penetrating the closed academic ranks of gentile legal scholarship prove quite difficult, but the dire state of international law after 1945 made this option hardly appealing from an intellectual point of view. It is only as a consequence of the nature and organization of legal studies in the United States (and not because of some intrinsic intellectual necessity) that the realist critique of international law had to carve out its own space in order to be heard. But IR theory nevertheless remained one specific answer to the general problem that scientific administrators and their allies within academia were confronted with after 1945: reconstructing the study of law on the basis of sociological—that is, "realist"—rather than normative foundations.

At the Rockefeller Foundation, this problem was clearly identified by Kenneth Thompson, who oversaw the organization of IR theory as part of a program on legal and political theory. In 1952, he wrote:

in the same way that American government has proceeded from the study of the American Constitution and the basic law to the examination of practical politics and pressure groups, so international studies became concerned with the study of trends in the foreign policies of separate nation-states. . . . Instead of beginning with the *international* structure and society, the new line of inquiry has emphasized the urgency of examining *national* goals and objectives as a logical point of departure.

(THOMPSON 1952, 439–440)

While IR theory was the answer to the problem of articulating law and sociology at the international level, the introduction of legal realism in the study of municipal law would be a longer process, which was also promoted under the umbrella of the program in Legal and Political Philosophy at the Rockefeller Foundation and culminating in the creation of the Law & Society Association in 1964 (Garth 2000).

In that sense, the 1954 conference has further implications for our understanding of discipline history. It suggests that a disciplinary landscape does not always need robust theoretical foundations in order to flourish and that its development may be better explained by a range of external factors—institutional support, availability of funding, critical developments within adjacent fields, alliances with outside stakeholders such as policymakers or bureaucrats, and a wealth of other issues that are too often absent from conventional intellectual histories. In the case at hand, the Rockefeller Foundation acted as the main broker procuring these resources and the main external organizer involved in shaping an academic space for the development of IR. The organizational forces behind such intellectual formations are all the more important since these intellectual fields often do not have a strong internal coherence and find it instead in the project that sustains them and that they are supposed to serve.

Second, taking into account all the groundwork performed upstream of the actual development of IR as a discipline may lead us to reconsider a number of taken-for-granted assumptions or at least to apprehend differently its subsequent unfolding. This is probably where the contrast with conventional intellectual histories is the starkest. While the latter may apprehend a discipline essentially as a corpus of texts, the former approach may help us understand how this corpus was constituted in the first place. Once again, intellectual histories tend to produce a coherence that is then transformed into a property of the corpus of intellectual productions under scrutiny, the field being then seen as a rational "dialogue" or "conversation" between different works or authors—but they often fail to gauge the extent to which such a conversation may be staged, when "staging conversations" falls precisely within the line of business and the discrete power of philanthropic foundations funding various academic ventures. Turning the spotlights from the disciplinary stage to the backstage logistics suddenly makes visible the work of identification, classification, and promotion that is involved in the constitution of disciplinary canons. We readily accept the special significance of certain texts within a discipline, but we rarely question the mechanisms that make them significant in the first place. How is the authority of texts adjudicated? For sure, they have intrinsic virtues— but these need to be discovered and acknowledged by specialized publics for these works to acquire some sort of canonical authority. This is to say that texts have authority only within specific interpretive contexts, and the shape and the extent of these contexts is of critical importance. There is not the slightest doubt that Morgenthau's works, for instance, are crucial for the self-understanding of the discipline of IR. At the same time, this importance is dependent upon a certain number of preconditions, in particular upon the *separation* of IR theory from other strands of literature. Thus, for anybody who takes the time to read Schmitt or Meinecke, Morgenthau may not appear as such an original thinker after all[16]—but then Schmitt or Meinecke are not taught in IR courses, which in part explains the position occupied by Morgenthau. Hence the importance of such events as the 1954 conference, which contributed to creating a space in which his works would not only find a consistent and dedicated readership but appear as intellectual pillars of a new discipline and be read within a self-contained space of reception, thus shaping their subsequent literary and academic career. Another reason why such archival material may be so illuminating is that it often redistributes the relative importance of the different actors involved: while Kenneth Thompson is arguably a marginal figure in the theoretical canon of IR (who ever had to read Thompson in an IR course?), the documents reproduced here—as well as many others that are not— reveal him as a central organizer of the entire field and probably Morgenthau's most talented impresario. Indeed, Thompson almost singlehandedly oversaw the international program of the foundation. One might reasonably ask whether, had he not played a crucial role within the Rockefeller Foundation for several decades, the field of IR would be the same, or whether it would exist at all. One might equally ask whether, in Thompson's absence, Morgenthau would have escaped from the institutional marginality that characterized his first years in the United States and gained the influence he later had.[17] Ultimately, we may learn as much about the history of IR from such garbled discussions as the 1954 conference as from reading the "classical" works in the discipline.

It is therefore an altogether different intellectual history that is attempted here, one that seeks to relate the official history of IR to its more obscure origins rather than to a genealogy of Great Ancestors. In other words, one might say in Platonic terms that it tries to move from the "clear sky of eternal ideas," which usually shines over disciplinary history, to the chiaroscuro of the cave where the actual action takes place. It is surprising that such documents are so rarely exploited. All academics have participated in gatherings similar to the 1954 meeting, where budget constraints, political decisions, promotion opportunities, off-the-cuff ideas, and institutional strategies are coated with the gloss of intellectual necessity and scientific progress. Yet academics write disciplinary history as if such meetings never take place or have any epistemic effects. The denizens of the cave seem indeed quite reluctant to talk about their natural habitat, and they much prefer to have others believe that they inhabit a region of pristine ideas and celestial doctrines. This book does not take their word for it and is very much about what happens inside the grotto of discipline formation, rather than in the skies of intellectual history. Maybe our reader will now consider that the transcript is interesting after all, especially if it looks like an exercise in spelunking! But before descending into the cave, a few words about the historical context of the 1954 conference are in order.

FROM SOCIAL SCIENCE TO ANTISCIENCE: THE SSRC COMMITTEE ON INTERNATIONAL RELATIONS EXPERIMENT AND THE ROCKEFELLER BID FOR IR

The Rockefeller-sponsored conference on international relations held in 1954 was not the first of its kind. It differed from the numerous meetings convened since 1945 in order to map out and rethink the field, as the 1954 conference sought to ground the field in a theory and institutionalize it. Most of these previous meetings were essentially survey exercises, taking stock of the new international situation and reassessing accordingly the priorities in the study of international affairs. In 1948, however, the Social Science Research Council established a stable "Committee on International Relations" that worked toward a greater integration of the field into the social sciences. This important if short-lived precedent deserves special scrutiny because it charted what could have been an alternative direction for IR. Had this attempt not failed, leaving the field in abeyance and allowing the Rockefeller group to develop its own perspective, IR would probably have evolved into an entirely different discipline.

The original idea for the SSRC committee was debated in April 1948 during a meeting at Yale University convened by Frederick Dunn after initial discussions with Pendleton Herring, the president of the SSRC. The meeting was attended by Quincy Wright, who taught international law at Chicago, where he was in many ways Morgenthau's rival; Grayson Kirk, a political-science professor at Columbia and the author of an important report on the state of the field in the late 1940s; the liberal economist and former State Department employee Leo Pasvolsky, from the Brookings Institution; Malcolm Davis of the Carnegie Endowment for International Peace; William Fox; and the Harvard political scientist Rupert Emerson. The purpose of this gathering was "to consider the advisability of establishing a committee on international relations under the auspices of SSRC" that would "map the whole area of research in international relations, and then suggest the subjects on which research should be concentrated in relation to both the need of the Department of State *and to a philosophical and theoretical attitude toward international relations which the Committee itself would have to define.*"[18] The proposal was met with enthusiasm by the participants, and the committee was eventually established on July 23, 1948, with Dunn as its chairman. Its purpose was to foster the integration of the field of international relations around issues that the committee deemed important. Its primary tasks were to establish regular contacts between directors of existing research institutions to share information about current research and map the gaps in research coverage. But the committee also exercised a steering role, as its mandate was not confined to drawing up lists of what was being and should be done across U.S. campuses: indeed, as the SSRC made clear, "an undiscriminating and extremely comprehensive list would probably offer little guidance." The committee was thus expected to identify priorities and needs and to formulate what it believed were projects deserving "a high priority."[19] More significantly, the proposal set forth by Dunn and Herring made it clear that, in fulfilling its different functions, the committee would "aid in bringing the analytical skills of all the social sciences to bear upon the problems of international relations."[20]

If the initial membership included mostly scholars involved in the postwar rethinking of international relations, it was soon enlarged to include social scientists. Invitations to join were extended to James W. Angell, the economist from Columbia; the Harvard anthropologist Clyde Kluckhohn; and the social psychologist Dorwin Cartwright, who had just overseen the move of his MIT-based Research Center for Group Dynamics to the newly founded Institute for Social Research at the University of Michigan. The final composition of the committee was indicative of the whole philosophy of the project, which hoped to have the social sciences inform the study of international affairs by creating a dialogue between IR scholars and social scientists. The participation of Kluckhohn and Cartwright, in particular, suggests that the committee placed high hopes in the scientific contribution of behavioralism in solving some of the pressing issues of the day. Kluckhohn was starting his work on "value orientation" and how it affected intergroup relations; Cartwright was pioneering the psychological study of group dynamics. This interest in the behavioral and psychological aspects of international relations was further bolstered in 1950, when Gabriel Almond saw an opportunity to do "research in political behavior on the international level," focusing on the structure of public opinion and in particular on the role of "opinion elites."[21] Dunn was enthused by the project, which he thought could lead to a summer study group on the "attentive public," opinion elites, and foreign affairs. Even though it seems that the committee did little more than express its interest in the project, that it supported this kind of research agenda is highly revealing of its general orientation. Although the interwar reliance on democracy and public opinion to strengthen international law had failed, the social sciences could provide effective tools for rational control over a public opinion that, as recent events had demonstrated, was volatile and potentially dangerous. The focus on opinion elites rather than general public opinion in Almond's project is telling of the crisis of confidence and anxiety that plagued postwar liberalism and its vision of modernity,[22] but it also speaks to the hopes invested in the social sciences as the solution to the problem of international understanding.

Needless to say, the task of the committee was daunting. It brought together exponents of very different intellectual strands in the naïve expectation that their interactions would somehow produce a theoretical synthesis. It met irregularly, first in October 1948, then in May 1949. The result of the discussions it held on emerging trends in IR was summarized in "The Present Course of International Relations Research," an article that Dunn published in *World Politics* in October 1949. The article has all the attributes of a committee work: it is an exercise in diplomatic synthesis between diverging research orientations, reflecting a committee composition rather than a sound intellectual agenda. While Dunn acknowledged that the field was characterized by "a movement from reform to realism," it also pointed at the contribution of the social sciences to the understanding of the forces shaping political behavior—in particular sociology, anthropology, psychology, and psychoanalysis (Dunn 1949, 88). A "considerable degree of division of labor" was therefore "inescapable" in the study of international relations. The problem, however, was that the proper proportions of this division of labor were far from clear. Dunn oscillated between calls for collaboration between students of international politics and behavioral social scientists and the advocacy of a unifying conceptual scheme devised by scholars proficient in both domains. In the meantime, he foresaw "cooperative research adventures" and remained aware of the difficulties of institutionalizing such cooperation: "It has often been demonstrated that picking pieces of knowledge from various disciplines and cooking them together in one dish does not necessarily make a good pie" (89). Finally, reflecting on the role played on the committee by Kluckhohn and Cartwright, Dunn emphasized the importance of "value analysis," not in the sense of a moral or ethical reflection (as was the case with the scholars involved with the Rockefeller-sponsored 1954 conference) but as something that could be studied with the tools provided by cutting-edge empirical social-science research. Ultimately, the SSRC Committee on International Relations was promoting an interdisciplinary vision of the field, where the division of labor between specialists of various disciplines was not really conducive to theory building or disciplinary autonomy.

The committee disbanded in July 1950, after Dunn was designated to represent the SSRC at the national commission to UNESCO. But the reasons for the early termination of its activities were obviously deeply seated. It was built on two different constituencies: a group of IR scholars (Fox, Wright, Earle) and a group of social scientists representing what would soon be labeled "behavioralism." Their respective perspectives on how to understand and analyze international politics did not sit well together, especially since Morgenthau's *Scientific Man Versus Power Politics* had driven a massive wedge between them a few years earlier. A few months before the membership of the committee was discharged, Dunn confessed to Herring that he did not feel that, with the present membership, the committee could do much to develop the field of international relations. He thought that "the most promising line of development would be through emphasizing the contribution that research in social relations might make to the study of international relations."[23] In the end, the focus on value orientations and on the domestic determinants of foreign policy (government structures, interest groups, party politics, etc.) could not coexist with the realist vision of the state not as a pluralist arena but as a sovereign and quasi-ontological reality that would later permeate IR theory. Nor could the connivance between the social sciences and the progressive idea of modernization coexist with the pessimistic outlook characteristic of realism. The incompatibility between liberalism and historical pessimism sealed the fate of the SSRC initiative. A few years later, this tension would be definitely arbitraged in favor of the behavioral approach to international affairs, as the SSRC would conduct its work in this area through the Committee on Comparative

Politics, established in 1954 around Gabriel Almond, Lucian Pye, and other exponents of the behavioral social sciences and modernization theory.[24]

The SSRC committee was the last attempt at keeping international relations focused on its interwar concern with the role of public opinion on the international behavior of states, albeit in a modernized form, by relying on the scientific study of political behavior. This failure to turn IR into a province of the social sciences was also the end of a distinctly liberal approach to the analysis of international relations, and it paved the way for a "theory" that was premised on the impossibility of a scientific rationalization of politics and unmistakably influenced by Morgenthau.

Although they were different branches of the same philanthropic constellation, since the SSRC was created in 1923 with Rockefeller monies, the two institutions followed very different approaches to international relations in the 1950s. This contrast is captured suggestively in the opposition between Leo Pasvolsky and Nelson Rockefeller over American foreign policy. While working as assistant secretary to Cordell Hull at the State Department, Pasvolsky (who later sat on the SSRC committee) played a crucial role in chartering the United Nations. In favor of a strong UN system, he was critical of regional arrangements that might subvert it and therefore was bitterly opposed to Nelson Rockefeller, who defended the strengthening of the Inter-American system. While Pasvolsky was guarded against such "spheres of influence," which fueled rivalries, Rockefeller was an outspoken advocate of the relevance of the Monroe Doctrine and of its priority over any multilateral arrangements (Schlesinger 2003, 175–178). The bitter fight between Pasvolsky and Rockefeller concentrates in a nutshell the opposition between an approach to international affairs based on developing instruments for conflict resolution and one that focused on power politics—or, to put it in other words, between the rationalism of the social sciences and the grounded and partial perspective of political realism. The Monroe Doctrine was regarded by realists such as Carl Schmitt and Morgenthau as a genuinely *political* understanding of the national interest, as opposed to the abstractions of internationalism.[25]

At any rate, when the Rockefeller Foundation defined its program in international relations in the mid-1950s, it was dealing with a field in which the social-science option was increasingly problematic, if not a losing one. Earlier, as the SSRC Committee on International Relations was being established, the Rockefeller Foundation was already developing an understanding of recent research trends in IR that was clearly at odds with the SSRC efforts to find a social-scientific fix to international disputes. An internal report written in 1948 by Bryce Wood, a consultant who was a professor of political science at Swarthmore College and later joined the SSRC,[26] saw realism as the emerging trend in IR research and advised the Rockefeller Foundation to move its program away from interwar international cooperation and focus instead on matters of national interest.[27] This shift in perspective, however, also implied a new intellectual and academic agenda that refuted the rationalist implications of the behavioral approach to the study of international politics. While the SSRC was busy trying to foster a better integration between international relations and the social sciences, Wood was suggesting that the emerging realist trend was premised on the "possibility that force and not social science will be employed to solve disputes." What the "theory" of IR would soon encapsulate was precisely this fundamental rejection of rationalist approaches to politics and the principled acceptance of conflict—or, to put it in other words, enmity—as an existential dimension of human life. It would take several years and many theoretical adjustments to bring the new discipline back into the sphere of American academic social science. But that is another story . . .

ORGANIZATION OF THE BOOK

The purpose of this book is primarily to make public the background discussions that preceded the gradual expansion of international studies into a quasi-discipline backed by a theory of international relations. Some of this primary-source material is presented here. But in order to discuss its significance for the subsequent development of the discipline, the primary-source material is also the focus of eight contributions by scholars representing different intellectual traditions, from realist IR scholars to historians and political scientists. Although very diverse in their approach, the following chapters touch upon common themes.

The first two contributions underscore the importance of the 1954 debate for the subsequent evolution of the discipline. In his chapter, Robert Jervis emphasizes the central role of morality in the early discussion of IR theory, making the case that a genuine understanding of realism cannot divorce it from this normative background. But the issue of morality in politics, says Jervis, should also be understood in the context of the cold war, where moral principles and claims could be used as weapons. This is to say that the 1954 exercise in theory building involved stakes that were anything but theoretical. What the participants meant by "theory" had a highly practical value: "To a very large extent," Jervis writes, "the theorists and practitioners around the table spoke the same language." The theory of international relations, therefore, was not so much an abstract model as it was a praxeology, formalizing the rules that, in the view of the participants, did or should guide good statesmanship (and the ambiguity here is crucial). In that sense, Morgenthau was absolutely right to insist on realism being a matter of prudence, wisdom, or "informed hunches" rather than a science. Yet, Jervis points out, the fact that IR theory was developed at the intersection of the academic and the political fields entails fundamental consequences for its epistemic status, and the difficulties into which the discussion ran when it touched upon the nexus between description and prescription, or theory and policy, should be taken seriously: to the extent that realist theories are also the software used by politicians to inform their actions (or, as Jack Snyder writes in his contribution, to the extent that they constitute the "mental furniture" of policymakers), they can be consciously defeated or realized. Realism, Jervis writes, can become a "self-fulfilling" or a "self-denying" prophecy. Once it is assumed that political actors operate on the basis of realist principles, such a "theory" becomes reflexive and falls into strategic calculations where contravening the theory becomes a consequence of holding it true. Such paradoxes hint at the specific nature of IR theory: once it is widely shared, its validity is compromised. Jervis's analysis is extremely useful here, as it points at the social dimension of the epistemology of IR: as a "theory," realism is true as long as its diffusion is restricted, for its value is indexed on its scarcity. Hence the necessity to control its diffusion, which was a major concern of the participants in the 1954 conference. IR theory thus reaches back to the tradition of politics as an *arcanum*, a wisdom shared by a few selected men. The realist scholar is more of a *Geheimrat*, a secret adviser to the Prince, than a social scientist dealing with public knowledge. His remoteness from the public is indeed crucial to his function, and the insulation for domestic politics is an important aspect of what the "theory" stood for. As Nitze conceded in the paper he prepared for the conference: "Under Mr. Acheson a serious effort was made to separate consideration of the national interest in a given context from consideration of the probable domestic popularity or the domestic political feasibility of a given course of action." That the 1954 conference on theory was held behind closed doors only serves to underscore that realism was essentially a reclusive, if not a secretive, project.

If realism did not sit well with the notion of a general democratic public, it was particularly ill suited for the American public. Jack Snyder also points at the uneasy relationship between realism and postwar political culture in the United States. Such pillars of realist wisdom as "no crusading," "will to power," or "national interest" were not congenial to the liberal tradition. The project of developing a specific "theory" of international relations separate from the general representations of politics (whether lay or academic) was also a way for policymakers to move beyond what many disparaged as the naïve assumptions of folk liberalism. This went hand in hand with a certain distrust of the democratic masses: "the fickleness of the democratic public was a central concern of the postwar American realist project." At a time when the historian Louis Hartz was reminding his fellow citizens that in America liberalism was a natural phenomenon, realism clearly appeared as an unnatural import that had to be assimilated. Yet, as Snyder points out, this project effectively took roots. In part, this successful transplant is due to its usefulness: realism provided strategic guidance in an era that required expanded engagement with other powers, and it was also an ideological justification for the authority of a specific policy elite. But early realists also made certain ideological adjustments, as they "needed to show how their brand of prudent consequentialism [was] consistent with universally held liberal values." The emphasis on values and the discussion of the tensions between politics and morality that characterize much of the 1954 discussion must be seen as part of this cultural translation. This tension between realism and democracy also overlapped with the tension between the different meanings of theory. Snyder rightly emphasizes that the confusion in the discussion of normative versus empirical theory stemmed from the fact that realism eroded such distinctions. Unable to distinguish clearly between the normative and the descriptive, realism actually conflates the real and the legitimate: what is is what should be. A whole theory of sovereignty and a whole theory of law are encapsulated in this conflation. But in any case, this predisposed realism to be an ideology of the status quo, a theory that deferred to the powers that be and privileged equilibrium and balance—certainly not a transformative vision. Finally, a third tension characterized the realist project: while premised on a universal lust for power that made power maximization the main rationale of human action, realist IR theory also embodied a form of prudence and called for restraint. These series of tensions within IR— between realism and democracy, between normative and descriptive theory, between maximization and prudence—were already at the center of the 1954 discussion and they have informed the subsequent evolution of the discipline. They have not found and probably cannot find a satisfying solution: IR theory is a discourse that constantly navigates these tensions. Ultimately, what Jervis and Snyder suggest is not that the discipline is still trapped within the 1954 debate but rather that the discipline *is* that debate.

The following chapter, by Brian Schmidt, provides us with the larger disciplinary context of the 1954 conference and in particular with a detailed analysis of the previous state of the field, which was characterized by a focus on international law (albeit a pragmatic one contrary to the simplistic representations serving the realist argument). Schmidt suggests that the shift to a focus on "international politics" introduced a new element and triggered a "disciplinary crisis." This crisis should be understood as a transformation of the entire field rather than as the consequence of some "Great Debate." Schmidt shows indeed that some key players—Grayson Kirk, Kenneth Thompson, and William T. R. Fox, among others—contributed to creating a distorted image of interwar scholarship that persists to this day, the purpose of which was to establish the legitimacy of the "realist" approach by disparaging an earlier orientation of the field toward problems of international law and organization. This operation, which had become explicit by the late 1940s, gave indeed some credence to the idea of a Great Debate. Yet, debate there was, Schmidt tells us, and the label is not totally wrong, but it is over the course of these postwar debates that the retrospective construct of an "idealist" scholarship took shape, before being taken at face value by a discipline that had fully endorsed realism and its lore. Schmidt shows that the main function of the theory of IR that the Rockefeller Foundation promoted in the 1950s was precisely to effectuate the transition to international politics, thus securing the central tenets that realists advanced about the nature of politics and establishing their control over the field. Schmidt also points out Morgenthau's role as one of the main intellectual architects of this transition and analyzes the ambiguities of his theoretical project. Although the notion of power politics that Morgenthau defended referred to a prerational stratum of the human psyche, Morgenthau included the assumption of rationality in his project of a theory of international politics. But he did so in a quasi-Weberian fashion, as an ideal-typical device needed by the theorist, a compass for political action that did not reflect the deep nature of politics. The theory of international politics that was discussed in 1954 was thus built upon a contradiction or at the very least a constitutive ambiguity: the theory of IR could not be a "science of politics."

The self-understanding of the discipline of IR through a sequence of "great debates" is central to Ole Wæver's contribution to this volume. Drawing upon the theory of speech acts and its application to the history of political theory by the Cambridge School, he suggests that, notwithstanding their accuracy as historical descriptors, the "great debates" that punctuate the discipline are also moves made by IR theorists in specific situations or in specific stages in the development of their field. In that sense, they are not necessarily true or wrong but, rather, performative or not. The 1954 conference was thus a complex instance where the fight against the "scientific" method in the study of politics—the "second great debate"— overlapped a strategy that sought to achieve scientific credibility for IR. The result was a compromise on a weak notion of "theory" that was ultimately self-contradictory with a number of premises on which the realists operated.

This question is further developed by Nicolas Guilhot, who focuses on the process of demarcation that allowed international relations to carve out a disciplinary space for itself. Reviewing postwar academic debates in political science, he suggests that IR theory did not emerge from disciplinary differentiation and specialization but rather from a contest over the nature of the politics. The intellectual movement that promoted the development of a distinct *theory* of international relations must in fact be understood as a normative statement as to what the entire discipline of political science should have been. The experience of World War II emboldened those scholars who viewed power as an irrational and existential given that could be only very partially understood through rational categories. More importantly, they saw the tendency to analyze politics through the lens of empirical social science as committing the same fallacy that liberal internationalists had committed during the interwar period: assuming that the conflictuality inherent to politics could be overcome by a rational fix or some sort of social engineering. Yet, unable to resist the hegemony of behavioralism over political science, they settled for the control of a smaller disciplinary territory, one limited to international politics. Guilhot's central argument is that, as an intellectual project, IR theory was difficult to decipher because it was making an antiscientific argument while at the same time strategically using the language of science. Many of the misunderstandings that took place in the 1954 debate stemmed from this premise. Such misunderstandings were further compounded by what should be ultimately regarded as the failure of early realism: if the language of science made IR theory more palatable to the academic audience of the 1950s, it also made it vulnerable to a gradual inclusion within the social sciences, which is precisely what realism had sought to resist in the first place.

If Morgenthau is very much a central character of the 1954 conference, Anders Stephanson explores the variety of realism developed by the conference's most conspicuous absentee, George Kennan, who nevertheless managed to have an indirect voice in the discussion by sending a paper that he had recently penned. For Kennan too, realism was "a rule of thumb, a way of being towards the world of international politics" rather than a full-fledged theory. After exploring Kennan's vision of international politics after 1945 and, through Kennan, the problematic relationship of realism to the cold war, Stephanson draws our attention to the role of moral values in realism. However, rather than considering values abstractly, he suggests that they refer to an underlying community attuned to the tension between morality and political action. Kennan thus helps us understand the socializing functions of the realist talk about morality and the political nature of the realist project: realism is based on an "elite morality" secluded from the deceptive influence of the democratic populace. The quest for a theory of international relations should thus be resituated within a wider pedagogical project that occasionally surfaces in the 1954 transcript and clearly figures on the agenda. What Kennan and other conference participants envisioned was indeed a form of state nobility made not of technical experts but of men of sound judgment. IR theory was meant to provide a form of education that was not based on the scientific routinization of technical solutions—rather, it formalized a certain conception of statesmanship; it was essentially a praxeology that was not fit for abstraction. The "theory" would not only ensure the transmission of a knowledge that was fundamentally atheoretical but also allow a specific group to secure control over this transmission process. But the need to confine the conduct of foreign policy to an "organic elite" was also grounded in a typically realist understanding of the relationship between norms and action: only the adherence to common normative standards would ensure that the moral dilemmas of politics did not become a paralyzing consideration in the conduct of foreign policy. Obviously, as Stephanson points out, the realist political vision is "un-American" in its rejection of legalism, moralism, and historical confidence, but it is also, for the same reason, an unfeasible project. Kennan's own trajectory is telling in this respect, as his role would rapidly be confined to commenting upon—and more often than not, railing against—American foreign policy while abandoning any attempt at articulating the tenets of his realism.

In his chapter, Inderjeet Parmar develops the idea of a policy elite and relates it to the notion of foreign policy "establishment." With the United States projected into a new hegemonic role after 1945 and the expanding needs of imperial foreign-policy making, the control over the personnel involved in the conduct of foreign affairs became a crucial issue. For the realists who gathered in Washington in 1954, grounding the theory of international relations in the social sciences would have reduced policy making to a technical expertise and changed the nature of the group in charge of it. By fostering a rather conservative vision of statesmanship that valued good judgment and character, the Rockefeller Foundation contributed to securing the control of the old establishment over foreign policy at a time of transformation and expansion of the American state. Parmar shows that the efforts to build a theory of international relations that would, as Thompson put it, rationalize the "jet stream of contemporary events" about international affairs should be understood as part of the cold-war reshuffling of the relationship between academics, intellectuals, and policymakers. But the role of the Rockefeller Foundation must also be analyzed in the framework of a longer history of efforts deployed by philanthropic foundations to strengthen state capacity. In particular, the Rockefeller event built upon previous experiments with realism, such as the Yale Institute for International Studies created in 1935, created with the financial support of the foundation and directed first by Nicholas Spykman and then by Frederick Dunn. Two important members of the Yale Institute, William T. R. Fox and Arnold Wolfers, would be key players in the 1954 conference. Because of these precedents, the 1954 conference can also be viewed as a part of a wider effort at building "the intellectual infrastructure of globalism." In this sense, the real significance of the 1954 gathering should not be searched in the minutiae of its theoretical debates but in its having simply taken place: whether it was conclusive or not in terms of theory, it was another step toward a greater integration of scholars and policymakers.

The relationship between scholarship and policy making is also at the center of Philip Mirowski's chapter, albeit in a different way. Mirowski resituates the rise of realism to self-consciousness against the backdrop of the interwar crisis of liberalism and the complex ideological realignments it triggered (of the kind that Walter Lippman underwent before he attended the 1954 Rockefeller gathering). As a reaction against liberal social reformism applied to international affairs and the idea of scientific administration, realism belongs to a wider intellectual constellation that also witnessed the emergence of postwar neoliberalism in the United States and that Mirowski characterizes as an instance of "reactionary modernism." Although realism and neoliberalism are arguably quite different in their outlook, both are premised on a distrust of the masses, especially in a democratic context, and on a critique of liberal government (whether because of its totalitarian tendencies or because of its incapacity to understand the political). Both movements, moreover, were heavily influenced by European émigré scholars. But the similarities between realism and neoliberalism cut deeper: for realists and neoliberals alike, the world is characterized by a complexity or a contingency that nullifies any possibility of centralized rational comprehension. There is no position from which a sufficient or reliable knowledge of the state of the world allowing for rational policy action can be obtained. As Arnold Wolfers quipped a propos IR theory during the 1954 conference: "the right and correct theory would have to be a theory of God." Planning, social engineering, comprehensive reform: realism and neoliberalism converged to undermine the whole notion of modern government. While the neoliberals sought to outsource the gathering and processing of information to the market, which they understood as a decentralized information processor, and thus to remodel politics after the market, the realists redescribed politics as a prudential practice operating in conditions of limited knowledge and rationality. While these positions were obviously different and even opposed in some respects, as Mirowski suggests, they were responses to the same issue: how does a modicum of political rationality obtain? To the extent that the political is not reducible to "reason," what is political rationality? How should government be exercised both in the domestic and the international arenas when it can only partially know its object or predict its outcomes? This, Mirowski shows, is the *problématique* common to both realism and neoliberalism, and it is also the reason why there is much to be gained by studying them jointly. In developing the parallel careers of Morgenthau and Hayek, Mirowski points out that realism and neoliberalism were not only similar in their diagnosis. They also shared important practical and organizational commonalities. For all their contempt for liberal social engineering, Morgenthau and Hayek both relied upon organizations that carefully planned and engineered the diffusion of their doctrines. The Rockefeller Foundation and the Mont Pèlerin Society both played major roles in the development of realism and neoliberalism but relied on principles that entirely belied these ideologies. What was at stake in both endeavors was the reconstruction of political rationality after 1945 and, in different ways, an attempt at insulating politics from democracy by either outsourcing it to market mechanisms or by entrusting it to a small elite of wise men aware of the irrational nature of politics and who showed only contempt for a domestic sphere from which "the political" had disappeared as democratization had progressed. In both cases, a counterelite was needed to counteract the influence of liberalism. The development of realism as IR theory, therefore, is part of the reinvention of modern politics after 1945 and of a grammar of politics that is still very much ours today.

NOTES

1. For a definitive statement on traditional intellectual history, see Skinner et al. (2001) and Tully (1988).
2. See, for instance, Schmidt (1998, 2002).
3. The quotation is from the *Discourses*. See Machiavelli (1997, 416): "In order for a sect or a republic to live for long, it is often necessary to bring it back to its original purpose." Translation mine.
4. See, for instance, Craig (2003), Williams (2005, 2007b), and the recent issue of *Constellations* (2007) on realism, with articles by Maurizio Viroli, William Scheuerman, and others. See also Bell (2008a).
5. The same is true of "idealism." See Ashworth (1999).
6. See, in particular, Recchia (2007).
7. See Epp (1991), Guilhot (2010), and Loriaux (1992).
8. See, for instance, Morgenthau (1945).
9. See the chapters by Schmidt and Guilhot in this volume.
10. There is an important literature on the renewal of American social science under the impetus of European intellectual migrations. As for IR, the contribution of this cohort is noteworthy: John Herz, Hans Kelsen, Klaus Knorr, Hans Morgenthau, Stefan Possony, Sigmund Neumann, Hans Speier, Nicholas Spykman, Robert Strausz-Hupé, Arnold Wolfers, and Karl Deutsch are only a few of the sixty-four German-speaking scholars who ended up teaching in U.S. political-science departments during the period under consideration. See Söllner (1988).
11. Toynbee to Willits, May 1947, pp. 1–2 Folder 61, Box 7, Series 910, Research Group (RG): Rockefeller Foundation Archive, Rockefeller Archive Center, Sleepy Hollow, N.Y. (hereafter designated RAC).
12. Kenneth W. Thompson, "Theory of International Politics," December 28, 1953, p. 2, Box 7, Series 910, RG 3, Rockefeller Foundation Archive, RAC.
13. Ibid., 3. Among the "younger men" in the seminar, the rapporteur played a special role, as he was in charge of keeping a record of the discussion. His name was Kenneth Waltz.
14. Some other readers will immediately object that these foundations are not to be found in freewheeling discussions such as the 1954 conference but in important works such as Morgenthau's *Principles and Problems of International Politics* or *Politics Among Nations*, with its famous "six principles." Yet, as it is argued below, such works may become "foundational" only retrospectively, within a disciplinary space that makes their reputation, ensures their diffusion, and elevates them to the rank of canonical works. They are in fact a product of disciplinary mechanisms (teaching, syllabi, etc.), not the cause behind the emergence of disciplines. Hence, Morgenthau's works may not have been so important, and certainly not "foundational" of anything, had the 1954 meeting not taken place and had the Rockefeller Foundation not decided to promote the "theoretization" of the study of international relations.
15. See "The Theoretical and Practical Importance of a Theory of International Relations," transcript, 265 (appendix 2 of this volume).
16. Scheuerman (1999, 244) aptly described *Scientific Man Versus Power Politics* as a "popularized version of Schmitt." As for Meinecke, Morgenthau was accused of having abundantly plagiarized him.
17. On Morgenthau's difficult adaptation to the U.S. academic context, see Frei (2001).

18. Folder 2283—International Relations 1948–1950, Box 202, Series 1 (Committee Projects), Subseries 58 (Committee on International Relations), Accession 2, SSRC Archives, RAC. Emphasis mine.

19. "Proposal for a Social Science Research Council Committee on International Relations," p. 2 Folder 4768, Box 403, Series 200S, RG 1.1, Rockefeller Foundation Archives, RAC.

20. Ibid., 3.

21. Dunn to Herring, March 13, 1950. Folder 2283, Box 202, Series 1, SSRC Collection, Rockefeller Archive Center, Tarrytown N.Y.

22. On this underlying liberal anxiety, see Gilman (2003).

23. Pendleton Herring, interoffice correspondence, 24 April 1950, Series 1, Subseries 58, Accession 2, Box 202, Folder 2283, SSRC Archives, RAC.

24. On the Committee on Comparative Politics, see Cammack (1997) and Gilman (2003, chap. 4).

25. On the role of the Monroe Doctrine in realist thought, see Morgenthau (1950, 1952) and Scheuerman (1999, 161–168). See also Siegelberg (2008, 359).

26. Interestingly, Bryce Wood, like Pasvolsky, had worked as an administrative assistant at the Department of State during the war (1942–1943). But, contrary to Pasvolsky, he was siding with Nelson Rockefeller.

27. The Wood report is analyzed in more detail in chapter 5.

REFERENCES

Ashworth, Lucian M. 1999. *Creating international studies: Angell, Mitrany, and the liberal tradition.* Aldershot: Ashgate.

Bell, Duncan, ed. 2008a. *Political thought and international relations: Variations on a realist theme.* Oxford: Oxford University Press.

——. 2008b. Introduction: Under an empty sky—Realism and political theory. In *Political thought and international relations: Variations on a realist theme*, ed. Duncan Bell, 1–25. Oxford: Oxford University Press.

Bourdieu, Pierre. 1976. Le champ scientifique. *Actes de la recherche en sciences sociales* 2: 88–104.

——. 1997. *Les usages sociaux de la science.* Paris: INRA.

Butterfield, Herbert. 1959. *The Whig interpretation of history.* London: G. Bell and Sons.

Cammack, Paul. 1997. *Capitalism and democracy in the Third World: The doctrine for political development.* Leicester: Leicester University Press.

Constellations. 2007. Realism then and now. *Constellations: An International Journal of Critical and Democratic Theory* 14.

Craig, Campbell. 2003. *Glimmer of a new Leviathan: Total war in the realism of Niebuhr, Morgenthau, and Waltz.* New York: Columbia University Press.

Dunn, Frederick S. 1949. The present course of international relations research. *World Politics* 2: 80–95.

Epp, Roger. 1991. The "Augustinian moment" in international politics: Neibuhr, Butterfield, Wight, and the reclaiming of a tradition. *International Politics Research Papers.* Aberystwyth: Department of International Politics, University College of Wales.

Foucault, Michel. 2001. Nietzsche, la généalogie, l'histoire. In *Dits et écrits I. 1954–1957*, 1004–1024. Paris: Gallimard.

Frei, Christoph. 2001. *Hans J. Morgenthau: An intellectual biography*. Baton Rouge: Louisiana State University.

Garth, Bryant G. 2000. James Willard Hurst as entrepreneur for the field of law and social science. *Law and History Review* 18: 37–58.

Gilman, Nils. 2003. *Mandarins of the future: Modernization theory in cold war America*. Baltimore, Md.: The Johns Hopkins University Press.

Guilhot, Nicolas. 2010. American Katechon. When political theology became international relations theory. *Constellations: An International Journal of Critical and Democratic Theory* 17.

Koskenniemi, Martti. 2002. *The gentle civilizer of nations: The rise and fall of international law, 1870–1960*. Cambridge: Cambridge University Press.

Lang, Anthony F., ed. 2004. *Political theory and international affairs: Hans J. Morgenthau on Aristotle's* The Politics. Greenwood, Conn.: Praeger.

Loriaux, Michael. 1992. The realist and Saint Augustine: Skepticism, psychology, and moral action in international relations thought. *International Studies Quarterly* 36: 401–420.

Machiavelli, Niccolò. 1997. *Discorsi sopra la prima deca di Tito Livio*. In *Opere I*, ed. C. Vivanti. Torino/Paris: Einaudi-Gallimard.

Mirowski, Philip. 2004. *The effortless economy of science?* Durham, N.C.: Duke University Press.

Morgenthau, Hans J. 1945. The evil of politics and the ethics of evil. *Ethics* 56: 1–18.

——. 1946. *Scientific man versus power politics*. Chicago: The University of Chicago Press.

——. 1950. The mainsprings of American foreign policy: The national interest versus moral abstractions. *American Political Science Review* 44: 833–854.

——. 1952. What is the national interest of the United States? *Annals of the American Academy of Political and Social Science* 282: 1–7.

Recchia, Stefano. 2007. Restraining imperial hubris: The ethical bases of realist international relations theory. *Constellations* 14: 531–556.

Scheuerman, William E. 1999. *Carl Schmitt: The end of law*. Lanham, Md.: Rowman & Littlefield.

——. 2007. Was Morgenthau a realist? Revisiting *Scientific Man Versus Power Politics*. *Constellations* 14: 506–530.

Schlesinger, Stephen C. 2003. *Act of creation: The founding of the United Nations*. Boulder: Westview Press.

Schmidt, Brian C. 1998. *The political discourse of anarchy: A disciplinary history of international relations*. Albany: State University of New York Press.

——. 2002. On the history and historiography of international relations. In *Handbook of International Relations*, ed. W. Carlsnaes, T. Risse, and B. A. Simmons, 3–22. London: Sage.

Siegelberg, Mira. 2008. Between regionalism and universalism: Carl Schmitt in postwar America. Unpublished paper. Cambridge, Mass.: Harvard University.

Skinner, Quentin, et al. 2001. Political philosophy: The view from Cambridge. *Journal of Political Philosophy* 10: 1–19.

Söllner, Alfons. 1988. Vom Völkerrecht zur *Science of International Relations*. Vier typische Vertreter der politikwissenschaftlichen Emigration. In *Exil, Wissenschaft, Identität: Die Emigration deutscher Sozialwissenschaftler 1933–1945*, ed. I. Srubar, 164–180. Frankfurt am Main: Suhrkamp.

Thompson, Kenneth W. 1952. The study of international politics: A survey of trends and developments. *Review of Politics* 14: 439–440.

Tully, James, ed. 1988. *Meaning and context: Quentin Skinner and his critics.* Princeton, N.J.: Princeton University Press.

Wight, Colin. 2002. Philosophy of social science and international relations. In *Handbook of international relations*, ed. W. Carlsnaes, T. Risse and B. A. Simmons, 23–51. London: Sage.

Williams, Michael C. 2005. *The realist tradition and the limits of international relations.* Cambridge: Cambridge University Press.

——. 2007a. Morgenthau now: Neoconservatism, national greatness, and realism. In *Realism reconsidered: The legacy of Hans J. Morgenthau in international relations*, ed. M. C. Williams, 216–240. Oxford: Oxford University Press.

——, ed. 2007b. *Realism reconsidered: The legacy of Hans J. Morgenthau in international relations.* Oxford: Oxford University Press.

MORALITY, POLICY, AND THEORY
Reflections on the 1954 Conference
ROBERT JERVIS

T HE 1954 Conference on International Politics reveals a deep concern with the interrelations among international relations (IR) theory, the practice of foreign policy, and morality. The participants
might be disappointed at how little progress we have made since they met,
but they probably would not be surprised. These questions have concerned
people from the time of Thucydides, and the fact that they remained pressing in 1954 indicates that they cannot be fully solved and that we should
not be embarrassed to be still discussing them.[1] This gives me humility
about my own remarks but does not stop me from making them.

MORALITY

Although some versions of realism denied any role for morality, most realists have seen that statesmen did not and should not put it aside. This was
obviously the case for E. H. Carr, John Herz, Hans Morgenthau, Reinhold
Niebuhr, and Arnold Wolfers, to name only five of the most prominent
realists, three of whom participated in the conference. Indeed, the conference opened with Wolfers asking that the "moral problem" be discussed
first, and Niebuhr replied that he was delighted that most of the prepara-
tory papers had talked about the relations between theory and practice.[2]
There were several reasons why they saw morality as the linchpin here.
Perhaps most important was that the participants believed that understanding had to start with human nature.[3] Most realists shared the common Western belief that humans were inherently evil or at least had the
potential for evil within them. For some theorists like Niebuhr, this view
can be traced to the Bible. For others, a simple look at history sufficed. For
scholars today, evolutionary psychology can be deployed. In the mid-1950s,

with the memory of Hitler still fresh, with Stalin just having died, and with the behavior of Joseph McCarthy looming large, it would have been hard to build coherent thoughts without this foundation.

This understanding meant that realists believed both that national survival at times required doing evil and that statesmen had to minimize this possibility and avoid becoming evil. Leaders had to fight some of the impulses they were sure to harbor, had to resist the easy rationalization that the requirements of national security always trumped other values, and had to avoid corrupting their personal or national souls. Furthermore, this struggle would never end, because politics, especially international politics, always contained multiple conflicts and posed multiple dangers. The utopia that for liberals would dawn with the universal reign of democracy and free trade and for Marxists would appear with the triumph of communism were for realists false hopes, ones that would bring disaster if they were pursued to the exclusion of other considerations. Morality then could only play a useful role if leaders were aware of their own immoral impulses and the concomitant danger of confusing narrower with broader interests. National egoism and self-righteousness were among the most disturbing and dangerous forces in international politics. It was all too easy for any country, perhaps especially a democracy, to universalize its own values and outlook, to think that it knows what is best for the entire world, and to disguise (to itself as much as to others) the selfish nature of its behavior.[4] Leaders and nations that fell into these traps would behave immorally while simultaneously thinking that they were the most moral of actors. The very fact that many actors convince themselves that they are abiding by the highest moral standards gives realists reason for looking at the topic with great care.

To say that people have the capacity to do great evil implies that they can do good as well, although determining what is good and what behavior contributes to it is of course contentious and difficult. But while denying the perfectibility of human beings, one of the animating forces behind realism is the belief that states can minimize evil and make the world better or at least see that it does not degenerate into constant strife and injustice. Realists then would not be surprised by the modern findings from psychology and neuroscience that people have an inborn sense of morality. In an era in which the academic division of labor had not gone as far as it has today, realists were also deeply concerned with their state's domestic regimes and societies. The point of politics, after all, was to make the lives of individuals and communities better. Since the external world influenced the internal one, it was hard to see how a good society could develop in a deeply malign environment. States had to survive, but the point of survival was to help the inhabitants thrive.

These concerns were particularly pressing in the mid-1950s, so much so that they hardly needed to be discussed. The participants in the conference saw the Soviet Union as evil, but they did not waste time explicating this. For them bipolarity, although important, was not the root of the matter. Evil was much of what the cold war was about. Had the Soviet Union been benign, there would have been much less international conflict and less reason to fear the limited expansion of Soviet power. During World War II, one reason for American wariness toward Great Britain was that the latter was fighting not only to defeat fascism but also to retain the British Empire. For most Americans, including realists, subjugating a large portion of the earth's population was not something the United States wanted to uphold, and while combating it could not be done at the cost of losing the war, neither should the United States cooperate with this endeavor. Although realists certainly did not call for a crusade to end British imperialism—some shared the prevalent racism, and even if there had been no Soviet menace none of them favored crusades—neither were they insensible to the fundamental idea that states should serve people. Any inclination to view that relationship the other way around was banished by the Nazi example.

Realism sometimes is viewed as synonymous with cynicism, given its view that states seek power and care first, if not solely, about themselves and their citizens. There is something to this, but the common next step of viewing cynicism as being in conflict with morality is not warranted. In fact, for Niebuhr, Morgenthau, and their colleagues it was their cynicism that permitted them to see that moral dilemmas in politics could not be easily elided and that one of the gravest dangers in politics was the attempt to do so. Cynicism is compatible with morality, and is indeed necessary for it, because by acknowledging the primacy of the national interest it allows us to see that this can and often does conflict with other values and goals. In the interwar period and to a lesser extent in the years after 1945, realists believed (with some reason) that liberals and idealists were prone to make the world worse because of their mistaken belief that there were no conflicts between what was good for the country and what was best for the world. One of Carr's major contributions was to point out that many people in Great Britain in the 1920s and 1930s assumed that the status quo had moral superiority (Carr 1946). Although Carr initially deployed this and other arguments to argue for appeasing Hitler,[5] the general point is extremely important: states that have gained a favorable position in the international system tend to conclude that their country is uniquely wise and just and that those who are seeking to displace them are morally inferior.

Morgenthau similarly argues that what he calls nationalistic universalism is a terrible force in world politics in part because states so imbued believe that they are carrying out the will of God or its secular equivalent (Morgenthau 1978, chap. 20). This can be seen as simply a generalization from Napoleon, fascism, and communism. But one of his less familiar but parallel claims cuts closer to the bone. He argues that bourgeois liberalism is not universally valid but stems from particular historical circumstances, and that because Western leaders are generally unaware of this, they assume that their outlook and values are universal (Morgenthau 1946, 50–53).[6] Leaders of these countries are not cynical, and that is a problem, because their lack of awareness of the roots of their beliefs leads them to consider their outlook and policies to be highly moral. Greater cynicism would have permitted a more accurate view of others and themselves; it would have led leaders and the public to see that their values were necessarily parochial and that they often faced difficult moral choices and judgments. People who understand this are better able to control themselves and act with moderation than those who think they are acting for the good of humankind.[7]

Four aspects of the 1950s heightened the realists' concern with moral tensions. Most obviously, the cold war brought with it the perception of a sharp contrast between Soviet and Western standards and behavior. This involved a clash with an arguably evil state and also raised the danger of a gap widening between America's principles and its actions. The cold war was a nasty struggle, and the sources of dispute and means of influence were principles as well as power. As Melvyn Leffler (2007) put it, the cold war was largely a struggle "for the soul of mankind." This made it imperative that the West not mimic Soviet tactics, but the nature of the conflict required the United States to exercise power in a way that other states (and some moralists) would find objectionable.[8] Second and relatedly, there was a real danger that the extreme competition would undermine democratic processes and values. Although by the early 1950s some of the fears that the United States would turn into a "garrison state" had dissipated, one of the main reasons why President Eisenhower was so set on reducing the defense budget was the belief that if he did not, much of what the United

States was striving to protect would be lost. As he put it at one National Security Council meeting, "We could lick the whole world . . . if we were willing to adopt the system of Adolf Hitler. . . . [We are] engaged in defending a way of life as well as a territory, a population, or our dollar" (State 1984, 519, 521).[9] Third, the emerging doctrine of nuclear deterrence involved making credible the immoral threat to kill tens of millions of innocent Soviet citizens. Even to people who accepted the destruction of German and Japanese cities during World War II, this was difficult to contemplate. The question of how these threats, let alone their implementation, might be squared with our consciences vied for attention with the challenge of whether we could make the threats credible enough that they would never have to be carried out.[10] Finally, with the independence of India and Pakistan, France's war to keep control of Indochina, and the stirrings in Africa, the future of colonialism was an obvious question. The immorality of foreign rule, however, clashed with the immoralities that could follow from early independence and with the need to support Britain and France. Policies in this area somehow had to balance and combine pragmatism and morality.[11]

THEORY AND POLICY

Questions such as these would not have been so pressing if the realists had been concerned only with developing theories. These could be entirely derived from and applied to the past, be highly abstract, and even seek to avoid questions of foreign policy entirely. This indeed is what Kenneth Waltz did with his neorealist *Theory of International Politics* (although as we will see, even this enterprise was influenced by policy concerns). But realists were traditionally involved with what their states should do, and those at the 1954 conference were no exception. Indeed, the participants included Robert Bowie, Dorothy Fosdick, and Paul Nitze, people who were more practitioners than theorists. Even for people such as Morgenthau and Wolfers, I think the notion of a theory that had few implications for how states in general should behave or for what the United States should do in its current situation would have had little value and perhaps little meaning.

Context and personal experiences played a large role here. The participants in the conference had just been through one of the most destructive wars in history, one that many people believed could have been avoided by appropriate statesmanship. The cold war had just started, and it had already witnessed a series of crises that had started a prolonged and surprising limited war in Korea and could have triggered another world war as well. In World War II, many scholars had served in the government, few questioned the legitimacy of the Western cause, and all were now facing the enormous intellectual challenge of understanding a world that was new and threatening. The gap between IR theory and policy making being much narrower than is now the case, theorists saw their task as relevant to policy, and policymakers, at least those like Bowie and Nitze, hoped for guidance from scholars.[12] In this light, it is not surprising that the head of the Rockefeller Foundation, which sponsored the conference, was Dean Rusk, who had left the State Department two years earlier and would return as its secretary six years later. To a very large extent, the theorists and practitioners around the table spoke the same language. Indeed, although the transcript reveals individual voices, if the names were not attached it would be hard to tell whether the speaker was a theorist or a practitioner.

The members of the group realized that developing and applying theories was extraordinarily difficult and that the links between these and particular cases could be tenuous and remote. Thus even a good theory could not be counted on to chart the way through the perilous waters that the United States found itself in. But there were aspects of the policy-theory relationship that they did not fully grasp.

Let me start with the other side of this coin: some of the problems they did raise were less troublesome than they believed. The participants questioned whether true theory was possible, in part because statesmen have free will and can break IR laws in a way that objects cannot break the law of gravity, in part because when dealing with a fairly small number of actors the exceptional behavior of any one of them can have wide-ranging effects, and partly because national leaders may not be rational. These objections are not entirely well founded. The fact that a person can choose what to do does not necessarily make it impossible for observers to predict and explain her behavior. Indeed, in some cases, observers can understand the person's behavior better than the person herself does. Unless the person wants to behave differently than the theory expects merely to embarrass the theorist (President Johnson was notorious for reacting to accurate news leaks by doing the opposite, just to show that the reporter was wrong), choice and theories of behavior can coexist, although the latter may need to be probabilistic and at times specific to particular actors.

For many of the same reasons, theorizing is not made impossible by the fact that we are dealing with relatively few actors and that events can be shaped by who is in office and exactly what they do.[13] As Waltz pointed out, economists can theorize about markets that are oligopolistic as well as about markets with innumerable buyers and sellers (Waltz 1959, 91–94; 1979). The tools required are different and involve strategic interaction, an approach that was just being developed when the Rockefeller conference met, and so this is an area in which I think we can point to progress, if not to the final word.[14]

The participants are similarly too pessimistic about the implications of the problematic nature of rationality in politics.[15] It can simultaneously be true that people are not fully rational and that we derive valid and useful propositions from the assumption that they are. Milton Friedman's argument to this effect has had an enormous influence, and Waltz's theory of international politics explicitly argues for this approach (Friedman 1953). Indeed, even Waltz's critics find other grounds on which to attack him. The quest for honor and glory, so important in international politics before the middle of the twentieth century, is hard to square with many notions of rationality because it is inconsistent with considering alternative courses of action and making careful calculations. But we still may be able to understand and generalize about the behavior of actors who are driven by these concerns (Kagan 1995; Lebow 2008). More recently, psychologists have found that people's propensity to take risks operates in a way that violates the rules of rationality. But this leads to prospective theories that have proven enormously powerful for predicting a wide range of human behavior, including international politics.[16] Theories require not rationality but regularities, and only if behavior is without a pattern will we necessarily be stumped.

OVERLOOKED PROBLEMS: PRACTICE, PRESENTISM, AND PREFERENCES

Several problems in the relationship between theory and practice were not discussed at the conference, although I think they are obvious enough so that they could have been. In some cases, these problems are now more salient because of new developments in theory. In other cases, it is a different intellectual atmosphere that brings them to the surface, while in still other cases the experience of the last half-century is responsible. Most obviously, if theorists become deeply involved in advising or even contemplating policy, they may get distracted from their theoretical tasks. There are only twenty-four hours in the day, and careful theorizing can be a full-time operation. It took Waltz about fifteen years to write his *Theory of International Politics*. Government advising and serving in Washington can be fascinating, gratifying, and highly seductive. The time may be well spent, but it is time spent.

There is another side to this coin, however. Working on policy issues can stimulate theorizing. This was true for the development of ideas concerning deterrence, nuclear strategy, and strategic interaction.[17] Although the validity of this work is subject to debate, it is clear that it has had an enormous influence on IR and indeed on the discipline of political science in general. In the twenty years following the conference, Bernard Brodie, Glenn Snyder, William Kaufmann, Thomas Schelling, and others developed what probably was the most rigorous, widely ranging, and stimulating corpus of theoretical work in the field. While some of them wanted to build IR theories, all were deeply concerned about protecting the United States and its allies while simultaneously avoiding World War III. These concerns were not merely those of any informed citizen but were worked out by wrestling with detailed and sometimes technical questions, often in the form of classified studies. Thus many of our concepts in this area grew out of the RAND study, led by Albert Wohlstetter, which had the mundane task of figuring out the most efficient configuration for basing American bombers and their associated refueling tankers. Less well known is that much of what became Schelling's *Arms and Influence* was drafted as a 1962 report to the government on how to cope with the strategic challenges over the next decade.[18] It is hard to believe that this work would have been written without the immediate stimulus of policy concerns and the close contact with policymakers.

But this contact had its costs, in part because it focused attention on bargaining and the use of threats. Although rewards, reassurances, and conciliation were not entirely neglected, and indeed Schelling stressed that they were a necessary part of deterrence, broad areas of international politics such as other instruments of influence, seeking and enlarging the common interest, and diplomacy, were squeezed to the margins. These were precisely the areas that Morgenthau had stressed in *Politics Among Nations*.[19]

A second and related interaction between policy and theory is that even those who do not advise the government are likely to be strongly influenced by the events of the era and the day. The focus on the polarity of the system, and especially its impact on the likelihood of war, followed the rise of the two superpowers. Considered in the abstract, it would have been possible for scholars in the 1930s to have taken up this subject. But it would have seemed like a waste of time; indeed, it never would have occurred to them. Similarly, the growth of realism obviously was entangled with the cold war; revisionism about the origins of this conflict was sparked by the war in Vietnam (although this approach was unable to explain the self-defeating American policy); and the subfield of international political economy (IPE) developed rapidly in the wake of the American abandonment of the gold standard, the growth of OPEC, and the oil boycott following the 1973 Mideast War. The other side of this coin is that things that do not happen lead to subjects being ignored. The role of religion in international politics, for example, received little attention until the emergence of "political Islam." Civil wars are important and interesting analytically but were only intensively studied during the Vietnam conflict (when the subject was considered under the heading of "counterinsurgency" or "internal war") and fell back into neglect until these conflicts returned to the newspapers in the 1990s. Similarly, it is no accident (to borrow a phrase from a different intellectual tradition) that only after the end of the cold war did scholars start to study unipolarity.

This "presentism," to apply a somewhat pejorative label, obviously has costs. Theorizing should have a strongly internalist drive as we try to work out the problems and implications of alternative theories. Current events are only one part of world politics, which has a long history and many possible futures. Why should we be preoccupied by the current situation? On the other hand, it is hard for people who are fascinated by international politics to entirely shield themselves from the characteristics of our age, and the broad topics of concern perhaps last just long enough for us to make significant progress without continuing past the point at which we have exhausted the possibilities. Furthermore, the frequent surprises that appear as events unfold is a reminder of our fallibility and a prod to think more carefully.

That scholars' agendas would be set in part by pressing issues may have seemed so obvious to the participants that they did not need to discuss it. However, it is more surprising that they did not talk about the ways in which policy concerns could create personal and national biases. The latter are still largely unexplored, at least by American scholars. As Stanley Hoffmann pointed out thirty years ago, the discipline of IR is largely an American enterprise, and when other countries do it, they do it differently (Hoffmann 1977). Although part of the reason involves the different intellectual trends within countries, it is likely that their positions in the international system play a role as well. Is it entirely an accident that many British scholars stress the importance of culture, norms, and ideas and see American theorizing as excessively focused on material strength and weakness? Is there not a trace here of the British hope to play Greece to the American Rome?[20]

INDIVIDUAL PREFERENCES

I want to discuss the effects of policy preferences on individual theorists at greater length. Two pressures are at work, the first clearly corrupting and the second debatably so. First, scholars can bend their views in order to curry favor with members of the policy elite. They may provide rationalizations for their policies and bolster their views in return for gaining access and perhaps office. Henry Kissinger continually flattered Nixon, although the extent to which he skewed his policy advice, let alone changed his own beliefs, is far from clear. Condoleezza Rice has said that she learned more from President Bush than she taught him, and indeed she does seem to have abandoned much of her realism, even if the line between wanting to please and being persuaded is hard to draw. Seeking power may exert as strong a pull as holding it. Although he never served in the government, Morgenthau appears to have altered his views in the 1950s in order to gain favor with the Democrats (Craig 2003).

More interestingly, a scholar's policy preferences usually affect a great deal of his or her theorizing. Even if we can logically distinguish between facts and values, it is hard to believe that we can ever fully succeed in being objective, especially when the topics under investigation are highly charged and the evidence is ambiguous. Would we really expect a scholar who deeply believes that the American interest is best served by a liberal internationalist policy to explain events in the same way that an isolationist or a unilateralist would? I like to think that my explanation for the Bush Doctrine is unaffected by my distaste for it, and although I am gratified that proponents of the policy see some merit in my arguments, there are components that are inextricably linked to my critical stance toward it (Jervis 2005). Scholars' preferences may play a role even in their most abstract theories. Morton Kaplan's systems theory clearly bears the marks of his view of how the United States should conduct the struggle with the Soviet Union (Kaplan 1957).[21] A more interesting and subtle case is Waltz's *Theory of International Politics*, which indicates that under bipolarity the superpowers do not have to engage in costly conflicts on the peripheries and so leads to the prescription that the United States did not need to fight in Vietnam. But it is not clear whether Waltz arrived at the advice through his abstract theory or if his distaste for the war came first (Waltz 1967).

Furthermore, in some areas our evaluation of political behavior and our explanation of it will logically be linked. While an academic would not use a title as provocative as What's the Matter with Kansas? (Frank 2005), one's explanation of why poor and middle-income people vote Republican does depend on one's view of what their "true" interests are. To most liberals— and I suspect it makes a difference to research that most social scientists are liberals—it is a mistake for these people to vote Republican, and this leads to a search for explanations of why and how noneconomic considerations have risen to the fore, how the Republicans have framed issues and elections in a way that allows them to win, how the media distorts the parties' views, and how people get socialized into what Marxists would call "false consciousness." Someone who believes that Republican policies lead to freedom and high economic growth that benefits people in all income brackets will naturally be drawn to very different explanations (for example, Caplan 2007). Indeed, it is the belief that Republican policies cost the poor a great deal of money that makes their voting Republican a puzzle that requires an explanation rather than being straightforward rational behavior.

In many cases, those who believe that a policy is appropriate will find it self-explanatory. Realists believe that states follow their national interests, so when they do so little further comment is needed. For those who opposed the Vietnam War, the puzzle is why the United States fought; for those who thought it was possible and important to win, the puzzle is why the United States did not see the enterprise through. But in some cases, it is not quite this simple. Policies believed to be appropriate may call for an explanation if the observer doubts that all other leaders or countries would have behaved in this way. Thus both those who favor the Iraq War and those who oppose it may reject realist arguments that explain behavior in terms of the external environment in favor of a view that focuses on Bush's special characteristics. For those who agree with Bush, these are his leadership, courage, and insight; critics point to his ignorance and blinkered ideology. Note, however, that it is only critics who see the war as both unfortunate and a sharp break from the past who seek to explain it in terms of the peculiar nature of the situation or leader. A radical critic who believes that the United States in particular, capitalist states as a category, or big states in general tyrannize small ones would find this episode reprehensible but not puzzling.

DESCRIPTION/PRESCRIPTION

A somewhat less obvious aspect of the tension between policy and scholarship is created by the tendency for the latter to be both descriptive and prescriptive.[22] Realists in general and Morgenthau in particular argue that their theories not only describe, explain, and predict national behavior (that is what makes them good theories) but also offer guidance to policymakers. Thus Morgenthau spent half his time explaining that states follow their national interests and the other half lecturing American leaders that they should do so. But had he really discovered laws of international politics, he would not have to explain them to the very people about whose behavior he was generalizing: if I drop my pencil, I do not have to tell it that it must fall to the floor in obedience with the law of gravity. In the early years of the cold war, realists spent considerable energy refuting idealists who placed excessive faith in world public opinion and the United Nations and paid insufficient attention to economic and military power. This advice did not sit well with realist theories that not only indicated the importance of such power but left little room for leaders to believe otherwise.

I fell into this trap when I echoed Morgenthau and others in asserting that marginal differences in the nuclear balance did not matter but did not bother to confront the implications of the embarrassing fact that leaders in both the United States and Soviet Union had adopted a quite different view (Jervis 1984, 1989). If nuclear superiority was not meaningful in the sense of being able to be translated into political advantage, why did I and others have to tell American leaders not to worry about possible Soviet nuclear superiority or bother to pursue it themselves? Indeed, as long as the leaders adhered to their benighted outlook, then our arguments could not fully apply, and nuclear superiority, though "objectively" meaningless, could indeed have political influence, which then disconfirmed our empirical arguments. What this means is that when the state does not do what the scholar thinks the relevant theory indicates is appropriate, it simultaneously harms the country and embarrasses the theory.[23]

Those who stress the importance of international institutions similarly make claims that are both normative and empirical. As a result, when leaders or countries neglect institutions or act in violation of them, this behavior is not only seen by institutionalists as inappropriate, but it also constitutes an exception to, if not a violation of, the theory. The other side of this coin is that critics of realism run into difficulties when they argue that we can tell that realist prescriptions are incorrect by the fact that states that follow them often come to misfortune, usually by engaging in excessive conflict. But to attribute many of the world's woes to states following realism implies that it is a good description of their behavior, if not of the outcomes of that behavior.

This raises the possibility that theories may be self-fulfilling prophecies. During the cold war, some strategic theorizing may have been of this nature. The United States (and perhaps the Soviet Union as well, although this is harder to say) often seems to have behaved in accord with many of Schelling's expectations. But was the theory correct only because American leaders came to appreciate it? Richard Nixon (unsuccessfully) tried to put pressure on North Vietnam and the Soviet Union by leading them to believe that if the war were not successfully concluded, he might act irrationally (Haldeman 1968, 82–83, 98). He called this his "madman theory," and at first glance this seems to be a confirmation of Schelling's argument that bargainers will employ the tactic of the "rationality of irrationality." But in fact he may have learned some of it from Henry Kissinger, who in turn picked it up from Schelling and Schelling's student, Daniel Ellsberg. This is much of the reason why Nixon put the Strategic Air Command on alert in the fall of 1969. Although he did so in secret, the expectation was that the Soviets would detect it and become extremely worried. In fact, they did not even notice until later and even then thought it was related to the heightened Sino-Soviet conflict (Burr and Kimball 2003). (An interesting side issue here is whether the Soviet interpretation would have been closer to or further from what Nixon intended had they read Schelling—and knew that Nixon had as well. More broadly, if not only the state but its adversary follows the theory, will the results be the expected ones—and will they be in the state's interests?)

Self-fulfilling prophecies may make the theory valid, but this does not mean that the results will be good for the country or for the world. To continue with the nuclear-strategy example, Schelling argued that mutual vulnerability could create the "reciprocal fear of surprise attack" (that is, each side expects that the adversary is about to attack it and believes that the adversary has a symmetrical fear) and that this could produce a mutually undesired war. The irony is that this understanding, which I believe is in some sense objectively correct, could have made the world more dangerous. Mutual vulnerability (which arguably existed during the period when Schelling developed the idea) is troublesome only when one or both sides understand it.[24] Warner Schilling notes that theories about the causes of war can be the causes of war.[25] If everyone believes that war is inevitable under certain circumstances, it is very likely to occur. In fact, this is a large part of the explanation for World War I; if the participants had entered the July crisis with a different mindset, peace might have been preserved.

Indeed, one reason why social constructivists not only disagree with realism but feel that it is pernicious is their belief that acting according to realist precepts increases international conflict. Furthermore, for them the explanation for why states act this way is that leaders have learned to be realists, if not in the classroom, then through their general experience. In the slogan of the 1960s, realism is part of the problem, not part of the solution. Only by convincing people that realism is false can the world be made better.[26]

Theories can constitute self-denying prophecies as well, and this can occur in simple or complex ways. To start with the former, understanding the dangers that the theory points to can lead states to avoid it. Thus in response to the new understanding of the dangers of vulnerability, the United States (and, to a lesser extent, the Soviet Union) protected their systems in order to decrease the incentives to strike first and also pursued stabilizing forms of arms control. Countries may also have learned from theories of regional integration, but in a way that dismayed the theorists. According to a perhaps apocryphal story, when Joseph Nye interviewed a Central American leader about the prospects of regional integration in the late 1960s, he replied: "Ah, Professor Nye, we have learned from Professor Ernst Haas that if we take small steps toward economic cooperation, this will produce pressures for extensive regional integration, and because we do not want that, we will not take these limited measures." Because Haas' spillover theory said that European integration had operated through processes that the leaders did not discern and that benignly led to greater integration (Haas 1958), understanding it could lead people to steer clear of the entire process.

Although these are self-denying prophecies, it is not quite that belief in the theories invalidates them. Rather, people change their behavior so that the independent variables specified by the theory no longer arise. Nevertheless, the effect is still that patterns disappear once they are understood.

Erik Gartzke (1999) develops a more subtle and far-reaching analysis of this phenomenon.[27] If knowledge diffuses rapidly, there is little that scholars will know that national leaders will not. If the former can understand when wars will occur, then the latter will be able to do so as well. Since war is usually not desired, the patterns expected by our theories should not be present, because states will act in a way that nullifies them. In our theorizing we are then like Lewis Carroll's Red Queen, who stays in place even though she is running as fast as she can. Scholars will never be able to develop good theories about the occurrence of wars unless they can keep them secret. But what is bad news for theory may be good for policy, the world, and the values that scholars hold, because theorizing may reduce the level of violence and other forms of costly conflict. Scholars would continue to be ridiculed for being out of touch with the world and unable to solve real problems but in fact would be making enormous contributions.

More broadly, theorizing that attempts to tell "what works" is inhibited if not defeated by the endogeneity problem. In IR and many other areas of social science, in order to improve the world, it is crucial to know what policies are effective. If social scientists ran the world (granted, this is a disturbing thought), they could perform experiments, randomly distributing differing policies and then drawing inferences about their effects. But in the world we deal with, policies are not random (although in our more cynical moments we may wonder if they are); they are chosen by policymakers because of their expected costs and benefits, which presumably are seen as more favorable that those of the alternatives. This reduces our ability to determine the effect of the policy, because it is very hard to separate treatment effects from selection effects, to use current terminology. For example, a finding that the use of force tended to be less effective than the application of economic sanctions would not mean that policymakers should rely more on the latter in the future. Their predecessors obviously thought about the expected outcomes of alternative policies and chose accordingly, and the greater success of sanctions may be attributed to their having been applied to easier circumstances. The policy that is used is thus endogenous to the interaction in that rather than being employed at random (which would allow us to determine its effect), it is built into the selection of cases. Our ability to test theories is limited by the fact that we are studying people who are acting on the basis of their own theories of these phenomena.

This does not have to stop us in our tracks, however, because with adequate data we can control for many possible confounding factors. Thus Page Fortna (2004) shows that endogeneity cannot explain the fact that the deployment of peacekeeping forces is associated with the maintenance of postconflict peace because peacekeepers are deployed under conditions that are less rather than more propitious, and Christina Davis (2003) similarly demonstrates the efficacy of treating agricultural issues in forums that involve multiple issues by showing that this is done when the conflict is high, not low.[28] But these operations are difficult and cannot be entirely secure. Theorizing about the effectiveness of policies chosen by theorizing actors is a particularly complex endeavor.[29]

CONCLUSION

I am not sure that we are much closer to solutions to the conundrums of morality, policy, and theorizing than were the participants in the 1954 meeting. It is certainly the case that my own thoughts cannot be parsimoniously summarized, so in concluding I will just point to pitfalls and areas for further exploration. Discussions of morality in international politics often fail to separate the author's own moral judgments from the analysis of why people have made the moral choices that they did. Many scholars, especially historians, use current knowledge and standards to render moral judgments rather than try to understand the situations, actions, and actors being described.[30] Perhaps even more than in other areas, humility is in order here. When I walk home from my office, I pass a monument honoring a nineteenth-century doctor because "his brilliant achievement carried the fame of American surgery throughout the entire world." Today we view his experiments and practices as reprehensible. What ideas and principles that we hold dear will be seen as monstrous by our successors?

"Pure" theorizing is valued both by the IR discipline and by many of us. I myself would be deeply gratified if I could develop a theory of the balance of power in the eighteenth and nineteenth centuries, or if I could develop a true (if not *the* true) understanding of the cold war, even if these theories said nothing about current problems. But most of us were drawn to international politics not because we were excited by a theory or even a discussion of the past but by reading the newspapers (or now by reading blogs or seeing videos). Even those who do not want to scurry to Washington have strong views on what should happen there. This gives great motivation and excitement to our field, but we should not expect to be able to give great advice, nor should we underestimate the dilemmas created by the interplay between policy and theory.

NOTES

1. More parochial concerns are constant as well: "'Elder statesmen' in the field of theory frequently lack the time for research because of the increasing burden of other activities." Arnold Wolfers, "Theory of International Politics: Its Merits and Advancement," 284 (appendix 6 of this volume).

2. The links among theory, practice, and morality are highlighted by Dean Rusk when he notes: "We are talking about three kinds of theory: 1) normative theory; 2) general behavioral theory; and 3) theory which forms the basis of action in concrete cases." "Conference on International Politics," transcript, 242 (appendix 1 of this volume).

3. One reason why morality drops out of Waltz's neorealism is that his theory requires few assumptions about human nature (Waltz 1979); for discussion, see Keith Shimko (1992).

4. Niebuhr saw the dilemma clearly: "We lose by our moral pretenses. We have too narrow a statement of moral principles. In this sense, moral pretense is a self-defeating thing. Yet it a necessary part of social, moral, and political cohesion" ("Conference on International Politics," transcript, 245–46; see also his conference paper, "The Moral Issue in International Relations" [appendix 4 of this volume]).

5. He removed the relevant sections from his book when it was republished in 1946, remarking that he had "recast phrases which would be misleading or difficult to readers now far remote from the original context, . . . modif[ied] a few sentences which have invited misunderstanding, and . . . remove[d] two or three passages related to current controversies which have eclipsed or put into a different perspective by the lapse of time" (Carr 1046, vii).

6. For a related argument about the United States in particular, see Hartz (1955).

7. I think Niebuhr would call this hypocrisy rather than cynicism, but I do not think the substance of my claim differs from his: Niebuhr, "The Moral Issue in International Relations"; also see Wolfers (1979). To take a case outside of IR, throughout most of history and most of the world slavery was not only common but considered a normal part of life, unpleasant but not needing any special justification. The Europeans (and their American offspring), however, were guided by general principles that were in conflict with holding fellow humans as slaves. They therefore had to justify the practice with an elaborate ideology of racism that could make them feel comfortable with this practice. They could not simply be cynical about exploiting the labor of others in this way. The result was to make slavery more vicious and to leave the residue that still plagues us.

8. See the discussion in "Conference on International Politics," transcript, 243–48, especially the comments by Niebuhr.

9. The term and concept of the garrison state was developed by Harold Lasswell (1937; 1940–1941) before the cold war.

10. The first session of the conference ends with Nitze questioning whether the lessons of the Korean War still applied because now "we are not alone in having thermonuclear weapons. There is the H-bomb" (transcript, p. 251).

11. In discussing decolonization, Wolfers said: "We think that chaos is so terrible that wherever we see it we are on the side of order. This may leave western states in an opposite camp from those who are demanding change," to which Niebuhr replied: "In some cases we are forced to choose between liberty and order. How are you going to prefer one to the other?" "Conference on International Politics," transcript, 244.

12. As Nitze put it, "practitioners make little theories out of big theories." Ibid., 241.

13. For a strong and convincing restatement of this position, see Daniel Byman and Kenneth Pollack (2001). For the argument that dictators are different from democratic leaders, see Stephen Rosen (2005), in particular chapter 5.

14. Some of my previous work (Jervis 1997) combines the perspectives of strategic interaction, evolution, and ecology to develop ideas about politics and society.

15. See "Conference on International Politics," transcript, 254–55. A deeper set of problems concerning whether a state should behave rationally if others do not was not raised at the conference (although Morgenthau hinted at it on 254) and will be put aside here as well.

16. For a summary, see Rose McDermott (2007, 69–75, 139–141, 266–270).

17. I am drawing here on Jervis (2004).

18. Schelling (1966). See also Schelling Study Group, "Report on Strategic Developments Over the Next Decade for the Inter-Agency Panel," October 12, 1962, National Security Files, Box 376, John F. Kennedy Library, Boston. This was officially a committee draft, but the language and ideas are unmistakably Schelling's.

19. Morgenthau criticized a great deal of nuclear strategy in his important article "The Fallacy of Thinking Conventionally About Nuclear Weapons" (1976). While much of what he said is correct and has influenced my own thinking, the fact that it strongly argues against much American strategic policy should not obscure the fact that it reinforces rather than contradicts the arguments of Brodie, Snyder, and Schelling.

20. For the importance of national differences, see Ole Wæver (1998). As Walter Lippmann put it at the conference, "great political theories are designed as advice to someone as to how to act. They are always within a system and are arranged around the facts of the situation. If you were a Guatemalan, you would construct a different political theory." "Conference on International Politics," transcript, 251.

21. For a general demonstration of the impact of the issues of the day on historians' views of the past, see Combs (1983).

22. Some of the subsequent discussion is taken from my "Bridges, Barriers, and Gaps: Research and Policy" (Jervis 2008). Also see Jervis (1994), Kuklick (2006, 78, 88, 190), and Oren (2009, 283–301).

23. Thus John Mearsheimer acknowledges that "anytime that a state behaves in a strategically foolish fashion, it counts as a clear contradiction of my theory" (Mearsheimer 2006, 112). See also Mearsheimer (2001, 3, 11–12, 35). For a somewhat different and interesting analysis, see Trachtenberg (2003).

24. In fact, when it was explained to the Strategic Air Command leaders, they rejected it, partially because they thought it was a theorist's fantasy and partly because they had good reason to expect warning of any premeditated Soviet attack and would have preempted.

25. Personal conversation.

26. In fact, leaders often are not realists. In his belief in the domestic sources of foreign policy and the expectation that international politics can be transformed, George W. Bush certainly is not. Neither was Ronald Reagan, who not only believed that the Soviet threat stemmed from its evil domestic system but also joined with Mikhail Gorbachev in seeking to abolish nuclear weapons.

27. William T. R. Fox also saw this problem: see "Conference on International Politics," transcript, 256, 259–60.

28. Also see Mitchell and Hensel (2007).

29. It becomes even more complex when we deal with the strategic interactions among actors: see Jervis (1997, chap. 6).

30. Two recent and excellent exceptions are Bess (2006) and Conway-Lanz (2006). For an exchange about the moral judgments and moralizing in the discipline of history, see Jervis (2001) and Schroeder (2001). Also see Jervis (2009).

REFERENCES

Bess, Michael. 2006. *Choices under fire: Moral dimensions of World War II*. New York: Knopf.

Burr, William, and Jeffery Kimball. 2003. Nixon's secret nuclear alert: Vietnam War diplomacy and the Joint Chiefs of Staff readiness test, October 1967. *Cold War History* 3: 113–156.

Byman, Daniel, and Kenneth Pollack. 2001. Let us now praise great men: Bringing the statesman back in. *International Security* 25: 107–146.

Caplan, Bryan. 2007. *The myth of the rational voter: Why democracies choose bad policies*. Princeton, N.J.: Princeton University Press.

Combs, Jerald. 1983. *American diplomatic history: Two centuries of changing interpretations*. Berkeley: University of California Press.

Conway-Lanz, Sahr. 2006. *Collateral damage: Americans, noncombatant immunity, and atrocity after World War II*. New York: Cambridge University Press.

Craig, Campbell. 2003. *Glimmer of a new Leviathan: Total war in the realism of Niebuhr, Morgenthau, and Waltz*. New York: Columbia University Press.

Davis, Christina. 2003. *Food fights over free trade: How international institutions promote agricultural trade liberalization*. Princeton, N.J.: Princeton University Press.

Fortna, Virginia Page. 2004. *Peace time: Cease-fire agreements and the durability of peace*. Princeton, N.J.: Princeton University Press.

Frank, Thomas. 2005. *What's the matter with Kansas? How conservatives won the heart of America*. New York: Metropolitan Books.

Friedman, Milton. 1953. The methodology of positive economics. In *Essays in positive economics*, ed. Milton Friedman, 3–46. Chicago: University of Chicago Press.

Gartzke, Erik. 1999. War is in the error term. *International Organization* 53: 567–587.

Haas, Ernest. 1958. *The uniting of Europe*. Stanford, Calif.: Stanford University Press.

Haldeman, H. Robert. 1968. *The ends of power*. New York: New York Times Books.

Hartz, Louis. 1955. *The liberal tradition in America*. New York: Harcourt, Brace, & World.

Hoffmann, Stanley. 1977. An American social science. *Daedalus* 106: 41–59.

Jervis, Robert. 1984. *The illogic of American nuclear strategy*. Ithaca, N.Y.: Cornell University Press.

——. 1989. *The meaning of the nuclear revolution*. Ithaca, N.Y.: Cornell University Press.

——. 1994. Hans Morgenthau, realism, and the scientific study of international politics. *Social Research* 61: 858–860.

——. 1997. *System effects: Complexity in political and social life*. Princeton, N.J.: Princeton University Press.

——. 2001. Diplomatic history and international relations: Why are they studied so differently? In *Bridges and boundaries: Historians, political scientists, and the study of international Relations*, ed. Miriam Fendius Elman and Colin Elman, 399–402. Cambridge, Mass.: The MIT Press.

———. 2004. Strategic studies: Ideas, policy, and politics. In *The evolution of political knowledge: Democracy, autonomy, and conflict in comparative and international politics*, ed. Edward Mansfield and Richard Sisson, 100–126. Columbus: Ohio State University.

———. 2005. *American foreign policy in a new era*. New York: Routledge.

———. 2008. Bridges, barriers, and gaps: Research and policy. *Political Psychology* 29: 572–577.

———. 2009. International politics and diplomatic history: Fruitful differences. Keynote address at the First Williams/H-Diplo Conference on New Scholarship in American Foreign Relations, April 17–18, 2009, Williams College. http://www.h-net.org/~diplo/roundtables/PDF/Williams-Jervis-Keynote.pdf.

Kagan, Donald. 1995. *On the origins of war and the preservation of peace*. New York: Doubleday.

Kaplan, Morton. 1957. *System and process in international politics*. New York: Wiley.

Kuklick, Bruce. 2006. *Blind oracles: Intellectuals and war from Kennan to Kissinger*. Princeton, N.J.: Princeton University Press, 2006.

Lasswell, Harold. 1937. The garrison state versus the civilian state. *China Quarterly* 2: 643–649.

———. 1940–1941. The garrison state. *American Journal of Sociology* 46: 455–468.

Lebow, Richard Ned. 2008. *A cultural theory of international politics*. New York: Cambridge University Press.

Leffler, Melvyn. 2007. *For the soul of mankind: The United States, the Soviet Union, and the cold war*. New York: Farrar, Straus & Giroux.

McDermott, Rose. 2007. *Political psychology in international relations*. Ann Arbor: University of Michigan Press.

Mearsheimer, John J. 2001. *The tragedy of great power politics*. New York: Norton, 2001.

———. 2006. Conversations in international relations: Interview with John J. Mearsheimer (part I). *International Relations* 20: 105–123.

Mitchell, Sara, and Paul Hensel. 2007. International institutions and compliance with agreements. *American Journal of Political Science* 51: 721–737.

Morgenthau, Hans. 1946. *Scientific man versus power politics*. Chicago: University of Chicago Press.

———. 1976. The fallacy of thinking conventionally about nuclear weapons. In *Arms control and technological innovation*, ed. David Carlton and Carlo Schaerf, 256–264. New York: Wiley.

———. 1978. *Politics among nations*. 5th ed. New York: Knopf.

Oren, Ido. 2009. The unrealism of contemporary realism. *Perspectives on Politics* 7: 283–301.

Rosen, Stephen. 2005. *War and human nature*. Princeton, N.J.: Princeton University Press.

Schelling, Thomas. 1966. *Arms and influence*. New Haven, Conn.: Yale University Press, 1966.

Schroeder, Paul. 2001. International history: Why historians do it differently than political scientists. In *Bridges and boundaries: Historians, political scientists, and the study of international relations*, ed. Miriam Fendius Elman and Colin Elman, 409–16. Cambridge, Mass.: The MIT Press.

Shimko, Keith. 1992. Realism, neorealism, and American liberalism. *Review of Politics* 54: 281–301.

Trachtenberg, Marc. 2003. The question of realism: A historian's view. *Security Studies* 13: 156–194.

U.S. Department of State. 1984. *Foreign relations of the United States, 1952–1954.* Vol. 2, part 1: *National security policy.* Washington, D.C.: Government Printing Office.

Wæver, Ole. 1998. The sociology of a not so international discipline: American and European developments in international relations. *International Organization* 52: 687–727.

Waltz, Kenneth. 1959. *Man, the state, and war.* New York: Columbia University Press.

——. 1967. The politics of peace. *International Studies Quarterly* 11: 199–211.

——. 1979. *Theory of international politics.* Reading, Mass.: Addison-Wesley.

2

TENSIONS WITHIN REALISM: 1954 AND AFTER

JACK SNYDER

THE 1954 Rockefeller-funded meeting of realism's luminaries seems on first inspection to have been a rambling step backward in coherence and clarity from Hans Morgenthau's elegant paradigmatic statement of 1948, *Politics Among Nations*. The conference documents reveal unresolved ambivalence toward science and democracy and anxiety about realist morality, yet little concern is shown about a taken-for-granted philosophical pessimism. On further reflection, however, what is interesting about the 1954 meeting is precisely the unresolved tensions in realist thought, which are present but smoothed over in Morgenthau's text and with which all subsequent reformulations of realism have had to struggle.

For realists, international relations is shaped by a struggle for power, which defines the constraints within which law, morality, and ideals must operate. Realists see the logic of power as incontrovertible—more "real" than the artifices of universalistic law, morality, religion, or utopian hopes for progress. The logic of power makes inexorable demands, which states ignore at their peril. Yet the common sense of many people—especially the broad American public—apprehends the world not through the prism of power but through standards of right and wrong. In contrast, realists evaluate the rightness of behavior based on its pragmatic consequences in a competitive field of struggle against powerful opponents who lack common legal or moral standards. In the view of realism's founders, this perspective, counterintuitive and distasteful to many, could be grasped only though theory, which uproots unreflectively idealistic habits of mind. Such a theory had to be based on the proper philosophical assumptions, they insisted, and should not be confused with an overly rationalistic, optimistic approach to applied social science, which assumes that all political problems can be solved through diligent data collection and "can-do" social engineering. These differences in outlook between the knowing elite and the naïve masses have placed realists in an uneasy relation to democracy. As Robert Gilpin (1996) put it, "nobody loves a political realist."

The foregoing description of the essence of realism and its place in American society marks out four dilemmas that have pushed and pulled the development of American realist thought about international relations: realist pessimism versus liberal optimism, idealistic universalism versus consequentialist situational ethics, "scientific man versus power politics," and the stance of elites toward public opinion in making foreign policy (Morgenthau 1946). Different schools of realist thought have dealt differently with these recurrent problems, but for all schools, these issues have been defining.

None of the successive waves of realist thought has decisively resolved these continuing dilemmas. Nonetheless, realism has established itself as a powerful presence in American thinking about foreign affairs, despite both its poor fit with American political culture and America's temptation as a relatively unconstrained superpower to indulge its ideological preferences in foreign affairs. In the face of sustained challenges from various forms of liberalism and idealism, surveys show that realism remains neck and neck with liberalism as the two most prominent paradigms in American research and pedagogy on international relations.[1] Even its most intense critics acknowledge this by treating realism as their principal target, the alternative explanation that they feel they must confront.

In the wider arena of public debate and high politics, however, a pure form of realism never prevails for long. Especially in the amoral-seeming variant associated with Henry Kissinger, realism goes against the grain of liberal idealist Wilsonianism. Rhetorically, liberal internationalism remains the default position of American foreign policy. But the American public is also cost conscious in its attitudes toward foreign affairs, so realist voices of prudence are rarely shut out of policy discourse entirely (Dueck 2006). The bulk of foreign-policy professionals in government approach their work with a loosely realist sensibility. Realism is part of their mental furniture, most likely having read Hans Morgenthau or Kenneth Waltz in International Politics 101. Perhaps more important, realism resonates with their boss's wariness of getting blamed for a costly failure.

Realism's relatively high degree of success as an intellectual and ideological program, given the odds against it in the American context, is due to two factors. First, it provides a useful way of thinking about the basic questions of international politics. If it were not on America's intellectual menu, it would have to be invented. Second, realist thought in America has embodied a number of qualities needed for any successful intellectual and ideological program. It has sustained a continuous research program connected to its core concepts but has retained the flexibility to adapt creatively to changing political circumstances and intellectual challenges. It has taken care to nourish its theoretical roots while also remaining highly engaged in debates in the political world outside of academe. It offers a product that delivers. As a result, nowadays even some public intellectuals whose ideas are the antithesis of realism, such as neoconservatives who advocate the spread of democracy by military force, try to appropriate the cachet of the realist label (e.g., Krauthammer 2004; for a critique, see Fukuyama 2004).

In the following sections, I will trace developments in American realist thought, showing how successive variants of realism have dealt with its recurrent intellectual and ideological dilemmas. Five variants, or phases, will be examined: the founding generation, including the 1954 group; the adaptation of realism to the management of containment and deterrence under bipolar parity; the emergence of theoretically rigorous neorealism in the academy; the debate between offensive and defensive realists; and the turn after the cold war to an eclectic "neoclassical" realism. In doing so, I will try to shed light on why these recurring problems remain so prominent in realist thought, what accounts for variations in the way realists resolve them, and how these trends enlivened the realist tradition and contributed to its relative success.

THE FOUNDERS

American realists' own story of origins emphasizes the need to wake the American people up to the realities of world politics at the end of World War II: to shake them out of their Wilsonian utopian daydreams, to steel them against the tendency to slip into a disappointed isolationism, and to steady them in their support for a prudent international leadership role. Realism's critics might tell the story of origins differently: realism reflected a cultural pessimism, a worship of the state, or an authoritarian-personality syndrome transported by émigrés from Old Europe, which thrived in—and perpetuated—the fearful climate of U.S. cold-war domestic politics (Ashley 1984). There may be an element of truth in these criticisms, but they are far too harsh. My own view is that realism fulfilled a necessary function in the international and domestic political setting of post-1945 America, providing a needed intellectual anchor for American global policy. To carry out this task, America's foreign-policy elite (the so-called

Wise Men, including Dean Acheson, George Kennan, and Paul Nitze) needed realism as a guide for strategy and statesmanship and also as an ideology justifying their expertise, authority, and autonomy (Issacson and Thomas 1986; Lewis Gaddis 1982, chaps. 2 and 4).

This initial phase was well captured by the discussions at the 1954 meeting, which convened to take stock of the theoretical basis for realism's authority claims and to consider ways to institutionalize it in the academy. The foundational realist watchwords were power struggle as reality, national prudence as morality, philosophical theory as the appropriate type of science, and deference to realist "Wise Men" as keepers of the cold-war consensus.

No Crusading

Other contributors to this volume note that the founding realists were trumping up a "nondebate" with Woodrow Wilson's absent idealist ghost. It is unclear who, if anyone, is the idealist anti-Morgenthau of comparable intellectual weight in the immediate postwar period. Despite the realists' decision to pitch their critique at the level of high theory, their real target seems to be not some actual theoretical opponent but the wider foreign-policy elite and what public-opinion scholars call "the attentive public."

In Morgenthau's list of the eight "rules of diplomacy," *no crusading* comes first (Morgenthau 1948, 439). Walter Lippmann's 1943 book *U.S. Foreign Policy* had decried the boom-and-bust oscillations between messianic Wilsonian efforts to make the world safe for democracy and isolationist backlashes in which the United States retreated from its responsibilities in the global game of power politics. These cycles were blamed not so much on idealistic thinkers and international lawyers as on naïve American public opinion (Lippmann 1943).The tenets of realism were aimed at the misconceptions that led to these dangerous oscillations.

On some points, the realists made an airtight, nearly unanswerable case. Oscillations caused in part by uncompromising idealism and legalism had helped botch the peace after World War I and hindered practical efforts to prevent World War II. It was also difficult to argue with Morgenthau's second rule of diplomacy, that objectives had to be pursued with adequate power, or with the view that results count in morality.

On other points, however, the foundational realists made some choices that were questionable on intellectual or ideological grounds. Often their choices seem needlessly pessimistic and are skeptical that prudent policy could lead over time to change for the better in international politics.

The Will to Power

For example, Morgenthau is unnecessarily wedded to the idea of man's will to power as the mainspring that drives his conceptual system. His list of discussion topics for the 1954 meeting places the "nature of man" in second position right after "international relations theory."[2] Also high on the list, ahead of the balance of power, is nationalism. In *Politics Among Nations*, Morgenthau argued that, through nationalism, the powerless masses "project those unsatisfied aspirations [to wield power] onto the international scene" (Morgenthau 1948, 74). A vastly subordinated theme, presented in a way that makes it seem like a consequence of the will to power rather than a cause of struggle in its own right, is the lack of a sovereign power over states and their consequent resort to war and balancing alliances as means to survive (Morgenthau 1948, 125–133). This choice to play up man's fallen nature and to subordinate the structural problem of survival in anarchy was surely not an ideological advantage for the realists, since it played into the hand of neoisolationists and Asia-Firsters who condemned the Marshall Plan and European alliances as entanglement in the corrupt power politics of decadent Europe. The most plausible explanation for the choice is simply the philosophical pessimism in Morgenthau's and Reinhold Niebuhr's thought, which preceded their engagement with American foreign policy (Frei 2001). Later realists, unencumbered by this philosophical baggage, would make radically different choices that fit better in an American setting.

The National Interest

A second important conceptual choice was the founding realists' emphasis on the national interest. At one level, the attractiveness of this move is obvious both intellectually and ideologically. The realists were making a case against counterproductive cosmopolitan internationalism, so what could be a more natural move than to anchor their case in the national interest? However, they did this in a way that addresses the moral concerns of the cosmopolitans: basing policy on the national interest is actually better for everyone, not just for one's own nation, than is a hollow, dangerous cosmopolitanism. Theirs is no Germanic idealist glorification of the state, nor a cramped pandering to selfish interest, but a well-worked-out argument that contemporary realists might benefit from revisiting.

According to Morgenthau, only communities bound together by a dense web of reciprocity are able to sustain altruism within the group without degenerating into two deformations: masking self-interest as the universal good and imposing local values as if they were universal values (Morgenthau 1951). In discussing the impossibility of basing foreign policy on universalistic principles, Morgenthau notes that "no single nation is powerful enough to pursue its own ends without including the interests of others," including their distinctive moral outlook.[3]

When states claim that they are acting in the interests of others, they are either lying or fooling themselves, these realists believe. Niebuhr, in *Moral Man and Immoral Society*, had warned that social order requires coercion. The exercise of power leads to hypocrisy, masking self-interest as altruism and trying to justify the interest of the part as the interest of the whole. The ruling class does this domestically, and strong nations do the same internationally (Niebuhr 2001, 11, 17). Echoing this theme, Arnold Wolfers told the 1954 group that moralism in politics can easily become an ideological pretense cloaking more self-interested objectives.[4]

But this very emphasis on moralism's harm to the other lets cosmopolitan considerations reenter the discussion through the back door. Some participants in the conference seek to reconcile realist empirical theory, based on power and self-interest, with a rational view of a broader social interest. Nitze argues for an enlightened self-interest in which "the expedient and the moral merge." Dorothy Fosdick offers up the example of free trade, which makes everyone better off.[5] This realist tradition is far from being hard edged and ruthless. Its tone is one of prudent stewardship of the international order, where effective charity begins at home.

Democracy and Realist Diplomacy

Since the fickleness of the democratic public was a central concern of the postwar American realist project, it is not surprising that the participants in the 1954 meeting repeatedly return to the question of the compatibility of democratic domestic politics with the requirements of realist diplomacy. Part of this concern stems from the inexorable tradeoff that the participants perceive between liberty and order and between justice and peace.[6] As realists, their instinct is to prioritize order and security over liberty and justice. Paul Nitze states flatly that "tyranny is preferable to chaos."[7] Yet Hans Morgenthau (1946, 169, 174, 176) abhors the "totalitarian philosopher" Hobbes, partly on moral grounds, but partly for reasons of political expediency. In *Scientific Man Versus Power Politics*, he asserts than even "practical" people need "meaning" and "ethics" to direct their lives, and that a philosophy wins out in the marketplace of ideas only if it captures what "the man in the street" feels (Morgenthau 1946, 7–8). In a liberal democracy, realists need to show how their brand of prudent consequentialism is consistent with universally held liberal values.

In general, however, the realists seem confident that a realist-led government could be "the leader and not the slave of public opinion" (Morgenthau 1967, 142). Morgenthau's agenda of discussion topics includes "foreign policy and domestic politics" as well as "democratic control of foreign policy," but he places them at the bottom of his list.[8] Nitze tells the group that it is not true that public opinion, interest groups, and congressional factions unduly hamstring the making of foreign policy. He quotes Keynes's view that ideas, not vested interests, are decisive.[9] The implication is that the realists are doing reasonably well in the domestic war of ideas.

Theoretically, the founding generation of realists did not demarcate the international and domestic political spheres as sharply as later realists have sometimes done. Morgenthau wrote that "domestic and international politics are but two different manifestations of the same phenomenon: the struggle for power." The two spheres differ in "cultural uniformity, technical unification, external pressure, and above all hierarchy," but this is a difference "of degree, and not of kind" (Morgenthau 1948, 21). He cites the *Federalist Papers* on domestic factions to illustrate the universality of the logic of the balance of power.[10] Realist causal mechanisms such as divide and rule, compensation, and alliance making characterize both domains (Morgenthau 1948, 128–129; Morgenthau and Thompson 1985, 189–192).

As we have seen, both Niebuhr and Morgenthau based their theories of the national interest and political ideology on underlying theories of the national state. Unlike some later realists who tried to construct a theory of international politics without opening up the black box of the state, the founding realists tried to integrate their theories across these realms. Indeed, they thought that foreign-policy problems—including nationalism, idealism, and self-deluding hypocrisy—often emerged from domestic politics.

Assumptions About Science and Theory

The participants in the 1954 meeting understandably showed deference to Niebuhr in moral philosophy and to Morgenthau on questions on science and theory. The intellectual background of both men predisposed them to favor a philosophically and morally grounded social theory that failed to draw a sharp boundary between "is" and "ought" (Frei 2001). They understood theorizing to be a rationalist pursuit of moral and empirical generalizations, but they warned against taking rationalism too far. Humans are not merely rational, they believed, and complex historical concatenations of events could not be easily subsumed under general laws established by statistical methods. They were far less materialist than many subsequent realists would be. Morgenthau devoted many pages of his 1948 text to the nature and measurement of material power, but he stressed that power is a "psychological relationship," stressed that "a nation is . . . not an empirical thing," was as interested in prestige (the reputation for power) as in material capability, and did not reduce the former to the latter (Morgenthau 1948, 57, 73). Thus, the founders were ambivalent about science, theory, rationality, and materialism in ways that allowed their successors to make different choices yet still retain a toehold in the realist intellectual tradition.

Separate sections of the conference agenda were devoted to normative and empirical theory, yet the boundaries between the two were repeatedly eroded during the discussion and in the writings of some of the participants. Niebuhr said that for a realist, "theory is something that describes reality," yet "theory may also consider what should be."[11] Morgenthau argued that both normative and empirical theory are similar in seeking general principles that shape politics. An empirical theory of international politics, he contended, "would in its generality look something like the regulative principles of normative theory."[12]

This isomorphism between generalizing normative and empirical theories is not necessarily a source of comfort to the realists. Indeed, Morgenthau saw generalizing empirical theory as facing a "problem similar to that of normative theory," in that history is made up of ambiguities, unique events, and complex concatenations. Still, history also contains an element of rationality and regularity that makes it susceptible to theory.[13]

Both Morgenthau and Niebuhr worried about equating general theory—whether normative or empirical—with rationalism.[14] Rationalism—especially liberal rationalism—is dangerous, because it fails to capture humankind's full nature, which encompasses biology and spirituality as well as reason, and thus it "distorts the problem of ethics" (Morgenthau 1946, 5). "Politics must be understood through reason," writes Morgenthau (1946, 10), "yet it is not in reason that it finds its model." Politics is not "simple, consistent, abstract," like scientific reason, but "complicated, incongruous, concrete." A person may be a "scientist by choice or chance," but he is a "moralist because he is a man," and besides, a man who "wants to be master" (1946, 168). Scientific rationalism, including the kind of moralism rooted in strict logical consistency, therefore has a "moral blindness" that is alien to the "moral strength of the [true realist] statesman" (1946, 10). "Scientific schools become religious sects" (1946, 167).

And whereas moralistic rationalism leads to practical disaster in its belief that "the morally wrong cannot be politically right" (1946, 36), rationalism that exempts politics from morality leads to the emptiness of *raison d'état* (1946, 176). The scientism of Machiavelli and Hobbes, says Morgenthau, has "lightning" that illuminates political reality "but no fire" to inspire and direct political action in a constructive direction. "Moral issues demand an answer," despite attempts to make politics and ethics a merely empirical science (1946, 169). In short, the one-sided errors of both the rationalist moralists and the rationalist scientists are to be avoided.

The realist founders were committed to a form of philosophical theorizing that was highly selective in its commitment to science, rationality, and materialism. These choices were surely sincere, because they reflect the intellectual backgrounds of Niebuhr and Morgenthau. Nonetheless, the commitment to a form of rationalist science was also tactical. "No political thinker can be heard who would not, at least in his terminology, pay tribute to the spirit of science, and by claiming his propositions to be 'realistic,' 'technical,' or 'experimental,' assume their compliance with scientific standards," Morgenthau noted in *Scientific Man Versus Power Politics* (1946, 31). Subsequent generations took heed of this warning and were influenced by the founders' theoretical style. While the conflation of moralism and empiricism in realist theory was extirpated in later realism, realism retained a sharp evaluative edge that much social science lacks. And the resistance to behavioralism and statistical induction continues to characterize much realist scholarship for reasons that can only be explained by intellectual path dependence.

"REALIST" PRUDENCE AND PRESTIGE STRATEGIES IN THE HIGH COLD WAR

Following in these founders' footsteps were a generation of security-policy intellectuals who brought a realist-seeming sensibility to the management of power politics in an era of bipolar military parity. Their watchwords were containment through military alliances, nuclear deterrence through the balance of terror, and theories of strategic interaction as the intellectual tool for mastering the logic of power competition.

The avowed realist Henry Kissinger, like Morgenthau an émigré escaping from the harsh power politics of Europe, exemplified this moment in American strategic thought. The hero of Kissinger's dissertation book, *A World Destroyed*, was Prince Metternich, the archrealist Austrian statesman who craftily manipulated the European balance of power after Napoleon's defeat to protect status quo states from the destabilizing plans of revisionist powers (Kissinger 1964). In spirit at least, the book provided a model of how a realist might approach a problem like cold-war containment. Kissinger wrote a much more widely influential study for the Council on Foreign Relations, *Nuclear Weapons and Foreign Policy*, which argued in favor of a military strategy of limited nuclear war. Like Morgenthau, Kissinger stressed the Clausewitzian principle that war must be an instrument of policy and was too important to be left to the generals (Kissinger 1957; see also Morgenthau 1948, 442–443). The realists' morality of political consequences extended even to nuclear war.

Another commonality between Kissinger and Morgenthau was a concern for prestige as the reputation for power. Both considered power to be above all a psychological relation that depended on projecting an image of credibility in the use of power as well as restraint in its use. Kissinger, like many mainstream strategic thinkers of the day, thought that extending nuclear deterrence to allies and containing communist expansion meant jealously protecting America's reputation for living up to its commitments to allies. They feared that credibility was indivisible and so felt that they needed to make good on promises to shore up dubious, peripheral allies, such as South Vietnam, lest failures tarnish their reputation in the eyes of linchpin allies such as West Germany.

This way of thinking had a realist pedigree dating back to Morgenthau's concern for prestige in *Politics Among Nations*, yet Morgenthau himself rejected reputational arguments for fighting in Vietnam. Morgenthau defined prestige as the reputation for power and anchored it firmly in the underlying realities of material power. Kissinger's more general concern for the credibility of commitments opened the door to psychological and rhetorical analyses that risked coming unmoored entirely from realism's central concern with the material realities of power competition. More like Morgenthau, George Kennan had been skeptical about competing militarily with communism for control of the developing world on the realist grounds that the periphery lacked the military-industrial capacity to affect the world balance of power. In contrast, some other key figures who were realist enough to be invited to the 1954 meeting favored global containment, in part on prestige grounds. If the United States allowed dominoes to fall to communism, especially states to which it had made commitments, its reputation for power would be tarnished and a procommunism bandwagon might ensue. Paul Nitze had argued for global containment in these terms in NSC-68 (Lewis Gaddis 1982, 92). His boss, Secretary of State

Dean Acheson, later said that like "most other educators . . . we made our points more clear than the truth" in order to mobilize support for global containment inside the government (Acheson 1987, 375). During the Vietnam War, Secretary of State Dean Rusk, who paid for the 1954 meeting as President of the Rockefeller Foundation, feared what a falling-domino effect would do to U.S. reputation. Kissinger likewise gave huge weight to reputational dangers in Vietnam. Before withdrawing from Vietnam, he felt, the United States had to show that it had been a "good doctor" over the long haul for a sick patient, even if the patient eventually died.

Because Kissinger has unimpeachably realist roots, it is sometimes assumed that all his ideas were realist. However, by looking at the ideas of other deterrence theorists, such as his contemporary Thomas Schelling, it is clear how detached much of this kind of thinking was from realism. In *Arms and Influence*, the economics-trained game theorist Schelling argued that under conditions of mutually assured nuclear destruction, the balance of material power was equal and therefore neutralized in determining the efficacy of military threats. What mattered under those conditions was the balance of resolve, which hinged not on material advantage but on projecting an image of willingness to risk a nuclear escalation that would be disastrous to both sides. His analyses were dominated by such nonrealist concepts as the use of rhetoric to inflate one's stakes in a conflict (and therefore to boost one's perceived resolve), "the threat that leaves something to chance," and the relinquishment of control over one's action (in tension with the basic realist tenet of prudence).

This whole mindset was at odds with realist thinking. Deterrence and containment theorists depicted an international system whose expected dynamic was falling reputational dominoes rather than balancing against a rising power. To a large extent, these thinkers believed that psychological manipulations created rather than reflected material-power configurations. They counseled fighting for symbolic purposes in regions that had no military-industrial potential. In other words, the deterrence theorists and game theorists, no matter how realist their pedigrees, were flirting with ontological idealism. Even Kissinger, who tried to extricate himself from the logic of the domino theory by "letting Asians fight Asians," allowed reputational thinking to mire the United States in Vietnam for Nixon's entire first term. Academic realists, dismayed by the results of the oversold reputation theory, eventually blew the whistle on what they saw as a corruption of realism and innovated variants that were more anchored in material-power balancing. As Kenneth Waltz (1979, 208) put it, "others may have to worry about the credibility of our commitments, but we don't. Our credibility is their problem, not ours."

NEOREALISM

A third phase of realist thought, overlapping the second and important mainly in the academy, was the development of neorealism by Kenneth Waltz. As early as his 1954 Columbia University dissertation, which became the syllabus standby *Man, the State, and War*, Waltz rejected Morgenthau's stress on human nature and the will to power (Waltz 1959). Instead, Waltz explained the recurrence of war and balance-of-power politics as the result of security competition in anarchy. His 1979 *Theory of International Politics* articulated this argument in deductive social-science terms, dominating academic realist discourse and shaping debates throughout the IR field ever since.

Theory of International Politics rejected the founding realists' theoretical style in many respects but retained significant marks of that tradition. *Man, the State, and War* was anchored in a reading of the classics of European political theory but treated them more as a guide to empirical than to normative insight. Even in this early period, Waltz was moving away from Morgenthau's style of theory, which conflated "is" and "ought." Rhetorically, *Theory of International Politics* broke radically with the earlier realists' philosophical style, finding better metaphors for the balance of power in general systems theory and oligopoly theory. This placed Waltz's brand of realism closer to the mainstream of deductive theorizing in American social science, including its dominant rationalistic current—a move that placed realism on firmer ground in the academy.

Nonetheless, Waltz retained some of the realists' traditional ambivalence about rationality. He refrained from claiming that states and statesmen were always rational in their strategic calculations, arguing only that the international system could generally be modeled as if leaders were rational, since socialization and natural selection would correct or weed out those who failed to get it right the first time (Waltz 1979, 74–77, 107–111, 127–128). Waltz also retained the realists' traditional disdain for atheoretical inductive strategies of inference as practiced by some statistically minded behaviorist scholars. Finally, although Waltz did not dwell on moral issues in his book, which bent over backward to be a pure exercise in social-science theory, the theme of socialization through inexorable punishment as a result of the inescapable logic of the balance-of-power system arguably implied a commitment to traditional realist consequentialism in morality.

Theory of International Politics was a brilliant exercise in theory construction that resolved many of the contradictions and shortcomings of the realist founders' writings. However, it gave rise to at least two nagging problems. First, the theory girded its pristine elegance with a stout belt of limiting assumptions. Waltz insisted that his theory explained only a few basic outcomes at the level of the international system—why wars recur, why balances of power recurrently form, and why bipolar distributions of power are more stable (or more peaceful, in a later restatement) than multipolar ones. It was not a "theory of foreign policy" that could explain or predict particular choices of particular countries at particular moments— for example, whether to form a balancing alliance against a threat or to pass that buck to other states. Ironically, this kind of study of general systemic patterns might have happily occupied statistically minded researchers, but since most realist scholars were policy oriented and inclined toward qualitative historical case-study research, they wanted a systems theory that could also work as a theory of foreign policy in specific cases. As a result, realists struggled to find ways to add variables to Waltz's spare theory that would allow more determinate predictions of strategic behavior in specific cases yet be theoretically compatible with Waltz's scheme. Close to the hard core of the theory, these variables included military technology and geography. Additions more loosely connected to the core were perceptions of power and threat, including misperceptions rooted in psychology and in domestic political ideologies (Jervis 1978; Walt 1987; Van Evera 1999, chap. 7; Christensen and Snyder 1990).

A second problem was the tension between Waltz's relentlessly pessimistic rhetoric about war and power competition (part of the realist legacy) and his logical deduction that much aggressive behavior was pointless and indeed self-defeating. Because the balance of power punishes aggressors, Waltz said, "winning leads to losing." For some readers, including self-described realists, this led to what they saw as a contradiction in Waltz's discussion of a hot-button issue: the strategic logic of decisions to fight small wars in nonindustrial territories under conditions of bipolarity, such as the war in Vietnam. Waltz argued that multipolar systems were less stable than bipolar ones, because of the uncertainty in multipolarity over who would stop an aggressor. Since passing the buck was impossible in a system of only two powers, Waltz contended that aggressors would be less likely to stumble by miscalculation into large, system-destabilizing wars

(Waltz 1979, 171–172). Playing out this logic, Waltz argued that bipolarity should see lots of low-level competition in the periphery, since challenges mounted by one superpower would necessarily trigger resistance by the other, but this very predictability of resistance would keep the competition from getting out of hand. Many realist readers, however, thought that this violated the realists' materialist dictum that the goal of containment was "the division of industrial Eurasia," a goal to which backward Vietnams were irrelevant. Waltz himself, like Morgenthau, opposed the Vietnam War in part for this reason, as a chapter in *Theory of International Politics* makes clear (e.g., Waltz 1979, 206). From the vantage point of 1979, nobody—not even Waltz—was comfortable with a theory whose logic said Vietnam-style wars were inevitable. Soon Waltz's realist students were writing prominent articles on "why the Third World doesn't matter" (Van Evera 1990a, 1990b).

These two unresolved tensions in neorealism—the lack of a theory of foreign policy and the seeming contradiction that anarchy both requires and punishes aggression—led to further innovations in realist thought.

OFFENSIVE AND DEFENSIVE REALISM

A fourth phase of realism, again prominent mainly in the academy, was a debate between "offensive realists" such as John Mearsheimer and Fareed Zakaria and "defensive realists" such as Stephen Van Evera, Stephen Walt, and myself. The offensive realists criticized Waltz for failing to push the logic of anarchy to its logical culmination: whereas Waltz had said that states seek at a minimum to survive and at a maximum to dominate the whole system, Mearsheimer argued that the logic of competition compels states to maximize power, which means never passing up an opportunity to expand the state's sphere of influence (Waltz 1979, 91, 118; Mearsheimer 2001). In contrast, the defensive realists pushed Waltz's argument in the opposite direction. They seized on Waltz's observation that, in a balance-of-power system, "winning leads to losing" as states gang up to resist the most powerful, most aggressive state. Thus, the defensive realists contended that the fundamental logic of competition in anarchy typically creates incentives for prudent self-restraint, not aggression, and smart statesmen should anticipate that. Consequently, instances of self-defeating "overexpansion," such as German and Japanese aggression in the world wars, should be explained not by the logic of anarchy but by misperceptions and domestic political pathologies that led these states to defy the logic of the balance-of-power system (Snyder 1991; see also Zakaria 1992, a critique that sets this in the context of defensive realism more generally).

Despite their dissatisfaction with aspects of Waltz's arguments, both offensive and defensive realists rejected the human-nature realism of Morgenthau and accepted as their starting point Waltz's theory of the anarchical structure of international politics. The debate between offensive and defensive realists is not about the motivations of states, since both emphasize the survival motive yet acknowledge predatory motives as well. It is also not a debate about policy preferences: while offensive realists have been more pessimistic about international trends than have defensive realists, the two approaches have typically shared a preference for a U.S. grand strategy of selective engagement and "offshore balancing." To some modest extent, it is a debate about the incentives and disincentives for aggression that international anarchy creates. More fundamentally, it is a debate about the need to introduce perceptual and domestic political factors to explain choices that are anomalous or causally underdetermined by the strategic circumstances facing states. Defensive realists are like the early realist founders—Lippmann, Morgenthau, and Niebuhr—in articulating explicit theories of the domestic politics of foreign policy, but they are unlike the founders in seeing democratic public opinion as an enforcer of realist prudence in foreign policy against self-interested or ideological elites.[15]

The Motives of States: Security, Power, or Conquest?

A superficial reading might create the impression that defensive realists see states as mainly motivated by the desire for security, whereas offensive realists see them as motivated by the need to maximize power or simply by a desire to expand. This impression would be incorrect. Everyone on all sides of this debate portrays states as having a range of motivations in which security, power, and expansion are interrelated.

Defensive realists are well aware that states expand to increase their power and wealth when they can. In *Myths of Empire*, I wrote: "much imperial expansion is unproblematic: the strong conquer the weak because it pays" (Snyder 1991, 10). Van Evera argued that the cult of the offensive encouraged both the greedy and the fearful to attack. Conversely, Mearsheimer says that "survival is the primary goal of great powers" (Mearsheimer 2001, 31). "The 'security dilemma,'" he continues, "reflects the basic logic of offensive realism." In this situation, states strive to "maximize relative power . . . because power is the best means to survival in a dangerous world." Therefore, "only a misguided state would pass up an opportunity to become a hegemon in the system because it thought it already had sufficient power to survive" (2001, 35–36).

Defensive realists do not normally use Morgenthau's and Mearsheimer's language of "maximizing relative power," a term that Waltz explicitly rejected in favor of maximizing their chance of survival (Waltz 1979, 226). However, there is no reason why the defensive realists or even Waltz could not adopt this terminology. When states form balancing alliances against an aggressor, they are simultaneously increasing their chance of survival and increasing their power relative to what it would have been without the alliance. Bismarck, for example, argued against preventive war on the grounds that it would unnecessarily provoke enemies and thus undermine Germany's relative power. As for the claim that only a foolish state would pass up an opportunity at hegemony (even regional hegemony), the rub is in defining what constitutes an opportunity. This brings us a bit closer to the heart of the dispute between offensive and defensive realists, but still not as close as some may think.

Incentives for Aggressive Behavior in Anarchy

In *Myths of Empire*, I defined the central difference between offensive and defensive realism in terms of their views of the structural incentives for aggression in anarchy: "'aggressive [i.e., offensive] Realism,' asserts that offensive action often contributes to security; . . . 'defensive Realism,' contends that it does not" (Snyder 1991, 12). Still, the difference on this score should not be exaggerated. Defensive realists acknowledge that circumstances sometimes allow conquest, as when the strong conquer weak states that lack allies. That is why attackers, especially democratic ones, usually win their limited wars. However, grandiose hegemonic bids almost never succeed, because they nearly always provoke insurmountable resistance.[16] Defensive realists also concede that expansion may be needed for the sake of security in some unusual conditions, for example, if military technology really does make offense easier than defense, if relative power is dramatically shifting, or if limited conquests can achieve autarky or geographically defensible borders. Conversely, an offensive realist such as Mearsheimer readily points out that states are not constantly on the attack because circumstances often make it imprudent to do so. Prudent states, which is to say power-maximizing states, are aware of the limitations of their power, he says. They anticipate the possible balancing reactions of other states, they avoid arms races that would leave them worse off, they are stopped by water, they bide their time until they are stronger, and they look for opportunities to pass the costs of balancing against aggressors onto others (Mearsheimer 2001, 37, 157–162). In other words, much of the time states behave exactly as defensive realists say they should. "There is no question that systemic factors constrain aggression, especially balancing by threatened states," Mearsheimer notes, adding, "but defensive realists exaggerate those restraining forces" (2001, 39, 188, 304).

This is a dispute not about theoretical principles but about empirical probabilities. It is as if defensive realists think the offensive glass is 20 percent full and the offensive realists think it is 30 percent full. They may read incentives differently one time out of ten, but in most situations they agree about how a smart state should and will behave. That is why both offensive and defensive realists typically favor a strategy of offshore balancing for the United States, why they both tended to oppose the Iraq War, and why the defensive realist Stephen Walt has no trouble writing books and articles with Mearsheimer.

Nonetheless, on World War I Mearsheimer does differ substantially with the defensive realists and even with other strictly structural realists such as Dale Copeland, who calls it a preventive war instigated by Germany to forestall Russia's impending rise. Mearsheimer, denigrating Russia's army as only "the fourth best" in Europe before 1914, mainly argues the opposite, claiming that Germany was so strong after 1903 that it could make a grab for regional hegemony, the offensive-power maximizer's Holy Grail (Mearsheimer 2001, 188, 304). He admits that this gives rise to a puzzling anomaly: why did Germany not gamble on a war for hegemony during the 1905 Moroccan Crisis, when Russia's revolutionary turmoil created the prospect of an easy German victory over France? All he can say is that they made a mistake.

In contrast, defensive realism has a ready explanation: in 1905, German strategic mythmaking was still largely in the hands of cynical manipulators such as Chancellor Bernhard von Bulow, who played the nationalist card for public consumption but never confused the myths of empire with his real foreign-policy assumptions (Snyder 1991, 86; Berghahn 1999, 315). After 1911, however, Germany's new generation of leaders had internalized more of this nationalist rhetoric and become more entrapped in the mass nationalist mobilization that they and their forebears had spawned. They got caught in the rhetorical blowback as well as the strategic logic of the offensive Schlieffen Plan, which fit the self-serving organizational ideology of the military but not the national-security interest of the German people.

Perceptual and Domestic Origins of Strategic Biases

This leads to the third alleged difference between offensive and defensive realism: namely, that defensive realism introduces perceptual or domestic political factors to explain why states deviate from what structural logic would dictate, in particular why they often behave too aggressively for their own good (Zakaria 1992; Van Evera 1999; Christensen and Snyder 1990). There is no question that defensive realists often do this. Robert Jervis brings in cognitive biases that exacerbate the security dilemma or other conflict spirals. Van Evera and I introduce self-serving organizational and domestic political ideologies. But now, with the argument that the Israel lobby shaped President George W. Bush's strategy in invading Iraq, Mearsheimer is doing exactly the same thing (Mearsheimer and Walt 2007). And Randall Schweller, a critic of defense realism's status quo bias, similarly brings in domestic variables to explain why states sometimes are not aggressive enough (Schweller 1996, 2006).

John Vasquez and others have argued that this represents a "degeneration" from structural realism's ultraparsimonious explanatory hard core, and perhaps it is (Vasquez 1997; Vasquez and Elman 2003). Nonetheless, it is a complication that explains a lot with a theoretically coherent amendment that retains realism's focus on calculations about the implications of anarchy and power relations. These strategic ideas also feed back into the structural hard core when misperceptions of power incentives create facts on the ground that have real strategic consequences. Germany's Schlieffen-type posture actually did make Germany more vulnerable to the rise of Russian power than it would have been if it had prepared to fight according to a more defensive plan. And of course the misperception of offensive advantage had real consequences when the offensives bogged down in the reality of trench warfare. Moreover, defensive realists argue that states with open public debate learn to correct their strategic errors when the facts pour in. Thus, defensive realism depicts a close relationship between structural power realities and the perceptions of them. If this is a degeneration, it is one that lies close enough to the theoretical hard core.

A theoretical mistake worse than adding perceptual factors is causal underdetermination. That is the characteristic mistake of offensive realism: circumstances that might plausibly lead toward one behavior (say, gambling on war) might just as plausibly lead to the opposite behavior (say, prudent self-restraint), yet no additional variables are adduced to explain why the former is chosen. Mearsheimer's explanation for German behavior in World War I is a good example. A powerful, prosperous, largely secure state goes out of its way to make enemies of all of its neighbors, provokes a simultaneous land and naval arms race that it cannot win, refuses to give up on a hegemonic contest that is bleeding it white, and ultimately succumbs when the strongest power in the world throws its weight on the scales against it. Why does it do this? Nationalism? Militarism? Strategic misperception? No, says Mearsheimer: it is just that Germany was strong enough to think that it had a chance for regional hegemony, and it would have been foolish to let the opportunity pass by. Even without the benefit of hindsight, offensive-realist reasoning seems incomplete to explain Germany's gratuitously self-defeating behavior.[17]

The debate between offensive and defensive realism thus reflects two main tensions that characterized American realism since its early days. The first is the tension between the relentless striving to maximize power and the need to exercise prudence. Both offensive and defensive realists tried to reconcile those seemingly contradictory themes, and despite differences in substance and rhetoric, they have advanced arguments with a good deal of overlap.

The second is the tension between realism and democracy. Whereas Lippmann and most of the founding realists argued that fickle, idealistic public opinion was the bane of a consistent, pragmatic foreign policy, defensive realists have argued that mature democracies are the *best* realists. Mature democratic states necessarily have a well-institutionalized free marketplace of ideas in which policy expertise is widespread and strategic ideas are held up to scrutiny and criticism. Moreover, the average voter in a well-functioning democracy has the incentive and the means to enforce a cost-conscious prudence on governmental leaders. Although defensive realists do not argue that democracies never make mistakes, they argue that democracies are better at correcting them than are other regime types (Snyder 1991; Van Evera 1999; Reiter and Stam 2002; for a critique, see Kaufmann 2004).

Some friendly liberal critics of defensive realism say that the arguments are good but the label is wrong. Instead of seeing defensive realism as a degenerative form of neorealism, they suggest labeling it a hybrid of realism and liberalism (Legro and Moravcsik 1999). So perhaps it is.

NEOCLASSICAL REALISM

The fifth and most recent trend in realist thinking is neoclassical realism, which rejects the theoretical parsimony of neorealism in favor of a more eclectic analysis that shows how the state's international power position interacts with its political ideas, culture, and domestic politics to shape its foreign policy. Whereas Waltz said he had devised a general theory of re current patterns in international politics, not a theory of specific states' foreign policies, neoclassical realists explicitly aim at that goal.

Many neoclassicals are like offensive realists in retaining the causal priority of the international power position of the state, even while featuring domestic politics in their analysis (Rose 1998). Some of them are also like the founding realists in their emphasis on the state's need to mobilize and steer public support for foreign policy. For example, Thomas Christensen's *Useful Adversaries* argues that both the Truman administration and Mao Tse-tung demonized each other as a tactic in mobilizing public support for national-security programs that would strengthen them against the Soviet Union (Christensen 1996). In this case, international competition required domestic tactics that reduced the flexibility of foreign policy. This echoes the defensive realists' concept of "blowback," wherein elites' nationalist, imperialist, or militarist propaganda takes on a life of its own and traps them in their own rhetoric. A key difference is that for neoclassicals the motive for the rhetoric is to gain popular support to accomplish necessary international tasks, whereas for defensive realists the rhetoric is typically a self-serving effort to justify elite parochial interests in national-security terms.[18]

Other neoclassicals bring in domestic politics and culture to explain variations in policy preferences over time and across strategic subcultures. The international setting may load the dice in favor of some domestic and cultural patterns, but purely domestic factors may also play a role. For example, Colin Dueck's analysis of American grand strategy in the twentieth century is anchored in the materialist, realist facts of American power preponderance and distance from foreign threats, yet it also stresses American liberal messianism. As a result of America's international position and domestic principles, says Dueck, four strategies repeatedly vie for predominance over U.S. policy: liberal and realist isolationism and liberal and realist internationalism. Rising threats spur internationalism. Domestic political culture insures that internationalism generally takes a liberal form. However, power and distance permit the United States to indulge in the geopolitical luxury of limited liability in the pursuit of liberal ideological objectives such as democracy promotion and humanitarian intervention. As a result, America often leaves the objects of its help high and dry. Dueck's eclectic argument, which he describes as being "neoclassical realist," prominently emphasizes the state's international power position yet seems little constrained by any of the specific theoretical commitments of any of the earlier realist schools of thought.

Neoclassicals are like most other realists in privileging qualitative, historical methods but often unlike them in adopting inductive strategies of interpretation. Although some, like Dueck, make arguments that have policy implications, their policy stances have been quite varied. Rather than being driven by policy concerns, they mainly seem driven by the wish to combine a broadly realist sensibility with a flexible methodology that allows them to remain close to the data of their cases.

REALISM'S CONTINUING RELEVANCE

"Realism" has continued to enjoy wide currency in nonacademic policy circles and in public discourse about American foreign policy. During the George H. W. Bush presidency, policy making was in the hands of realist protégés of Kissinger: Brent Scowcroft, James Baker, Colin Powell, and Lawrence Eagleburger. They fought a limited war over security and resources against Iraq but kept Saddam Hussein in power to balance Iran. They shunned humanitarian intervention in Bosnia, where they had "no dog in that fight." And they agreed to humanitarian intervention in Somalia only because they thought it would be easy and perhaps because it would give them political cover for not intervening in Bosnia (Western 2005).

During the George W. Bush presidency, realism was a ubiquitous buzzword whose meaning was bent to support every policy and its opposite. Neoconservatives sometimes called their policy of preventive war against rogue states "democratic realism"—"democratic" because it sought to spread democracy, "realist" because it advocated the use of military force— though in fact their arguments had virtually nothing in common with any of the realist approaches that I have discussed here (e.g., Krauthammer 2004). The Bush administration's National Security Strategy study likewise dressed up forceful democracy promotion with the buzzwords of realism, speaking of "shifting the balance of power in favor of freedom." Condoleezza Rice, in her speech releasing the study, reminisced about the debates between realists and idealists during her days as a Stanford IR professor, saying that in Washington she had learned that all policies must be realistic and grounded in an idealistic social purpose.[19] Meanwhile, almost all academic realists, including the offensive realist Mearsheimer and his defensive realist co-author Stephen Walt, opposed preventive war in Iraq.[20] President Bush himself claimed that skeptics "who call themselves 'realists' . . . have lost contact with a fundamental reality" that "America is always more secure when freedom is on the march."[21]

In the wake of the disappointments of the Bush Middle East policies, realism's cachet is arguably greater than ever. Prudence and pragmatism are in. It is no longer true that nobody loves a political realist.

Despite that United States has often provided an unfriendly climate, realism is thriving, both in theory and in practice. It has established itself, along with liberalism, as one of the two dominant paradigms of IR study in U.S. universities. Indeed, it remains an indispensable reference point even for approaches that disagree with its assumptions. Realism has adapted creatively to illuminate such diverse, timely topics as civil war, mass killing, unipolarity, U.S. foreign policy, and terrorism (Posen 1993; Valentino 2004; Pape 2006; Walt 2005; Dueck 2006). Realists of various stripes (neoclassical, structural, offensive, defensive) retain a common core of insights that has proved its continuing relevance.

By now, several generations of officials, journalists, politicians, businesspeople, and voters have been schooled in realism's classic texts. Realist terminology—albeit often distorted and abused—has established a firm toehold in public debate. Although the Vietnam era and the rise of neoconservatism have long since ended the realist Wise Men's monopoly over mainstream policy making and public discourse, cadres with loosely realist outlooks still provide much of the staff of foreign-affairs bureaucracies.

One reason for this success is that realism speaks to issues that perennially face the United States as the leading power in the international system: the balance between assertive leadership and prudential self-restraint, as well as the morality of social purpose tempered by a necessary ethics of consequences in a strategic environment. A second reason is that realists— including the founders and their successors—addressed these perennial, seminal issues with a combination of flexibility and rigor that kept their debates lively and relevant. The 1954 conversation may be judged a success because of its fruitful contradictions.

NOTES

1. Maliniak et al. (2007) report that one-quarter of U.S. international relations specialists consider themselves committed to the realist paradigm in their research; one-third are committed to the liberal paradigm. The two paradigms are roughly equal in curricular attention.

2. Morgenthau, "The Theoretical and Practical Importance of a Theory of International Relations," 266–77 (appendix 2 of this volume).

3. "Conference on International Politics," transcript, 245 (appendix 1 of this volume).
4. Ibid., 244.
5. Ibid., 245.
6. Ibid., 243–44.
7. Ibid., 243.
8. Morgenthau, "The Theoretical and Practical Importance of a Theory of International Relations," 266–67 (appendix 2 of this volume).
9. Nitze, "The Implications of Theory for Practice in the Conduct of Foreign Affairs," 277–78 (appendix 5 of this volume).
10. See Morgenthau (1948, 127); making this same point more recently is Boucoyannis (2007).
11. "Conference on International Politics," transcript, p. 242.
12. Ibid., 249.
13. Ibid., 248–49.
14. Ibid., 249.
15. The following subsections draw on Snyder (2008).
16. A major exception is the conquest of the Chinese Warring States system by Chin. See Tin-bor Hui (2005).
17. For this argument, see Snyder (1991, 70–75).
18. In addition to Christensen, another argument of this kind is Kupchan (1994).
19. "Dr. Condoleezza Rice Discusses President's National Security Strategy," Waldorf Astoria Hotel, New York, October 1, 2002.
20. Mearsheimer and Walt (2003). See also the advertisement opposing an invasion of Iraq signed by prominent realists in the *New York Times*, September 26, 2002.
21. George W. Bush, "Remarks by the President at the United States Air Force Academy Graduation Ceremony," June 2, 2004.

REFERENCES

Acheson, Dean. 1987. *Present at the creation*. New York: Norton.

Ashley, Richard K. 1984. The poverty of neorealism. *International Organization* 38: 225–287.

Berghahn, Volker R. 1999. War preparations and national identity in imperial Germany. In *Anticipating total war: The German and American experiences, 1871–1914*, ed. Boemeke et. al, 307–326. Washington, D.C.: German Historical Institute.

Boucoyannis, Deborah. 2007. The international wanderings of a liberal idea. *Perspectives on Politics* 5: 703–727.

Christensen, Thomas J. 1996. *Useful adversaries: Grand strategy, domestic mobilization, and Sino-American conflict, 1947–1958*. Princeton, N.J.: Princeton University Press.

Christensen, Thomas J., and J. Snyder. 1990. Chain gangs and passed bucks: Predicting alliance patterns in multipolarity. *International Organization* 44: 137–168.

Dueck, Colin. 2006. *Reluctant crusaders: Power, culture, and change in American grand strategy*. Princeton, N.J.: Princeton University Press.

Frei, Christoph. 2001. *Hans J. Morgenthau: An intellectual biography*. Baton Rouge: Louisiana State University Press.

Fukuyama, Francis. 2004. The neoconservative moment. *National Interest* 76: 57–68.

Gilpin, Robert G. 1996. Nobody loves a political realist. *Security Studies* 5: 3–29.

Hui, Tin-bor. 2005. *War and state formation in ancient China and early modern Europe.* New York: Cambridge University Press.

Issacson, W., and E. Thomas. 1986. *The wise men: Six friends and the world they made: Acheson, Bohlen, Harriman, Kennan, Lovett, McCloy* New York: Simon and Schuster.

Jervis, Robert L. 1978. Cooperation under the security dilemma. *World Politics* 30: 167–214.

Kaufmann, Chaim. 2004. Threat inflation and the failure of the marketplace of ideas: The selling of the Iraq war. *International Security* 29: 5–48.

Kissinger, Henry A. 1957. *Nuclear weapons and foreign policy.* New York: Council on Foreign Relations.

———. 1964. *A world restored.* New York: Grosset & Dunlap.

Krauthammer, Charles. 2004. *Democratic realism: An American foreign policy for a unipolar world.* Washington, D.C.: American Enterprise Institute, Irving Kristol Lecture.

Kupchan, Charles A. 1994. *The vulnerability of empire.* Ithaca, N.Y.: Cornell University Press.

Legro, Jeffrey W., and Andrew Moravcsik. 1999. Is anybody still a realist? *International Security* 24: 5–55.

Lewis Gaddis, John. 1982. *Strategies of containment.* New York: Oxford University Press.

Lippmann, Walter. 1943. *U.S. foreign policy: Shield of the republic.* Boston: Little, Brown.

Maliniak, D., A. Oakes, S. Peterson, and M. Tierney. 2007. The view from the ivory tower: TRIP survey of international relations faculty in the United States and Canada. Williamsburg, Va.: College of William and Mary, Program on the Theory and Practice of International Relations. http://www.wm.edu/irtheoryandpractice/trip/surveyre porto6–07.pdf.

Mearsheimer, John J. 2001. *The tragedy of the great powers.* New York: Norton.

Mearsheimer, John J., and Stephen M. Walt. 2003. An unnecessary war. *Foreign Policy* 134: 50–59.

———. 2007. *The Israel lobby and U.S. foreign policy.* New York: Farrar, Straus & Giroux.

Morgenthau, Hans J. 1946. *Scientific man versus power politics.* Chicago: University of Chicago Press.

———. 1948. *Politics among nations.* New York: Knopf.

———. 1951. *In defense of the national interest.* New York: Knopf.

———. 1967. *Politics among nations.* 4th ed. New York: Knopf.

Morgenthau, Hans J., and K. W. Thompson. 1985. *Politics among Nations.* 6th ed. New York: McGraw-Hill.

Niebuhr, Reinhold. 2001 [1951]. *Moral man and immoral society.* Louisville, Ky.: Westminster John Knox Press.

Pape, Robert. 2006. *Dying to win: The strategic logic of suicide terrorism.* New York: Random House.

Posen, Barry. 1993. The security dilemma and ethnic conflict. *Survival* 35: 27–47.

Reiter, Dan, and Allan C. Stam. 2002. *Democracies at war.* Princeton, N.J.: Princeton University Press.

Rose, Gideon. 1998. Neoclassical realism and theories of foreign policy. *World Politics* 51: 144–172.

Schweller, Randall. 1996. Neorealism's status quo bias: What security dilemma? *Security Studies* 5: 90–121.

———. 2006. *Unanswered threats: Political constraints on the balance of power.* Princeton, N.J.: Princeton University.

Snyder, Jack. 1991. *Myths of empire: Domestic politics and international ambition.* Ithaca, N.Y.: Cornell University Press.

——. 2008. Defensive realism and the "new" history of World War I. *International Security* 33: 174–194.

Valentino, Benjamin. 2004. *Final solutions: Mass killing and genocide in the twentieth century.* Ithaca, N.Y.: Cornell University Press.

Van Evera, Stephen. 1990a. Why Europe matters, why the Third World doesn't: American grand strategy after the cold war. *Journal of Strategic Studies* 13: 1–50.

——. 1990b. The case against intervention. *Atlantic Monthly* 266: 72–80.

——. 1999. *Causes of war: Power and the roots of conflict.* Ithaca, N.Y.: Cornell University Press.

Vasquez, John A. 1997. The realist paradigm and degenerative versus progressive research programs: An appraisal of neotraditional research on Waltz's balancing proposition. *American Political Science Review* 91: 899–912.

Vasquez, John, and Colin Elman, eds. 2003. *Realism and the balancing of power.* New York: Prentice Hall.

Walt, Stephen M. 1987. *The origins of alliances.* Ithaca, N.Y.: Cornell University Press.

——. 2005. *Taming American power: The global response to U.S. primacy.* New York: Norton.

Waltz, Kenneth N. 1959. *Man, the state, and war: A theoretical analysis.* New York: Columbia University Press.

——. 1979. *Theory of international politics.* Reading, Mass.: Addison-Wesley.

Western, Jon. 2005. *Selling intervention and war: The presidency, the media, and the American public.* Baltimore, Md.: The Johns Hopkins University Press.

Zakaria, Fareed. 1992. Realism and domestic politics. *International Security* 17: 177–198.

3

THE ROCKEFELLER FOUNDATION CONFERENCE AND THE LONG ROAD TO A THEORY OF INTERNATIONAL POLITICS

BRIAN C. SCHMIDT

T HIS CHAPTER is devoted principally to exploring the initial phase of the long road to a theory of international politics that the field of international relations began to embark on in the late 1940s and early 1950s. As world war engulfed the international system for the second time in twenty years, IR experienced a profound disciplinary crisis. Contrary to the conventional wisdom, I argue that it was the lack of an explicit theory of international politics and not the failure of the League of Nations to prevent World War II that precipitated one of the field's early and recurring identity crises. The role of theory, in a fundamental sense, is to specify and demarcate a bounded domain of activity. As generic or universal claims about what kinds of things exist, theories answer the basic ontological question of what is to be explained. The very act of defining international relations, both as a distinct realm of political activity and as a separate and autonomous field of study, is inherently theoretical. Thus it is understandable that in the absence of a general theory of international politics, a host of critical questions began to be raised in the 1940s about the disciplinary status of the field as well as about the analytical distinctiveness of its subject matter.

The principal focus of the chapter is the 1954 Rockefeller Foundation–sponsored Conference on International Politics, which represented a defining moment in the field's history. I will pay special attention to the seminal role that Hans J. Morgenthau played in developing an explicit theory of international politics. The conference clearly reveals the self-conscious attempt on the part of the attendees to construct a theory of international politics. Moreover, the proceedings of the conference indicate that all of the participants were firmly convinced that the field was in desperate need of a theory. The stated purpose of the conference was "to discuss some of the fundamental problems involved in theoretical approaches to international politics."[1] The conference can be viewed as the dawn of what Yale Ferguson and Richard Mansbach (1988, 3) describe as the elusive quest for a theory that would "unravel the arcane secrets of world politics." Many of the same obstacles and dilemmas that continue to confront those seeking to develop a theory of international politics were present at the 1954 conference. The 1954 conference, however, was unique in that at that point, the attempt to construct a theory was a relatively novel development in the field's history. In this regard, the conference represents the beginning of what Stanley Hoffmann (1959) described as the long road to a theory of international relations.

My main intention is to develop an appropriate disciplinary context for understanding some of the issues and concerns that gave rise to the 1954 conference. This requires briefly revisiting the interwar period of the field's history. Orthodox accounts of the interwar period describe it as a time when the field was dominated by an "idealist paradigm," and scholars were engrossed in the utopian quest to create a pacific order whereby the League of Nations, international law, and disarmament would rid the world of war. However, a new cohort of disciplinary historians has systematically challenged this orthodox view and collectively argued that the interwar period cannot in any meaningful sense be construed in terms of idealism or utopianism (Long and Wilson 1995; Wilson 1998; Schmidt 1998; Ashworth 2002). While it is certainly the case that the scholarship of the interwar period has been grossly mischaracterized, there was, nevertheless, a glaring omission among the early participants in the field: namely, the absence of any self-conscious, explicit attempt to formulate a substantive theory of international politics. This lacuna contributed to a disciplinary crisis in the 1940s, when a number of new scholars reacted to what they perceived to be the field's amorphous and ill-defined character and began to advocate that international politics be the core of the field.

Yet in order to make international politics the core, it was increasingly acknowledged that the field was in need of a theory. Some of the leading scholars in the 1940s and 1950s, many of whom attended the 1954 conference, responded to the disciplinary crisis by attempting to construct a general theory that could explain the main events unfolding in the realm of activity designated as international politics. Although the conference deliberations indicate that there was little consensus on the exact meaning and purpose of theory, there was, especially when compared to the previous generation of scholars, a basic agreement that theory was absolutely necessary. There was a recognition that many of the problems the field was facing arose from the lack of a theoretical core to guide research and teaching. It was in this context that the long road to a theory of international politics commenced.

Curiously, it was the Rockefeller Foundation's Division of Social Sciences, under the direction of Kenneth Thompson, that played an influential role in fostering the analytical shift away from international law and international organization to international politics. Nicolas Guilhot explains that after World War II, the Rockefeller Foundation began to lose interest in the "legalist approach" to international relations and in strategies that placed a premium on the role of education in mitigating international conflict (Guilhot 2008). Instead, the foundation became interested in the work of the early realists, who were emphasizing the role of power and conflict in international politics. It was the Rockefeller Foundation that lent crucial support to the early endeavor to develop a theory of international politics. The 1954 conference was just one element of the Rockefeller Foundation's Division of Social Sciences mandate to "encourage theoretical studies in the field of international politics."[2] Guilhot argues that the Division of Social Sciences, under the direction of Thompson, was especially interested in promoting the work of those who were resisting the behavioral revolution that was sweeping across political science and the social sciences. The fact that the early realists were opposed to a science of politics and were resolute that international politics constituted an autonomous realm of activity helps explain why they received support and financial assistance from the Rockefeller Foundation. And one also cannot discount the special role that Thompson played in promoting the work of realists in general and Morgenthau in particular.

THE INTERWAR PERIOD REVISITED

Of all the self-images of IR, none is as pervasive as the notion that its early period of development was dominated by an idealist or utopian approach to studying international politics. According to this version of the field's history, the genesis of IR was rooted in an idealist moment after World War I, when scholars were apparently more concerned with finding utopian solutions to the problem of war and peace than with analyzing the cold hard facts that constitute the daily practice of international politics. This view of the interwar period is reinforced by the equally popular assumption that the field experienced a "Great Debate" during the late 1930s and early 1940s that resulted in a significant paradigm shift from "idealism" to "realism." The idealists apparently envisioned everlasting peace, and thus World War II was seen as a glaring anomaly that represented a severe crisis for the idealist paradigm. Eventually, it was replaced by the realist paradigm, which was superior in its ability to explain the ubiquitous struggle for power among nations. The systematic repudiation of the ideas of the interwar "idealists" by the members of the realist school, most famously in E. H. Carr's *The Twenty Years' Crisis*, has been construed as marking the field's first "Great Debate."

A new critical literature on the disciplinary history of IR has pointed to a sharp disparity between the actual discourse of the interwar period and the images that have been presented of it in the secondary literature. It is noteworthy that the prevailing image of the interwar period as a time when the field was dominated by "idealism," "utopianism," and "legalism" comes from surveys that were written after World War II and that continue to be popularized today. Cameron Thies (2002, 173) is largely correct when he writes that the "realists constructed 'idealism' and included it within their own version of disciplinary history to cement their identity as a community of researchers and show the progress of realism over 'idealism.'" By the end of World War II, a body of self-reflective literature on the state of the field began to appear. While ostensibly offering an account of the field's history, the primary intention of this literature was, more often than not, to diagnose the current problems in the field and to recommend new directions to follow. These surveys revealed a noticeable dissatisfaction with the overall direction of IR. Disconcerting questions were raised about whether or not IR was a discernable field of study with a distinct subject matter. Conflicting opinions on what the field should be studying were expressed. The surveys also conveyed a growing skepticism about the adequacy and relevancy of international organization continuing to serve as the predominant framework for studying international relations.

Grayson Kirk, who was an internationally renowned professor of international relations and president of Columbia University from 1953 to 1968, wrote one of the first book-length surveys of the postwar trends in IR, which was sponsored by the Council on Foreign Relations and supported by the Rockefeller Foundation. According to Kirk, the refusal of the United States to join the League of Nations led the interwar scholars, whom he maintained were strong partisans of American membership in the League, to "redouble their efforts at indoctrination." Kirk argued that as a result an

emphasis upon what has been variously called "sentimentalism," "idealism," and "Utopianism," dominated the teaching in the new field, and a wholly disproportionate amount of time and energy was given to discussing "international cooperation," while analyses of the forces of conflict in society, and of the institution of war, were subordinated and tainted with the stigma of moral reproach.

Kirk concluded that this emphasis on utopianism "cast a shadow of academic disrepute over the new field" (1947, 4), to disastrous effect. Kirk was united with the cadre of postwar scholars who sought to make international politics the field's new nucleus. Guilhot (2008) claims that Kirk's survey, along with a report by Bryce Wood in 1947, was instrumental in changing the direction of the type of work that the Rockefeller Foundation would subsequently sponsor and fund.

Kenneth Thompson shared Kirk's disparaging views of the interwar IR scholarship and he, along with his close friend and colleague Hans Morgenthau, would come to play a major role in championing the cause of both IR theory and political realism. This was evident in a 1952 review article that Thompson published, titled "The Study of International Politics: A Survey of Trends and Developments," which exhibited the predilection to denounce the scholarship that he believed characterized the interwar period. Thompson argued that the study of international relations had evolved through four general stages. The first stage was when the study of diplomatic history was dominant. According to Thompson (1951, 435), "the price which was paid for this rigorous, objective and non-generalized approach to the field was the absence of anything corresponding to a theory of international relations." He dubbed the second phase the "current events point of view," in which the role and function of the IR scholar was to interpret and explain current events. The third stage was inaugurated after World War I and, according to Thompson, it was reformist in character, in that the "mission of students in the field had been to discover the goals and objectives toward which international society ought to be tending" (436). He argued that this stage shared three fundamental characteristics. First, it was dominated by a spirit of optimism. Second, research was focused exclusively on international law and organization. And third, "it was widely believed that everything international was good, and everything national bad." Following World War II, the field had reached a fourth stage, in which "the study of international politics replaced the study of international organization as the guiding concern and fundamental point of reference in international relations" (439).

Kirk and Thompson were not alone in either their condemnation of the interwar scholarship or their perception that the field was experiencing a shift away from international organization toward international politics.

Writing in 1949, William T. R. Fox, who received his doctorate from the University of Chicago and was one of the original faculty members who helped create the Institute of International Relations at Yale University, commented, "what is today in the United States conventionally known as international relations is a subject different in content and emphasis from its counterpart of even two decades ago" (Fox 1949, 67). To help make his point, Fox provided a highly distorted and rhetorical characterization of the analytical model used during the interwar period. According to Fox, the "analytical model used for investigative purposes was a world commonwealth characterized by permanent peace" (77). Most of the dominant characteristics that he associated with the interwar period were similar to those that Carr had critiqued in *The Twenty Years' Crisis*: the assumption of a basic harmony of interests, a pervasive faith in reason, the efficacy of education, and legalistic prescriptions for peace.

What is perhaps most interesting about Fox's interwar survey were his comments about what was missing from the field. As a result of what he perceived to be an internationalist bias in the field, Fox argued that that there was a disproportionate focus on studying "'good' international things like collective security and peaceful change and 'bad' national things like nationalist attitudes, imperialism, and the munitions makers." Consequently, Fox continued, "there was a corresponding underemphasis on 'bad' international things like the Third International and 'good' national things like American security" (1949, 74–75). The net result, according to Fox, was that the interwar scholars failed to study the politics of the contemporary state system. He did, however, note that there were a few scholars writing at the end of the interwar period who did not fit the mold. Fox specifically mentioned the work of Charles A. Beard, Frederick S. Dunn, Quincy Wright, Frederick Schuman, Harold Laswell, Edward Mead Earle, Harold Sprout, Nicholas Spykman, and Arnold Wolfers. The work of these scholars, Fox claimed, helped move international politics to the center of focus. In another article that he wrote on the teaching of international relations in the United States, Fox recollected that "there has been, at least since the 1930s, wide acceptance of the proposition that prescriptions for national policy and definitions of the national interest ought to be appropriate for the world we live in rather than for the one we wish we lived in" (1968, 19). This proposition rested on recognizing the centrality of power, which he argued was gaining more and more adherents. Dwight Waldo, who undertook a major postwar survey of political science, concurred and described the situation in IR in terms of "movement away from 'idealism' toward 'realism'; by bringing to the centre of study the concepts of power and politics" (Waldo 1959, 56).

INTERNATIONAL POLITICS

The increasingly prevalent but by no means unanimous view expressed in the post–World War II surveys was that international politics now constituted the core of the field (e.g., Wolfers 1947; Dunn 1950; Kirk 1947; Fox 1949; Thompson 1952; Waldo 1959). Thompson (1952, 442) was a strong advocate of this view, arguing that "international politics has become the focal point of present-day research and teaching partly because of the march of events in the 1930s." He defined international politics as "the study of rivalry among nations and the conditions and institutions which ameliorate or exacerbate these relationships" (443). Kirk had also concluded that international politics represented the "nucleus of the modern study of international relations." According to Kirk (1947, 10), "international politics deals with those forces which mold the foreign policies of national states, the manner in which they are exercised, and the influences which limit their effectiveness." Central to both Thompson and Kirk's view of international politics, and politics more generally, was the presence of conflict.

This view became increasingly prominent after World War II, especially by those who identified themselves as belonging to the realist school. Their conception of international politics was state-centric; IR was concerned with the political dynamics arising from the interaction of separate political units (states) existing in an environment lacking centralized authority. One of the early endorsements of this view was put forward by Frederick S. Dunn in an article titled "The Scope of International Relations," which appeared in the very first issue of *World Politics*. Beginning in 1935, Dunn was a professor of international relations at Yale. Following the disbanding of the Yale Institute of International Studies in 1951, Dunn accepted the position of Albert G. Milbank Professor of International Law and Practice at Princeton University, where he also took on the responsibility of director of Princeton's new Center of International Studies until his retirement in 1961. The purpose of Dunn's article was "to state certain propositions about the nature and scope of IR which seem to represent the present views of some mature scholars in the field" (Dunn 1948, 143). Dunn, like many of his colleagues, found it difficult to provide a definitive answer to the question of whether IR should be regarded as a separate and autonomous field of inquiry. He did, however, argue that the "distinguishing characteristic of IR as a separate branch of learning is found in the nature of the questions with which it deals." These questions, according to Dunn, "arise in the relations between autonomous political groups in a world system in which power is not centered at one point" (144).

Dunn argued that in light of the complete breakdown of the interwar system, the twin assumptions of rationalism and the inevitability of progress toward peace that had led scholars to focus on formal governmental structures and institutional devices could no longer be justified. Now that rationalism was no longer the standard assumption, Dunn claimed that researchers were turning "to a more careful observation of international politics in action and of the forces influencing political beliefs and actions" (Dunn 1950, 81). According to Dunn, the uniqueness of studying international politics, and what justified differentiating it from domestic politics, stemmed from the fact that it "is concerned with the special kind of power relationships that exist in a community lacking an overriding authority." This being the case, the IR specialist is interested in the "conflict, adjustment and agreement of national policies" (Dunn 1948, 144).

Although Dunn accentuated the anarchical character of international politics and the role of conflict and rivalry in the relations among autonomous political units, he did not discount the normative commitment to improve the condition of international life. He both recognized and accepted that the study of IR was in many ways dedicated to understanding the conditions that could lead to the obsolescence of war. The commitment to improving the practice of international politics was noticeable in Dunn's *Peaceful Change: A Study of International Procedures* (1937). But, according to Dunn, the difference between the interwar and postwar scholars was that the former conceived of "ideal social systems in which wars did not exist," while the latter "give primary attention to the ascertainable facts of international life and the forces and conditions that influence behavior among nations, as well as the ways in which these can be used for desired ends" (Dunn 1948, 145).

There was a growing realization that in order to establish international politics as the core of IR, a substantive theory needed to be developed. Many reached the conclusion that in the absence of a general theory, questions and doubts about the disciplinary status of IR as well as about the analytical distinctiveness of its subject matter would persist. This was clearly recognized by Stanley Hoffmann in 1959, when he wrote that "the problems we face in our field can be solved only by far more systematic theoretical work than has been done in the past—a conviction shared by most writers." He continued, "it is the possibility of considering international relations as a largely autonomous field, within the sprawling and loose science of politics, which explains the need for theory" (Hoffman 1959, 346). As more scholars began to recognize that it was the lack of theory that was responsible for the field's various problems, the search for a general theory of international politics commenced. Writing in 1960, J. David Singer stated that "one of the most promising developments in the intellectual growth of a discipline is the appearance of a concern for theory on the part of its students and practitioners." He added, "without theory we can have only the barest shadow of a discipline" (Singer 1960, 431).

THE ROCKEFELLER CONFERENCE ON THE THEORY OF INTERNATIONAL POLITICS

The literature on IR theory grew rapidly after World War II. Conferences were organized around the theme of IR theory, and formal study groups dedicated to developing a theory of international politics were institutionalized, with the financial support of the Rockefeller Foundation, on both sides of the Atlantic. This is the appropriate context for appreciating the significance of the 1954 Conference on Theory of International Politics. Kenneth Thompson and Dean Rusk, who were both working at the Rockefeller Foundation, invited a group of prominent scholars and practitioners to meet at the Statler Hotel, in Washington, D.C., on May 7 and 8, 1954, to discuss the general subject of theory in international relations.[3] In addition to Thompson and Rusk, Robert Bowie, Dorothy Fosdick, William T. R. Fox, George Kennan, Walter Lippmann, Hans J. Morgenthau, Reinhold Niebuhr, Paul H. Nize, Don K. Price, James B. Reston, and Arnold Wolfers were invited to attend the meetings. On the other side of the Atlantic, the British Committee on the Theory of International Politics was formed in 1959 with financial assistance provided by the Rockefeller Foundation and the personal support of Thompson. The original members of the British committee, which was attached to the University of Cambridge, included Herbert Butterfield, Martin Wight, Desmond Williams, Donald Mackinnon, Adam Watson, William Armstrong, Hedley Bull, Michael Howard, and Geoffrey Hudson.[4] The British committee would outlive the "American committee" and lay the foundation for what has become known as the English School of international relations. Tim Dunne, in his authoritative disciplinary history of the English School, argues that it was disputes between theorists and practitioners in the American committee that led to its early dissolution. The British committee, on the other hand, "remained detached from policy issues" and had a longer and more productive history (Dunne 1998, 90).

The purpose of the 1954 Washington conference was "to allow a group of scholars and political analysts to meet informally to discuss some of the fundamental problems involved in theoretical approaches to international politics."[5] One of the principal motivations for holding the meeting came from the new literature that was being published on IR theory. Rusk, who at the time was the president of the Rockefeller Foundation, begins the proceedings by noting that "there currently tends to be a trend toward a more lively interest in theoretical and conceptual problems illustrated in the study of international politics and emerging in theories of politics, economics, law and human behavior." He adds that from the point of view of the Rockefeller Foundation, we are not only "anxious to learn what the state of the field is intellectually," but also "if we can do anything about it."[6] Thompson expresses his concern that while scholars of international law and international organization were being supported by the American Society of International Law, the Carnegie Endowment for International Peace, and the World Peace Foundation, "scholars in the field of international politics have not enjoyed similar opportunities for considering together their problems and the developments in their field." As a consequence of this, Thompson argues that "the work in the theory of international politics has not been distinguished by the number of laborers in the vineyard nor has there always been agreement among scholars regarding the merits of the work."[7] By agreeing to cover the expenses of the conference, the Rockefeller Foundation sought to assist those who were actively seeking to develop a theory of international politics, which, as mentioned previously, was in accordance with the foundation's official policy "to encourage theoretical studies in the field of international politics."[8]

While the literature on IR theory expanded rapidly after World War II, there was, at the same time, little consensus on many of the key issues involved in the theoretical enterprise. Thompson summarized the situation in the following manner: "the present state of theory in the field of international politics is compounded of vigorous debate, intellectual growth, and little unanimity on points of detail" (Thompson 1955, 746). While all of those who presented papers at the conference agreed on the necessity of theory and believed in the possibility of constructing a theory of international politics, there were noticeable differences of opinion on a number of important topics. There was, for example, ambivalence about science and disagreement on whether or not it was possible for IR to achieve greater certainty and predictive capabilities by utilizing the scientific techniques of the natural sciences. This disagreement, which was most noticeable in some of the exchanges between Arnold Wolfers and the other members of the conference, would increasingly polarize the field between those championing the behavioral revolution and those rejecting it. There were also disagreements about what theory can and cannot do, especially in regards to helping practitioners conduct foreign policy. Indeed, a case can be made that the theory-practice issue is one of the overarching themes of the conference deliberations, a theme that no doubt was elevated by the presence of several foreign-policy practitioners. Finally, it is obvious that normative and ethical concerns are paramount as the participants debate the relative merits of normative and scientific theory. Thus much like today, intellectual ferment and debate rather than tranquility and consensus characterized international theory in 1954.

HANS J. MORGENTHAU'S THEORY OF INTERNATIONAL POLITICS

The participants were asked to consider four major questions in the papers that they prepared for the conference:

1. The possibility, Nature and Limits of a Theory of International Politics;
2. The Relevance and Uses of Theory in International Politics, especially for the Conduct of Foreign Policy;
3. Problems and Issues in a Theory of International Politics including the Moral Issue, the National Interest, etc., etc.; and
4. The Status and Future Work in this Field.[9]

It is instructive to focus briefly on the answers that Hans J. Morgenthau provided to some of these questions, as the other conference participants clearly recognized that he had made great strides in developing a general theory of international politics, even if they did not agree with all of his points and arguments. As Michael C. Williams acknowledges in his new book, *The Realist Tradition and the Limits of International Relations*, "no assessment of the development of International Relations can overlook the importance of Morgenthau in the intellectual evolution of the field, and his role in placing Realism at the centre of that evolution" (Williams 2005, 82). The focus of Morgenthau's early work in the United States was on developing an explicit theory of international politics. At the time of the conference, Morgenthau had already published three major theoretical books: *Scientific Man Versus Power Politics* (1946), *Politics Among Nations* (1948), and *Defense of the National Interest* (1951). The opening sentence of the second edition of Morgenthau's classic text *Politics Among Nations* represents a milestone in the development of IR, as he announces "this book purports to present a theory of international politics" (Morgenthau 1955, 3). This is the first book in the field to unequivocally take on the task of setting forth a general theory of international politics. Morgenthau felt that it was imperative to develop a theory of international politics, for without a general theory, the field would continue to lack intellectual focus and direction. For Morgenthau, "a theory is a tool for understanding. Its purpose is to bring order and meaning to a mass of phenomena which without it would remain disconnected and unintelligible."[10] In this manner, Stefano Guzzini has perceptively argued that Morgenthau's theory of realism should not be understood "just as one theory among others, but as one theory which contributed to legitimately demarcate an independent discipline from other social sciences" (Guzzini 1998, 2). Morgenthau's theory of realism had the effect of carving out a distinct subject matter that helped establish the disciplinary boundaries of IR.

While Morgenthau recognized the absolute necessity of theory, he also acknowledged many of the obstacles that stood in the way of developing a theory of international politics. The difficulty of the task was confirmed by the fact that so few attempts had been previously made to develop such a theory. Morgenthau wrote, "it is significant that, until very recently, no explicit theory of international relations has existed; nobody even considered the possibility of writing a theory of international relations" (1964, 106). He completely agreed with Martin Wight's analysis that international theory was "marked not only by paucity but also by intellectual and moral poverty" but remained much more optimistic than Wight about the possibility of developing a theory of international politics (Wight 1960, 38). For Morgenthau, it was revealing that each of the previously predominant ways of studying international relations—history, reform, pragmatic manipulation—were all alien to theory. He argued, however, that each of these approaches actually presupposed a theoretical conception of international politics; the problem was that they failed to do so in an explicit and coherent manner. According to Morgenthau, what was presently most necessary was a theory that accentuated politics. "The recognition of this primacy of politics cannot but lead to the suggestion that, among legitimate predominant interests upon which international relations as an academic discipline might be focused, international politics should take precedent over all others" (Morgenthau 1958, 100).

All of the conference participants agreed with Morgenthau that the foremost obstacle to constructing a general theory of international politics was the ambiguity of the subject matter itself. Morgenthau explains that, on the one hand, the material consists of a series of unique events that only occur once. Yet, on the other hand, he argues that "these same events are also specific instances of general propositions, and it is only as such that they are susceptible to theoretical understanding." According to Morgenthau, the task of theory is "to detect in the welter of the unique facts of experience that which is uniform, similar, and typical. It is its task to reduce the facts of experience to mere specific instances of general propositions, to detect behind them the general laws to which they owe their existence and which determine their development."[11] Morgenthau concedes that it is often difficult to determine the line demarcating the unique from the general, and a spirited exchange among the conference participants takes place on this issue. Because of the ambiguous nature of politics, Morgenthau issues a warning to those who were tempted to ignore this fact in their attempt to impose scientific standards on the study of international politics. For Morgenthau, "a theory of international relations which yielded to that temptation would become a metaphysics, superimposing a logically coherent intellectual scheme upon a reality which falls far short of such coherence."[12]

While Morgenthau was aware of the ambiguity of historical events and of the difficulty of differentiating between the general and the particular, he argued that it was the assumption of rationality that allowed for the possibility of a theory of international politics. For Morgenthau, it was the rationality of the IR theorist, of the foreign-policy practitioner, and even of the activity of international relations itself that made a theory of international politics possible. Morgenthau argues that "what makes a theory of international relations possible in spite of the ambiguities of its subject matter is the rationality in which both the mind of the observer and the object of observation, that is, international relations, partake."[13] He held that one of the central tasks of theory was to sort out the rational from the contingent elements so that a degree of order could be discerned from the otherwise random and unconnected events that make up international relations. A crucial function of theory, for Morgenthau, was "to detect in the welter of the unique facts of experience that which is uniform, similar, and typical" (1959, 19). Thus, on one level, the assumption of rationality was defended on the grounds that it was what allowed for the possibility of a theory of politics. Morgenthau wrote that political realism "shares with all social theory the need, for the sake of theoretical understanding, to stress the rational elements of political reality; for it is these rational elements that make reality intelligible for theory" (1955, 7).

In the political sphere, the central concept for Morgenthau was interest defined in terms of power. This concept, according to Morgenthau, "allows the observer to distinguish the field of politics from other social spheres, to orient himself in the maze of empirical phenomena which make up the field of politics, and to establish a measure of rational order within it" (1959, 17). The key concept of interest defined in terms of power provided a rational map that could be used as a tool to approach political reality. In one of the field's most famous metaphors, Morgenthau likened a theory of international politics to a map: "Such a theory is a kind of rational outline of international relations, a map of the international scene. . . . Such a map then will tell us what are the rational possibilities for travel from one spot on the map to another, and which road is most likely to be taken by certain travelers under certain conditions."[14] Morgenthau did not adopt the assumption of rationality simply to develop an academic theory of international politics. For Morgenthau, one of the main aims of a theory of international politics was to better inform those who were responsible for conducting foreign policy. According to Morgenthau, "a theory of international relations presents not only a guide to understanding, but also an ideal for action. It presents a map of the international scene not only in order to understand what that scene is like, but also in order to show the shortest and safest road to a given objective."[15]

Morgenthau held that a rational foreign policy was by its very nature a good foreign policy, because rationality was a precondition of a prudent foreign policy. As such, his theory necessarily contained a normative element. This might help explain why Morgenthau was so quiet during the discussion that the conference participants had about the different types of theory, especially regarding the difference between a normative and a general theory of politics. For Morgenthau, a general theory of international politics had the practical aim of helping foreign-policy practitioners make better-informed decisions. Rationality was valued for its capacity to help provide a coherent picture of the international scene and to foster successful foreign policies. In *Politics Among Nations*, Morgenthau wrote, "political realism considers a rational foreign policy to be good foreign policy; for only a rational foreign policy minimizes risks and maximizes benefits and, hence, complies both with the moral precept of prudence and the political requirement of success" (1955, 7).

CONCLUSION

Morgenthau was confident that his realist theory provided the field with a general theory of international politics that demarcated international relations as an autonomous realm of activity. This, he believed, was one of the core functions of theory. He was, nevertheless, guarded about what theory could and could not do. It was on the basis of Morgenthau's erudite understanding of politics that led him to appreciate the limits of what a theory of international politics could accomplish. It was this understanding that put him at odds with the liberal rationalists of the interwar period and the post–World War II behavioralists who were calling for a scientific theory of politics. For Morgenthau, a science of international politics was simply impossible because "politics is an art and not a science, and what is required for its mastery is not the rationality of an engineer but the wisdom and moral strength of a statesman" (1946, 10).

Following the 1954 conference, a cleavage increasingly developed between those like Morgenthau who were advocating a realist theory of international politics and behavioralists advocating a science of politics. It was in the midst of the controversy generated by the behavioral revolution that a follow-up conference, once again financially supported by the Rockefeller Foundation, was held in 1957 at the Institute of War and Peace Studies of Columbia University.[16] The central question that the participants of the second conference were asked to consider was: "how does one go about making statements of a general character in International Relations that are true, useful, and hitherto not yet obvious?"[17] A wide range of answers were offered, and they were largely a function of whether a particular scholar endorsed a normative, empirical/scientific, or rational theory of international politics. This would prove to be the last meeting of the "American Committee on International Relations."

The importance of the 1954 Conference on Theory of International Politics was in spurring the members of the field of IR to develop a general theory of international politics. The conference itself was a testimony of the recognition that emerged after World War II that theory was an absolutely essential component of IR. While recognizing the centrality of theory to the study of international relations, significant differences existed among the conference participants on a range of issues relating to the purpose and functions of theory, the nature and content of theory, the limitations of theory, and the different types of theory. The fact that a small group of scholars that were selected personally by Thompson and the Rockefeller Foundation could not come to a consensus on these issues did not represent an auspicious beginning for what would become a very long road to a theory of international politics. Yet the conference provided a strong foundation for subsequent work on a theory of international politics. Thomson concluded his summary of the conference proceedings with the following recommendation: "a spirit of mutual respect must increasingly animate good theoretical work" (1955, 746). Unfortunately, this has not always been the case as scholars have continued the elusive quest for a general theory of international politics.

NOTES

1. Kenneth W. Thompson, "Conference on Theory of International Politics," May 7, 1954, Folder 69, Box 8, Series 910, Research Group (RG) 3, Rockefeller Foundation Archives, Rockefeller Archive Center, Sleepy Hollow, N.Y. (hereafter designated RAC).
2. "Grant in Aid," May 17, 1954, Folder 61, Box 7, Series 910, RG3, Rockefeller Foundation Archives, RAC.
3. Thompson (1955) provides a detailed account of the main themes and issues of the conference.
4. For the definitive account of the British committee, see Dunne (1998). The papers from the first meeting of the British committee are published in Butterfield and Wight (1966).
5. Thompson, "Conference on Theory of International Politics."
6. "Conference on International Politics," transcript, 240 (appendix 1 of this volume).
7. Thompson, "Conference on Theory of International Politics."
8. See "Grant in Aid," May 17, 1954, Folder 61, Box 7, Series 910, RG3, RF.
9. Thompson, "Conference on Theory of International Politics," 1.
10. Hans J. Morgenthau, "The Theoretical and Practical Importance of a Theory of International Relations," p. 7 Folder 69, Box 8, Series 910, RG3, Rockefeller Foundation Archives, RAC.
11. Ibid., 3.
12. Ibid., 4.
13. Ibid., 5.
14. Ibid.
15. Ibid., 7.
16. The papers from the Washington meeting appear in Fox (1959). The participants included Paul Nitze, Hans Morgenthau, William T. R. Fox, Kenneth Waltz, Charles Kindleberger, Arnold Wolfers, and Reinhold Niebuhr.
17. "Columbia University International Politics Seminar," p. 2 Folder 4218, Box 493, Series 200, RG1.2, Rockefeller Foundation Archives, RAC.

REFERENCES

Ashworth, Lucian M. 2002. Did the realist-idealist great debate ever happen? A revisionist history of international relations. *International Relations* 16: 33–51.

Butterfield, Herbert, and Martin Wight, eds. 1966. *Diplomatic investigations: Essays in
the theory of international politics*. London: Allen and Unwin.

Dunn, Frederick S. 1948. The scope of international relations. *World Politics* 1: 142–146.

——. 1950. The present course of international relations research. *World Politics* 2:
80–95.

Dunne, Tim. 1998. *Inventing international society: A history of the English School*. New
York: St. Martin's Press.

Ferguson, Y. H., and R. W. Mansbach. 1988. *The elusive quest: Theory and international
politics*. Columbia: University of South Carolina Press.

Fox, William T. R., ed. 1959. *Theoretical aspects of international relations*. Notre Dame,
Ind.: University of Notre Dame Press.

——. 1949. Interwar international relations research: The American experience. *World
Politics* 2: 67–79.

——. 1968. The teaching of international relations in the United States. In *The American
study of international relations*, ed. W. T. R. Fox, 14–35. Columbia: University of South
Carolina.

Guilhot, Nicolas. 2008. The realist gambit: Postwar American political science and the
birth of IR theory. *International Political Sociology* 2: 281–304.

Guzzini, Stefano. 1998. *Realism in international relations and international political
economy: The continuing story of a death foretold*. London: Routledge.

Hoffmann, Stanley H. 1959. International relations: The long road to theory. *World Politics* 11: 346–377.

Kirk, Grayson. 1947. *The study of international relations in American colleges and universities*. New York: Council on Foreign Relations.

Long, D., and P. Wilson, eds. 1995. *Thinkers of the twenty years' crisis: Interwar idealism
reassessed*. Oxford: Clarendon Press.

Morgenthau, Hans J. 1946. *Scientific man versus power politics*. Chicago: University of
Chicago Press.

——. 1955. *Politics among nations: The struggle for power and peace*. 2nd ed. New York:
Alfred A. Knopf.

——. 1958. *Dilemmas of politics*. Chicago: University of Chicago Press.

——. 1959. The nature and limits of a theory of international relations. In *Theoretical aspects of international relations*, ed. W. T. R. Fox, 15–28. Notre Dame, Ind.: University
of Notre Dame Press.

——. 1964. The intellectual and political functions of a theory of international relations.
In *The role of theory in international relations*, ed. Horace V. Harrison, 99–118. Princeton, N.J.: D. Van Nostrand Co.

Schmidt, Brian C. 1998. Lessons from the past: Reassessing the interwar disciplinary history of international relations. *International Studies Quarterly* 42: 433–459.

Singer, J. David. 1960. Theorizing about theory in international politics. *Journal of Conflict Resolution* 4: 431–442.

Thies, Cameron G. 2002. Progress, history, and identity in international relations theory:
The case of the idealist-realist debate. *European Journal of International Relations* 8:
147–185.

Thompson, Kenneth W. 1952. The study of international politics: A survey of trends and developments. *Review of Politics* 14: 433–467.

———. 1955. Toward a theory of international politics. *American Political Science Review* 49: 733–746.

Waldo, Dwight. 1959. *Political science in the United States of America: A trend report.* Paris: UNESCO.

Wight, Martin. 1960. Why is there no international theory? *International Relations* 2: 35–48.

Williams, Michael C. 2005. *The realist tradition and the limits of international relations.* Cambridge: Cambridge University Press.

Wilson, Peter. 1998. The myth of the "first great debate." *Review of International Studies* 24: 1–16.

Wolfers, Arnold. 1947. International relations as a field of study. *Columbia Journal of International Affairs* 1: 24–26.

4

THE SPEECH ACT OF REALISM
The Move That Made IR

OLE WÆVER

THE SIMPLE question addressed in this chapter is: *What were they doing?*

This remarkable group of hyperinfluential, realist theorists of IR met to discuss how to further the production of *theory* in IR, the documents say. But what did they do? What became the place of this theorizing in the history of the discipline of international relations? They did not only further theory; they also shaped the discipline and its theories in particular ways.

To ask "what were they doing?" really includes three different questions: one about the intentions of the people present at the workshop in 1954, a second one about the intentions *of the texts* that they produced (a subtle distinction asserted vehemently by Quentin Skinner; more on this below), and a third about the effects of their actions.

The first part of this chapter makes a general argument about how to write the history of IR theory, and focuses on what status to assign to the so-called great debates of the discipline. This is an important question, because the debates could be a possible way to frame the speech acts of the papers and discussions in 1954. On this basis, the second half of this chapter discusses five different interpretations, five main axes or focal points that could be structuring their debates, and these all turn out to be, to varying degrees, elements of a combined interpretation. By seeing this combination—the move made at this cross-section of debates—it becomes possible to understand what these realists *did*. And some of the—surprisingly—long-term effects on the discipline of IR can be traced back to this crucial instant.

1. DEBATING DEBATES—DOING
DISCIPLINARY HISTORY

International relations tends to recount its history in terms of "great debates"—a sequence of three or four major debates starting with the one between the "realists" and the "utopians" (or "idealists") in the 1930s or 1940s. This framing is by no means uncontroversial. In fact, the dominant attitude to this convention today is that it is something of a bad habit: that this excessive focus on polarized alternatives and large, loosely defined "paradigms" inhibits intellectual growth. References to "great debates" these days are mostly negative. Also within the specialized subfield (or sub-sub-field) of disciplinary history, the story of great debates has fallen out of favor, and they are mostly treated as myths to be debunked.

I will question this dominant derision of the "debates" in three steps. The first, which will only be briefly summarized, sees a naïvety in assuming that great debates are recurrent "mistakes," a "bad habit," and not an integral element of the intellectual and social structures of the discipline. Second, the major section in this first part of the paper reconstructs a more sociologically sound conception of great debates, with the help of theorists such as Randall Collins and Quentin Skinner. Finally, I look briefly at the debate on the first great debate among disciplinary historians and restate the legitimate conclusions to be drawn from their historical investigations of the actual debate.

1.1. Debates for a Reason

Much of the diagnostic and prescriptive literature on the state of the discipline laments the dominance of debatism. It is pointed out, with much justification, that it is unproductive for intellectual clarification and assessment of theories to focus on large, unwieldy, and loosely coupled "paradigms" and ill-defined metalevel disagreements (Puchala 2002; Hellmann 2003; Waltz 1997).

However, very often the argument is made in a form that implies that we are here talking about a kind of pure, personal choice—that debates as a form of self-reflection and self-description can be handled purely by deciding individually about how to pursue enlightenment. This is sociologically naïve. If great debates have been a recurrent pattern, they are probably not extraneous, isolated occurrences—they are part of the structure of the IR discipline. Exactly how the pattern of great debates fits in the peculiar social and intellectual structure of IR as a discipline has been explored elsewhere

(Wæver 1998, 2003, 2007), and for the present purpose, it suffices to point to the embeddedness of the pattern in relations of hierarchy, power, and coordination. Furthermore, debates are not a sign of disintegration, as assumed especially by quasi-positivists in their longing for a cumulative-consensus science. Debates are as much a form of integration, and historically IR has been focused and has agreed on a specific set of main theories and overarching questions more so than, for example, sociology and comparative politics. (Very likely, the prominence of great debates is on the decline, and the discipline of IR is currently moving toward less integration [Wæver 2007]. But that is in the present context only a morbid irony and not really relevant to the argument pursued.) A third observation to be drawn from this observation is that the social organization of this particular discipline has been focused on theory. The high degree of coherence, focus, and social regulation has been achieved through a relatively clear hierarchy of key journals, and these journals both favored a dominant format of theory-anchored empirical studies (and a more limited number of pure theory articles) and were mostly run by leading theorists or their protégés. IR is not necessarily "more theoretical"—or, for that matter, theoretically more sophisticated—than neighboring disciplines, but the *idea* of theory has been powerful and instrumental.

1.2. The Sociology of Debates, Theories, and Moves

Next we must establish a sustainable, microsociological understanding of "debates." These are usually treated as metaphysical, free-floating entities and thus become very easy to denounce. However, it is possible to conceptualize debates with a microtheoretical foundation in meaningful practices by researchers.

Before I turn to more elaborate theories, the argument can be made on its own terms: studying (and teaching) the great debates helps not only to understand the pattern, not only to track *what theories* are in the field, but also to understand *what is in* those theories, that is, how they are structured. And by understanding why they look the way they do, it also becomes easier to get deeper into their inner logic and thus to work with them.

Theories are shaped by their immediate social setting, that is, the academic scene (and only to a much lower degree by external factors relating to political developments); they are not developed in an ideal process of "learning" and adjusting as previous theories generate anomalies or weaknesses (Kuhn 1962; Lakatos 1970). The academic scene is much more combative, and there are always a (limited) number of theories competing.

Therefore, the landscape or "fronts" explain to a very large extent what a given theory is "up to," that is, why particular challenges are seen as decisive for this theory. To prove A or redefine B is important *because of* what this will mean in the current main fights. Therefore, one can best get to the heart of a theory by understanding what it was designed *to do* originally— and for that you need to have a good, graphic depiction of what the scene was like. As Peter Berger notes, in a phrase attributed to "a somewhat cynical colleague," "the goal of every scholarly enterprise is to blow someone's theory out of the water" (2002, 1).

To understand a theory implies knowing why it was created (that way), and this follows from understanding its context. In other words, to understand neorealism, it helps to have the IR scene of the 1970s as setting and see how Waltz intervened most cleverly and strategically with his structural relaunch of realism. Similarly, Keohane constructed his neoliberalism on the basis of rational egoism and as a theory that says but a few important things, as a strategic move in relation to a discipline in which Waltz had by then triumphed. After Keohane's intervention, the standards of evaluation were transformed accordingly. That certain elements of poststructuralism came to be defining in an IR context (different from poststructuralism elsewhere) had a lot to do with the battle lines and constellations among IR theories (Wæver 1996). Wendt's theory is statecentric for theory-internal reasons (having to do with the structure-agency debate) but surely also for relational reasons—it thus becomes a companion to Waltz and Keohane, the third book on that top shelf.

Contextual events—wars, changes of zeitgeist, funding patterns, 9/11— will be woven into the story, but the *understanding* of the main theories is enhanced more by coming to grips with their meaning as theoretical interventions than from contextual factors.

This argument about the importance of debates exists in the shape of a much more general (and far-reaching) model. Randall Collins, in his remarkable book *The Sociology of Philosophies: A Global Theory of Intellectual Change* (1998), develops a general theory of how intellectual work can be understood through the networks of—in his case—philosophers. This allows him to trace philosophical thought in ancient Greece; China; Japan; India; medieval Islamic, Jewish, and Christian traditions; and modern Europe. Not "only" that, but he explains it all in a conception that covers both the "micro" level of the movements and moves of individuals and (more problematically; cf. Goodman 2001) the "macro" level of the large patterns. The core is intellectual conflict, which is "always limited by focus on certain topics, and by the search for allies" (Collins 1998, 1) and produces "the law of small numbers" (Collins 1998, 38, 81). The number of positions that succeeds in gaining general attention (and constitutes the active schools of thought that reproduce themselves for more than one or two generations) is typically *three to six*. There have to be rival positions, thus there are always at least two, and then it is easy to find a third position in contrast to both. The upper limit is around six, because the need for allies and the scarcity of attention tend to make processes of multiplication beyond this self-defeating.

Probably Collins generalizes too lightly (even with the nuances made possible by 1,100 pages). The theory is applicable to philosophy and sociology but not as easily so to more monoparadigmatic natural sciences or more fragmented disciplines like parts of the humanities. Therefore, the sociology of the social sciences needs to supplement Collins's magisterial grand theory with a differentiation among disciplines (e.g., drawing on Whitley 2000). However, when mapping IR in more detail (Wæver 2003), it turns out that IR happens to be rather like philosophy (and some parts of sociology) in this respect, so Collins *is* actually quite applicable to us. The intellectual law of small numbers works on us too. Or at least it used to.

External factors matter, but it is important to avoid unsustainable reductionism or functionalism, where social factors determine science in a direct sense, which is hard to square with the actual practices and motivations of researchers. Collins works in a three-step procedure from the inside out. Social factors do not work on theories directly but rather indirectly through their effects on the "micro-core."

1. Theories are most shaped by their immediate social setting, the academic scene. The core is never an individual as such but always "a conversation," and the driving motivations are rarely about external factors directly but about moves to be made vis-à-vis other scholars and their theories—Collins's "intellectual law of small numbers."

2 The organizational base: universities, publishers, churches, regal patrons, and other suppliers of material resources.

3. The largest structure, the political and economic forces that feed these organizations. This includes the events that we write about, that is, international relations, which has been a favored cause in many reflections on the history of the discipline, where it is here stressed that changes like the rise and fall of power centers influence the discipline but do not directly translate into theory.

One layer does not reduce to another; least of all do the contents of the philosophies reduce to the outermost material and political conditions. Intellectuals maneuver within their own attention space, reshaping the tools at hand from past and current controversies internal to their own sphere, while energized by the structural opportunities opening up in the material and political world surrounding them.

(COLLINS 1998, 622)

At the outermost causal layer, the geopolitical and economic rise or fall of states shifts the location of resources, expanding the material bases for some intellectual networks at the expense of others. Networks realign; new philosophical positions appear.

(COLLINS 1998, 623)

Intellectual life, like everything else, takes place in a series of embedded levels. Start at the centre with a human body charged with emotions and consciousness. Around him or her is the intellectual network and its dynamics, the market opportunities for ideas which open up at particular times. Creativity comes to those individuals optimally positioned to take advantage of these opportunities.

(COLLINS 1998, 51)

With this approach, there is a route for social factors to influence science, but always through the mechanisms closer to researchers. And the theory is thoroughly social, even if the core arena is one where intellectual moves are made and battles are fought, alliances formed, and positions built through theorizing.

Obviously, this does not exclude the fact that in a specific situation such as the 1954 conference, it was important for the academic participants to relate to policy. The main warning is in relation to the elements that structure their basic academic contributions, their main works, and their major commitments. A question about the kind of theory that ought to be put forward is shaped in relation to the academic world. Policy relevance is ultimately causally relevant to the extent that it translates into power within academe.

When developing fuller stories of disciplinary history, there is something important to be gained from all of the generations of sociology of science, including complex combinations of internal and external as well as social and cognitive (Mirowski 2004; Wæver and Tickner 2009). However, with regard to the more limited question addressed in this article, the emphasis will be on how much can be achieved with an approach like Collins's, especially if expanded on by core ideas borrowed from Quentin Skinner.

Skinner, and more generally the so-called Cambridge School in conceptual history, has developed a powerful approach to the study of the history of political thought and theory. Originally, it was not developed for recent history, as in our case, but in order to recover the author's intentions in writing classic works of political theory. Studying Hobbes, the guiding question would be what *Leviathan* did to the intellectual landscape of the time and thereby to political options and definitions. The approach is too often summarized as "contextualism," which has led to strange discussions where Skinner's approach is sometimes assimilated to externalist explanations (and contrasted to internalism, then linked in IR discussions to a retracing of debates in the discipline as practiced by Gunnell [1993] and Schmidt [1998, 36–37]). This is rather absurd given the centrality in Skinner's approach of the textual moves at the heart of what one text does in relation to other texts. This is developed on the basis of speech-act theory.

"I argue that, if we are to write the history of ideas in a properly historical style, we need to situate the texts we study within such intellectual contexts and frameworks of discourse as enable us to recognise what their authors were *doing* in writing them" (Skinner 2002, 7). Because of its focus on "doing *in* writing them," the investigation does not go to underlying motives in the sense of personal inner feelings but to what the text tries to do.[1] To understand this, one needs to be aware of the general theoretical or disciplinary situation at the time. This "contextualism" means that one does not read Hobbes as giving answers to timeless, deep questions that should then be compared to answers from two thousand years earlier or two hundred years later; it means that his works should be understood in terms of the difference they made, when made. This means, for instance, that one should not overemphasize the leading works that might stand now as defining for that period but should also read possibly "minor" works in the history of political thought, if they mattered then, when they were written. This way, one can reconstruct the intellectual landscape and see why particular moves were important and effective in changing the terms of debate for others.

Texts become participants in debates in the following way:

The types of utterances I am considering can never be viewed simply as strings of propositions; they must always be viewed at the same time as arguments. But to argue is always to argue for or against a certain assumption or point of view or course of action. It follows that, if we wish to understand such utterances, we shall have to find some means of identifying the precise nature of the intervention constituted by the act of uttering them. . . . We need to see it not simply as a proposition but as a move in an argument. So we need to grasp why it seemed worth making that precise move by way of recapturing the presuppositions and purposes that went into the making of it.

(SKINNER 2002, 115)

When the text at hand is not a written, published one but a transcript like our document in this project (reprinted in appendix 1), the meaning of meaning has to be slightly redefined. The text *is* not in itself a move in the collective process of meaning making—what we see in the 1954 workshop is rather a *move in the making*. The intention of the text is the strategizing shown in relation to other texts in the surroundings as well as the debates that go on in the room. Intentions of persons can in some ways be better assessed in this case than with normal texts—we get a clearer sense of the people involved in the process, but still it is always problematic to go too deeply into questions that are more mental than mediated, more about consciousness than communication (in Niklas Luhmann's terminology), or more about perceptions than discourse. The main emphasis will therefore be on the intentions of the text in the present case, despite the particular complexities having to do with its status.

1.3. The Fairly Great Debate on the "First Great Debate"

IR has witnessed an increased reflexivity on the issue of how to write IR history and what is at stake in doing so (Schmidt 1998, 2002; Guzzini 1998; Holden 2001, 2002, 2006). In these reflections, one empirical case is a privileged reference point: the first great debate. In addition to the arguments made in the general historiographic writings, a number of specialized historical studies have increasingly built a revisionist consensus against the previously dominant image of the first debate (especially Quirk and Vigneswaran 2005; also Wilson 1998, 2003; Ashworth 2002, 2006).

Whereas the traditional rendition of this foundational "debate" saw realists and idealists/utopians pitted against each other throughout the 1930s and into the 1940s (with the realists ultimately prevailing), the revised story goes like this: The interwar period actually saw very little debate along these lines, and there certainly were no discernable "schools." Probably, it is still fair to say that the dominant scholars were not realists and that a lot of the leading representatives of the new discipline of IR held some of the views later ascribed to the "utopians," but few if any held all of them, and they certainly did not think of themselves as a group, school, or paradigm. Carr construes the straw man of "utopians" in order to inaugurate his realism. Several of the scholars so labeled actually responded to the attacks, but Carr did not reply to his critics (Long 2003).

Other writers, including Morgenthau (1946), carried out relatively parallel attacks on both the philosophical foundations of "idealism" and the foreign-policy doctrines as such, however without presenting it at this stage in the terms of two contrasting IR perspectives. In *Scientific Man Versus Power Politics* (Morgenthau 1946), the index lacks an entry for "realism" (or, for that matter, "international politics/relations" or "theory"—whereas "realism" is in both *Politics Among Nations* [1948][2] and Carr's *Twenty Years' Crisis* [1939], "international politics" in the former, and "theory" in none of them).

In the 1940s, it became standard operating procedure for realists to point out the contrast between realists and idealists. At this time, no theoretical debate took place either, because very few scholars tried to uphold anything akin to the idealist position.

Quirk and Vigneswaran (2005) then make their most fascinating observation: it was in the *second debate* that the idea of "great debates" was cultivated (although Quirk and Vigneswaran here seem to ignore Morgenthau's 1952 attempt to define "another great debate" around the national interest). Their astute observation is that the first great debate was promoted to mythic status to increase the legitimacy of the second debate! By being placed into the same category as this famous period in the history of the discipline, the leading participants in the second debate enjoy an elevated status.

The curious interaction of the debates—with backward historical causality—is reiterated in (what is called) the third debate, because it has the peculiar role of distorting the *chronology* of the first debate. Whereas previous observers had been aware that the IR works of the first debate only appeared in the 1940s (1939 in the case of Carr), the depiction in the third debate of the sequence pushes the first debate decisively (and incorrectly) back to the interwar period.

All of this is interesting in relation to my sociology of the discipline, because it reinforces the point that debates as an *institution* have been crucial to IR. The most important in the present context is where this historical revision for the status of the first debate actually leaves the first debate.

The new historical literature on the first debate has mostly summarized its own findings in terms of three errors it finds in the traditional story:

1. The idealists/utopians were not a group, and many of them did not hold the views ascribed to them.
2. There was no active exchange at any time, neither in the interwar nor in the immediate postwar period.
3. The most important texts that instigated the distinction appeared from 1939 and into the 1950s, that is, during and right after World War II, not during the interwar period.

However, whether it should be concluded on this basis that the first debate was a myth depends on what it means for a debate to be real. It is a myth *too*—the stereotyped version à la Carr has had an impressive grip on the discipline since then and has been reenacted over and over again to settle all kinds of debates that really were not similar to the original one (Walker 1992). But this does not mean that it is a pure invention without any connection to what realists did at the time—quite the contrary!

One can think of four different meanings of the "existence" of a debate:

1. *An accurate description of the majority of researchers of the day.* The universe of scholars actually consisted of "idealists" and "realists" who self-identified as members of these respective groups. This is probably an overly naïve empiricism that underestimates the structure of academic universes, where some scholars define the situation more than others and the number of adherents is less important than the meaning created mostly by certain leading scholars.

2. *A dominant "map" at a given time.* Many scholars do other things, take up middle-ground positions, apply one specific theory, and so on, but their idea of their overarching options are defined by these dominant, debating positions. Although not everyone fits into these positions or identifies with them, a large part of the research community refers and relates to this structure as defining the major alternatives available.

3. There are not two parties that agree to have a debate. Instead, *one of the poles constitutes itself by positing this axis.* The debate is thereby real as speech act, as textual practice. To the extent that this succeeds, this situation will often gradually transform into situation number 2.

4. *It is the dominant narrative about the past of the discipline, and as such it is effective in the present.* This comes close to tautology and becomes

trivial if the meaning of a past debate being real is only its ghostly presence at a later stage.

With this perspective, it seems reasonable to reinterpret the findings of the first-debate revisionists in terms different from their own conclusions. The first debate is certainly of type 3 and possibly of type 2 as well.[3] The relative one-sidedness is common to those kinds of debates: they are not necessarily ongoing "debates" between two sides; rather, they are constructed in the speech act of one theory, which thereby defines the other.

The reality of the first debate furthermore shows in the way that realism is shaped by it. Ironically, the downgrading of debates runs the risk of strengthening the image that realists usually prefer, that is, that of a timeless tradition. In the standard textbook presentation, realism *runs itself* throughout the millennia—and the first debate is one of its most heroic periods. A critical history of the first debate allows us to see how we got a particular form of realism in the mid-twentieth century. If the first debate is denounced, the intention might be to undermine all aggregate positions, but the more likely effect is that the particular, historical formation of *this* realism gets lost, collapsing us back into the image of realism as such.

Hedley Bull (1972) has pointed out that postwar realism came to differ from "traditional realism" exactly because it was born by giving different answers to the questions of the interwar "idealists." Most importantly, the moral question was framed completely differently. Partly due to the form of the debate with the idealists, and partly because of the general political context (the twentieth century, democracy, the United States), there was not much full-fledged "Machiavellianism" pleading for amoralism as such. Instead there was a highly moral argument for the superiority of an approach rooted in power compared to one rooted in law, wishful thinking, or moralizing (cf. Liska 1977, 1981). The argument was not that one should not care about moral questions but that policies ignoring power were proven to lead to wars or appeasement (or both), whereas a policy that took the national interest as its guiding star was more likely to manage the international situation well and thus serve both one's own interests/ values and the systemic preference for peace. (After all, *Politics Among Nations* was subtitled *The Struggle for Power and Peace.*) It was a moral argument for putting moral arguments in a particularly circumscribed position. And this would hardly have been the case if twentieth-century American realism had been born in a "debate with" or "move against" another opponent.

The combined conclusion to all of part 1 is that debates exist. They have been an integrated part of the discipline of IR; they are not metaphysical abstractions but can be given a sociologically sound interpretation in terms of scholarly behavior. And although the heroic story of the first debate that has long dominated IR was deeply flawed, the revisionist historians have not really shown that no debate took place, only that it did in a very different form (and at a different time) than is usually assumed. Thus, as we will move to the reading of the 1954 texts, we will have recourse to the category of "debates." And we have some more rigorous tools and principles, especially derived from the speech-act theoretical historical model of Skinner.

2. THE STATUS ANGST OF THE MODERN (AMERICAN?) SOCIAL SCIENCES

Section 4, below, the second main part of this article, will use the above understanding of "debates" to interpret the 1954 workshop and its meaning for the history of IR as a discipline. However, it is first necessary to reflect briefly on another kind of dynamic. "Debates" are basically internal to a discipline and driven by competition among different networks and orientations within it. However, sometimes acts seem to be made about and on behalf of the discipline at large—and internal debates can be about defining the identity of the discipline.

Generally, in writings on the history of the social sciences, a theme that is often emphasized is the fight for becoming (or remaining) credible as science. This typically implies a hierarchy where the natural sciences are the real sciences. Economics has almost made it to this status, and the other social sciences try to emulate economics, which in turn is emulating (allegedly) the natural sciences. What seem to be at first debates among different theories are interpreted in many of the most penetrating analyses of disciplinary history as struggles over the identity of a discipline—and not only competition between different identity projects but rather projects aimed at securing an identity for the discipline as such (e.g., Wagner et al. 1991; Ross 1992; Gunnell 1993; Farr et al. 1995; Schmidt 1998; Guzzini 1998).

Attempts to define a discipline can often be seen as attempts to stake out "territory," but this is less about a "land grab" and more about forming secure, defendable borders. It is a challenge to become well defined enough to count as a meaningful academic enterprise.

A major problem with much of this literature is that the analyses are presented as if this were normal rather than occurring under exceptional conditions. This amounts to assuming that a discipline acts on the basis of collective rationality, although such an assumption has no microtheoretical basis. It makes sense only if the discipline in a quite integrated format has strong "representatives" or "leaders." Most of the time, a discipline is less driven by concern for survival or relative status, but claims on behalf of the discipline are made in order to strengthen one program vis-à-vis another. (Again, see the previous section, because the social environment that matters to most scholars is the immediate one, that is, their colleagues and competitors within their own discipline or even subfield, not the struggle "for IR" within academe at large or even "society.") We should, however, allow for the possibility of those rare moments of clear leadership, but only when specific groups have secured a relatively tight grip of the discipline, whereas under normal circumstances, claims of this kind are to be interpreted as internal to a discipline. (And thus, much can be learned from those historical writings, even if their status as general interpretations has to be seriously challenged.) Why both sides of this picture have to be taken into account will become clear below, in our case analysis.

3. INTERLUDE: STRUCTURAL SLIPS IN RECOUNTS OF REALISM

Before I turn to the operational usage of the above framework for the issue at hand, let me briefly note the absence of this kind of study. Some of the best extensive studies of "realism" actually make methodological noises similar to the above, such as M. J. Smith's and Jonathan Haslam's (the latter even with direct reference to Skinner), but actually end up betraying these principles, because they operate with a longer realist tradition (Smith 1986; Haslam 2002). Then, naturally, the particular phenomenon of postwar American realism is only to a secondary degree resituated in its unique context and is primarily treated as a moment in the longer history of realism. (This is even more strongly the case for books—otherwise very helpful—that discuss in a contrasting mode three to five more or less timeless traditions: Wight [1992], Boucher [1998], Donelan [1990], and many others).

Much of the very helpful and inspiring literature that comes forth these years on single realist authors (or occasionally on two or three in one book) are mostly interested in tracing their philosophical roots—not least whether to read them in relation to European or American traditions or to this or that European philosopher (e.g., Bain 2000; Scheuerman 2007). In the best cases, this is extended into attempts to find forgotten value in their approaches and use them for interventions in the current political or academic situation (for particularly successful examples, see Williams [2005] and Tjalve [2008]). However, this rarely allows their moves in the particular time and place to be seen in their own context, and especially not as IR moves (although Tjalve [2008] is an important study that places Niebuhr and Morgenthau in their contemporary context in the United States, but more as public intellectuals than as IR theorists, and Guzzini [1998] is careful in distinguishing the different moves made during different periods but makes relatively less of alternative approaches during the early periods).

4. WHAT WAS DONE AT THE MAY 1954 CONFERENCE

The central question to ask about the transcript and the workshop papers from 1954 is: how did the intellectual landscape and the social situation for IR look to the participants, and what were the changes they tried to achieve?

Methodologically, that we are dealing with a transcript and unpublished papers written for the meeting raises interesting possibilities and challenges. An advantage of the transcript form is that you can almost get the tone, sense what is controversial, apprehend where the familiar disagreements are, and so forth. It is also possible for the participants to refer to others outside the room in a format different from published work. On the other hand, one cannot apply the normal Skinnerian principles directly, because we are not dealing here with "acting in writing." The texts are not acts and moves in the most immediate sense, because they are not located in the public process of exchange of arguments as an article or a book can be. When looking at the workshop in an action perspective, the question is therefore primarily to understand how the participants saw the challenge. The disciplinary actions in the narrow sense were constituted by what they—mostly individually—did in the following years, as well as what they did not do, and by the way actions in the conference shaped the discipline indirectly by shaping these "public" actions.

Therefore, the challenge is to find out by what fronts, opponents, debates, or issues they were guided and discover how the question of a "Theory of International Politics" was constituted before and after the event.

4.1. First Debate

The first candidate for a debate opponent is obviously "idealism." The standard story about the famous first great debate tells us that a number of the conference attendees were prominently involved in it. So, what is the role of the first debate in this seminar? They are not engaging in it as such, naturally—because the opponent is not present in the room. But it seems to be the taken-for-granted background. As Arnold Wolfers says, "the realist says that nations are after power. The idealist says they are worried about moral ends. This is the constant debate and the lesson of mankind" (242, appendix 1 of this volume).

They see themselves as a group relatively united on this issue, victorious in the debate and basically charged now with suppressing the inevitable recurrent attempts to make idealist mistakes. They do not, however, see themselves as confronting a serious academic opponent. (This, to state the obvious, confirms the interpretation above about the first debate as real—as a *realist operation*—and not necessarily a debate in the traditional sense.) The first debate in this role is an important condition for understanding the situation—it is a crucial background but is not what animates the event.

They do refer to themselves as "realists" (not constantly, but both Niebuhr and Wolfers do so on 242). More importantly, however, is an implicit, unquestioned assumption: they are now the representatives of the discipline. There are few references (see section 4.4 below, on the second debate) to behavioralists *in IR*: only a mention in a memorandum by Kenneth Thompson that the journal *World Politics* has been taken over by the behavioralists (something echoed in the transcript, 257–61). But when talking about teaching, Ph.D.s, and textbooks toward the end, it is assumed that *they*, the realists, can speak on behalf of the discipline; what their kind of people do is what IR is. More revealing than specific passages like this is the general tone—and what is not said. There is a general absence of any distinction between their strivings and a wider discipline. Whereas later periods would see constant references to different programs or approaches within IR, the 1954 conference attendees simply feel entitled to speak on behalf of the discipline. "We are IR" and "we are realists" are overlapping presuppositions.

This in itself does not explain the form of their textual acts, but it is an important first step.

4.2. Foreign Policy

A second possibility for a driving debate could be one over American foreign policy. We often find that a theory debate really stands in for political disagreements. In that case, we should find a structure in the arguments where alternatives are defined in foreign-policy terms or follow disagreements over foreign policy. (This is, for instance, the case in what Morgenthau labeled "Another 'Great Debate': The National Interest of the United States" [Morgenthau 1952], but it really was not "another" debate but rather an echo of the first debate.) In the conference, however, we do not find discussions over different clear alternative lines in foreign policy.

Rather, in relation to policy, the picture at the 1954 conference is one of constant operational errors, a weakness of overarching vision, and therefore a need to improve on policy by a recourse to *their* input. Does this mean that they find it realistic to come up with a theory that really guides and assists policy? The policymakers in the group clearly ask for this again and again, but the theorists are not inclined to promise much. Ironically, they come closest in the discussion on moral theory, where there is much intimation that one should be able to specify better the aims of U.S. foreign policy theoretically. But in the part on a "general theory of international politics," the leading theorists are quite careful when they suggest what theory can do vis-à-vis policy. (More could be said here about the theory-practice issue, which they dance around several times, but this is addressed in other chapters of this book, and for the present purpose, it is more important to suggest the way in which this dimension interacts with the others.)

The picture is not of a theory that can be taught to policymakers or delivered as a manual. Rather, it is often hinted that the theorists have an ability to achieve a kind of understanding that is complementary to that of policymakers (whose particular abilities are strongly acknowledged). Albeit with a strong emphasis on the limits of theory, it seems that what is suggested here is that, by virtue of their ability to sort the particular from the universal and thereby *handle* theory without overestimating its applicability in specific cases, these theorists should be listened to more.

Thus, the interaction of the first two elements (with the third also beginning to be felt) is that because these realists *are* IR, and because policy needs to listen to *them*, it is important that their discipline, IR, gains a status and a credibility that would allow it to pronounce with sufficient authority on matters of policy and influence policy processes.

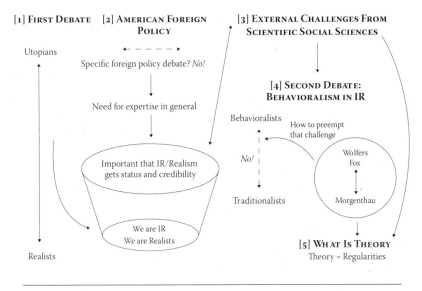

FIGURE 4.1

4.3. Scientific Credentials for IR

In this quest for academic status, the "scientific" revolution is beginning to be seen as a troubling trend of the times. If IR/realism wants to gain scientific credentials, this must happen within the context of increased disciplinary requirements. The scientific status of the discipline within the hierarchy of the (social) sciences has to be fought for in a situation where the other social sciences also start to establish themselves as modern, scientific disciplines.

This point (in contrast to the next) is not about behavioralism in IR specifically but in the social sciences in general: behavioralism not as IR but as an alternative *to* IR. Actually, it is not behavioralism as such but the more general movement of "scientific social science," covering "theory" as well as science through method or empiricism. After all, only the year before, David Easton had published *The Political System: An Inquiry Into the State of Political Science*; political science too was on a quest for a theory.

Take Dean Rusk's statements opening the conference: "There currently tends to be a trend toward a more lively interest in theoretical and conceptual problems, illustrated in the study of international politics and emerging in theories of politics, economic, law and human behavior" (240). The trend as such is manifested in other fields. The question put to the group is:

given the current situation characterized by this general trend, where do we stand in international politics; that is, where does this group representing international politics stand?

Morgenthau speaks later (257) about "the general social science tendency toward a particular conception of what is scientific. Everything qualifies as scientific that can be described in a particular social science jargon or pressed into a social science conceptual framework. Everything that cannot is not scientific and hence inferior."

This development in the general social sciences influences the text in two ways. First, it sets the difficult conditions for the quest for scientific status, and then it potentially spills into the discipline in the form of behavioralist or "scientific" IR.

4.4. The Second Great Debate

This brings us to the so-called second great debate in IR. Is the active axis the one between traditionalists and "behavioralists"?

Nicolas Guilhot (2008 and in this volume) has argued that this debate is crucial to the 1954 workshop. This is in many ways true and important. However, this observation and interpretation should not be overstated, or rather, it should not only be shaped as an attempt to project the second debate backward in time. Although it is interesting to note, as does Guilhot, that the two debates thereby come to overlap in time, contrary to the sequence established in the disciplinary narrative, it would be misleading to interpret the seminar in terms of a second great debate in a direct sense.

There are some good, clear textual examples of a "second-debate" interpretation of the workshop in Thompson's *American Political Science Review* article that followed and commented upon the workshop (1955), but interestingly, these examples are far less clear in the papers and the transcript.

On a note of method, we can assume here that dealing with a transcript and not a published article makes a difference. If we were reading an article, it would be fair to assume that it could well be that the real opponent was not named. For tactical reasons, one might not want to elevate an alternative approach to a higher status (just as an incumbent politician avoids debates with a challenger because of the risk of granting him thereby an equal status). With a transcript, it is more likely that the group would, among itself, in private, be explicit if a crucial part of their situation was made up of other powerful schools. This would usually appear explicitly, because in candid exchanges within the group, one would want to justify one's arguments with reference to what matters to the group (unless some more complex psychological mechanism should be preventing this, but this would require an elaborate justification to be argued here).

The behavioralists are mentioned a few times—they are neither absent nor strongly present. And one really has to stretch the categories to make the discussion in the group one where behavioralism is one of the positions *in the room*. This is precisely what Thompson (1955) attempts. He presents the workshop as a debate between two wings represented by Morgenthau on the one side and Wolfers (sometimes backed by Fox) on the other. (He attempts something similar already in his memo for the conference, where he summarizes the papers circulated in these terms.) This is an odd move indeed. Wolfers is an unlikely behavioralist. He was trained mostly in law (and economics and political science), became famous first in the United States for a work of diplomatic history (Wolfers 1940), and published in 1962 his main work of theory, a collection of essays that pushed for theoretical rigor in some sense but clearly from within the classical tradition and without help from any modern methods (Wolfers 1962). Niebuhr (1962) wrote in the preface to that book that "Dr. Wolfers is a 'political philosopher' rather than a 'political scientist'" and obviously meant this as praise.

How is it, then, that Wolfers sometimes takes a position in the debates that is only slightly different from Morgenthau's and that even defends the value of works such as those published in *World Politics*? This seemingly has to do with the way in which one can relate to something external to the group rather than with the kind of work represented by the participants themselves. The difference between Wolfers and Morgenthau is less about their individual type of IR and more about a political difference in how they generally dealt with differences. Wolfers generally sought compromises with policymakers on foreign-policy issues in order to gain influence in a way that Morgenthau would never do (Thompson 1980, 97–107), and he generally seems to have been interested in political maneuvering and finding medium positions. The difference between Wolfers and Morgenthau here can probably best be interpreted as a "political" difference about how to handle the challenge from behavioralism—an existing challenge outside IR that was likely to become an internal one.

This is illustrated in figure 4.1 by the long arrow in part 4—the second debate, which does not happen—and then the shorter arrow between Wolfers and Morgenthau, which is really a preemptive second-order debate about how to meet or prevent the bigger challenge.

4.5. What Kind of Theory?

The final issue to be outlined here has to do with the kind of theory, and therefore the kind of discipline, that was to be developed. In this area, the most striking feature of the transcript is the weakness of the debate. Here we have all these great minds meeting, and what do they come up with about theory? Not a lot. The debate is not very cumulative or precise. Some rather simple statements about theory are never really probed or deepened, and most of the energy is spent on repetitive discussions over the possibility of moral theory and differences between theory and practice. The discussions about theory as such mostly move in circles in relation to the unique and the universal. How can this be?

Let us compare this conference with those of the "English School" in international relations, specifically, those discussions of its (little) sister organization, the British Committee on the Theory of International Politics. The British committee, which provided the institutional origin of the "English School," was set up by Rockefeller as a counterpart to the group we are discussing here. Their first book, *Diplomatic Investigations* (1966), was largely the committee's coming to terms with the very idea of international relations (or politics) as a field and the possibility and limits of *theory* (most famously pointed to by the reprinting therein of Wight's famous 1960 essay, "Why Is There No International Theory?"). It was thus largely a parallel enterprise to the meeting we are here discussing. Herbert Butterfield and Martin Wight (1966, 11–12) wrote in the preface to this book:

> The Rockefeller Foundation gave the group the name of the British Committee on the Theory of International Politics. "The theory of international politics" is a phrase without wide currency or clear meaning in this country. The group took it to cover enquiry into the nature of the international states-system, the assumptions and ideas of diplomacy, the principles of foreign policy, the ethics of international relations and war. This is a region that still calls for new approaches and for academic treatment. It marches with the domains of the political theorist, the international lawyer, the diplomatic historian, the student of international relations, and the strategic analyst.

And:

> It soon became clear to the members of the British Committee that within this ill-defined field they had different interests from their American colleagues. The connoisseur of national styles may notice the contrasts. The

British have probably been more concerned with the historical than the contemporary, with the normative than the scientific, with the philosophical than the methodological, with principles than policy.

Lots of people have read—in an English School context—this famous passage and nodded. Sure, that's how American IR is: scientific, method driven, and so forth. However, "American" here is a reference to "our" group, to these classically minded realists! One would usually expect them to take a position very close to the English School on theory. Very often, Niebuhr, Morgenthau, and several of the others have indeed been characterized as "more concerned with the historical than the contemporary, with the normative than the scientific, with the philosophical than the methodological, with principles than policy." But this is not how they sound in this meeting. What is theory? "When we speak of theory, we speak of general laws," says the most philosophical member of the group, Reinhold Niebuhr, on 240 of the transcript! At the beginning of the transcript, in Niebuhr's remarks and in Kenneth W. Thompson's introductory note, there is a marked difference between this view of general laws and the standard empiricist conception of theory as laws. Morgenthau especially talks about deeper constants in contrast to simple empirically observable regularities. This, however, is not explored or developed at all in the workshop.

In practice, they converge on talking about theory simply as regularities— "the uniformities and similarities in international politics" (Dean Rusk, on 248 of the transcript). This is a rapprochement to a general scientific ("behavioral") conception of theory.

Also, it is striking that when they—and especially Morgenthau—are asked to come up with illustrations of theoretical laws, the examples are curiously isolated "laws": "You should never make an alliance with a stronger nation" (249) and "why France opposes unification that would permit Germany to dominate" (252). These formulations are not deduced from deeper, more general theoretical principles but nevertheless are presented as laws—especially the first one—that stand on their own terms. It is hard to see where the theory of international politics is.

Morgenthau had at this time published the second edition of *Politics Among Nations* (1954)—although the (in)famous six principles of political realism would only follow in the third edition (1960)—so one could expect a more self-conscious and elaborate presentation of how this rational model forms the basis for more specific theorizing. There are some statements in the workshop that clearly draw on this theoretical format, but they are not developed as such. Nor do the participants spell out any other kind of theory.

Compare how Wight from the English School side tried more aggressively to push international theory in the political-theory sense, which we might also have expected from Niebuhr and to some extent Morgenthau: "By 'international theory' is meant a tradition of speculation about relations between States, a tradition imagined as twin of speculation about the State to which the name 'political theory' is appropriated. And international theory in this sense does not, at first sight, exist" (Wight 1960, 35).

In 1961, one year after Wight's paper appeared in the journal *International Relations*, Morgenthau wrote about it:

> While I cannot, of course, subscribe to the unqualified negativism of the title for both personal and professional reasons, I find the paper a most illuminating and penetrating discussion of the problem. Its fourteen pages contain more insights into the intellectual issues posed by theoretical concern with international relations than a whole shelf of books and articles which, following the fashion of the day, spin out theories about theories of international relations and embark upon esoteric methodological studies about how to go about theorizing about theories of international relations.
>
> (MORGENTHAU 1971 [1964], 282)

By then, the second debate was grinding on!

Morgenthau continued: "I take indeed a more sanguine view of the possibility of international theory than he does, finding that possibility in the very fact that 'international politics is the realm of recurrence and repetition.' It is this repetitive character of international politics, i.e., the configurations of the balance of power, that lends itself to theoretical systematization" (1971 [1964], 282). Regularities and repetition form the basis of theory.

A quarter of a century later, Waltz (1979) would emphatically make the argument that theory does not follow from "laws" in the sense of regularities as such. Theory is both more creative and must be seen as a system-level feature. Thus it must be unified and not simply a collection of isolated laws. It is common to say—in praise or critically—that Waltz moved realism from a more philosophical format to a modern concept of theory. However, in some respect he actually distanced himself from the behavioralist concept of theory and harked back to a deeper, integrated theory of realism close to what the leading voices in this workshop were in some sense struggling to express (Wæver 2009). Why did they not express themselves more in this format back then? It is too easy to simply assume, in hindsight, that they did not have the intellectual tools to do so at that time. The more likely reason has to do with whom they wanted to act vis-à-vis at the time, by contrast with the situation Waltz was in and with what he tried to achieve by his particular move. Their nemesis was to adopt a concept of theory from the time, which ended up creating a self-destructive tension within their own philosophical basis.

In relation to theory, the most puzzling part has to do with the arguments that were *not* made:

1. *Against* scientistic theory and for a more philosophical kind of theory. They did have a powerful argument in their own books, especially Niebuhr and Morgenthau. They had argued why a positivist conception of science is part of the problem, not the solution. This argument seemed impossible to make in this particular setting. It was not attractive to make it here, in a general situation that put a premium on "science" and on "theory" of a particular kind.

2. *Direct reference* to theory already produced, not least Morgenthau's *Politics Among Nations* (1948). It is barely mentioned in the workshop and alluded to only a few times. It is mentioned by Wolfers, but specifically as a textbook and in relation to teaching (256).

3. *Unfolding the more sophisticated methodology and conception of theory from Weber.* It has recently been argued convincingly by Stephen Turner (2004, 2006; Turner and Mazur 2008) that Morgenthau is methodologically much more consistent and sophisticated than is usually assumed—but he must be read through a Weberian lens. But then, it is striking how little this allows him to elevate some of the trivial discussions in the workshop— or even give intelligent answers to the policymakers when pressed by them.

In order to explain these curious absences, combining the five elements in my reading (and figure 4.1) proves to be a valuable strategy. They are not alternatives but elements of a combined story.

5. THE SPEECH ACT OF REALISM

Important pressures in the situation came from the general hegemony in society and not least from founding circles of a particular concept of science. The realist scholars tried to accommodate to this—which created the often confused and contradictory arguments of their seminar—because they had emerged from the first debate in a position of control. Due to the first debate, and because we are still before the second debate as such in IR, they can speak in the double capacity of "we are realists" and "we are IR." But they are trying to devise concepts of theory and science that allow them to become a respected discipline, not least in order to be able to speak with authority to policymakers. The result was the compromise formulation of theory as a collection of regularities, which might have seemed innocent at the time, as it combined superficially some core tenets of Morgenthau's theory (the most developed in the group) with formulations close to those of the behavioralists. In practice, however, this did not allow them to develop their own theory.

The speech act in this situation, the main move of these realists, was therefore to try to secure a continued dominance for realism = IR through adopting a concept of theory = regularities, which was not exactly their own but seemed—wrongly—functional for the purpose.

Nicolas Guilhot has argued very persuasively (2008) that the move by this circle of realist scholars was driven by the need to defend the territory of IR from being subsumed into a general behavioralist social science. However, I believe that he overemphasizes—or in a sense overrationalizes— their use of "theory" as a way to stake out their own territory. I almost say: I wish they did! They had in their repertoire their own concept of theory, which *could* have been used to defend a space for politics against "scientific man," in a way very similar to how "political theory" came to define a subdiscipline within political science at odds with the main trends of that same discipline (and thus not the "theory" *of* that discipline in the normal sense that one would expect in most sciences but as a pocket for a distinct tradition deviating from the mainstream [Hauptmann 2005]. Something similar has been seen in periods of the history of American sociology; cf. Abend [2008]). But they did not! If we look at what the realists said in this workshop and what they published in the years following, they did not launch a strong concept of theory in sense that "political theory" did: witness the "exchange" between Wight and Morgenthau. Instead they compromised with mainstream understandings of theory.

Textbooks and sloppy references often claim that realists in general are positivists. In most respects this is wrong, as witnessed by the critique from Carr, Niebuhr, and Morgenthau of Enlightenment rationalism and the performative understanding of the nature of reality, where truth is not simply a matter of "getting it" but of "making it"; that is, as a statesman you choose and create and thereby make objectivity (Morgenthau 1958, 1960,

1970, 1977, and especially 1962; Kissinger 1957; Niebuhr 1959). But in terms of theory, they did not define a clear front against the positivists. Ironically, Kenneth Waltz's neorealism (1979) actually engaged in a more hard-hitting confrontation with positivist, correlation-seeking, regularity understandings of theory (Wæver 2009). Usually, Waltz is seen as the scientistic second debate–influenced "rationalist" who discarded the classical heritage of ethics and politics for a thin social-science version of realism (Walker 1993; Wæver 1996; Donnelly 2000; Williams 2005). But in relation to positivist understandings of theory, one could just as well argue that forty-five years later he did one of the two things that the classical realists could have done: defend a distinct concept of theory tied to a deep and quite abstract understanding of the international. Their other option would have been the more "philosophical" option of defending international theory as something akin to "political theory." Instead, they constituted their kind of realism and, for a long time, mainstream IR as wedded to a hybrid of European-inspired political thinking—and a concept of theory as regularity.

Guzzini (1998) and others have shown how, although it was started by the "idealists" in small numbers, the consolidation of a discipline of IR was achieved by some key moves by the "realists" in the 1940s and 1950s. Notably, the realists fought to construct an independent object, international relations (see Guilhot 2008). But IR as we know it became constituted with a particular concept of theory that makes little sense if interpreted as a linear extrapolation of the convictions or aspirations of the realists as such. But seen in their relational context, we can understand what they did and why.

6. THE MOVE THAT MADE IR AS WE KNOW IT

It would naturally be excessive to claim that something hugely important happened in this workshop. But some very important things happened to and were caused by these figures during this period, and the workshop offers a glimpse into this larger process. It is also, in some sense, a place where things happened, although largely in the form of nonaction. What they did *not* do on this occasion ended up having long-term effects on the discipline.

Because they did not advocate aggressively for some of the concepts of theory that they actually had access to but instead adopted a compromise format, they pushed the discipline of IR in the direction of a particular understanding of theory—theory as regularities—which has haunted it ever since. Even when we get to the master theorist, Kenneth N. Waltz, we can argue that the one revolution he failed to accomplish was really the one about the nature of theory. Chapter 1 in *Theory of International Politics* (Waltz 1979) tries to move the discipline away from the dominant correlation-based conception of science, but few read this chapter, and the rationalism that he spurred in IR ended up fusing with exactly the kind of theory and method (King, Keohane, and Verba 1994) that he wanted to move away from. Waltz succeeded impressively in several other revolutions, but it is striking that his strongest failure is in what he probably feels strongest about: the theory of theory (Wæver 2009)—this is where the discipline seems thoroughly infused with a particular concept of theory. And one part of the explanation for this is that at a crucial moment, a powerful group of realist scholars met, and they could have unified around the promotion of a different concept of theory. But they did not.

The realist speech act *made IR* in several respects. It preserved IR as a distinct discipline (Guilhot 2008), and it constructed a field that for a long time was (and even is?) self-organizing around realism as its main tradition, even when later there would be an excess of critics compared to the number of defenders of the original core. Realism became defining for IR, and IR became what could be said to realists.

However, it also *made IR as we know it*. It was a particular IR that came out of this somewhat tactical move of talking about theory in an idiom not well integrated with the tradition that it was put to work for. The realists produced a discipline unable to think theory in other ways than the behavioralist one or its occasionally radical critique and deprived it of the kind of theory corresponding to the philosophical traditions they were otherwise drawing on. In the last instance, the story of these realists is as tragic as their own analyses: their actions led to the achievement of some of their goals, notably the securing of an independent discipline and a central position for realism, but in some central respects they produced the outcome of a discipline of IR organized around a concept of theory much closer to the kind of social science they disliked. Or in the language of neorealism: one should not expect outcome to correlate to intentions, because systemic effects introduce themselves and produce unexpected results. In this case only, the system is not the international one but the disciplinary matrix. Seeing these realist scholars in their disciplinary network of relations, we can see the tragic history of their making of the social science of IR.

I appreciate the many helpful comments from the participants in the Tarrytown 2007 workshop as well as from my colleagues in the department of political science, University of Copenhagen, who shared many helpful ideas in a research seminar on an earlier draft. As always, Cecilie Fenger did a great job on the references.

NOTES

1. "Doing *in* writing" is an important emphasis imported from Austin's original speech-act theory, where the quintessential speech act, the illocutionary type, is defined by what is done *in* saying something, that is, the act that is performed when the speech is given and uptake ensured (e.g., a promise is made), in contrast to the locutionary dimension of what the speech act "says" contentwise in a classical sense or the perlocutionary dimension, defined by the effects brought about by the speech act. In the Skinnerian context, this focus on "*in* writing" ensures that we focus on the change that is produced by the fact that these textual moves have now been made (e.g., by *Leviathan* existing) in contrast to the multitude of diverse effects more or less directly engendered by this. Too often, speech acts are understood in a perlocutionary sense in terms of effects external to the act, but the full and original potential of speech-act theory is best exploited by focusing on the illocutionary force of speech acts and therefore on what is done *in* the act (Austin 1975; Sbisà 2001; Wæver forthcoming).

2. First, second, third, fourth, and fifth editions have entries for "international politics" (including "different approaches to") and "realism in foreign policy, 3ff; different from other schools, 3,4, 9ff." Fifth revised (the last Morgenthau himself was involved with) has "international politics" (but not "different approaches to") and "political realism" (but not realism).

3. For a preliminary quantitative estimation of the debateness of the discipline during different periods, see Wæver (2010).

REFERENCES

Abend, Gabriel. 2008. The meaning of "theory." *Sociological Theory* 26, no. 2:173–199.

Ashworth, Lucian M. 2002. Did the realist-idealist great debate really happen? A revisionist history of international relations. *International Relations* 16, no. 1: 33–51.

Ashworth, Lucian M. 2006. Where are the idealists in interwar international relations? *Review of International Studies* 32: 291–308.

Austin, John L. 1975. *How to do things with words.* 2nd ed. Oxford: Oxford University Press.

Bain, William. 2000. Deconfusing Morgenthau: Moral inquiry and classical realism reconsidered. *Review of International Studies* 26, no. 3: 445–464.

Berger, Peter. 2002. Introduction: The cultural dynamics of globalization. In *Many globalizations: Cultural diversity in the contemporary world*, ed. Peter Berger and Samuel Huntington, 1–16. Oxford: Oxford University Press.

Boucher, David. 1998. *Political theories of international relations: From Thucydides to the present.* Oxford: Oxford University Press.

Bull, Hedley. 1972. The theory of international politics, 1919–1969. In *The Aberystwyth papers: International politics, 1919–1969*, ed. Brian Porter, 30–50. Oxford: Oxford University Press.

Butterfield, Herbert, and Martin Wight. 1966. Preface to *Diplomatic investigations: Essays in the theory of international politics*, ed. H. Butterfield and M. Wight. London: George Allen and Unwin.

Carr, E. H. 1939. *Twenty years' crisis, 1919–1939: An introduction to the study of international relations*. New York: Macmillan and Company.

Collins, Randall. 1998. *The sociology of philosophies: A global theory of intellectual change*. Cambridge: Belknap.

Donelan, Michael. 1990. *Elements of international theory*. Oxford: Clarendon.

Donnelly, Jack. 2000. *Realism and international relations*. Cambridge: Cambridge University Press.

Easton, David. 1953. *The political system: An inquiry into the state of political science*. New York: Knopf.

Farr, James, John S. Dryzek, and Stephen T. Leonard, eds. 1995. *Political science in history: Research programs and political traditions*. Cambridge: Cambridge University Press.

Goodman, Douglas. 2001. What Collins's *The sociology of philosophies* says about sociological theory. *Sociological Theory* 19, no. 1 (March): 92–101.

Guilhot, Nicolas. 2008. The realist gambit: Postwar American political science and the birth of IR theory. *International Political Sociology* 2, no. 4 (December): 281–304.

Gunnell, John G. 1993. *The descent of political theory: The genealogy of an American vocation*. Chicago: University of Chicago Press.

Guzzini, Stefano. 1998. *Realism in international relations and international political economy. The continuing story of a death foretold*. New York: Routledge.

Haslam, Jonathan. 2002. *No virtue like necessity: Realist thought in international relations since Machiavelli*. New Haven, Conn.: Yale University Press.

Hauptmann, Emily. 2005. Defining "theory" in postwar political science. In *The politics of method in the human sciences: Positivism and its epistemological others*, ed. George Steinmetz, 207–232. Durham, N.C.: Duke University Press.

Hellmann, Gunther, ed. 2003. Symposium: Dialogue and synthesis in individual scholarship and collective inquiry. *International Studies Review* 5: 123–150.

Holden, Gerard. 2001. The politer kingdoms of the globe: Context and comparison in the intellectual history of IR. *Global Society* 15, no. 1: 27–51.

Holden, Gerard. 2002. Who contextualizes the contextualizers? Disciplinary history and the discourse about IR discourse. *Review of International Studies* 28, no. 2: 253–270.

——. 2006. Approaches to IR: The relationship between Anglo-Saxon historiography and cross-community comparison. In *International relations in Europe: Traditions, perspectives, and destinations*, ed. Knud Erik Jørgensen and Tonny Brems Knudsen, 225–252. London: Routledge.

King, Gary, Robert O. Keohane, and Sidney Verba. 1994. *Designing social inquiry. Scientific inference in qualitative research*. Princeton, N.J.: Princeton University Press.

Kissinger, Henry A. 1957. *A world restored: Metternich, Castlereagh, and the problems of peace, 1812–1822*. Boston: Houghton Mifflin Company.

Kuhn, T. S. 1962. *The structure of scientific revolutions*. Chicago: University of Chicago Press.

Lakatos, I. 1970. The falsification and the methodology of scientific research programmes. In *Criticism and the growth of knowledge*, ed. I. Lakatos and A. Musgrave. Cambridge: Cambridge University Press.

Liska, George. 1977. Morgenthau vs. Machiavelli: Political realism and power politics. In *A tribute to Hans Morgenthau*, ed. K. Thompson and R. J. Myers, 104–111. Washington, D.C.: New Republic Book Company.

——. 1981. The vital triad: International-relations theory, history, and social philosophy. *Social Research* 48, no. 4 (Winter).

Mirowski, Philip E. 2004. The scientific dimensions of society and their distant echoes in American philosophy of science. *Studies in the History and Philosophy of Science* 35 (June): 283–326.

Morgenthau, Hans J. 1946. *Scientific man versus power politics*. Chicago: University of Chicago Press.

——. 1948. *Politics among nations: The struggle for power and peace*. New York: A. A. Knopf.

——. 1951. *In defense of the national interest*. New York: A. A. Knopf.

——. 1952. Another "great debate": The national interest of the United States. *American Political Science Review* 46, no. 4: 961–988.

——. 1958. The commitments of a theory of international politics. In *Dilemmas of politics*, ed. Hans J. Morgenthau, 47–53. Chicago: University of Chicago Press.

——. 1960. *The purpose of American politics*. New York: A. A. Knopf, 1960.

——. 1962. The difference between the politician and the statesman. *Commentary* (January). Reprinted in *Politics in the twentieth century*, by H. J. Morgenthau, 343–350. Chicago: University of Chicago Press, 1971.

——. 1964. The intellectual and political functions of a theory of international relations. Address given at the University of Maryland, March 1961. In *Politics in the twentieth century*, by H. J. Morgenthau, 282–298. Chicago: University of Chicago Press, 1971.

——. 1970. *Truth and power: Essays of a decade, 1960–70*. New York: Praeger.

——. 1977. Fragment of an intellectual autobiography: 1904–1932. In *A tribute to Hans Morgenthau*, ed. K. Thompson and R. J. Myers, 1–17. Washington, D.C.: New Republic Book Company.

Niebuhr, Reinhold. 1959. *The structure of nations and empires: A study of the recurring patterns and problems of the political order in relation to the unique problems of the nuclear age*. New York: Scribner.

——. 1962. Foreword to *Discord and collaboration: Essays on international politics*, ed. Arnold Wolfers, vii–viii. Baltimore, Md.: The Johns Hopkins University Press.

Puchala, Donald J., ed. 2002. *Visions of international relations: Assessing an academic field*. Columbia: University of South Carolina Press.

Quirk, Joel, and Darshan Vigneswaran. 2005. The construction of an edifice: The story of a first great debate. *Review of International Studies* 31, no. 1: 59–74.

Ross, Dorothy. 1992. *The origins of American social science*. Cambridge: Cambridge University Press.

Sbisà, Marina. 2001. Illocutionary force and degrees of strength in language use. *Journal of Pragmatics* 33, no. 12: 1791–1814.

Scheuerman, William E. 2007. Was Morgenthau a realist? Revisiting *Scientific man versus power politics*. *Constellations* 14, no. 4: 506–530.

Schmidt, Brian C. 1998. *The political discourse of anarchy: A disciplinary history of international relations*. Albany: State University of New York Press.

——. 2002. On the history and historiography of international relations. In *Handbook of international relations*, ed. Carlsnaes et al., 3–22. London: Sage.

Skinner, Quentin. 2002. *Visions of Politics*. Vol. 1: *Regarding Method*. Cambridge: Cambridge University Press.

Smith, Michael Joseph. 1986. *Realist thought from Weber to Kissinger*. Baton Rouge: Louisiana State University Press.

Thompson, Kenneth W. 1955. Toward a theory of international politics. *American Political Science Review* 49, no. 3: 733–746.

——. 1980. *Masters of international thought: Major twentieth-century theorists and the world crisis.* Baton Rouge: Louisiana State University Press, 1980.

Tjalve, Vibeke Schou. 2008. *Realist strategies of republican peace: Niebuhr, Morgenthau, and the politics of patriotic dissent.* New York: Palgrave.

Turner, Stephen. 2004. Morgenthau as a Weberian. In *One-hundred-year commemoration to the life of Hans Morgenthau (1904–2004),* ed. G. O. Mazur, 88–114. New York: Semenenko Foundation.

——. The importance of social philosophy to Morgenthau and Waltz. In *Twenty-five year memorial commemoration to the life of Hans Morgenthau (1904–2005),* ed. G. O. Mazur, 174–193. New York: Semenenko Foundation, 2006.

Turner, Stephen, and G. O. Mazur. 2008. Morgenthau as a Weberian methodologist. *European Journal of International Relations* 15, no. 3: 477–504.

Wæver, Ole. 1996. The rise and fall of the inter-paradigm debate. In *International theory: Positivism and beyond,* ed. Steve Smith, Ken Booth, and Marysia Zalewski, 149–185. Cambridge: Cambridge University Press.

——. 1998. The sociology of a not-so-international discipline: American and European developments in international relations. *International Organization* 52, no. 4: 687–727.

——. 2007. The structure of the IR discipline: A proto-comparative analysis. Paper presented at the ISA Convention, Portland, February 26–March 3, 2003.

——. 2007. Still a discipline after all these debates? In *International relations theories: Discipline and diversity,* ed. Tim Dunne, Milja Kurki, and Steve Smith, 288–308. Oxford: Oxford University Press.

——. 2009. Waltz's theory of theory. *International Relations* 23, no. 2: 201–222.

——. 2010. Measuring debateness and mapping frontiers—Great debates in IR, 1947–2009. Paper for *International Studies Association,* New Orleans, February.

——. Forthcoming. Theorising security politically: Speech act theories of securitisation between socio-linguistic pragmatics and prescriptive philosophy.

Wæver, Ole, and Arlene B. Tickner. 2009. Introduction: Geocultural epistemologies. In *Global scholarship in international relations: Worlding beyond the West,* ed. A. B. Tickner and O. Wæver, 1–31. London: Routledge.

Wagner, Peter, Björn Wittrock, and Richard Whitley, eds. 1991. *Discourses on society: Shaping of the social science disciplines.* Yearbook in the Sociology of the Sciences 15. Dordrecht: Kluwer.

Walker, R. B. J. 1992. *Inside/outside: International relations as political theory.* Cambridge: Cambridge University Press.

Waltz, Kenneth N. 1979. *Theory of international politics.* New York: McGrawHill.

——. 1997. Evaluating theories. *American Political Science Review* 91, no. 4: 913–917.

Whitley, Richard. 2000. *The intellectual and social organization of the sciences.* 2nd ed. Oxford: Oxford University Press.

Wight, Martin. 1960. Why is there no international theory? *International Relations* 2, no. 1: 35–48.

——. 1992. *International theory: The three traditions.* Teaneck, N.J.: Holmes & Meier.

Williams, Michael C. 2005. *The realist tradition and the limits of international relations.* Cambridge: Cambridge University Press.

Wilson, Peter. 1998. The myth of the "first great debate." *Review of International Studies* 24: 1–15.

——. 2003. *The international theory of Leonard Woolf.* New York: Palgrave.

Wolfers, Arnold. 1940. *Britain and France between two wars: Conflicting strategies of peace since Versailles.* New York: Harcourt, Brace and Company.

——. 1962. *Discord and collaboration: Essays on international politics.* Baltimore, Md.: The Johns Hopkins University Press.

5

THE REALIST GAMBIT

*Postwar American Political Science and
the Birth of IR Theory*

NICOLAS GUILHOT

A PERUSAL OF American political-science debates in the immediate postwar period suggests that both political scientists working on domestic issues and scholars of international relations had similar concerns: the confidence in the future development of the discipline was tainted by uncertainties about methods, anxiety about the nature and the boundaries of the field, and envy for the scientific status achieved by the discipline of economics. That such concerns were shared suggests that the study of international relations did not constitute a separate field within or outside political science. These disciplinary identities were still in flux, as no clear-cut distinction of method had yet set these fields apart. By the mid-1950s, however, a number of scholars, policy practitioners and public intellectuals were engaged in an important effort at defining international relations as a separate field based on a distinct *theory* of politics. How and why an important swathe of political science dealing with international politics was demarcated by advancing claims as to the specificity of its theoretical perspective is the question that I address in this article.

More often than not, the role of a line of demarcation is to put an end to territorial conflict. In the postwar years, IR was generally considered to be an interdisciplinary field located on the margins of political science, with no method of its own—a sort of commons, as it were, plowed by various disciplines ranging from economics to geography. Yet, as political science and other disciplines became increasingly integrated under the research standards that would define "behavioralism," the territorial status of IR became contentious. As a correspondent of the *American Political Science Review* observed in 1948, "the study of international politics reflects the present tendency toward the consideration of social science as a whole and away from its artificial division into separate compartments" (Fifield 1948,

1190). This tendency, however, had important implications for the status of the field: in the absence of a theory of IR, such theory would be dictated from outside, as the field would become a province of the social sciences. For some, this was a promising professional perspective: for example, this vision of IR as a policy science driven by empirical research methods inspired the work being done at Yale and later Princeton under the leadership of Frederick S. Dunn (Dunn 1948; Lasswell 1951). Others, however, resented the methodological imperialism of the behavioral revolution. They considered the promise of an empirical science of politics an illusion: for them, politics was not entirely rational and could not be comprehended by scientific rationalism. They believed the study of power politics to be premised, as an influential report of the late 1940s put it, on "the possibility that force and not social science will be employed to solve disputes" (Wood 1947, 24). The limits of rationalism was a theme that ran deep within the disciplinary conversation of the 1940s and 1950s: in some quarters, politics and science were seen as alternatives, if not as opposites, and Morgenthau's *Scientific Man Versus Power Politics* (1946) provided the flagship statement for this epistemological position. For these scholars, the development of a behavioral science of politics amounted to nothing less than the suppression—or, to use Morgenthau's term, the "repudiation"—of politics.

In this chapter, I argue that the *theory* of international relations was developed by this latter group as a way to secure a space for its alternative vision of politics and scholarship. It initially emerged as a normative statement on what political science should be, not as a discourse of specialization. Unable to contrast the positivist trends transforming the discipline, these scholars settled for controlling a smaller but independent disciplinary territory. The "theorization" of IR was essentially meant to delineate this territory and make it immune to the cues of behavioralism. A second line of argument suggests that the battle over method was also a battle over politics. Those involved in the development of IR theory were not so much opposed to science per se as they were deeply suspicious of the *liberal* faith in the power of science to subdue political conflict. Because politics was ultimately impervious to rationalization, its best rational rendition was under the form of prudential maxims, not scientific principles. This gave an important role to practitioners in the development of a theory. Also, implicit in this vision of politics was the idea that policy making should not be the preserve of rationalist experts but of men of judgment: men breathing the tragic atmosphere of international politics, able to navigate the "moral dilemmas" of politics, but also aware that the truths of international politics could not be easily accepted by the public of democratic polities. The nascent discipline ensured the permanence of an elitist and conservative tradition that deeply shaped its politics.

IR theory is thus better understood as a case of intellectual irredentism, resisting its own integration into American social science. Like the leaders of any separatist movement, early IR theorists referred to traditions and historical lineages that had been repressed under the rule of pragmatism and empirical social science (whether Augustine, Machiavelli, or a prerationalist views of politics). But despite their traditionalist gesturing, they also had to use modern means of propaganda in order to make their case: they had to speak the language of science and claim that they were laying out the "general laws" of politics. Nobody seemed to have been more aware of this strategic constraint than Morgenthau himself, when he observed that "no political thinker can expect to be heard who would not, at least in his terminology, pay tribute to the spirit of science" (Morgenthau 1946, 31). By paying this tribute, early IR theorists were in fact subverting the dominant spirit of science at the time: the "theory" that they sought to defend did not rest on the assumptions of empiricism and rationalism, as it sometimes may have sounded, but on the Germanic tradition of *Staatslehre* and on a prerationalist view of politics and the state that sought a new audience in 1950s America by speaking the compulsory language of science, albeit with "a thick German accent" (Bull 1972, 39; see also Koskenniemi 2002; Söllner 1987).

This opening gambit is what makes the nature of early IR theory so elusive. The confluence of different meanings into the project of building a "theory" was obviously premised on cultural misunderstandings, and the disciplinary conversation of the 1950s was marred by a good deal of confusion as to what "theory" meant. But such misunderstandings may have been the very condition for the reception of an intellectual tradition that was not congenial to American liberalism and its reliance on rational-scientific knowledge to solve policy issues. Nothing illustrates this better than the perceptive analysis of the transformation of IR into an "American social science," by an émigré scholar who had himself promoted, almost twenty years earlier, the theoretical autonomy of IR as an explicit defense against the "policy scientism" that, according to him and many others, plagued the analysis of international politics in the United States (Hoffmann 1959, 1977). If Stanley Hoffman saw clearly through the original context in which IR theory took shape, it is not least because he took part in it and sided with the critics of scientism. But this state of affairs was confusing enough for contemporaries, and it should not come as a surprise that it also perplexes current commentators, most of whom consider IR as a so-cial science while it actually originated as a reaction *against* the social sci-ences (George 1994; Hollis and Smith 1990; Smith 1987). Even sophisticated historical works tend to overlook the antipositivist, antitechnocratic impe-tus behind IR theory. In his recent study of defense intellectuals, Bruce Kuklick (2006, 187), for instance, suggests that "professorial realists" only provided a "lexicon" that smuggled RAND rocket science into the univer-sities. More tellingly, most constructivist, postpositivist, normative, reflex-ive, or critical approaches to IR implicitly or explicitly posit an image of the discipline as a *positivist* social science beyond which they pretend to move (Neufeld 1995). Ironically, this is exactly what Morgenthau, Niebuhr, and others deplored fifty years ago when they sought to establish IR as an inde-pendent disciplinary field.

In recovering the defensive, antipositivistic purpose of the theory of international relations, this chapter takes stock from a disciplinary histori-ography that has renewed our understanding of political science and interna-tional relations (Adcock et al. 2007; Gunnell 1988; Gunnell 1993b; Guzzini 1998; Kahler 1997; Long and Wilson 1995; Schmidt 2002; Schmidt 2007; Wæver 1998) and from a recent revival of interest in Morgenthau (Frei 2001; Williams 2007). While this literature has often recaptured the com-plexity of postwar realism, it also tends to take for granted the existence of a distinct "field" of IR as a self-evident framework of analysis, even when such a framework was not the one under which the actors under scrutiny operated. Such internalist accounts fail to see that IR debates were mean-ingful only in relation to a much wider disciplinary context. When Colin Wight (2002, 23) argues that the field of IR is "structured around a set of deep contestations over the very idea of science itself and the extent to which IR can, and should, be a science," his argument is correct because it applies to the study of politics in general, not exclusively to international politics. It is thus necessary to consider the emergence of a distinct field of IR as a process led by scholars who sought to articulate an alternative view of politics but could do so only through increased field differentiation vis-à-vis mainstream political science. IR theory was less a specialized sector of political science than a specific view of what the overall discipline should be about. It should therefore be understood as the outcome of the "boundary work" (Gieryn 1999) that any scientific field must perform to establish itself. By emphasizing this pragmatic dimension of theory building, this article shifts the focus onto the qualitative break represented by the development of theory in the 1950s, against the tendency to dilute it into a realist "tradition" spanning centuries if not millennia (Lebow 2003; Molloy 2006; Williams

2005). It suggests that IR took shape as a specific response to the political-science debates of the late 1940s, at odds with the general direction in which the discipline was evolving. While this perspective represented the views of a minority, it successfully mobilized extradisciplinary resources to reinforce its position, in particular those resources offered by the Rockefeller Foundation. There, the early IR theorists could rely upon the unflinching support of Kenneth Thompson, an officer in the Division for the Social Sciences, a former student and colleague of Morgenthau, and a realist himself. This chapter suggests that these efforts at defining a "theory" of international relations turned out to be a failure but also that it did not matter so much: what really defined the "theory" was its opposition to the integration of the discipline under the behavioral paradigm. The real consensus was on what IR should *not* be. The focus of the theory, in the last instance, was its repudiation of a liberalism masquerading as value-free social science and rooted in the tradition of Enlightenment rationalism: early IR theorists explicitly conceived of their discipline as a modern counterenlightenment.

POLITICAL SCIENCE AND INTERNATIONAL RELATIONS AFTER 1945

The lack of differentiation between political science and international relations is one of the striking aspects of postwar disciplinary debates. Whether they studied domestic or international politics, most scholars of the time belonged to a single disciplinary field. The study of international politics was identified as one of the thriving areas of political science after 1945. The collaboration between political scientists and government agencies during the war had widened the interest of the profession in all things international. Dramatic international developments and soaring enrollment numbers following the demobilization contributed to creating a strong demand for courses in international relations. Summing up wartime developments in the discipline, Carl Friedrich observed that "among the more specialized organizations, those in the international field are most numerous, and indeed are highly significant for the progress of political science in the United States" (Friedrich 1947, 985). For sure, the thriving field of international relations may seem poorly defined compared to an established discipline that had its own association since 1903, a dedicated journal, and academic departments in prestigious universities. A lot of ink was spilled trying to delineate the contours of the expanding field of international relations by defining its core contents and research methods. In most accounts, practitioners and observers alike concurred that it had strong affinities with political science but that it also needed to mobilize other branches of the social sciences, such as geography, economics, international law, diplomatic history, social psychology, and anthropology. "The IR specialist," according Klaus Knorr, "is a specialist in one of the basic fields, ordinarily political science, who is compelled to draw upon the relevant research work of specialists in other subsidiary fields" (Knorr 1947, 552). The specificity of IR resided not in a method but rather in the particular assemblage of materials and techniques it represented, in the "patterns of equipment" it brought to bear upon the study of power (Dunn 1949, 85).

These perplexities were not confined to a neatly delineated field of IR. The discussions about its nature only reflected locally a status anxiety that was felt throughout the discipline of political science. In the late 1940s, IR appeared to "command . . . no methodology of its own" (Knorr 1947, 552), but neither did political science. Writing the same year as Knorr, Friedrich (1947, 980) pointed out that "the development of a central core of sound theory is perhaps the greatest need of American political science today. Its most obvious weakness in comparison with economics is the lack of interest of political scientists in the development of such an agreed foundation in theory." A 1948 report by the research committee of the American Political Science Association tried to cast the situation in a more optimistic light and considered that "there is no longer any single technique—methods and designs must be blended and kept in elastic touch and mutual penetration" (Griffith 1948). The situation does not seem to have substantially improved in the early 1950s when Harold Lasswell (1951, 133) pointed out "the existence among academicians of conflicting conceptions of the scope and method of political science." Because the discipline was defined by its "subject-matter" rather than by an agreed-upon method, "most valuable work has been done by other than academically trained political scientists" (ibid.). The same criticism was addressed to international relations, to the extent that the field was also defined by "the nature of the questions" that it dealt with rather than a consensual methodology, which resulted in much relevant work being done within neighboring disciplines (Dunn 1948, 144). In 1955, Morgenthau seems to have formulated a common complaint when he lamented the "inorganic growth and haphazard character of political science," a discipline that had developed "not by virtue of an intellectual principle germane to the field, but in response to pressures from the outside" (Morgenthau 1955, 437). His criticism of the state of IR, however, was couched in the very same terms. A few years later, Stanley

Hoffman (1959, 348) deplored that "without theory, we will have to take whatever other disciplines w[ill] see fit to dump onto our plate, and we will have indigestion from smörgåsbord." In other words, the lack of a theoretical core was a generic problem of political science that, by extension, also marred IR but was not specific to it. This has important implications for the argument followed here, for it means that the protracted search for a theory was not so much about clarifying the professional identity of IR as it was part of a discipline-wide conversation involving all the branches of political science. Postwar statements about IR theory must be understood primarily as contributions to a wider contest over the nature and the method of political science itself.

What was at stake in these debates was the legitimacy of political science as a scientific project. That this project was in crisis was something that many contemporaries acknowledged and tried to address. Pondering what the discipline had to offer in the current world situation, Quincy Wright (1950, 2) started by pointing out "the insistence by many that a science of politics is impossible," an objection that he then proceeded to counter. Writing a few years later, Fred Kort, a political scientist at the University of Connecticut, stressed "the contested status of the science of politics" and the fact that exponents of scientific aspirations remained "on the defensive" as they grappled with the twin problems of the unpredictability of human behavior and the difficulty of ascertaining what the criteria of a science of politics would be (Kort 1952, 1140). Most of these discussions revolved around two contested issues: the role of values and the problem of the rationality of politics.

The possibility of a science of politics was indexed on the prevailing conception of science at the time, and this conception was premised on value relativism. A true science did not pronounce upon ultimate ends, only on the causal sequences allowing for their realization. As long as science was considered to be part of a modernizing historical process that could be described as progress, value relativism was not an issue. Yet, after World War II had witnessed the power of science and technology unleashed at the service of the darkest purposes, narratives of historical progress could no longer be taken for granted. An increasingly vocal critique of value relativism and positivism, articulated in particular, but not exclusively, by émigré scholars, set the stage for the postwar debate on political science. For these critics, value relativism had prevented the social sciences from discriminating between democracy and totalitarianism. Morally blind, unable to resist being harnessed to the most sinister political projects, the social sciences had been in no position to contribute in any meaningful way to the fight against fascism, when they did not serve it. Arnold Brecht, a legal scholar who had found refuge at the New School in 1933, opened his report on a 1946 round table on relativism in political theory with a dramatic personal note:

> modern science and modern scientific methods . . . have led to an ethical vacuum, a religious vacuum, and a philosophical vacuum. . . . For they have offered little or nothing to distinguish between good and evil, right and wrong, justice and injustice. All social sciences are involved in this calamity, but none has been so deeply affected as political science, which had to face the new creeds of Communism, Fascism, and Nazism as political phenomena of tremendous power. They settled down in the area abandoned by science, taking full advantage of the fact that, scientifically speaking, there was a vacuum.
>
> (BRECHT 1947, 470)

Whether they deplored the demise of the social sciences, like Brecht, or suggested that there was a dialectic connivance between scientific positivism and totalitarianism, like members of the Frankfurt School, émigré scholars leveled a charge that forced political scientists defending the traditional image of the discipline to make explicit a number of methodological assumptions previously taken for granted (Gunnell 1993a). The charge against value relativism was indeed at odds with the basic image of science in the United States: true science stemmed from a commitment to empiricism, rational inference, and an objectivism untainted by the assumption of normative preferences. Value relativism, in fact, was the very criterion of science. Faced with the rejection of value relativism, many political scientists struggled to maintain the image of a value-free social science in a context where normative orientations could no longer be ignored, solicited as they were by the ideological tensions of the cold war. Harold Lasswell, for instance, considered that the preference for democratic values was "obvious" and that it did not need, therefore, to "interfere with objectivity" in scientific activity (Lasswell 1951, 135). Taking a rather exceptional position among émigré scholars, Hans Kelsen (1951, 641, 646–647) defended in no uncertain terms the principle of value-free political science: the scientist "must not presuppose any value," and this "principle of objectivity applies to social science as well as to natural science, and in particular to so-called political science." If scientific statements involved the endorsement of values, they would become "political ideology," and "there will never be a real political science." Closer to international relations, Wright (1950, 3–4) distinguished between the value relativism of "pure science" and an "applied science" that could "assume the values of a particular group and seek formulae useful in achieving these values." These latter values could be of the most general kind—such as human welfare—and political science could move freely between its status as a pure science and its practical applications. In his article on the possibility of a scientific study of politics, Kort suggested that both natural and social phenomena were subject to the same scientific method of inquiry. The difference was in the "lower degree of probability" that hypotheses could achieve in political science, because of the number of uncontrolled variables intervening (Kort 1952, 1151). To a large extent, behavioralism would be the explicit formulation and defense of a number of assumptions that were implicit in traditional American social science but became increasingly contested in the postwar years (Adcock 2007; Gunnell 1993b).

The second issue that the proponents of a science of politics had to deal with was the rationality of their subject matter and, more broadly, the relation between reason and power. Here again, the discussion must be resituated against the backdrop of the war and the unprecedented combination of bureaucratic rationality and calls to irrational impulses that distinguished the exercise of power in fascist and Nazi regimes. As the rational nature of politics could no longer be taken for granted, and as the state could no longer be considered as the embodiment of a rational good, the problem was to determine whether politics could be entirely characterized and accounted for through rational categories. This discussion crystallized around the notion of "power." Power, of course, was not a new subject in the discipline, but it is fair to say that its connotations changed in the postwar years. Closely associated with "realist" political analysis, the notion of power was usually used to stress the incapacity of scientific rationalism to comprehend politics. It gave a strong leverage to those who wanted to detach political science from the naturalistic model of scientific analysis. Analyzing politics or the state "in terms of power" generally meant introducing irrational elements such as psychological drives, charisma, or a deep-seated *libido dominandi*. In a programmatic article on the study of power in which he discussed recent trends in American political science, Franz Neumann made the case that power was an "elusive concept." Because it was not merely physical coercion but also an appeal to rational and emotional faculties, its "two-sided character . . . already marks political science off from natural sciences. It makes it impossible (even if it were desirable) to measure power relationships as one measures the behavior of external nature" (Neumann 1950, 162). The new focus on power, in other words, was very much the symptom of the crisis of confidence that affected scientific rationalism. In September 1951, the *American Political Science Review* dedicated a special section to the issue of "Political Science and Political Power," in which the issues at stake in the vogue of power politics, both for political science at large and international relations, became visible. Writing about "the present-day tendency to think and to speak of the state almost exclusively in terms of power," Walter Sandelius (1951) accepted the view that the reality of power was more than just physical coercion: "the power of propaganda, of prestige, and the like are variously documented and analyzed in the search for political realities." Citing Morgenthau's view of power as "the evil lust for domination over men," he proceeded to mount a defense of scientific rationalism by refuting the idea that what was historical or psychological was not rational. Ultimately, the analysis of power could still be conducted within the framework of scientific rationalism. At the other end of the spectrum, Thomas Vernor Smith (1951, 699) expounded a social-Darwinist, ontological view of power as ubiquitous and running through nature and society alike but finding in nationalism and the national interest its highest moral expression. This antirationalist manifesto, written by a philosopher, embodied a lot of what was wrong with the metaphysical view of power. The dramatization of power politics resulting in a vision of interstate relations as essentially inimical was quickly described as a "German view" that could be traced back to Schmitt or Ratzenhofer and could not be endorsed (Wolfers 1949, 181). For most in the political-science profession, the focus on power politics entailed the risk of moving away from the standards of naturalistic science and regressing to speculative and ideational constructions or, worse, to some kind of *Lebensphilosophie* associated with reactionary German romanticism.

IR scholars obviously took part in these debates, but they did not speak with one voice. The diversity of their views matched the different positions found within the political-science profession at large, bearing witness to the lack of specificity and autonomy characterizing the field of IR. Yet they participated in this discussion in the context of a growing uncertainty as to the identity of their own field. As the demand for IR courses grew, many political scientists were "not at all certain about what material to cover or what approach to use" (Fifield 1948, 1189). This context triggered a protracted discussion about the study of international relations, and the late 1940s saw a protodisciplinary conversation take shape in journal articles, conferences, and reports of various kinds (Schmidt 2007). The twin issues of relativism and rationalism thus resonated within an ongoing reflection about the nature of international politics. The framework of this discussion was a relative consensus about the fact that IR was primarily defined by its topic and not by its method. It was "applied science" (Wolfers); "an unsystematic putting-together and presentation of material" from other fields, a "hodgepodge" (Gurian); it commanded "no methodology of its own" (Knorr); maybe it was only "the non-domestic side of the traditional disciplines" (Dunn). A few years later, Quincy Wright (1955, 33) still claimed that IR was based on "at least eight disciplines," and Stanley Hoffman stated that it was a "flea market" (1959, 348). Such perplexities were not confined to IR, of course, as similar doubts assailed other regions of political science, if not the whole discipline. But by making IR an applied field where analytical tools were imported from the social sciences, interdisciplinarity tended to impose the dominant criteria of scientific rationalism prevailing in other disciplines. Most scholars seeking to strengthen IR by promoting the application of social-science research techniques to the study of international politics therefore subscribed to value relativism as a principle of scientific work. They also tended not to advocate disciplinary autonomy, in the name of the same ideal of scientific unity. Arnold Wolfers (1947, 24–26), for instance, considered that "discussing whether international relations constitutes a separate discipline" was a moot point, since "the problem is how to apply the resources of the social sciences most effectively to matters concerning international affairs." And "as a social scientist," the student of international relations had "no special competence to judge the moral merits of ends or means" and was therefore committed to the ideal of value-free social science. Similar views, mitigated by a commitment to social reform characteristic of the "policy science" approach, ran through much of Frederick Dunn's writing during the same years, and in particular the idea that IR should be subjected to the same criteria of validity as any other science, meaning logical induction and subsequent testing of hypotheses through empirical research (Dunn 1948, 1949).

Yet the realist troops were split on these matters. If many saw the future of the field within the orbit of a scientific method cutting across traditional disciplines, others were quite dismayed by such prospects. Early proponents of a theory of international relations were not parsimonious of critical pronouncements upon political science and were aware that the institutional location of international relations within political-science departments was a thorny issue. The "advisability of this solution," Morgenthau sternly wrote (1952, 655), depended upon "whether a department of political science actually puts the study of politics in the centre of its endeavors or whether— as most of them do—merely offers a disparate collection of courses whose common denominator is a vague and general relation to the activities of the state." The emphasis on power politics required an altogether different approach, one remote from the functional analysis defended, for instance, by Lasswell. The scholars opposed to value relativism and to the rationalist view of power sought to move the field away from its interdisciplinary stage, which subjected it to the dominant trends in political science. It gradually became clear that the only way to achieve this was to pursue theoretical autonomy. The rejection of relativism and rationalism thus provided the common denominator for the forces that converged into the project of building a theory of international relations.

One of the earliest objections against considering IR as a mere subfield of other social sciences was formulated by Waldemar Gurian. Armed with impeccable realist credentials (he had been a close disciple of Carl Schmitt), Gurian was the founder of the Catholic *Review of Politics* at Notre Dame and a German émigré. Writing in 1946 about the study of international relations, he cautioned that the objections against considering IR a separate branch of knowledge should not be accepted. IR may have no method of its own, Gurian conceded, but it was nonetheless defined by "a special point of view" focusing on the relations between separate political units. These units did not have to be states: they were first and foremost communities of purpose, and thus could be supranational organizations like the Catholic Church or the labor movement. In this watered-down rendition of an existential concept of the "political" as the primary focus of IR, Gurian could not fail to attack the dominant conceptions of science, which were preventing IR from developing in the way he adumbrated: the instruction of IR should be "free of a spirit of relativistic nihilism" and acknowledge that "views on the nature of men become decisive" (Gurian 1946, 280). The same year, Morgenthau's *Scientific Man Versus Power Politics* made a much more adamant case for the specificity of international politics and the inadequacy of the scientific method. Later, he would explicitly connect the project of a theory with the rejection of value relativism: the "denial of the existence and intelligibility of a truth about matters political that exists regardless of time and place implies a denial of the possibility of political theory" (Morgenthau 1955, 452).

An important milestone in this conversation was a series of regional conferences organized by the Council on Foreign Relations in April and May 1946 and supported by the Rockefeller Foundation, whose conclusions were summarized in a volume later published by Grayson Kirk, a professor of government at Columbia University (Kirk 1947). Compared with interwar surveys (Ware 1938), the Kirk report was characterized by its criticism of the infatuation of academics with Wilsonianism: a "disproportionate amount of time and energy was given to discussion of 'international cooperation,' while the analyses of the forces of conflict in society, and of the institution of war, were subordinated and tainted with the stigma of moral reproach." Much of interwar scholarship thus amounted to "propaganda," however well meaning (Kirk 1947, 4). The report also expressed dissatisfaction with the division of the field between international law, international organization, and international politics: to the extent that law and international forums could become politicized at any time, international politics was really "the nucleus" of the field. While leaving open the question of the disciplinary status of IR, Kirk also advocated "a special method and approach" and suggested that its real focus should be power politics (Kirk 1947, 10–12). If the Kirk report provided "a kind of consensual springboard into the second postwar era" (Olson and Groom 1991, 108), it was in part because it was ambiguous and could be construed in different ways. On the one hand, it still subscribed to the view of IR as an interdisciplinary enterprise whose subject matter was "drawn from a variety of specialized fields" (Kirk 1947, 15). Yet it criticized the reformist inclinations of IR and made clear that the field revolved around the political, understood as a phenomenon that could displace the orders of morality and law. Although the Kirk report sanctioned the dominance of the realist mood, it did not do much to arbitrage between its internal divisions. This was probably unavoidable, due to its nature as a synthesis document reflecting the views of the profession. But it certainly emboldened the active minority that opposed the widespread acceptance of value relativism and rationalism in the study of politics, which had resulted from the methodological subordination of international relations to other disciplines. Although the scholars of that persuasion fought an uphill battle against the opinion prevailing in such prestigious centers as Yale's Institute of International Studies or Princeton's Woodrow Wilson School of Public and International Affairs and against the general direction in which political science was developing, their inferiority was compensated for by the support that they received from the Rockefeller Foundation. By assembling a network of scholars who shared similar views but belonged to different institutional or disciplinary areas, the foundation contributed to the emergence of an intellectual counterforce to the confident liberalism of the 1950s and its scientific manifestations in the study of international politics. As the hub of this network, the Division for the Social Sciences of the Rockefeller Foundation acted as the midwife of IR theory.

THE ROLE OF THE ROCKEFELLER FOUNDATION
IN THE RUN-UP TO IR THEORY

In retrospect, the support granted by the Rockefeller Foundation to realist scholars may seem puzzling. Why would a foundation support the intellectual current that called into question the key premises of its past activities? The idea of scientific reform based on the use of rational knowledge to solve social conflicts was anathema to critics of scientific rationalism such as Morgenthau. It embodied all the illusions of the liberal pretense to master the historical process through technical means. Moreover, postwar realism primarily defined itself against the legalist approach to international relations that was the stock in trade of philanthropic foundations. In the wake of the nineteenth-century peace movement, foundations had played an important role in articulating the key instances of the legalist vision, such as international arbitration, customary law, disarmament, and peace conferences (Boyle 1999). Inspired by late-Victorian liberalism and its belief in the political benefits of free trade, this vision saw in the development of modern economic forces the foundation of a rational world order (Ashworth 1999). In the United States, it resonated with the interests of the new industrialists and their legal advisers, who believed that they could apply to international relations the same rationalization that they had brought to economic production. Just as their vertically integrated trusts had put an end to ruthless competition, international organizations would in due time eliminate conflict and irrational behavior and generate a common legal culture. This vision was also the matrix of the academic study of international relations. Until World War II, most of the surveys of the field were indeed commissioned by or for philanthropic foundations, while research and teaching in the universities reflected primarily legalist concerns (Fox 1968). The Rockefeller Foundation was no exception: since the 1920s, its mission in the field of international relations had been to "facilitate the amicable adjustment of national differences" and to promote "continuous conference among nations" (1930, 227; 1932, 278). In 1945, its Division of Social Sciences still considered that raising education about international relations contributed to peace by avoiding misconceptions.[1] And in 1946, its most important financial appropriation still went to the League of Nations, then poised to become the United Nations—making its support to realist critics of international reform all the more paradoxical.

Two major factors explain the support granted by the Rockefeller Foundation to the realist vision of international affairs. The first is the rethinking that took place within its Division for Social Sciences after 1945. The invigorated critique of the policy-science model that implicitly defined much of American social science was heard at the foundation, which had longstanding ties with the émigré scholars who usually formulated it. The crisis of scientific rationalism placed at the service of social reform was very much the crisis of the philanthropic model, and this crisis led to a reappraisal of previous programs by the Division for Social Sciences. The second factor, analyzed in the next section, is the nature of the Program on International Relations that was established in 1953–1954: the program was based on a de facto alliance with Hans Morgenthau, whose views of the field of IR and of the need for a theory it entirely endorsed. The Rockefeller Foundation thus became not only the architect of a new academic field but also a player occupying a very specific position within this field. However, it would be misleading to assume that, by supporting a realist theory of international relations, the Rockefeller Foundation was reneging on its earlier commitment to reform through international law. Its officers saw realism as the continuation of preexisting legalistic approaches to international affairs. This perception rested in part on a sociological continuity: as Alfons Söllner (1988, 164–165) observed, the German émigrés who ended up teaching international relations in U.S. political-science departments were generally trained as jurists. They gave realism the credentials it needed for appearing as superior to, and improving on, the legalist vision of international affairs. As international law had "stumbled down from [its] high estate" after 1945, realism was seen as a promising redefinition of work in the area of international law, characterized by a "vigorous sociological approach" that insisted that "the legal rule be seen in relationship to a given social reality."[2] In the field of municipal law, this new course would later culminate in the creation of the Law and Society Association in 1964, also supported by the Rockefeller Foundation as a direct offshoot of the legal realism of the 1950s (Garth 2000). Moreover, if some Rockefeller programs, such as Legal and Political Philosophy, where international relations were rooted, tended to promote theoretical work "as a counterweight to the growing power of social science in the study of politics" (Hauptmann 2006, 648), this reflected not only the convictions of some program officers but also a strategy of experimentation and diversification of the philanthropic portfolio, in a context where the development of a behavioral science of society remained a key objective of the foundation's scientific programs.

The reappraisal of IR programs started early on. In his 1945 memorandum on the foundation's policy in the field of IR, Joseph Willits, the director of the Division for Social Sciences, expressed mixed feelings about past achievements. The massive investments made in developing international studies (almost $10,000,000 from 1926 to 1945) appeared in retrospect as "an infinity of small dabs at many things."[3] More significantly, the traditional emphasis on the education of public opinion was now questioned: with the rise of mass media and their increased coverage of world affairs, "adult education" programs were no longer an area where the foundation could make a difference. Instead, it should identify the "points of strategic importance" for international relations in the new postwar context. Along with other institutions, such as the Social Science Research Council, which established a Committee on International Relations Research in 1948, the Rockefeller Foundation became part of the disciplinary conversation of the 1940s as it sought to generate reliable surveys of current work and foster the development of the field. In this context, it financed the 1946 cycle of regional conferences organized by the Council on Foreign Relations and subsequently took its cues from the Kirk report.

The translation of the Kirk report into operational guidelines was the work of Bryce Wood, a consultant asked to write an internal report for the foundation outlining possible courses of action (Wood 1947). The foundation, he suggested, had to decide whether it wanted to continue support for expertise in international law and research on international organization, which he defined as "strictly non-political international activities," or whether it would instead seek to strengthen the capacities of the making of U.S. foreign policy. The question raised was really about the possibility, as the international situation was becoming increasingly polarized, to maintain the prewar internationalist perspective and to stay outside of politics. He suggested that, while peace efforts remained worth supporting, the reorientation of Rockefeller programs from the international to the national level was not only desirable but, in fact, already underway. This process had already begun in 1935, Wood argued, when the foundation had made a grant to the Yale Institute of International Studies, which was one of the early receptacles of realism in the United States.[4] This decision was part of a wider trend, which consisted in "the strengthening of anti-totalitarian foreign policies" next to the traditional interest in international peace (Wood 1947, 28). In the postwar context, this policy should be continued and expanded, Wood suggested. Beyond the circumstantial argument that the cold war forced politicization and that the experience of the Rockefeller Foundation with international law would not prevent it from being drawn into politics, the Wood report actually reiterated an idea that had been developed by the most ferocious critiques of legalism: law was not a bulwark against politics, because it could become politicized at any moment. It also made two further claims that strengthened the case for conceiving of IR theory as an *alternative* to social science. First, as a branch of knowledge, IR was concerned with the "possibility that force and not social science will be employed to solve disputes" (Wood 1947, 24); that is, it took for granted the limits of scientific rationalism. Second, Wood argued that the "anti-statistical nature of diplomacy" called for different methods: the secrecy of diplomatic transactions, the small number of statesmen, and other factors made international politics unfit for the kind of quantitative analysis that was gaining ground in other social sciences (Wood 1947, 44). The Wood report was an important policy document that paved the ground for the alliance between realists and the Rockefeller Foundation. It explains why support for the interdisciplinary option and for the scientific rationalism that came attached to it seems to have declined considerably by the early 1950s.[5]

Paving the way toward an autonomous discipline, the decision to strengthen a "theory of international politics" was taken in 1953 and officialized in the president's report to the trustees. The "Program for International Studies" drafted by Kenneth W. Thompson for the Division for Social Science was entirely pitted against the "aimless humanitarianism" of interwar scholarship, which it contrasted with the objective study of power politics. Only by shedding its past ways could the study of international politics reach the status of a scientific field of study. While acknowledging that "no serious student would presume to claim the study of international relations had arrived at the stage of an independent academic discipline," the program suggested that all the requirements were met: the field had a core focus (the state and power politics); efforts were made toward developing an appropriate methodology; and "inventories have been drawn up by individual scholars, universities and institutes, of topics and concrete projects which would best serve the development of general principles in the field and their validation through systematic inquiry."[6] Obviously, interdisciplinarity—what Thompson called "blending fragments of knowledge and isolated techniques from the humanities and the natural sciences"— was not the way forward.

MAPPING OUT THE FIELD: THE CHICAGO VIEW

If conversations within the Rockefeller Foundation pointed at the need to establish disciplinary autonomy, they did not specify in detail the lines along which the emerging discipline should develop. Yet, curiously, the views of IR theory promoted by the Rockefeller Foundation in the mid-1950s consistently echoed those of Hans J. Morgenthau. This is all the more surprising since earlier contacts between Morgenthau and the officers of the Rockefeller Foundation had not been good. In 1950, Morgenthau had approached the foundation with a proposal requesting support for his Center for the Study of American Foreign Policy at the University of Chicago.[7] Following consultations with Pendelton Herring, the president of the SSRC, who thought Morgenthau's work was "highly personal and dogmatic," and with Philip Mosely, who did not show more enthusiasm, the proposal was turned down. Morgenthau's strong views, which he expressed during a meeting with Willits, certainly accounted for this lack of understanding: he had criticized the "pragmatic and anti-philosophical" American tradition for the poverty of political philosophy in the country and attributed the crisis of the tradition of political thought to the "scientific spirit." "The Foundation," he suggested, "could make a great contribution, if it set up an institute of political philosophy, and break up the stranglehold which public administration has on political science and philosophy."[8] This early attempt at countering the social sciences, however, did not succeed.

The situation changed dramatically three years later, when Kenneth W. Thompson, a young political scientist at Northwestern, was hired as a consultant in charge of the IR program of the Rockefeller Foundation. The appointment of the man that Morgenthau considered "the best student he ever had"[9] and who reciprocated his admiration brought Morgenthau back into the good graces of the foundation, albeit indirectly, and gave him considerable intellectual influence over the formulation of the IR program. After joining the Division for Social Science as a consultant in 1953, Thompson subsequently became assistant director (1955–1957), associate director (1957–1960), director for social sciences (1960–1961), and vice president for international programs (1961–1974). Born in 1921, Thompson had studied history before joining the army as an infantry and counterintelligence officer. He later enrolled at the University of Chicago, where he took a Ph.D. in political science in 1950, with a dissertation on the political philosophy of Toynbee. More importantly, he was a disciple and close colleague of Morgenthau, with whom he had published the reader *Principles and Problems of International Politics* (Morgenthau and Thompson 1950). It is hard to overstate the role played by Thompson in aligning the IR program with the views elaborated in Chicago against the legalistic teaching of Quincy Wright. If Morgenthau was the thinker, Thompson was the academic entrepreneur and philanthropic manager who decisively contributed to establishing the discipline on a theoretical agenda inspired by Morgenthau.

The picture of the field that emerges from Thompson's papers bears witness to the strong antibehaviorist bias that oriented the foundation's Program for International Studies. His analysis of the academic landscape was crucial for determining the institutional loci and the research efforts on which the program would concentrate its resources. Writing at the end of 1953, Thompson observed that one of the obstacles to the development of a theory of international relations was the absence of appropriate outlets. *World Politics*, which had been founded in 1949 at Yale and whose editor was William T. R. Fox, had been "taken over by the behavioral scientists"; the *American Political Science Review* had obligations to "five or six fields"; and *International Organization* was essentially about "the factual description of United Nations affairs."[10] A month later, reporting to Dean Rusk on the foundation's Program in International Studies, Thompson delineated what he saw as the strategic alternative for the foundation. The old Yale group, which the foundation had supported since 1935, had migrated en masse to Princeton's Center of International Studies in 1951. But since 1943, these scholars had developed an interest in a practical approach to foreign-policy decisions. Decision making, however, was the kind of issue that lent itself most to the development of quantitative research tools and rational-choice methodologies after the war (Amadae 2003). The "Princeton school," Thompson wrote, had thus developed "behavioral constructs" that, he added somewhat scornfully, had aroused little interest.[11] Next to the behavioral approach to international politics, however, there was another school of thought that emphasized the national interest as the interpretive standard of rational political action. "If Princeton is the capitol [*sic*] city of behaviorism," Thompson went on, "Chicago and Columbia are the centers of this second approach at the present time."[12] "Is it of interest to the foundations and to scholarly progress in general that the growth of a 'party-line' at major institutions has been a dominant characteristic of the field? Or is this, to the contrary, a force contributing to progress through intense specialization? Can we steer a middle course between extremes?"[13] The question was purely rhetorical, and the conclusion was foregone: "If what is sought is diversity in approach then perhaps Columbia or Chicago or Stanford-Berkeley has much to offer."[14] Yet the middle course envisaged by Thompson proved rather partisan in then end.

A list of centers and scholars doing research in IR drafted in February 1954 sheds some light on what Thompson himself meant by "Chicago" and "Columbia."[15] At Chicago, the program considered exclusively the Center for the Study of American Foreign Policy. The department of political science, with its strong empirical tradition going back to Charles Merriam and its contribution to behavioralism, was simply excluded from the list, and virtually no mention was made of the work of Quincy Wright, who represented the legalist alternative to Morgenthau. This is quite significant, given that the department had provided cohorts of IR scholars to Yale's Institute of International Studies, and, through the institute, to Princeton, Columbia, MIT, and the RAND Corporation (Almond 2004). The Chicago side of things, in other words, was essentially a Morgenthau operation. As for Columbia, what Thompson had in mind was primarily the Institute of War and Peace Studies. Opened in 1952 under the direction of William T. R. Fox and established within the School of International Affairs, the institute's mandate was to deal with "basic research" on issues of national security rather than with policy making (Cowan 1954, 90–92). The other major figure at Columbia was Reinhold Niebuhr, at the Union Theological Seminary, another critique of liberalism and scientific rationalism. The same list of institutions and individuals reveals a bleak view of the work done at Princeton's Center for International Studies. The same bias drove the process of short-listing potential participants in the conversation that Thompson was staging on the "theory" of international relations. Names were initially circulated during informal discussions between Thompson, Wolfers, and Fox. None of the Princeton scholars suggested by Fox (Harold Sprout, Klaus Knorr, Frederick Dunn) were included in the shortlist, while some of Wolfers' suggestions (John Herz) were also discarded. The invitations extended to foreign-policy practitioners obeyed the same logic: the exhaustive Rockefeller listing of "academic competence in international relations" included a number of nonacademic institutions with an interest in foreign policy, such as the Council on Foreign Relations, the Brookings Institution, the Carnegie Endowment for International Peace, and the RAND Corporation. Among those, only the Foreign Service Educational Foundation was retained as a valid provider of participants. Often nicknamed the "Policy Planning Staff in Exile," the Foreign Service Education Foundation of 1954 was the fiefdom of Paul Nitze and also included George Kennan.

THE REALIST *METHODENSTREIT*:
THE 1954 CONFERENCE ON THEORY

The strategy pursued by the foundation officers was not limited to an "exploratory search" identifying scholars and research in the field. It entailed an exercise in social engineering by gathering like-minded scholars to discuss the content of the theory and its institutional dimension. A major step in that direction was taken in May 1954, with the organization of a "conference on international politics" convened to discuss the possibility and the nature of a theory of international politics, its relevance to foreign-policy making, and the institutional resources available: Ph.D. opportunities, publication outlets, regular seminars, departmental bases, relations with statesmen and policy makers, and so on. The 1954 conference is unique in that it gathered the luminaries of IR to have them discuss the nature, boundaries, and future of their field. The participants included Hans Morgenthau, Reinhold Niebuhr, William T. R. Fox, Arnold Wolfers, Dean Rusk, Paul Nitze, Kenneth W. Thompson, and Dorothy Fosdick, along with nonacademic observers of international affairs such as Walter Lippman and John Reston. Compared to the conferences of the late 1940s, the 1954 seminar was more selective: it excluded scholars associated with the study of international law and organizations. More importantly, it firmly located the interest in theory within a network of scholars and practitioners committed to the study of power politics. The gathering was clearly designed as a counterpoint to the reformist conferences of experts in international law and organizations.[16] A common theme running through the different contributions was the inadequacy of previous approaches to international politics and the need to strengthen a "theory." Morgenthau, for instance, claimed that none of the hitherto prevailing modes of dealing with the subject, "history, reform, or pragmatic manipulation," could claim scientific status, as they were not dealing with "general laws."[17] Arnold Wolfers pointed at political science and the social sciences in general as the relevant pool of tools for analyzing international affairs. Similar claims were made by William Fox and Kenneth Thompson. On the face of it, these debates seemed to suggest that, by contrast with the amateurish reformism of the past, the development of an academic interest in a *theory* of international politics was a bid for scientific supremacy.

The opposition between "scientific" realism and "idealist" internationalism is well known and belongs to the official lore of the discipline. As any foundational legend, however, it builds upon carefully selected historical facts but conceals others. A wholly different image takes shape when we understand the genesis of the discipline in its own terms, and the transcript of the 1954 conference provides a solid ground to assess them. Behind the rhetorical claims to "science" that supported the attack against the legal-historical approach to international relations lay oppositions that betrayed deep divisions within realism. In this context, the theoretical approach to international relations was first developed to insulate the field from the surrounding behavioral sciences. It was not meant to make it more scientific but, on the contrary, immune to science. A closer look reveals that realism provided a common language for ultimately divergent intellectual and ideological projects. Claims to scientific status in the analysis of international politics were made by two competing projects: classical realism and behavioralism. Morgenthau may indeed have heralded a "science" of international politics in some of his publications (Morgenthau and Thompson 1950), but this must be understood against the backdrop of the excoriating attack delivered against the social sciences in *Scientific Man Versus Power Politics*, where the belief in "the power of science to solve all problems" was portrayed as the cause of the "decay" of the Western world (Morgenthau 1946, vi). By modeling themselves on the natural sciences, the social sciences had produced the illusion of a mastery over society and of providing "scientific solutions" to the moral dilemmas of politics when, in fact, the kind of certainty they could produce was limited and irrelevant to such dilemmas. Far from subsiding, this polemic against the social sciences emerged as a rather consensual leitmotif of the 1954 meeting. Morgenthau, of course, could be expected to warn against the "social science tendency," which he regarded as "the greatest present pitfall" to theory building.[18] But he was joined by the other participants in his critique of behavioralism. Kenneth Thompson also identified objective, empirical, data-gathering social science as the main inhibition to theory.[19] In the paper he had prepared, Paul Nitze expressed "little patience with those behaviorist theories which maintain that there is no such thing as a better or worse decision in foreign affairs."[20] Because the social sciences claimed to be value free, they could not address the issue of moral judgment that constituted the essence of politics nor understand the nature of decisions that do not solve such dilemmas but simply put an end to them through robust action. They assumed, as Niebuhr vehemently argued, "that the proper 'scientific technics' can assure men mastery over their historical fate," when both the course and the meaning of history were not opened to human scrutiny.[21] Not all was to be discarded in the social sciences, however: Morgenthau envisioned them in a subordinate role limited to mining data for the theorist. The social-scientific approach, he concluded, "must be contained within very narrow limits."[22] The final report, written by Kenneth Thompson, devoted a whole section to the criticism of "presuppositionless social science."[23]

For all their talk about "general laws" of international politics or "rationality" in the conduct of international affairs, the scientific rhetoric of the realists remained ultimately a tactical weapon against liberal historians and legal scholars. But by the time they convened in Washington to discuss their discipline, this was already a foregone battle: in the mid-1950s, the real fight was *internal* to political-science departments, and it was a fight against the behavioral sciences. The two aspects were not unrelated: American social science had developed out of the social-reform movement of the turn of the century and produced the belief in the capacity of rational analysis and planning to achieve economic progress and overcome conflict (Ross 1991). Wilsonianism and the international-law movement extended this belief to the international sphere. The same rational methods used to harmonize domestic interests would solve the problems of international politics, and international relations would become a province of the social sciences. But this was precisely the liberal fallacy denounced by Morgenthau (1946, 108–109), a fallacy that assumed that "the social structures of international and domestic society are essentially identical" and that the former was also amenable to peaceful social engineering. The critique of interwar liberal internationalism, in the eyes of many classical realists, could not be complete without a simultaneous critique of the behavioral sciences, which were seen as responsible for the further depoliticization of social and international relations typical of liberalism (Söllner 1987).

The academic context in which IR developed was thus perceived as hostile. Behavioralism promoted a unified conception of the social sciences under the experimental method and promised unlimited scientific progress (Almond 1960; Dahl 1961). Such claims also involved a bid to institutional supremacy. In the run-up to the creation of the National Science Foundation in 1950, the sociologist Talcott Parsons had tried to have the new public agency endorse behavioral standards for social-science research (Klausner and Lidz 1986). In a similar fashion, Daniel Lerner and Harold Lasswell (1951) had stressed the methodological unity of the sciences of which international relations was part. As if this was not threatening enough, the new paradigm also benefited from the support of the Ford Foundation, which set up a "Behavioral Sciences Program" in 1952 and invested its massive resources in the institutionalization of the social sciences at home and abroad (Seybold 1980). The purpose of the 1954 conference therefore appears to have been essentially defensive. Reporting on the debates, Kenneth Thompson wrote that "theory in the study of international politics may deserve a special priority because of the stringency of the debate generated in part by the imperialism of competing approaches each claiming to have pre-empted the field."[24] The point of discussing "theory" was to establish a demarcation line vis-à-vis the behavioral sciences and to build into such theory the antibodies that would prevent the capture of international relations by the social sciences. The items on the agenda included a discussion not only of the "nature" of theory but also, more significantly perhaps, of the "limits" of theory: a clear reminder, against the cognitive pretensions of the social sciences, that power politics was restive to complete rationalization.[25] In fact, IR theory not only had limits: it was essentially *defined* by these limits. Niebuhr insisted on the necessity for theory to be open to the contingent. A "prudent self-interest" was the highest attainable degree of rationality and morality.[26] Morgenthau emphasized the incommensurability between theoretical statements and political practice. Politics was always about concrete decisions engaging with a world of contingencies: "A theory of international relations," Morgenthau wrote,

> must, then, guard against the temptation to take itself too seriously and to neglect the ambiguities which call it into question at every turn. A theory of international relations which yielded to that temptation would become a metaphysic, superimposing a logically coherent intellectual scheme upon a reality which falls far short of such coherence. *A theory of international relations, to be theoretically valid, must build into its theoretical structure, as it were, those very qualifications which limit its theoretical validity and practical usefulness.*[27]

The theory may provide a rational representation of a given situation, but the actual engagement was a matter of Machiavellian *virtù*, of a decision that cut across conflicting judgments. "Prudence," then, was also a moral precept. As Morgenthau put it in the course of the debates, "in reality you can only rely on a series of informed hunches."[28]

The only exception to this antibehaviorist consensus was Arnold Wolfers, whose case deserves a special mention. His views were somewhat at odds with the rest of the group, and the debates that ensued help illuminate the real stakes of a distinct IR theory. A Swiss, Wolfers (1892–1968) was trained as a legal scholar. He took his diploma in Zurich and practiced law before pursuing his doctorate in Giessen. Following a lecturing tour in the United States, he came to Germany in 1929 as a *Privatdozent* at the University of Berlin before becoming director of the Rockefeller-funded *Deutsche Hochschule für Politik*, also in Berlin, a school developing "modern" empirical social-science methods against traditional German historical-legal scholarship (Caplan and Rosenblatt 1983). Wolfers was already an old Rockefeller hand when he joined the faculty at Yale in 1933. Yet by the 1950s, the Yale group, and Wolfers himself, had developed an interest in behavioral methods. From the perspective of the behavioral sciences, the question of "theory" was solved in advance: no domain of human action could claim exemption from a universally applicable scientific method. Realists attracted by behavioral methodologies and by political "science" had no particular incentive to develop IR as a distinctive discipline. This explains why IR theory did not crystallize around Yale and Princeton, despite the important work done in these institutions. The views that Wolfers expressed in 1954 were essentially those he had held in the late 1940s, when he had called for the implementation of social-science techniques in the study of international politics, and they attracted much criticism: in the precirculated paper, he suggested that "the main job of the theorist *qua* theorist is . . . the creative elaboration of fruitful hypotheses which bear on the relationship between specified variables."[29] He reiterated this probehavioral position during the discussions, adding that the concept of political "behavior" allowed for a greater degree of certainty: "as soon as you begin to talk about behavior, however, you are pretty safe"—to which Morgenthau immediately quipped that such an analysis then became "meaningless."[30]

THE POLITICS OF THEORY

Underwritten by the Rockefeller Foundation, IR "theory" emerged in the mid-1950s as a symptomatic reaction to the evolution of American political science. This reactive aspect runs through the minutes of the 1954 meeting, which saw the emergence of an essentially negative consensus. What the "theory" of international politics exactly meant may not have been very clear to the participants in the May 1954 conference—in his subsequent report, Kenneth Thompson (1955, 746) wrote euphemistically that the state of theory was compounded by "vigorous debate" and "little unanimity on points of detail"—but the necessity of having a theory was unanimously recognized, as it provided a rallying cry for the opponents of behavioralism and more generally of the liberal vision of science as an instrument of rational social reform. Despite the inconclusive nature of the debates, therefore, the 1954 workshop was considered a very stimulating event worth replicating. Following the circulation of Thompson's report, William Fox wrote to say that Morgenthau, Niebuhr, Nitze, Wolfers, and himself were willing to engage in "more formal discussions," which hopefully would also involve English scholars such as Martin Wight or Herbert Butterfield, and asked for the support of the Rockefeller Foundation.[31] In order to secure the regular participation of Niebuhr, who was regarded as a major source of intellectual inspiration, it was decided that these regular discussions would take place at Columbia's Institute of War and Peace Studies. Starting in 1957, Columbia's interuniversity seminar gave a stable form to the network that had coalesced during the 1954 workshop and established the legitimacy of the theoretical agenda.[32]

More than it advanced research methods, the 1954 workshop brought into the open a lot of "unresolved problems" (Fox 1959, xi). But it also fostered the emergence of a group that, despite its diversity, developed a sense of collective identity and left its imprint on the discipline. The first IR *theorists* were united by their negative view of the social sciences: they saw in scientific rationalism the same utopian drive that characterized the legalist vision of the interwar years. As they traced back to the Enlightenment the cause of the crisis, their diagnosis became overtly political. The crisis, as Thompson reported, resulted from an "unfounded optimism" that "derived, undoubtedly, from the philosophy of the enlightenment and from its step-child, the peace-movement of the nineteenth century."[33] The time had come to reassert the legitimacy of self-interest, to shed the "cult of internationalism," and to accept a notion of the political that was built upon a pessimistic anthropology and the impossibility of progress. The point was no longer to redeem liberalism, as Niebuhr was still suggesting in the mid-1940s, but to reach beyond and against liberalism, to restore and rejuvenate a political tradition that emphasized the limits of rationalism and the hubristic dangers of reformism. "The paramount problem for contemporary study of international relations," Niebuhr suggested to the other conference participants, "is to supplant the illusions which we have inherited from the French enlightenment . . . with the wisdom of Edmund Burke."[34] Along with Burke, the other intellectual icon often conjured was Augustine: with its pessimistic anthropology, its denial of mundane progress, and the absolute separation it established between the universal values of the City of God and the relative claims of earthly kingdoms, Augustinism provided a "political language" for Anglo-American circles thinking about international relations in the wake of World War II, of which IR theory was arguably an important dialect (Epp 1991, 5). Much more than an academic critique of scientific rationalism and liberalism, therefore, IR gave an articulated form to a distinct political mood that explicitly considered itself as a form of counterenlightenment. While the upbeat liberalism of the 1950s was blossoming into the grand narrative of modernization theory (Gilman 2003), IR initially provided an academic niche for the discontents of the liberal consensus. In this respect, the participants in the Rockefeller-initiated conversation are a telling group, mixing émigrés of various persuasions

(Morgenthau, Wolfers), traditional conservatives (Kennan, Nitze), former liberals en route toward new forms of conservatism (Lippman), or Protestant neo-orthodoxy (Niebuhr). It suggests that the critique of liberalism imported by émigré scholars was not purely idiosyncratic, as it also offered a platform for American academics and intellectuals who did not recognize themselves in the postwar liberal consensus. In fact, the positions taken by members of this group during the cold war are also quite telling, as they tended not to align on the positions characteristic of the liberal "vital center." Kennan and Morgenthau became strongly opposed to the Vietnam War in the name of a limited notion of the national interest. Even Niebuhr, who, as the theologian to the "best and the brightest," played a decisive role in laying the ideological foundations of cold-war liberalism, ended up joining this position, in part after realizing the moral problems associated with the nuclear possibilities (Craig 2003). Here again, the opposition between IR theory and political science was perpetuated under different forms: as Ido Oren (2003, 153) pointed out, Morgenthau's opposition to the Vietnam War was not indicative of the dominant trends in political science, that profession being generally more supportive of the administration. The founding fathers of IR remained, indeed, critical of political science and of its policy implications, even though the discipline they had so powerfully contributed to establishing had by then reintegrated the realm of political science.

CONCLUSION: THE FAILURE TO LAUNCH OF A SUCCESSFUL SOCIAL SCIENCE

The emergence of IR was not a process of late professionalization along the lines defining the social sciences. It was the result of a disagreement over the nature of politics and, by extension, of political science. Initially located within the ill-defined fringes of the discipline, international relations started to differentiate itself when it formulated different answers to the same set of questions. In political science, the belief that the earlier development of the discipline was haphazard and driven by the practical issues of the day led many to look for a more systematic and scientific approach, which ended up carrying the day under the convenient label of "behavioralism." The same diagnosis led some IR scholars to develop a theory of politics entirely pitted against the image of science underpinning the development of the discipline in which they were grounded. In this process of growing divergence, IR became the repository for a political tradition critical of liberalism and, in particular, the reformist idea of scientifically informed policy advice. Rather, it viewed politics as an art performed not by technical specialists but by a few men of good judgment, an elite seasoned in the arcane wisdom of statecraft. This vision did not just inspire the small group of founding fathers brought together by the Rockefeller Foundation: it was embodied by it.

While I have focused on the early years of this process of differentiation and on the major actors involved in theory building, it is worthwhile keeping in mind that this project ultimately failed. Starting in the early 1960s, rational-choice methodologies rapidly made their way into the study of international politics, while the psychological, anthropological, or normative elements regarding human nature originally present in the theory were discarded in favor of systemic-structural notions producing the same effects. The latter operation was Kenneth Waltz's enduring legacy to the discipline. As IR gradually morphed into a social science, its origins were obliterated in favor of a standardized historical account presenting its development only as a "lag" in scientific development with respect to other branches of knowledge. What the archives and the transcripts of the early discussion about IR theory reveal, however, is a deliberate attempt at breaking away from the major tendencies at work within the social sciences, as well as the overtly political nature of this project.

In retrospect, the failure of the original vision of IR illuminates the extent of the gravitational pull that behavioralism exerted over postwar political science and suggests that the possibilities for alternative disciplinary discourses were ultimately limited. The parallel careers of IR and political theory are quite telling in this respect. John Gunnell (1993b) has cogently shown how political theory also took shape through a critical dialogue on the nature and scope of political science. IR theory was part of the same discursive matrix, and quite tellingly it was also developed by the Rockefeller Foundation under the umbrella of its program on Legal and Political Philosophy. But while political theory managed to escape the gravitational field of political science at the price of a complete disconnection between the two fields, IR was irresistibly drawn back into the behavioral atmosphere of the 1960s after its attempted launch in the previous decade. There are many reasons for this failure. The vision of IR theory as an alternative to the social sciences did not have the odds in its favor, as it had to steer a difficult middle course between opposites. In order to shed the remnants of its previous grounding in history and law, IR had to assert its scientific character. Based on the notion of power, the science of international politics was then developed within political-science departments.

But there, IR theory found itself sharing similar claims to "realism" with approaches that were fundamentally at odds with its ideological outlook and were encapsulated in the language of science characteristic of behavioralism. Therefore, once it became firmly anchored within political-science institutions, IR theory had to steer the other way and emphasize its antiscientific tendencies. This has led to a constant oscillation between the scientific and the metaphysical, the normative and the factual, and the descriptive and the prescriptive, and this oscillation found its most acute expression in the writings of Morgenthau, where, as perceptive commentators have observed, it became a redoubtable polemical weapon (Jervis 1994; Koskenniemi 2002). This, however, did not prove sufficient to establish a fully autonomous discipline. But the main reason may be something else: the failure to achieve complete disciplinary autonomy was in part because the postwar triumph of the "realist" approach to international politics concealed deep discords within the ranks of the realists themselves. Frederick Dunn, Arnold Wolfers, Klaus Knorr, and others were arguably realists, yet they also believed that the social sciences provided adequate tools for studying power politics. Not so the proponents of a theoretical approach to IR. Ultimately, as the position of Wolfers during the 1954 conference suggests, the project of IR theory gained a following on the basis of a misunderstanding over what theory stood for. The antiliberal, antiscientific message attached to it by Morgenthau, Niebuhr, Thompson, and others did not travel very far beyond the small group that crystallized around the Rockefeller Foundation. The strategic adoption of the language of science and the emphasis on theory building made its project difficult to decipher and easy to misinterpret. This eventually left the group unable to prevent the development of IR theory in a direction that it did not endorse. The realist gambit, ultimately, was a losing one. Yet, despite the subsequent development of the discipline, it was an opening move that set the field of international relations on a very particular path, one characterized in particular by a proximity to power that few other disciplines ever enjoyed.

NOTES

1.   Joseph H. Willits, "Memorandum on Postwar Policy in the Support of International Relations," May 14, 1945, Folder 67, Box 8, Series 910, Research Group 3, Rockefeller Foundation Archives, Rockefeller Archive Center, Sleepy Hollow, N.Y. (hereafter designated RAC).

2. Kenneth W. Thompson, "International Law as a Target Area in RF's International Relations Program," January 17, 1955, Folder 67, Box 8, Series 910, RG 3.1, Rockefeller Foundation Archives, RAC.

3. Willits, "Memorandum," 2.

4. On the Yale Institute, see Parmar (2002).

5. Joseph H. Willits to Dean Rusk, "Some points for intensive exploration," December 28, 1953, Folder 61, Box 7, Series 910, RG 3.1, Rockefeller Foundation Archives, RAC.

6. Kenneth W. Thompson, "A Program for International Studies."

7. Hans J. Morgenthau, "Application to the Rockefeller Foundation for aid in establishing a Center for the Study of American Foreign Policy under the direction of Hans J. Morgenthau Professor of Political Science at the University of Chicago 1950," Folder 4874, Box 411, Series 200S, RG 1.1, Rockefeller Foundation Archives, RAC.

8. Joseph H. Willits, interview notes from a meeting with Hans J. Morgenthau, August 16, 1950, Folder 4874, Box 411, Series 200S, RG 1.1, Rockefeller Foundation Archives, RAC.

9. Joseph H. Willits, interview notes from a meeting with Hans J. Morgenthau, September 14, 1953, Microfilm, Reel 1, RG 12.1–12.2, Rockefeller Foundation Archives, RAC.

10. Thompson to Willits, "Theory of International Politics," December 28, 1953, Folder 61, Box 7, Series 910, RG 3.1, Rockefeller Foundation Archives, RAC.

11. Kenneth W. Thompson, "Report to Dean Rusk on the RF's Program in International Studies," January 12, 1954, p. 8 Folder 61, Box 7, Series 910, RG 3.1, Rockefeller Foundation Archives, RAC.

12. Ibid., 10.

13. Ibid., 9.

14. Ibid., 8.

15. Thompson to Rusk, "Academic Competence in International Relations," February 17, 1954, Folder 61, Box 7, Series 910, RG 3.1, Rockefeller Foundation Archives, RAC.

16. Kenneth W. Thompson, "Conference on Theory of International Politics," May 7, 1954, Folder 69, Box 8, Series 910, RG 3.1, Rockefeller Foundation Archives, RAC.

17. Hans J. Morgenthau, "The Theoretical and Practical Importance of a Theory of International Relations," 263 (appendix 2 of this volume).

18. "Conference on International Politics," transcript, 257 (appendix 1 of this volume).

19. Ibid., 259.

20. Paul Nitze, "The Implication of Theory for Practice in the Conduct of Foreign Affairs," 279 (appendix 5 of this volume).

21. Reinhold Niebuhr, "The Moral Issue in International Relations," 272 (appendix 3 of this volume).

22. "Conference on International Politics," transcript, 257.

23. Kenneth W. Thompson, "Toward a Theory of International Politics," 1954, Folder 69, Box 8, Series 910, RG 3.1, Rockefeller Foundation Archives, RAC.

24. Ibid.

25. "Agenda II: Outline for Structuring the Discussion," Folder 69, Box 8, Series 910, RG 3.1, Rockefeller Foundation Archives, RAC.

26. Niebuhr, "The Moral Issue in International Relations," 270.

27. Morgenthau, "The Theoretical and Practical Importance of a Theory of International Relations," 265. Emphasis mine.

28. "Conference on International Politics," transcript, 254–55.
29. Arnold Wolfers, "Theory of International Politics: Its Merits and Advancement," 283 (appendix 6 of this volume).
30. "Conference on International Politics," transcript, 255. ·
31. Fox to Thompson, January 21, 1955, Folder 4128, Box 493, Series 200S, RG 1.2, Rockefeller Foundation Archives, RAC, 1.
32. Some of the seminar papers were later published in Fox (1959).
33. Thompson, "A Program for International Studies."
34. Niebuhr, "The Moral Issue in International Relations," 272.

REFERENCES

Adcock, Robert. 2007. Interpreting behavioralism. In *Modern political science: Anglo-American exchanges since 1880*, ed. R. Adcock, M. Bevir, and S. C. Stimson, pp. 181–208. Princeton, N.J.: Princeton University Press.

Adcock, Robert, Mark Bevir, and Shannon C. Stimson, eds. 2007. *Modern political science: Anglo-American exchanges since 1880*. Princeton, N.J.: Princeton University Press.

Almond, Gabriel A. 1960. Introduction: A functional approach to comparative politics. In *The politics of the developing areas*, ed. G. A. Almond and J. S. Coleman, 3–64. Princeton, N.J.: Princeton University Press.

——. 2004. Who lost the Chicago School of Political Science? *Perspectives on Politics* 2: 91–93.

Amadae, Sonja M. 2003. *Rationalizing capitalist democracy: The cold war origins of rational choice liberalism*. Chicago: University of Chicago Press.

Ashworth, Lucian M. 1999. *Creating international studies: Angell, Mitrany, and the liberal tradition*. Aldershot: Ashgate.

Boyle, Francis A. 1999. *Foundations of world order: The legalist approach to international relations, 1898–1922*. Durham, N.C.: Duke University Press.

Brecht, Arnold. 1947. Political theory: Beyond relativism in political theory. *American Political Science Review* 41: 470–488.

Bull, Hedley. 1972. The theory of international politics, 1919–1969. In *The Aberystwyth papers: International politics, 1919–1969*, ed. B. Porter, 30–54. Oxford: Oxford University Press.

Caplan, Hannah, and Melinda Rosenblatt, eds. 1983. *International biographical dictionary of Central European émigrés, 1933–1945*. Munich: K. G. Saur.

Cowan, L. Gray. 1954. *A history of the school of international affairs and associated area institutes of Columbia University*. New York: Columbia University Press.

Craig, Campbell. 2003. *Glimmer of a new Leviathan: Total war in the realism of Niebuhr, Morgenthau, and Waltz*. New York: Columbia University Press.

Dahl, Robert A. 1961. The behavioral approach in political science: Epitaph for a monument to a successful protest. *American Political Science Review* 55: 763–772.

Dunn, Frederick S. 1948. The scope of international relations. *World Politics* 1, no. 1: 142–146.

——. 1949. The present course of international relations research. *World Politics* 2: 80–95.

Epp, Roger. 1991. *The "Augustinian moment" in international politics: Niebuhr, Butterfield, Wight, and the reclaiming of a tradition*. Aberystwyth: Department of International Politics, University College of Wales.

Fifield, Russell H. 1948. The introductory course in international relations. *American Political Science Review* 42: 1189–1196.

Fox, William T. R., ed. 1959. *Theoretical aspects of international relations*. Notre Dame, Ind.: University of Notre Dame Press

———. 1968. *The American study of international relations: Essays by William T. R. Fox*. Columbia: University of South Carolina Press.

Frei, Christoph. 2001. *Hans J. Morgenthau: An intellectual biography*. Baton Rouge: Louisiana State University.

Friedrich, Carl J. 1947. Instruction and research: Political science in the United States in wartime. *American Political Science Review* 41: 978–989.

Garth, Bryant G. 2000. James Willard Hurst as entrepreneur for the field of law and social science. *Law and History Review* 18: 37–58.

George, Jim. 1994. *Discourses of global politics: A critical (re)introduction to international relations*. Boulder, Colo.: Lynne Rienner.

Gieryn, Thomas F. 1999. *Cultural boundaries of science: Credibility on the line*. Chicago: University of Chicago Press.

Gilman, Nils. 2003. *Mandarins of the future: Modernization theory in cold war America*. Baltimore, Md.: The Johns Hopkins University Press.

Griffith, Ernest S., ed. 1948. *Research in political science. The world of the panels of the research committee, American Political Science Association*. Chapel Hill: University of North Carolina Press.

Gunnell, John G. 1988. American political science, liberalism, and the invention of political theory. *American Political Science Review* 82: 71–87.

———. 1993a. Relativism: The return of the repressed. *Political Theory* 21: 563–584.

———. 1993b. *The descent of political theory: The genealogy of an American vocation*. Chicago: University of Chicago Press.

Gurian, Waldemar. 1946. On the study of international relations. *Review of Politics* 8: 275–282.

Guzzini, Stefano. 1998. *Realism in international relations and international political economy*. London: Routledge.

Hauptmann, Emily. 2006. From opposition to accommodation: How Rockefeller Foundation grants redefined relations between political theory and social science in the 1950s. *American Political Science Review* 100: 643–649.

Hoffmann, Stanley. 1959. International relations: The long road to theory. *World Politics* 11: 346–377.

———. 1977. An American social science: International relations. *Daedalus: Proceedings of the American Academy of Arts and Sciences* 106: 41–60.

Hollis, Martin, and Steve Smith. 1990. *Explaining and understanding international relations*. Oxford: Clarendon Press.

Jervis, Robert. 1994. Hans Morgenthau, realism, and the scientific study of international relations. *Social Research* 61: 853–854.

Kahler, Miles. 1997. Inventing international relations: International relations theory after 1945. In *New thinking in international relations theory*, ed. M. W. Doyle and G. J. Ickenberry, 20–53. Boulder, Colo.: Westview Press.

Kelsen, Hans. 1951. Science and politics. *American Political Science Review* 45: 641–661.

Kirk, Grayson. 1947. *The study of international relations in American colleges and universities*. New York: Council on Foreign Relations.

Klausner, Samuel Z., and Victor M. Lidz, eds. 1986. *The nationalization of the social sciences*. Philadelphia: University of Pennsylvania Press.

Knorr, Klaus. 1947. Economics and international relations: A problem in teaching. *Political Science Quarterly* 62: 552–568.

Kort, Fred. 1952. The issue of a science of politics in utilitarian thought. *American Political Science Review* 46: 1140–1152.

Koskenniemi, Martti. 2002. *The gentle civilizer of nations: The rise and fall of international law, 1870–1960.* Cambridge: Cambridge University Press.

Kuklick, Bruce. 2006. *Blind oracles: Intellectuals and war from Kennan to Kissinger.* Princeton, N.J.: Princeton University Press.

Lasswell, Harold D. 1951. The immediate future of research policy and method in political science. *American Political Science Review* 45: 133–142.

Lebow, Richard Ned. 2003. *The tragic vision of politics: Ethics, interests and orders.* Cambridge: Cambridge University Press.

Lerner, Daniel, and Harold D. Lasswell, eds. 1951. *The policy sciences: Recent developments in scope and method.* Stanford, Calif.: Stanford University Press.

Long, David, and Peter Wilson, eds. 1995. *Thinkers of the twenty years' crisis.* Oxford: Clarendon Press.

Molloy, Seán. 2006. *The hidden history of realism: A genealogy of power politics.* New York: Palgrave Macmillan.

Morgenthau, Hans J. 1946. *Scientific man versus power politics.* Chicago: University of Chicago Press.

——. 1952. Area studies and the study of international relations. *International Social Science Bulletin* 4: 647–655.

——. 1955. Reflections on the state of political science. *Review of Politics* 17: 431–460.

Morgenthau, Hans J., and Kenneth W. Thompson, eds. 1950. *Principles and problems of international politics: Selected readings.* New York: Knopf.

Neufeld, Mark A. 1995. *The restructuring of international relations theory.* Cambridge: Cambridge University Press.

Neumann, Franz L. 1950. Approaches to the study of power. *Political Science Quarterly* 65: 161–180.

Olson, William C., and A. J. R. Groom. 1991. *International relations then and now: Origins and trends in interpretation.* London: HarperCollins.

Oren, Ido. 2003. *Our enemies & US: America's rivalries and the making of political science.* Ithaca, N.Y.: Cornell University Press.

Parmar, Inderjeet. 2002. "To relate knowledge and action . . . ": The Rockefeller Foundation's impact on foreign policy thinking during America's rise to globalism, 1939–45. *Minerva* 40: 235–263.

Rockefeller Foundation. 1930. *Annual report.* New York: Rockefeller Foundation.

——. 1932. *Annual report.* New York: Rockefeller Foundation.

Ross, Dorothy. 1991. *The origins of American social science.* Cambridge: Cambridge University Press.

Sandelius, Walter E. 1951. Reason and political power. *American Political Science Review* 45: 703–715.

Schmidt, Brian C. 2002. On the history and historiography of international relations. In *Handbook of international relations*, ed. W. Carlsnaes, T. Risse, and B. A. Simmons, 3–22. London: Sage.

——. 2007. International relations and the quest for the authority of knowledge. Paper prepared for the annual meeting of the International Studies Association, Chicago, Illinois, March 2007. Unpublished manuscript.

Seybold, Peter J. 1980. The Ford Foundation and the triumph of behavioralism in American political science. In *Philanthropy and cultural imperialism: The foundations at home and abroad*, ed. R. F. Arnove, 269–303. Boston: G. K. Hall.

Smith, Steve. 1987. The development of international relations as a social science. *Journal of International Studies* 16: 189–206.

Smith, T. V. 1951. Power: Its ubiquity and legitimacy. *American Political Science Review* 45, no. 3: 693–702.

Söllner, Alfons. 1987. German conservatism in America: Morgenthau's political realism. *Telos* 72: 161–172.

——. 1988. Vom Völkerrecht zur *Science of International Relations*. Vier typische Vertreter der politikwissenschaftlichen Emigration. In *Exil, Wissenschaft, Identität: Die Emigration deutscher Sozialwissenschaftler 1933–1945*, ed. I. Srubar, 164–180. Frankfurt am Main: Suhrkamp.

Thompson, Kenneth W. 1955. Toward a theory of international politics. *American Political Science Review* 49: 733–746.

Wæver, Ole. 1998. The sociology of a not so international discipline: American and European developments in international relations. *International Organization* 52: 687–727.

Ware, Edith E. 1938. *The study of international relations in the United States*. New York: Columbia University Press.

Wight, Colin. 2002. Philosophy of social science and international relations. In *Handbook of international relations*, ed. W. Carlsnaes, T. Risse, and B. A. Simmons, 23–51. London: Sage.

Williams, Michael C. 2005. *The realist tradition and the limits of international relations*. Cambridge: Cambridge University Press.

——, ed. 2007. *Realism reconsidered: The legacy of Hans J. Morgenthau in international relations*. Oxford: Oxford University Press.

Wolfers, Arnold. 1947. International relations as a field of study. *Columbia Journal of International Affairs* 1: 24–26.

——. 1949. Statesmanship and moral choice. *World Politics* 1: 175–195.

Wood, Bryce. 1947. *The program of the division of the social sciences in the field of international relations*. Rockefeller Foundation.

Wright, Quincy. 1950. Political science and world stabilization. *American Political Science Review* 44: 1–13.

——. 1955. *The study of international relations*. New York: Appleton-Century-Crofts.

6

KENNAN: REALISM AS DESIRE

ANDERS STEPHANSON

REALISM IS un-American. Its few appearances in U.S. foreign relations have occurred on borrowed time. Realism *as policy* is thus generally unrealistic. Kennan sensed that. His defining moment was his period of policy-making glory in 1947–1949, when the promise (as he saw it) of an intelligent and well-directed effort, under his tutelage, to place the United States in the world on sound footing was replaced by ideological excess and ensuing cold-war phantasmagoria. That searing experience turned Kennan into a full-fledged realist critic whose realism was grounded in its own impossibility: for the next fifty years, crushed, he would consistently and coherently argue that, in the absence of realistic policy, the United States should do less rather than more, certainly less by way of expansionism, both cold-war expansionism and otherwise.[1] It is worth remembering that, as he was approaching his hundredth birthday and the end of his life, he was denouncing the upcoming "Operation Iraqi Freedom" in the most scathing and prophetic terms.[2]

What interests me, however, about this impossibility is less the political vicissitudes than the discursive (I use the word as though it had not been destroyed) position of realism as an impulse and desire in relation to what it imagined itself ideologically to be combating during the late 1940s and early 1950s. Realism, like the related "conservatism," is always reactive. It is only articulated, revealing itself as true and realistic, when there is a perceived onslaught of something distinctly and perversely unrealistic, abstract, radical, or silly. The real is or should be self-explanatory. It is its own justification, so to speak, needing only a proper assertion by means of illumination in times of would-be delusion. From Kennan's standpoint, then, the real acquires a certain clarity when Rooseveltian neo-Wilsonianism (as he saw it) is replaced by the hardheaded regime of General Marshall's State Department, the moment, in short, when he, George F. Kennan, largely came to define the domain of policy making, albeit with some severe constrictions that would soon prove fatal. If this was not quite a "realist" regime, it was nevertheless realistic enough to warrant optimism. Alas, already by 1949, intelligence had been forced aside or warped, turned into demeaning abnegation before a public increasingly led and dominated by appalling demagogues.

I have no intention of returning to the endless discussion of Kennan's own responsibility for this sequence. He would wrestle with that responsibility for the rest of his life, a responsibility that he recognized but never quite embraced. I leave aside what was manifestly wrong about his own analysis of the Soviet Union and the kind of threat it presented in 1945–1947, and how this complex of errors provided the most important ground, rather a firm ground to boot, for the very perversions, in his terms, that would mark the U.S. project known as the cold war. Here, instead, I am concerned with the changing targets of Kennan's realist impulse (or irritation) at home and the precise relation between that specific history and what one might call, a little clumsily, the *longue duree* of the self-conception of the United States in the world, an identity that achieves great clarity in the early cold war. My wager is that such an analysis will reveal something both about the place of "realism" in the incipient phase of IR and about the constitutive structure of U.S. "unrealism." Kennan's emerging realism, I will claim, was never an "-ism." Articulated against domestic targets, however, it forced him concurrently to see the Soviet problem anew and to develop his mature critique of cold-war policy.

It is indeed with the Soviet Union that we must nonetheless begin, though not with Kennan's analysis but rather his diagnosis of what was wrong with his own government's view of it (or, more precisely, what he took to be Roosevelt's concept). Kennan, it will be recalled, had shown no sympathy for the Grand Alliance of World War II or Roosevelt's putative intimacy with Stalin. The obvious convergence of military interests notwithstanding, Kennan favored a strict, narrowly construed approach defined in terms of interests, the counterpoint to what he essentially took to be the Soviet way. Roosevelt and Washington appeared by contrast to base the U.S. position on the dual and wholly fallacious premise that extensive wartime collaboration with Moscow would continue after the war and that this process would take place in some universalist neo-Wilsonian frame of legalism and the United Nations, an organization Kennan would later describe with some hilarity as "a fortuitous collection of social entities which happen at this stage in human history to enjoy a wide degree of acceptance as independent states."[3] Because, accordingly, he deemed his own government incapable of a realistic policy, he argued for the radical disassociation between the West and the Soviet Union at the line wherever their respective armed might happened to land at the end of the war. A deep freeze was better than illusory neo-Wilsonianism and self-defeating cooperation with Moscow.[4]

The diagnosis, then, is still situated chiefly at the level of a "realistic policy," by which is meant one adequate to the real circumstances. The real is simply not visible either to the domestic powers that be or to the public, the deeply ignorant public. This inadequacy of policy has two concrete aspects. First, there is a failure to grasp the realities flowing from the (alleged) nature of the Soviet Union and its policy. Second, there is the larger failure to grasp the realities of how world politics operate, a failure finding graphic expression in the project of superimposing what is inside, that is, law, procedure, predictability, transparency, and order, immediately onto the outside; in short, it is a wrongheaded resurrection of Wilsonian "idealism."[5]

Whether better knowledge, a more visible Real as it were, was structurally possible is a question on which Kennan still wavered. In early 1945, in the wake of Yalta, he was certainly pessimistic. The unexpected change of his own fortunes a year later, his return to the United States, and his dark and apparently vindicated analysis of Soviet intentions and the ensuing elevation to the highest echelons of policy making occasioned, not surprisingly, a commensurately brighter outlook. Stamped to a considerable degree by Kennan's presence, policy from 1947 eliminated entirely any remaining illusions about the Soviet Union and most of those concerning the universalist project of the United Nations.

Alas, adequation of concept and policy proved far from total. The very moment of Kennan's greatest success in 1947 was indeed also the beginning of a painful awareness that all was not well. Let us recall the dialectical unfolding. Initially, in late spring, there is the Marshall Plan, exhibit A in Kennan's intelligent design. It is followed in the summer by the publication of the X-Article in *Foreign Affairs*, seemingly the summa of Kennan's Soviet analyses and the advent, it soon appears, of something called "containment," supposedly the essence of what the Truman administration and the United States are doing in the world, though the word (it is little more than a word) is really not salient in the article, which in any case was a simplistic version of what Kennan usually said about the Soviet Union. Then, in the fall another and more assured realist, Walter Lippmann, picks the piece apart in a series of articles that, as a subsequent book, originates the notion of "the cold war." The impact on Kennan, if not the administration, is enormous. And so here one must ask why he was so powerfully stung by Lippmann's critique. It has largely to do with the old problem of universalism and its dialectical opposite, particularity.[6]

For when all was said and done, Lippmann's realist attack on containment was not only about the obvious "passivity" implied in the concept (i.e., merely countering initiatives by the other side and erecting useless walls) but also, significantly, about the problem of universalism in U.S. policy, as evidenced by the Truman Doctrine, which had been announced in March 1947. Thus the preeminent pundit connected the doctrine directly with Kennan's apparently global containment policy: in both cases, policy is reduced to countering communism everywhere on the conceptual basis of simple binaries. By way of positive contrast, Lippmann held forth the Marshall Plan, a particular, smart, and offensive play in a place of vital importance. Kennan had been a central figure in the articulation of that plan while, in admittedly not very energetic ways, criticizing the Truman Doctrine as the kind of general statement that was either meaningless or meant something that might come back to haunt one. Thus it is readily grasped that he was upset. Lippmann, however, was essentially right, and Kennan, without ever truly facing up to it, eventually came to incorporate the chastizing lesson in interesting ways.[7] Lippmann was right in no small part because he saw, morphologically, one might say, that Kennan had failed on a central realist tenet: that regimes are about "interests" and that interests are inherently particular and, moreover, translatable and comprehensible across borders both conceptual and geopolitical, whatever one's ideology happens to be. Interests are universally particular, so to speak. Kennan's authority originated in his field expertise in Soviet affairs, but as Lippmann detected, he had lost sight of the particularity of Soviet interests amid his obsession with Moscow's universalist claims, and as a result he had lost sight too of the particularity of U.S. interests. Lippmann, ever the Atlanticist, thus cleared the woods by pointing out that the outstanding problem was the actual presence of the Red Army deep inside central Europe and that this was scarcely something beyond address because of any ideological incommensurability: troops are troops, they are real and countable, and they are either there or they are not. Interested parties of all persuasions will understand this reality. So one bargains on the basis of interests to see what can be accomplished, but bargaining, that is diplomacy, was precisely what Kennan's analytical scheme excluded.[8]

The absence of such bargaining, the entrenched U.S. refusal to engage in traditional diplomacy, was indeed the constitutive feature of the emerging cold war, which Lippmann had just named. My present concern, however, is not the cold war specifically but the reprimand about particularity.

Gradually, Kennan began to realize what that reprimand was about, if not how the positing of a "total" threat might give rise to the call for an equally total response, which in turn by its very nature had to be formulated in universalist terms. The particular, in any case, becomes the central sign of Kennan's attempt to conceptualize the ills of the opposition inside and outside the administration to his developing stance.

His broad move to delineate this domestic line or division in early 1948 is still to see universalism in terms of the same old legalism he had always found in the political culture, the neo-Wilsonianism he disdained so much: dealing with the world as an undifferentiated totality whose problems could be solved by application of some "universalistic pattern of rules and procedures," some "legalistic and mechanical solutions" devoid of politics. Difference, "the power aspirations, the national prejudices, the irrational hatreds and jealousies," in short "the ugly realities," would be eliminated by fiat. Form would be imposed on actual content in order to conceal, in a quasi-Freudian sublimation.[9]

Against this dominant viewpoint, Kennan held forth "the particularized approach," defined symptomatically not as anything substantially positive but as the negation of legalistic universalism. Thus "skeptical of any scheme for compressing international affairs into legalistic concepts," this approach deems actual, inner content more important than outside form. And the content of that content is "the thirst for power," which can only be dealt with by means of "counter-force." Particularism, finally, refuses reification of the principle of national sovereignty (as typified in the United Nations) and has no trust in the mobilizing power of "peace" in the abstract. In sum, then, aside from not believing in legalistic universalism, particularism only asserts that the real always entails difference, sometimes disagreeable difference, and that conflict is about the acquisition of power. By implication, such struggles take place in specific circumstances that demand specific, or "particular," solutions intrinsically unsuited to simple generalization.

I note in passing here that the idea of "reality" as marked by a certain ugliness connects Kennan's political realism with the otherwise quite different realism of the artistic kind around the turn of the century: the insistence that the conventional prettifies the real, as it were, or that such "surface" accounts are not only incomplete but also missing something essential and constitutive about the real and its operation. The realist impulse in art, however, is (largely) a critique of the conditions that have generated that ugliness: illumination of the hidden, the will to truth, is a demasking of official ideology so as to rectify certain evils. Kennan's realism, on the contrary, coincides with the profoundly conservative notion that the real is undoubtedly and unavoidably ugly in many ways but also rational, fundamentally unchangeable, and certainly not subject to any utopian, abstract schemes of violent change. Recognizing the real in all its dimensions is not a critique but an account that makes possible a range of judicious, appropriate, and particular actions, ultimately for the purpose of maintaining in a larger frame such conditions as will allow the actually existing hierarchy to thrive.

Kennan offers these formulations before the decisive spring and summer of 1948—before, that is, the highly satisfying Italian elections in April 1948, the wholly unexpected but similarly satisfying Tito-Stalin split in the summer, the vast political success of the Berlin Airlift, and, in a different key from his standpoint, the concurrent, well-orchestrated campaign to turn the European division generated by the Marshall Plan into a military one by means of the incipient NATO. Over the next eighteen months, there was also the unfolding debacle for the U.S. position in China, a debacle that would prove deeply troublesome for the administration at home, leading to charges of inaction and incompetence. Digesting these events and having concluded that western Europe was relatively safe, Kennan began to worry that the division of the continent and Germany in particular in the name of the cold war would become permanent and permanently militarized. In the second half of 1948, then, he starts his journey toward becoming the remarkable critic of cold-war orthodoxy that he would be for the better part of his long life. As is well known, his outline of a genuine agreement with the Soviet Union on Germany failed miserably, and a year later he had been marginalized in a State Department now firmly in the hands of Dean Acheson. Paul Nitze had replaced Kennan as head of the Policy Planning Staff. NATO was becoming a fact. So was the Bundesrepublik. Kennan had been completely outmaneuvered.

At that point, at the end of the summer of 1949 and about to be kicked upstairs, Kennan began again to reflect on ways of doing international relations. He detected, historically, five main strategies, all of which still remained in some form: (1) world domination, the Roman/Byzantine model whereby no other power can be recognized as equal or legitimate, now exemplified by the Soviet Union; (2) rigorous isolationism in the manner of Switzerland; (3) limited power politics with limited means for limited aims, the standard European concept in modern history; (4) the mercantile and liberal concept, articulated chiefly by the United Kingdom and the United States, whereby the proper function of government is to protect and promote the private trading activities of its constituent individuals;

and, finally, (5) the multilateral legalism of the present moment in the United States, positing juridical equality and procedure at the heart of interstate relations, thus making "the realities of political and economic and military power" vanish behind a surface of rules and regulations. While the United States had privileged (2) and (4), it was now in principle pushing (5). Kennan himself, given the character of his taxonomy, was not surprisingly in favor of (3), the limited approach that in practical terms sought, as he put it, no "world domination" but only to "carve out a sufficiently large and deep area of U.S. influence to stay, and eventually remove, the threat of communism."[10]

As that minimal area was rapidly becoming universal or at least global in scope along with the ideology that legitimated it, Kennan nevertheless stopped short, curiously enough, from posing the question of whether it was really the United States rather than the Soviet Union that best represented the idea of world domination or world empire. His realism, in fact, always centered on the rather different notion of congenital ignorance and naïveté, spasmodic enthusiasms and utopian schemes. Thus, even while bemoaning the inordinate power of the United States, he would point out the immature, inexperienced nature of structure and execution in U.S. policy. What Kennan failed to see, ironically because of his realism, was that the United States could often create its own realities and do so rather successfully. That the frame might be wrong and the knowledge about a given actual situation might also be wrong, that policy might well rest on "errors," sometimes enormous errors, mattered less because the "realities" of power and the interests at stake conspired to make things work. To state the obvious: one need not be "right" to be successful if one is powerful enough. Thus while "in reality" there might not be a communist conspiracy in Guatemala for the CIA to nip in the bud, a coup and ensuing dictatorship in the name of freedom might be useful anyway (or so it can be argued).

Kennan, it should be said, was dimly aware of this, and he worried about it. A globalist United States was for him a dreadful prospect, and he grasped that it was becoming a reality. Yet its framing eluded him. It took several years for him to figure out that what he had taken to be the "unnatural" division of Europe would not in fact eventually be eliminated on account of some underlying "realities but might indeed serve real U.S. interests, not to mention Soviet ones."[11] Meanwhile, the cold war, despite, or perhaps because of, its vast and unreal "abstractions," might really be an extraordinarily efficient way of maintaining and extending U.S. power. The corollary here is also obvious. There would eventually be a reality check, to put it vulgarly, once the United States reached the jungles of Vietnam, where the abstractions Kennan so disdained were to exact a terrible price, though as always most of it was paid by the people on the receiving end.

This is fascinating, but it is not my present concern, which is Kennan's attempt at explicit realism in the early 1950s and how it related to his diagnosis of the United States. For the next four or five years, Kennan would make several *Ansätze* to articulate foundational ills and realistic alternatives. These exercises were both historical and conceptual. The former showed that, except for the initial period of the Founding Fathers, the United States had never been realistic in the sense of grasping the external real and dealing with it in its own terms. The latter came to focus on the concept of "national interest," which was at the forefront of contemporary debates largely because of the work of Hans Morgenthau. Kennan, even when he had taken refuge in 1951–1952 in the leisurely ivy environs of Princeton, never perused Morgenthau's tracts, or those of any other theorist for that matter, extensively. However, he did make a serious effort to figure out the nature and content of "the national interest" as a ground for realistic policy. In this endeavor he failed, as he recognized. There was no Archimedean vantage point from which that "national interest" could objectively be determined. It was always already going to be subjective and open to the vagaries of domestic politics. Thus it could only be a heuristic device, a rule of thumb, a way of being toward the world of international politics: nothing more and perhaps rather a bit less, though it was still better than the empty, negative, and competing concept of "national security."[12]

Pursuing theory, then, led him to reject Theory (and of course abstraction), which was always his instinct anyway. What remained of systemic realism in Kennan's version amounted to a praxeology based on two simple ontological premises. In the first place, the world was made up of discrete interests in conflict or potential conflict and having no a priori community of mediating norms. Second (and less conventionally), there were other kinds of groupings, constituted by cultural proximity, affinity, and what he liked to call "intimacy," within which different interests could coalesce organically and be adjudicated because of intuitive understanding. Notably, neither of these premises entailed any necessary place for the nation-state. Kennan found nationalism revolting as yet another abstract enthusiasm, and felt that its embodiment in state machines was the central historical reason that the twentieth century had gone so awry.[13] Nonetheless, he acknowledged that there was a dominant system of action, roughly based on the pursuit of power, that governed relations between states. His primary sphere of identification, however, is still cultural "intimacy," which may be smaller or greater than any given nation-state, depending on what was at stake.

From that vantage point, he found the notion of the "North Atlantic" stretching all the way to the Iranian border absurd (as indeed it was). The North Atlantic might in fact permit some kind of community, but it was surely limited to the Anglophone countries and perhaps seafaring Norwegians and Dutchmen. Central Europe was something altogether different. Orthodox Europe, especially of course the neo-Byzantine Soviet Union, was alien. With "Catholic Europe" he had some personal affinities, Presbyterian paragon though he was: he liked its supranational and hierarchical aspects and found appealing such archconservative regimes as Salazarist Portugal. No extensive dealings, at any rate, could take place between essentially different circles of intimacy. This is why he was always against anything but the most limited U.S. involvement with, or in, the embryonic third world, which he considered a disagreeable and profoundly foreign space better left to its own devices, especially since it was of little geostrategic interest anyway. Assumption of identity across boundaries of intimacy, then, was a grave mistake. Objective distance must find objective expression in the conduct of actual relations. It was a matter of courtesy if nothing else. One does not intrude.[14]

It was not, notably, the notion of intimacy in itself that Lippmann had taken exception to in the fall of 1947 but the auxiliary one that no diplomacy or interaction is possible when polarization is extreme. Kennan himself did not actually maintain that view a year later, when he was working out his proposition for a deal with the Soviets on neutralizing Germany. Still, he did maintain a modified version to the effect that, all things being equal, it is better not to have anything to do, beyond the absolute diplomatic minimum, with places of the alien kind. This was coupled with his fundamentally "negative" geostrategic position. What mattered was the coloration of the four clusters of the world that might, by virtue of military-industrial power, be or become a threat to the United States. One of these, the Soviet Union, was already hostile and a threat; the others (Japan, the still imperial United Kingdom, and Western/Central Europe/Germany) were all under U.S. control and hence posed no imaginable threats. Such a strategic view is negative (and realist) in that it counts only actual or potential physical threats and disregards the whole. The political character of the remaining centers should be of no intrinsic concern. Given their history, then, it would be an exercise in futility to try to impose any radical, alien schemes in the name of the allegedly universal truths of U.S. democracy on, for instance, Germany or Japan. The crucial thing was to see to it that they did not become allies of the Soviet Union or develop the capacity to threaten the United States independently. So what matters, if you will, is the particularities, not the totality or the universal. The totality has no efficacy and is thus of no intrinsic interest.[15]

The cold war, alas, is very much about the totality and universal, about security as the positive coloration of totality (more about which below). For now it is enough to note that, aside from his peculiar preoccupation with intimacy, these views are not novel. In fact, they are exemplary of a conservative practitioner of diplomacy; indeed they are the reification of that type itself. So to handle the delicate and unpredictable structures of international politics, one needed an elite of general education capable of judging particularities far from the madding crowd and certainly far from the idiocies of domestic, political culture: "men whose experience of the world has left them with a certain sense of the tragedy of things, of the unaccountability of the historical process, and the persistent tendency of brave undertakings to have irrelevant and eccentric endings." History is thus central not as a fountain of exemplary action but as a series of unrepeatable events or differences. "The sources of international tension," he argued, "are always specific, never general. They are always devoid of exact precedents or exact parallels."[16]

If pandering to popular political prejudice would do nothing to further a realistic foreign policy, then neither would condensing the posited system of interstate relations into abstract models. There was no need whatsoever, in short, for any expanding apparatus of academic IR in the manner typical of the social sciences, devoted as they were to ahistorical, predictive "modeling" of what states presumably do and do not do. Kennan, again, was always deeply skeptical, if not always hostile, to general concepts and generalization. Realism was for him not a body of knowledge or single approach but a way of being toward the world, a capacity or skill in adequating means and ends. Besides, "realism" as a term implied inimically some kind of general standpoint, if not a downright ideology.[17]

It is not surprising, therefore, that when Kennan abandoned his project of grounding realism, he also de facto abandoned realism as a systemic discourse. From then on, he would give prescriptive accounts of the *Realities of American Foreign Policy* (the indicative title of his 1954 book on the topic) while avoiding any systematic exploration of realism as such. For the next half-century, he would consistently propose "realistic" policies in critical contrast to the "unrealistic" ones that he thought dominant. Substantially, this was not classic "realism," with all its appeals to the balance of power and whatnot. It was a pragmatic, conservative call for prudence and limits. In the early 1950s, prudence to him meant avoiding the kind of formal commitments entailed in alliances across the universe, commitments that the United States, like any other great power, could and would not honor anyway in times of actual crisis. It also meant de-escalation of the nuclear arms race and many other things not pursued, such as mutual withdrawal from Germany. Overall, his central message, one at obvious odds with reigning cold-war precepts, was a call for "the much maligned and neglected process known as diplomacy," meaning "the sitting down together of two or three men in a room . . . to find in this way the real sources of tensions" and for the space for a mutual accommodation of fundamental interests.[18] Thus, over the decade, he developed a critique of the cold war as a policy orientation (he called it "an intellectual straight-jacket"),[19] though it was a critique that tended to center on counterproductive effects rather than on the deeper sources of the U.S. conduct, a wish for some ingenious and better-grounded policy-making process, some kind of geopolitical privacy.

Kennan, then, would never produce a full-fledged critique of the cold war as a U.S. project. When he sought structure at home, he ingrained historically derived utopianism. He also found dangerous excesses and imbalances, a reckless belief in technology and urbanism, destructive mass culture and consumptionism, and devastating environmental exploitation (we are in the 1950s here, when such views were anything but conventional). By the end of the decade, his political position, not only on the cold war, had gravitated publicly very far from the mainstream. His constitutive "interest" was always that of the West; but that West, or rather its principle, was in Spenglerian-Toynbeean decline, one sign of which was precisely the rise of the singularly immature and irrational United States, whose leadership of the so-called Free World was an anathema to him. Curiously, his organicist conservatism thus generated opinions that often coincided with those of the left. There was no fertile soil in the United States in either case. His only hope by then was in making broad appeals for the United States to do vastly less, since it was a society wholly unsuited to imposing itself on the rest of the world and indeed incapable of doing so. Excess at home paralleled excess abroad. Yet the "realities" he offered originated more in a sense of duty and obligation than in any hope that matters would really change. Wish fulfillment had been replaced by the unending commitment to taking a stand because one could do nothing else. Kennan never let his gloom and pessimism turn into resignation before the actually existing, as opposed to desired, reality. In this he remained indeed a good Calvinist, ceaselessly working to remake the degraded present.[20]

All of which should now be connected to the 1954 Conference on International Politics and, beyond that, to the grander question of realism and its conditions of possibility in the United States, why indeed realism should be "un-American." It is also interesting to relate this in turn to the cold war, which was at its height in 1954. To be a realist is, knowingly or not, to be against the cold war, because the cold war is an "American" project through and through, suffused with precisely the kind of "utopian" universalism that no realist worth his (we are dealing with men) salt could countenance with equanimity.

Realism, I have asserted, is reactive, if not actually parasitic. It requires something "ideal" or pious to react against. The elective affinities with conservatism are obvious (Hayden White, following Mannheim, established this long ago): there would have been no Burkean conservatism had there been no illegitimate, "utopian," and radical French Revolution (the American Revolution having been classified, by contrast, as the proper restitution of the ancient rights of Englishmen). There is no imperative to invoke the unchanging Realities of the Real unless someone is trying outrageously to impose some abstract, artificial, far-reaching scheme on that Reality. Burke, one recalls, constituted the Real and the True, that which is worth conserving, as the Christian Community of European States. Inside that community, one might well pursue a policy of equality and respect that was at the same time "realistic" in the sense of taking care of one's national interest. Vis-à-vis the outside, by contrast, one could do whatever necessary.

If realism is reactive, what does it react against in the U.S. context? A range of "American" characteristics, as we have seen from Kennan's struggles, immediately appear: legalism, idealism, abstraction, ethnocentrism, parochialism, moralism, presentism, internationalism, rigidity, crudity, hubris, and, not least, exaggerated optimism. What one has in mind is the tendency to translate what is (ideally) inside unproblematically to the outside with no understanding of difference or the subsequent need to differentiate and be subtle. For the real world is quite different, full of heterogeneities and insuperable problems. The towering shadow in the background is of course Woodrow Wilson. Nothing is taken to be as "American" as Woodrow Wilson. Wilsonianism is a benevolent, twentieth-century version of the French Revolution, the attempted imposition of abstractions on existing international realities that would admit of no such thing. At the same time, realists had to confront the historical fact that the non-Wilsonian period between the wars turned out to be an obvious disaster. While pressing at the time of the 1954 symposium, Wilsonianism today is no longer the central problem for realists. There is precious little legalism around now. "Abstraction," on the contrary, is a matter of another kind of imaginary projection, the imaginary projection of "freedom" onto a world of real difference. Wilsonian "self-determination" and "equality" have been replaced by the dichotomous and undialectical conflict between the free world and totalitarianism/slavery. That imaginary projection, furthermore, is put into action in very real ways on a globalist level, without any sense of limits and fundamental interests. The cold war of 1954, then, is being played out, arguably, in apparently "realistic" ways under the universalist umbrella: to do what it takes to combat a savage enemy everywhere requires not only potentially a "total" effort but really so. And this effort must occur under the thumb of a universalism, one where the Wilsonian thematic is replaced by the role of the United States as the successful Agent of Liberation in charge of the Free World. Nitze is the person most responsible for the explicit codification of this posture, which is the quintessential cold-war posture. For him, the exaggerations had been a fairly cheap price to pay for the success in putting the United States into the world in a sustained and uncompromising way: realistic if not realist.[21]

The first thing to underline, then, is that the cold war is not the problem of the congregation, though it hovers everywhere over the conference proceedings, present in its absence, so to speak. Nor is "realism" the problem. The participants, including the absent Kennan, can certainly be described as "realists" of one tinge or another, but it is anybody's guess how many would agree to sign up with something called "realism." It is hard to be against a "realistic" policy, but it is not equally obvious that one should favor a "realist" one. Most of the conference participants, meanwhile, would probably not deviate radically, if pressed, from the given constitutive frame of the cold war. Only Morgenthau might privately agree closely with Kennan, the most critical figure regarding foreign policy and certainly a figure of many unorthodox views on domestic society. But Morgenthau lacked Kennan's security clearances and impeccable cold-war credentials. Morgenthau was a German-Jewish conservative, an exile hounded out of safety again and again until he landed in south Chicago, and he had reason to be circumspect with his opinions, to be a bit of an intellectual cover-up artist. On actual policy questions, then, there would be considerable differences, though the nature of the convocation serves to keep them under wraps.

Yet everyone, even Nitze, found deeply disturbing the contemporary climate of oppressive, hysterical anticommunism. Kennan's notion of an "intellectual straightjacket" was not solely his private hobby-horse. Nonetheless, whatever the latent differences, the fact remains that not even the deviating Kennan had posed the problem of the conduct of U.S. policy in universalist terms of "the cold war" as such but had instead centered his attention on the structural shortcomings of the United States as a realistic actor in foreign relations. This was something on which all of the participants agreed, which is also why they had been called upon to pronounce on potential remedies.

Two concrete problems come to dominate the proceedings. Most immediately, one ponders what to do about ignorance, competence, and education in the field of foreign relations. Second, not necessarily related but irrepressible, is the problem of how to deal with the (cold-war) discrepancy between the ideal and the moral on the one hand and the shady exigencies of actual foreign policy on the other. Opinions on both accounts differ, though probably not as much as they would had the cold war been on the table. Kennan's views on education and competence have already been dealt with: the elite of judgment and experience would require no academic discipline of social science mirroring their practice simply because that practice is not subject to abstraction. A "most subtle and literate comprehension of world realities," subtle and literate sometimes meaning the pursuit, "deliberately and simultaneously," of "contradictory policies," moreover, is not "American," because what is "American" is inherently devoid of contradiction.[22] Similarly, Nitze registers the skepticism about the usefulness of "theory" one expects from a "practitioner," an actual policymaker. The skepticism of his interlocutors is directed more against the kind of theory that is now threatening to dominate the academy, an egregious form of social science called behavioralism. There is some awkwardness, indeed discomfort, here about the Rockefeller question as such. Is the problem in the U.S. posture really the absence of "theory"? If so, in what sense? Theory appears as a codeword for the absence of a proper conceptual frame for the appropriation of the real or realizable. At the same time, theory as pure abstraction is actually the enemy. Such conceptualization is by definition removed from the real. Comprehension of the real, at least the outside real, requires something else altogether. It is much easier to grasp in hermeneutical and phenomenological ways, as an experiential art of judgment involving particularities. In the end, the Rockefeller Foundation gets no real answer because there is none.

The other unavoidable problem appears in part because of Niebuhr's presence and overwhelming authority on the topic. Substantially, the question is how to be realistically moral without becoming moralizing and narrow minded, how to fight a bad enemy without descending to a similar game of dastardly deeds. This may now not seem as dated and boring an issue, what with the recent experience with "rendition" and torture, as it once did. More than forty years ago, at any rate, Le Carré disposed of it in *The Spy Who Came in from the Cold*: there is no general solution. A linked and more interesting issue, discernible here if not exactly explicit, is the tragic view of life, utterly alien to the congenital optimism of U.S. culture, the popular notion that one can do anything one wants and that there is a solution to every problem if one tries hard enough. This diagnosis generates a self-evident prescription, which is genuine, although again it is an answer that is no answer: realistic flexibility and clarity, and above all prudence. Niebuhr's Augustinian realism provides the perfect cold-war answer in this respect: evil exists in the world, even in ourselves, it is ineradicable and must thus, realistically, be recognized as such and dealt with in no uncertain terms, but not on the premise that we will ever overcome it in this world. The prescriptive upshot is that one must steer a judicious middle course between tragic resignation and utopian optimism, see the world for what it is and act accordingly. Put differently, the United States must conduct the cold war in a prudently anti-Soviet way, neither falling into isolationist introspection nor launching any headless schemes of "liberation." When push comes to shove, however, there is probably no agreement here in just how "limited" it was prudent to be.

Meanwhile, the absent Kennan dismisses the whole problem of immorality, cynicism, and Machiavellian calculus as a pseudoproblem, though for political and conceptual reasons he had a hard time explaining why. His properly organic elite, in short, would always do right. One would act naturally according to the standards of the community whence one stemmed and so by definition there could be no ethical conflict, at least not a fundamental one (some transgressions being inevitable in politics when dealing with the outside). His elite morality, accordingly, was inherently founded on community values along Aristotelian or consequentialist lines. Conversely, appeals to the abstract precepts of universal morality made no sense. Kennan talked darkly of "the 'moral' approach to foreign policy" as little more than "smugness, self-righteousness, and hypocrisy." Trying to universalize the particular was always to do violence to nature, difference, and heterogeneity.

In pushing the inquiry in that direction, Kennan is in turn pushed to test the limits of cold-war thinking overall. For the very defining component of the cold war is precisely its limitlessness on the ground that what was defined as universal in theory had to be imposed in practice, namely, the timeless truth of the United States as the norm of the universal. The particular is the universal, and universalizing itself is what the United States must do if "the world" is at stake. Doing otherwise is not to be "the United States." This is the reason why realism in the United States is always already under suspicion. Realism, one might say, universalizes the particularity as particularity (the world as a set of particularities and differences), whereas the United States universalizes the particularity (the United States itself) as the universal. This is also why no realist can ultimately accept the cold war as a frame. One can live with it and, in the manner of Paul Nitze, even use it for putatively realist(ic) purposes, but it will be a Faustian bargain.

This requires some elaboration. Realism assumes, first and foremost, that difference is a matter of identity and similarity. One can only be a realist by grasping the outside as inherently different but functionally similar, that the forces out there operate on equally "real" as opposed to "ideal" grounds. Moreover, the absence of a common normative ground beyond the recognition of the validity of difference makes such normative claims unwarranted in the process of adjudicating difference itself as conflict. Realism, then, assumes that identity and difference play out according to constituted "interests." Different interests have similar ways of taking care of their interests. Norms, one's own norms, enter into the proceedings, but only in a secondary manner, and though, all things being equal, one's own norms are better than those of the opposition, there is no ultimate court of appeal where that normative conflict can be settled. Weber and, behind him, Nietzsche were right.

The United States as a political entity can have no truck with this sort of viewpoint for the simple reason that "America" is grounded in a notion of absolute difference. If the end of history as emancipated humankind is embodied in the "United States," then the outside can never be identical or ultimately equal. Difference there is, but it is a difference that is intrinsically unjust and illegitimate, there only to be overcome and eradicated. Foreign policy, in sum, can never be about a play on the differences between identically constituted interests. I think of this as "ground," some ultimate foundation or overdetermining instance. And when that last instance comes, there can be no difference between the United States, or what it is supposed to represent, and what ought to be in the world at large. Actually existing difference between inside and outside thus opens up a space of potentially unlimited, "total" action. Realists would say, and did say, that this potentiality is a recipe for potential disaster and finally delusory, but if so, the delusion corresponded, as a result of historical accident, to phenomenal "real" power.

The roots of this self-conception, deluded or not, is not difficult to find. For the United States is conceived, launched, and invoked as the liberal end of history, an end that arrived already in 1776 or 1789 or, at the very latest, in 1865. One cannot improve on it. One can only debate the extent to which the present powers are in accord with that unchangeable point of reference. That end of history might be more controversial had not the United States essentially been a country of the Book. Whether it is the real Book or the Constitution (along with the rhetorically more powerful Declaration) or, more likely, a combination matters less than the monumental reality of the coded reference point, the lapidary text. An appeal is always possible, indeed inherently imperative, to the principles of the founding document. The United States, in referring to itself and the originary Book/ Text, certainly claims that it was the embodiment of timeless, universal principles, true everywhere and at all given times. One can pursue a simulacrum of realism for a while, but *one is always liable to be held to account.* Kennan learned this. Eventually, the less principled Kissinger did too. And perhaps it will come to apply to Barack Obama as well, a sophisticated pragmatist and a realist in a minor key.

Universalist claims, however, do not in themselves make realism unrealistic. Here it is instructive to compare the United States to the Soviet Union. The Soviet regime, also universalist in orientation, found strikingly little difficulty in combining such a position with a remarkably straightforward form of realism. (Kennan saw this but could never quite grasp it, in turn because he never quite grasped Soviet Marxism.) In part, it was a product of the philosophical realism of Soviet Marxism, the well-known base/superstructure division whereby real interests are material and what is said somehow epiphenomenal and immaterial expressions of that materiality. In the United States qua "America," one can never be that reductionist. Politicians may be corrupt and cynical, but the political in the sense of "America" is always pure. In a word, it is ideal. More fundamentally, however, there is a difference in the kind of universalism at hand. Whereas the Soviet Union, representing (it claimed) the penultimate stage of history, was locked in a dialectical struggle for the final liberation of humankind, the United States *is* that very liberation. It is the end, it is already a world empire, it can have no equal, no dialectical Other. What is not like the United States can, in principle, have no proper efficacy. It is either perversion or at best a not-yet. In effect, in Kennan's taxonomy, it is about world domination. Given the maximalistic norm of what is embodied in that absolute difference, realism becomes impossible. For the Soviet regime, however, dialectical contradiction is the very name of the game, the realist assumption that different interests exist, and exist in conflict, and exist in conflict rationally.

Absolute difference, to be sure, has not always been an actuality in the foreign relations of the United States. There have been several periods or moments when a line of continuity has appeared between the United States and the rest of the world (or more precisely the kind of world grasped as "civilized"): the Progressive Era (civilizational imperialism); World War II (Roosevelt's quite deliberate reworking of progressive precepts in the name of alliance between responsible Great Powers); the period between the mid-1960s and the mid-1970s when some kind of managerial Great Power structure was not only possible but rendered imperative by the exigencies of nuclear weapons, a moment that received its proper historical expression in the individuals Richard Nixon and Henry Kissinger; and the unabashed globalization of the 1990s. Obama represents yet another. These moments, however, occur on borrowed time: their premise is success or at least no debacle. When the last instance comes, as it always does, it is not about realism but utopia, which is why realism, pure realism, will always itself remain a utopia or a desire.

NOTES

1. The literature on Kennan is enormous and, at the scholarly level, quite good. By contrast, his place and image in the world of punditry and policy making is often a matter of wish fulfillment, if not downright fantasy, involving clichéd odes to the would-be "father of containment" and so forth. My own view is to be found in Stephanson (1989), which, in general, I still stand by. Kennan's two-volume *Memoirs* remain the best guide to his thinking, besides being literary classics in their own genre.

2. See his unflinching remarks in Eisele (2002).

3. Kennan memorandum to the Secretary of State, November 14, 1949, U.S. Department of State, *Foreign Relations of the United States* (henceforth *FRUS*) 1949, volume 2 (Washington, D.C.), 16.

4. His most succinct statement here is his letter to Charles Bohlen, January 26, 1949, George F. Kennan Papers, Box 28, Mudd Library, Princeton University (henceforth GFKP).

5. See, *passim*, Stephanson (1989, chap. 6).

6. Lippmann (1947), which is a compilation of his sustained critique of the X-Article. Lippmann, incidentally, says nothing about the cold war, the title notwithstanding, though his analysis is an excellent diagnosis of the elements in Kennan's position that actually came to define the U.S. project we know as "the cold war."

7. Kennan, then or after, could never reconcile himself with Lippmann's critique. I think it nagged him forever.

8. On Lippmann generally, see Ronald Steel's peerless study (Steel 1980).

9. The quotations here and in the following paragraph are from PPS/23, i.e., Policy Planning Staff paper no. 23, "Review of Current Trends in U.S. Foreign Policy," which Kennan submitted to the Secretary of State on February 24, 1948. It is available in FRUS, 1948, I: 509–529, but is most easily found at http://en.wikisource.org/wiki/Memo_PPS23_by_George_Kennan. The same sentiments are expressed in greater detail in Kennan's 1951 minor classic *American Diplomacy*.

10. Kennan, "The World Position and Problems of the United States," address at the National War College, August 28, 1949, GFKP, Box 24.

11. It was in the aftermath of his controversial Reith Lectures, delivered on the BBC in early 1957, where he argued once again the case for mutual "disengagement" by the United States and the Soviet Union in Europe, that Raymond Aron finally explained to him that the division, however absurd in itself, was actually really in the interests of both sides because it was stable and predictable. Lippmann would make the same point with equal force soon afterward. Kennan, the realist, says he was dumbfounded at having discovered this elementary reality (so to speak). See Kennan (1972, 252–255).

12. His various ruminations here, many in handwritten form, can be found in GFKP Box 26. The only authority that he dealt with extensively was Charles Beard and his *The Idea of National Interest*. Morgenthau and Lippmann are conspicuous by their absence, as are E. H. Carr, Friedrich Meinecke, and host of other potential but obvious references.

13. His distrust of nationalism goes back, in part, to his powerful attachment throughout to the example and principles of the Austro-Hungarian Empire, the Habsburg model of a multinational dynasty and state. He disliked all nationalism (and the territorial sovereignty that sometimes went with it) but above all nationalism in its Third World garb, the highest contemporary condensation, in his view: "Both these forces—the nationalist and the communist—are revolting; they have similar origins and traits; both are by nature hostile to us and incapable of contributing anything positive to the type of world we must seek." Memorandum for the Secretary, January 22, 1952, GFKP, Box 24. Rather than state/nation, or any state for that matter, Kennan's focus in thinking about the world and relations within it was always "civilization."

14. See Stephanson (1989, chaps. 4–6).

15. The first time he outlines this idea of the military-industrial centers in geopolitical terms is in an address: "Contemporary Problems of Foreign Policy," given at the National War College on September 17, 1948, GFKP, Box 17.

16. Kennan, "Notes for Essays," Spring 1952, 132, GFKP, Box 26; Kennan (1954, 36).

17. As a conservative (an organicist conservative for whom society was by nature an organism, a unity, and a totality), Kennan disliked "abstractions" in the sense of "unnatural" and "artificial" schemes imposed on actually existing realities. At the same time, however, he was much attached in a different register to the idea of the artificial appearance as opposed to actually existing reality, namely, in his devotion to form, ethical and aesthetic *form*, in the conduct of people and states: behave as though the beast in you does not exist and eventually the outer form will have subdued, if not finally conquered, the inner essence.

18. Kennan, "Notes for Essays," 132.
19. Kennan, off-the-record discussion, Overseas Writers Club, Washington, D.C., May 29, 1953, GFKP, Box 18.
20. On the moment of his cultural critique in the 1950s, see Stephanson (1989, chap. 7). Once the "sixties" happened, he lost his bearings momentarily, finding himself in odd company in his unequivocal critique of the Vietnam War and denouncing what he considered to be the egregious transgressions of the younger generation. His intense dislike of the mass culture of the 1950s could not in the 1960s find any new stable ground, though he achieved an ideal resolution of sorts in the 1970s onward in his consistent and courageous support for a denuclearized and peaceful relation with the Soviet Union.
21. For further explications along these lines, see Stephanson (2005, 2004, 2000).
22. Kennan, letter to Philip Jessup, April 9, 1953, copy courtesy of Dr. Larry Bland.

REFERENCES

Eisele, Albert. 2002. Hill profile: George F. Kennan. *The Hill* (September 25).

Kennan, George. 1951. *American diplomacy, 1900–1950*. Chicago: University of Chicago Press.

——. 1954. *Realities of American foreign policy*. Princeton, N.J.: Princeton University Press.

——. 1972. *Memoirs*. 2 vols. Boston: Little, Brown.

Lippmann, Walter. 1947. *The cold war: A study in U.S. foreign policy*. New York: Harper.

Steel, Ronald. 1980. *Walter Lippmann and the American century*. Boston: Little, Brown.

Stephanson, Anders. 1989. *Kennan and the art of foreign policy*. Cambridge, Mass.: Harvard University Press.

——. 2000. Liberty or death: The cold war as US ideology. In *Reviewing the cold war: Approaches, interpretations, theory*, ed. O. A. Westad, 81–100. London: Frank Cass.

——. 2004. The United States as cold war. In *Reinterpreting the end of the cold war: Essays, interpretations, periodizations*, ed. S. Pons and F. Romero, 52–67. London: Frank Cass.

——. 2005. Law and messianic counterwar from FDR to George W. Bush. In *Guidicare e punire: i processi per crimini di guerra tra diritto e politica*, ed. L. Baldissara and P. Pezzino. Naples: L'Ancora del Mediterraneo.

7

AMERICAN HEGEMONY, THE ROCKEFELLER FOUNDATION, AND THE RISE OF ACADEMIC INTERNATIONAL RELATIONS IN THE UNITED STATES

INDERJEET PARMAR

The risks we face are of a new order of magnitude, commensurate with the total struggle in which we are engaged. For a free society there is never total victory, since freedom and democracy are never wholly attained, are always in the process of being attained. But defeat at the hands of the totalitarian is total defeat. These risks crowd in on us, in a shrinking world of polarized power, so as to give us no choice, ultimately, between meeting them effectively or being overcome by them. . . .

The whole success of the proposed program hangs ultimately on recognition by this Government, the American people, and all free peoples, that the cold war is in fact a real war in which the survival of the free world is at stake. Essential prerequisites to success are consultations with Congressional leaders designed to make the program the object of non-partisan legislative support, and a presentation to the public of a full explanation of the facts and implications of the present international situation.[1]

Intellectuals, journalists, and state policymakers were in close conference at the Rockefeller Foundation amid alleged existential world crises in the (original) "year of maximum danger": 1954. "It is estimated that, within the next four years [by 1954, later revised to 1952], the USSR will attain the capability of seriously damaging vital centers of the United States, provided it strikes a surprise blow and provided further that the blow is opposed by no more effective opposition than we now have programmed."[2]

Many observers claimed that world conditions, rather than America's will to global power, demanded nothing less than the complete national mobilization of resources against the Soviet foe; the future of mankind depended upon the course of U.S. national security and foreign policies. The "novel" character of the "Red threat," its existential challenge to the free world, and its characterization as necessitating a fight to the finish through a long, possibly permanent, war (Melman 1985) all echo the threat-construction discourses about political Islam deployed by the George W. Bush administration after 9/11 (Jackson 2005; Campbell 1998).[3] Then as now, every section of society had a part to play in thwarting the enemy -at home and abroad, in churches, schools, workplaces, libraries, and universities. Intellectuals, journalists, and academics had special roles, particularly in ensuring that no subversive thinking infected the minds of the young. On the contrary, they were to ensure the production of young minds ready to wage the struggle for freedom in all aspects of life, especially through graduate programs suited to training in the foreign service and foreign policy–making apparatus. In addition, academics were to supply policy-makers with usable knowledge and understanding of the world and its strategic countries, regions, and underlying transformative social, political, and ideological forces (Almond 2002). Even more than that, academics were to strive to produce theoretical models and frameworks to make sense of the sheer volume of facts about the world that were becoming available to America's national-security managers from its official and unofficial representatives throughout the world.

The foreign and national-security policies that were going to save the world from the march of "communist slavery" or, as is argued here, to promote American global hegemony,[4] were based, at least in part, on assessments and analyses of the vast amounts of information that poured into the State Department. But how was the department to assess the information? How was it to use knowledge to make better decisions that would, with the deployment of appropriate means and vigorous mass-media campaigns, command the support of the American people? What could "ivory-tower" academics, whose very trade is knowledge, contribute to this? Could academic theories help make better policies and, thereby, secure peace and security under American world leadership?

In my view, the confluence of intellect and power, the meeting of ideas and action, and the networks of private actors and former, serving, and future officials of the American state constitute the core compelling interest in the 1954 Rockefeller conference. In principle, it suggests that ideas were seen to matter, that intellectuals' voices were worth hearing and their expertise valued and recognized at high levels of national power in the United States, and that intellectuals and their institutions made a difference. The composition of the meetings also suggests that in developing a better sense of America's national purpose, the conference might result in practical suggestions for improving the promotion to the general public of U.S. foreign and national-security policies. The year 1954 was a moment for reflection, an attempt to explore, and, for some, an attempt to overcome and iron out the boundaries of knowledge and power. This is usually an unhappy experience for both intellectuals and public officials, as this chapter suggests.

Validation for (some) students of power came in the form of Dean Rusk, the former public official, future secretary of state, current president of the Rockefeller Foundation. Paul Nitze, the main author of NSC-68 and former head of policy planning at the State Department, was an active participant. The dean of U.S. foreign-policy journalism, Walter Lippmann, was in attendance, as was the elder statesman of Christianity and foreign-policy politics, Reinhold Niebuhr. Dorothy Fosdick, the first senior woman in the State Department and later advisor and aide to U.S. Senator Henry "Scoop" Jackson, also attended.[5] They wanted to know what international relations as an emerging academic discipline could do for them: whether IR theory possessed the "key" to analysis and action. They interrogated elite university professors—Hans Morgenthau (Chicago), Arnold Wolfers (Yale), and William T. R. Fox (Columbia)—for days. The meeting was direct and the immediate outcome disappointing though instructive about the differing functions of academic theorizing and the needs of hard-pressed and hard-nosed national-security managers. However, there was much more going on here than meets the eye. The road to and from the 1954 conference is a story of the gradual—*although not linear and preplanned, but with an inner logic nevertheless*—conscious development by elements of a rapidly developing East Coast U.S. foreign-policy establishment of an academic discipline (international relations),[6] armed with a specific dominant theory—realism and its several variants, or, more accurately, *the sense of the need to deploy "hard power" as a basic factor in foreign relations*—at the core of which was a belief in the inevitability of interstate conflict, the role of force in world affairs, the necessity of wise statesmanship, total national mobilization, and the need for U.S. global leadership or hegemony (Barnett 1973; Roberts 1992; Parmar 2004; Shoup and Minter 1977).[7] The year 1954 seemed to be, at least in part, about giving a veneer of philosophical depth to American national interest–driven U.S. foreign policy, differentiating the United States from its supposedly uncultured and uncivilized communist enemy.[8] It was also about reconciling values and interests, pointing up the value-based origins of national interests themselves. This was, then, an attempt to continue the development, under new conditions, of a myriad of programs that had begun several decades earlier by elites that looked forward to "the American century." The development of IR is viewed here as part of an elite "project," however "messy" in practice, for U.S. global hegemony (Hoare and Nowell-Smith 1971; Augelli and Murphy 1988; Parmar 2002b).

WHY DID THE ROCKEFELLER FOUNDATION ARRANGE THE 1954 CONFERENCE?

It is clear that the Rockefeller Foundation and other such philanthropies (such as Carnegie) had a long-standing interest in four matters in regard to U.S. foreign affairs. First, and most broadly, the foundation wanted to strengthen U.S. power in the world. Second, and as a result, the foundation aimed at a unity of analysis and action in the U.S. foreign-policy arena, and was dedicated to fostering and consolidating intellectual networks that would produce better empirical knowledge, conceptual understanding, and practical decisions. Third, the foundation sought to improve the State Department's ability to assess threats, opportunities, and the sheer volume of facts upon which such assessments were based. Finally, the foundation wanted to assist in the determination of U.S. national interests and the role therein of core values.[9]

The Rockefeller Foundation was a state-oriented and imperialistic institution from its early twentieth-century Progressive-era beginnings. It was dedicated to state building and constructing a civil society that was supportive of federal executive power, especially in foreign affairs. Foundation elites looked forward to America taking political and moral leadership of the world. This mirrored the foundation's serious interest in domestic social reform and state building to that end. The Rockefeller Foundation's principle of "private action for the public good" frequently led the way in later extensions of state power and institutional capacities, thereby building the American state (Arnove 1980).

The Progressive-era roots of Rockefeller and other philanthropies are fundamental to understanding their sense of historic mission. Progressivism was characterized by elite attempts to come to grips with and to manage massive social, economic, and cultural transformations within the United States and to promote American power in a global context featuring intra-European military and imperial rivalries, rising nationalist and anticolonialist movements, and socialism. Order through reform at home and increased influence abroad were intimately connected in the minds and activities of Progressive-era philanthropies (Leuchtenberg 1952–1953; Wiebe 1980).

In a profound sense, the Rockefeller Foundation was a "state-spirited" organization sitting at the heart of the emerging East Coast U.S. foreign-policy establishment. As Antonio Gramsci observed, state-spirited leaders are the core elements of any thoroughgoing historically transformative movement: they see themselves as the state, as embodying the interests and values of the state, and as duty bound to solve the state's problems as if they were their own. In the terms of Eldon Eisenach (1994), foundations may be seen as "parastate" organizations that despite their private, voluntarist character were motivated to their core by state interests.

Given their historical, East Coast–elite origins at a critical time in American history, the foundations marked the emergence of a global consciousness within which the United States was historically best suited to a world-leadership role. Spreading the benefits of the American dream to the world was critical (Rosenberg 1982). As the twentieth century progressed, the relationship between state foreign-policy makers and philanthropic intellectual networks deepened and broadened, blurring the increasingly vague distinctions between state and society and between public policy and private actors. By the end of 1945, philanthropic foundations were thoroughly integrated into the foreign-policy establishment; they assisted America's rise to global hegemony by, among other things, establishing university-based foreign-affairs institutes, funding the work of key foreign-policy think tanks, sponsoring IR and area-studies programs, offering graduate training courses for foreign-service officers, and developing the research and analysis capacities of the State Department. Such efforts coincided with the expansionist objectives of the American state, with which foundation networks were intimately connected both ideologically and personally.

The Rockefeller Foundation sits well in Godfrey Hodgson's (1972–1973) definition of the U.S. foreign-policy establishment, which, Hodgson argues, is composed of groups of men who know one another, "who share assumptions so deep that they do not need to be articulated; and who contrive to wield power outside the constitutional or political forms: the power to put a stop to things they disapprove of, to promote the men they regard as reliable, and to block the unreliable." Hodgson further notes that "the true establishment man prided himself on his bipartisanship, his ability to get on with and work with right-minded fellows of either party." The core elements of the establishment include Wall Street lawyers and bankers, Ivy League academics, and the heads of the major philanthropic foundations (Coser 1965, 339).[10] Nelson Polsby (1993) supports elements of that definition by arguing that the establishment tends to be centrist, pragmatic, and focused on the executive branch, and it draws its members principally from the Ivy League, although it was also open to talented people "with the wrong family pedigree," part of the "genius of the American Establishment" (Holland 1991, 26).

Hodgson argues that the post–Pearl Harbor foreign-policy establishment was defined by a *history*, a *policy*, an *aspiration*, an *instinct*, and a *technique*. It was forged historically in organizations such as the OSS during World War II and the cold war and in the design of the Marshall Plan, United Nations, IMF, World Bank, and NATO. Its *policy* was broadly anti-isolationist and liberal internationalist, advocating restraint but admiring the use of hi-tech military force. Its *aspiration* was to the moral and political leadership of the world: heading "a single Western coalition holding the world in balance against the infidel is fundamental to this establishment." The establishment's *instinct* was for the "nonideological," pragmatic center ground, and its *technique* was to work through the executive branch—the National Security Council, Central Intelligence Agency, State Department, and the White House rather than Congress, electoral politics, or public opinion. In short, the post-1941 establishment was characterized by its pragmatism, centrism, elitism, multilateralism, and almost exclusive focus on the executive branch. This not only sums up the place and position of the Rockefeller Foundation but also of most of the invited members of the 1954 Rockefeller Conference.

As a strategic organization of the establishment, the Rockefeller Foundation viewed the academy and academics as a critical resource, as noted above. Broadly, the foundation *effectively* took a Gramscian approach to intellectuals' roles, though from a very different perspective: to promote the power of a capitalist-democratic state rather than to undermine it. The Gramscian view, along with orthodox Marxism, is founded on an economic analysis of power in capitalist societies. Capitalist corporations form the bedrock of economic power and, thereby, the basis of social, cultural, and ideological power in civil society. Unlike orthodox Marxists, however, Gramsci made a radical departure from this view in order to explain Western capitalism's relative immunity to revolution. Gramsci noted that there existed important protective layers of probourgeois culture, ideology, values, and institutions that had played a powerful role in shaping the minds of the masses in favor of the status quo and against violent revolution. In short, Gramsci made more explicit and more specifically developed what Marx had argued when he wrote that "the ideas of the ruling class are in every epoch the ruling ideas" (Miliband 1984, 162–163).[11] Gramsci, however, located ideological, political, and cultural struggle more centrally into Marxist thought, thereby creating space in the theory for those who are the principal sources and disseminators of new ideas and theories: the intellectuals.

In effect, Gramsci's argument is that there is no simple way to define capitalist, or national, interests—in economic or political terms—and that interests are a matter of intellectual debate and competing interpretations. It is the role of "organic intellectuals"—thinkers who are connected with the dominant class via, for example, the universities, church, mass media, or political parties—to develop, elaborate, refine, disseminate, and teach the dominant ideas, values, and norms, to make "natural" and "commonsense" what are, in reality, ideas that principally support the ruling class.

Similarly, politics and the state are not mere reflections of unequal economic relations: they are also sites of competition between rival ideas, values, policies, programs, and regimes. Through struggle, bargaining, compromise, and the building of enduring coalitions that cut across class, ethnic, and racial cleavages is formed the prevailing idea of "reality," the dominant concept that underlics a particular set of political, institutional, and economic arrangements: a regime. As political regimes—or hegemonic projects and alliances—are made up of cross-class coalitions, they require for their formation and sustenance public-opinion mobilizations to convince the masses, or at least a critical proportion of them, that they have a stake in current arrangements, something to gain, such as a steady, well-paid job and improved living standards, from supporting the regime. In short, the coalition—or historic bloc, in Gramscian terms—is generated and sustained by leadership based on the "consent of the governed" under the hegemonic leadership of politicians and intellectuals of the capitalist class.

The "consent of the governed" is too vital to political and social arrangements to be left to chance. It is engineered (Parmar 2000)[12] by intellectual, political, and cultural elites through numerous channels that involve not only the state—through, for example, political speeches, schools, and political parties—but also through the sort of organizations that Hodgson's establishment and Eisenach's parastates would recognize: the major private and public universities, the Council on Foreign Relations, and the great East Coast philanthropic foundations—Ford, Carnegie, and Rockefeller (Barrow 1990).

In Gramscian terms, hegemony is constructed by an alliance of state elites and private ruling-class organizations, including those led by intellectuals. Elite and popular authority are constructed by an alliance of state and private agencies in order to undermine the old order and to usher in the new. As noted above, central to the motivation of private elites is Gramsci's concept of "state spirit," which, although a fairly "conservative" sounding concept, infuses every successful social movement. State-spirited leaders contextualize themselves in the broad sweep of national and global historical development. their outlook "presupposes 'continuity,' either with the past, or with tradition, or with the future; that is, it presupposes that every act is a moment in a complex process, which has already begun and which will continue" (Hoare and Nowell-Smith 1971, 146–147).[13] According to Gramsci, such leaders and intellectuals may even come to believe "that they *are* the State" (Hoare and Nowell-Smith 1971, 16). It is to one such specific initiative intimately related to the 1954 conference—relating to Arnold Wolfers and William T. R. Fox—that this chapter now turns.[14]

THE YALE INSTITUTE OF INTERNATIONAL STUDIES

Starting in the 1930s, the Rockefeller Foundation played a leading role in financing university-based research programs in international affairs and in "non-Western" studies. It is important to emphasize that the two developments occurred together because they were part of a broader project that aimed at the same outcome: expanding American power. Foundation officials were early to recognize the changing position of the United States in world affairs. This required, they believed, a new foreign policy. This in turn required trained experts and officers who spoke foreign languages and knew the history, politics, and culture of societies that would enter the orbit of America's "national interest." University courses in international relations were important for educating these and other future leaders of community opinion—lawyers, bankers, and teachers—who could be expected to secure general acceptance of the United States in world affairs. According to Olson and Groom (1991, 75–76), without the intervention of Rockefeller and Carnegie, "the field of [international relations] could hardly have progressed as it did" in its formative years. The foundations, they suggest, alongside the Council on Foreign Relations, constituted a "critical institutional base affecting the way in which IR developed." The foundations were simultaneously also a powerful institutional base for the development of area studies (Engermann 1999).

The Yale Institute of International Studies (YIIS) represents an excellent example of early foundation intervention. The Yale Institute was created in 1935 with a five-year Rockefeller grant of $100,000.[15] The year 1935, which saw the first of a series of four Neutrality Acts, forbidding U.S. entanglements in foreign wars, was a critical year in the history of U.S. foreign relations and a daring year to begin, consciously or otherwise, an overtly globalist project.[16] From its inception, the institute aimed to clarify American foreign policy by focusing upon "the subject of power in international relations"—an area neglected by American scholars.[17] The institute aimed to take a "realistic" view of world affairs, to be useful to the makers of foreign policy, to produce scholarly but accessible publications, and to train academics for governmental service.[18] That it was later nicknamed the "Power School" by IR insiders is adequate testimony to Yale's successful institutionalization of realpolitik (Olson and Groom 1991, 99). Yale also had such senior academics as Frederick Dunn, Arnold Wolfers, and Samuel F. Bemis on its faculty.[19] In addition to the initial $100,000 in 1935, the foundation provided a further $51,500 in 1941 (to run over three years) and $125,000 in 1944 (to run over the following five years), a total of $276,500.20

The realpolitik approaches of those who directed the YIIS (Nicholas Spykman from 1935 to 1940 and Frederick Dunn from 1940 until after the war) clearly satisfied Rockefeller officials.[21] Consequently, the drafting of "abstract schemes of a new world order" and "ivory tower speculation"—the YIIS's annual report for 1942 stressed—were *not* on the agenda. Instead, the institute focused upon "basic research" to fill conceptual gaps in current thinking and knowledge of international relations.[22] By 1944, the institute was focusing even more upon "those questions which are likely to cause the *most trouble*, such as Anglo-American and Western-Soviet relations, for American foreign-policy."[23]

The memoranda and records of the Yale Institute bear out its effective realism. One document, for example, reports that the United States could no longer "take a free ride" in the conduct of European affairs. While Britain's international hegemony had effectively ended, Britain still constituted a key "bridgehead" to Western Europe. Consequently, Britain's continued survival was in America's national interest, to the point of war if necessary. Europe, the report noted, had to be kept "in balance" and a new Napoleon or Hitler prevented. America had to engage in the "dirty game of power politics" if she were not to be dragged into another foreign war. Interestingly, the report recognized the dangers of Soviet expansionism while also acknowledging the USSR's legitimate security concerns.[24] While the Soviets ought to be decisively checked territorially, it would be a mistake, the memorandum warned, to oppose them by countering every movement for social reform. That would only convince Western liberals and radicals of the "reactionary" character of Anglo-American policy and "drive [them] ... into the arms of the doctrinaire Bolsheviks." Finally, the memorandum argued that the American economy had become the major factor in global prosperity. Not only must future U.S. economic policies assist the regeneration of Europe (and so keep Britain and France "going concerns"), but they must also run the American economy "responsibly." American domestic prosperity would create a stable market for the world's products and thereby add to global security. This imperialistic posture was endorsed by an internal foundation review of key books produced by the YIIS during the war.[25]

Both Arnold Wolfers and William Fox were deeply significant in developing the YIIS but were also themselves influenced by the institute. Fox, for example, later claimed that it was only after joining the YIIS in 1943 that he "realize[d] how ill-equipped I was to think about the responsible use of power by the United States" (Ramos 2003, 169). Wolfers, on the other hand, found Yale a ready platform for making influential contacts in the worlds of intelligence and policy making. During the war, Wolfers was a consultant with the OSS, National War College, the Institute of Defense Analysis, the Department of the Army, and the State Department (Thompson 1980, 98). In addition, Wolfers and other YIIS colleagues lectured on geopolitics at the School of Military Government, in Virginia (Ramos 2003, 165). After the war, Wolfers was a recruiter at Yale for the CIA. Kenneth W. Thompson, another of the 1954 conferees, argues that Wolfers was the most policy oriented of the Yale group and "had an insatiable yearning for the corridors of power." In fact, Thompson felt that Wolfers might have compromised his scholarly independence as a result of that yearning (Ramos 2003, 166).

However much the Yale Institute cherished its "independence," its usefulness to government was its first priority. In August 1944, Dunn told Joseph Willits of the Rockefeller Foundation that the YIIS had set up a committee (with State Department representation) to consider how universities might "produce good decision-makers."[26] Two years earlier, the YIIS's annual report noted the first of several meetings with U.S. War Department officials concerning Near Eastern policy. "It was intended," the report stressed, "as a test of the possibility of quick mobilization of academic knowledge and its application to practical questions of policy." The 1941–1942 report further noted that numerous "foreign area courses" had been established at Yale to increase the awareness of foreign societies, that the institute was sending information to the U.S. government "on demand," and that YIIS graduates were performing valuable roles within several government departments, notably the departments of State and War, the Board of Economic Warfare, and the Office of the Coordinator of Inter-American Affairs, which was headed by Nelson Rockefeller.[27]

The War Department asked the Yale Institute to establish a School of Asiatic Studies for army staff officers, which it duly did in the summer of 1945. Meanwhile, the State Department and the YIIS established a joint committee, with Dunn as chairman, to improve the training of foreign-service officers. The impact of such government connections was accepted within the broader political-science community by the formation of a "politico-military relations" panel by the American Political Science Association, under the chairmanship of Bernard Brodie (a YIIS member).[28] The institute approached foreign-policy problems from a perspective not dissimilar to that of the State Department. One of the most telling examples appeared in its 1943 annual report, in a discussion of the importance of the Middle East to the United States. Security, the report noted, was not merely a military question: it also required a watchful eye on the peoples and resources that bordered strategic sea routes and military bases. The Yale Institute proposed an investigation of industrial development, the "rise of nationalism," and "race and population pressures as they affect the stability of these regions," with a view to "early remedial action by the United States."[29] This was not only an early indication of the importance of national security–oriented area-studies programs that developed within and alongside the development of IR but was also symptomatic of the close interconnections between foundation-funded research initiatives (Morton 1963). IR's development cannot profitably be seen in isolation from those other developments.

The institute produced many books on the Far East, Anglo-American relations, and the place of Africa in American security policy. Over a half-century later, two stand out: William T. R. Fox's *The Superpowers: The United States, Britain, and the Soviet Union—Their Responsibility for Peace* (1944), which introduced the term "superpower" into the language (Reynolds 1991, 173; Olson and Groom 1991, 100); and Nicholas J. Spykman's *America's Strategy in World Politics: The United States and the Balance of Power* (1942). Gabriel Almond (2002, 2) argues that Fox's book "defined the structure of the postwar system of international relations."[30] According to the historian John Thompson (1992, 401), Spykman's study was the "most thorough analysis of America's strategic position made in these [war] years," the thrust of which was "that American interests demanded intervention in the war to restore the balance of power in Eurasia." (It was written before the Japanese attack on Pearl Harbor.) Spykman argued that total war characterized twentieth-century warfare. The United States, therefore, had to be prepared for a global strategy that combined and integrated the key factors of power: military preparedness, economic vitality, political

efficiency and mobilization, and ideological clarity. Spykman also abol-
ished the distinctions between peacetime and war: "total war is permanent
war." Finally, and most profoundly, he argued that there is "*no region of the
globe [that] is too distant to be without strategic significance, too remote to
be neglected in the calculations of power politics.*" Total, permanent war on
a global scale: this was Yale's contribution to U.S. grand strategy (Ramos
2003, 267). Interestingly, the universalistic views of U.S. national interests
and security expressed by Spykman, a hard-core realist, seem quite close
to the "containment thesis" as developed by Paul Nitze in NSC-68 and applied in the disastrous war of aggression against Vietnam, with the full support of Dean Rusk, secretary of state to presidents Kennedy and Johnson.

Both books received considerable praise and sold well. According to its
publisher, Harcourt, Brace, Spykman's book sold almost ten thousand copies within three months. In a letter to the Rockefeller Foundation, the
publisher argued that even these figures failed to give "an adequate idea" of
the books' importance. The letters he received suggested an "influence
quite disproportionate to the numbers sold." Indeed, Spykman's book, the
publisher argued, "may be considered one of the really influential books of
our decade."[31]

Isaiah Bowman, a respected Rockefeller Foundation advisor and political geographer, commented that Spykman's book ought to be read in a
million American homes and at least annually by official foreign-policy
makers. A foundation reviewer suggested that it sold well in Washington,
D.C.,[32] and the foundation's social-sciences director wrote that it was a
"great" book that deserved "prayerful study." Olson and Groom (1991, 99)
argue that Spykman's book continued to be influential because it "held
great appeal for Pentagon post-war planners."

The influence of the YIIS was also built through the teaching of international relations at undergraduate and postgraduate levels, mainly through
the establishment in 1935 of a major in international relations, offering a
BA degree. YIIS researchers were expected to carry out teaching as part of
their core functions. The IR major was built principally around the theme
of national security and war. As the course guide summarized it: "War as
an instrument of national policy. Preparation for war in peacetime: mobilization of national resources. The conduct of war and its problems of social
control. Military, economic, political, and propaganda instruments of war"
(Ramos 2003, 240).

During the 1940s, the U.S. Navy offered courses at Yale on war strategy and the "Foundations of National Power," coordinated by Princeton's
Edward Mead Earle. This particular course was also offered at five other

universities, including UCLA, Northwestern, Princeton, and the University of Pennsylvania, indicating the further dissemination of this line of thought and enquiry across the United States. Inevitably, there was some student resistance to the attachment to "power," "force," and "war" in these programs at Yale, especially from students who matriculated in IR classes in preparation for Christian missionary or peace-building work. Spykman wrote in his report to the Rockefeller Foundation in 1939: "The rather realistic approach to the subject at Yale sometimes shocked their [Christians'] youthful idealism but this only occurred after their arrival, and it did not deter them from recommending the treatment to others." As Paulo Ramos argues, "the conversion to realism was taking place."[33]

Student numbers in IR at Yale were modest before the war (seventeen in 1937–1938, rising to fifty-two in 1939–1940) but increased to eighty-eight in 1942–1943, stabilizing at about eighty after 1945. Ramos (2003, 243) estimates that around six hundred students majored in IR at Yale from 1935 to 1951. Between 1935 and 1945, Yale graduated twenty-seven MA and doctoral candidates. Well-known IR alumni include Bernard C. Cohen, Lucian Pye, and William C. Olson (Ramos 2003, 372). Other alumni went on to join important U.S. foreign policy–related institutions such as the Council on Foreign Relations, the Foreign Policy Association, U.S. Tariff Commission, the Foreign Service, and State Department (Ramos 2003, 243).

The role of the U.S. State Department in more closely orienting the teaching of IR at Yale to the State Department's concerns is interesting. In 1944, a committee was set up to investigate "what the educational process can do to produce good decision-makers in the field of international relations," mainly to improve the caliber of graduate students entering government service and to provide in-service training to practicing diplomats (Ramos 2003, 245).

That the influence of the YIIS reached much farther than the academic world was important to its Rockefeller Foundation sponsors. Its work was respected by other foreign-policy "influentials" and by policymakers. The State Department showed by their regular liaisons how important they believed its work to be. External advisers such as Jacob Viner and Isaiah Bowman continued to enthuse about the institute whenever the foundation asked for an assessment. Its research center and seminars attracted well-known academics such as the political scientist Harold Lasswell, journalists such as Hanson Baldwin of the *New York Times*, and State Department–connected men such as Grayson Kirk, a member of the Council on Foreign Relations' War-Peace Studies Project. By 1945, the institute was broadcasting on the radio (American Broadcasting System's Blue Network) on the "problems of peace" prior to the San Francisco Conference, with former Undersecretary of State Summer Welles presiding.[34] YIIS members were also engaged as consultants by the State Department at the San Francisco Conference on International Organization in 1945.[35] The YIIS contributed significantly to the diffusion of the realist paradigm in America and Europe and helped generate what Olson and Groom (1991, 106–111) call a new "consensus of power" in the discipline of international relations.

The institute's "independent" status also helped legitimize its views. Specifically, there was little public acknowledgement of its continuous connections with either the foundation or with the state. The institute trained hundreds of undergraduates and dozens of graduate students for state service or academia, furthering the influence of its realist approach. By 1948, the YIIS began a journal, *World Politics*, and ran one of the most prestigious programs of postgraduate research and training in America.[36] The experience of the Yale Institute demonstrates the valued place of utilitarian knowledge production—knowledge as technology—in Rockefeller's institutional and funding culture. It explains why the 1954 conference was organized and funded by the foundation even if its aims were to rein in somewhat the excessive realism of YIIS, which by 1951 had moved to Princeton.[37]

THE 1954 CONFEREES' BIOGRAPHIES

The list of 1954 conference participants is instructive: it is a mixture of leading academics, journalists, and past, serving, and future public officials, representing the increasingly incestuous worlds of knowledge construction, news, and policy making. They were, in the main, keenly interested in America's struggle against the Soviet Union and the necessity of U.S. global leadership. This emerges as a key subtext of the entire set of conference documents available in the Rockefeller archives. Yet the lines between the three categories of conferee ought not to be drawn too starkly: there was a "revolving door" between the three worlds, and all the conferees had some policy-making or at least policy-related experience. The analysis below of the conferees' biographies demonstrates this and thereby fleshes out the Gramscian concept of state-spirited organic intellectuals. It also shows the high degree to which the conferees were interconnected or operated in elite networks.

The eleven conferees were, had been, or would be very well connected with U.S. state agencies ranging from the State Department and the Department of Defense to the Central Intelligence Agency. Put slightly differently, this group comprised the sort of people who operated within the boundaries of "thinkable thought" in American foreign-policy and national-security circles, and they were destined to be a part of the debate in those policy areas for decades to come, even if they opposed the Vietnam War, for example, as "flawed," as Morgenthau did.[38] They were part of an elite—not necessarily by birth but by personal achievement—whose significance rested not just with holding public office but with their continuous proximity, in numerous institutions, to public officials and other policy influentials. Nine members of the group had over twenty-five long-term connections with various agencies of the American state related to its foreign affairs or national security. The least connected of the group to the state was the journalist James Reston (*New York Times*), who had served with the Office of War Information during World War II. Even Reston, however, was very close to several administrations and to Henry Kissinger, Nixon's secretary of state. His fellow journalist, Walter Lippmann (*New York Herald Tribune*), had served in the Department of War during World War I, as a member of President Wilson's inquiry in 1917–1919, and as a delegate to the Paris Peace Conference in 1919. He is considered by many to have been the most respected foreign-affairs commentator of the twentieth century (Thompson 1980).

Conversely, other conferees, such as Paul Nitze and Dean Rusk, had long periods of service in the state and should certainly be regarded in career terms as "men of the state." Dean Rusk, who served two terms as secretary of state (1961–1969), served four presidents. He was a hawkish proponent of the Vietnam War (Cohen 1980). Nitze served presidents Roosevelt, Truman, and Eisenhower in the 1940s and 1950s, Kennedy and Johnson in the 1960s, Nixon and Ford in the 1970s, and Reagan in the 1980s. He was truly a servant of the American state. As head of policy planning in Secretary Acheson's State Department, Nitze was the principal author of NSC-68, the report that called for a massive U.S. rearmament program—tripling the federal military budget. Nitze was also instrumental in the public promotion of NSC-68 through the formation of the Committee on the Present Danger (CPD)—a group of hawkish liberal internationalists that included James Bryant Conant, president of Harvard, and Robert Bowie, another 1954 conference participant. The CPD masterminded among the public what NSC-68 had done in the Truman administration: bludgeoned the "mass mind" of top government, as Dean Acheson had wanted. Nitze recognized the fundamental significance of public-opinion mobilization in decisively shifting U.S. national-security policy (Sanders 1983).

It is remarkable that six members of the group had served or were otherwise associated as advisers with the Policy Planning Staff of the State Department: Paul Nitze (director, 1950–1953), Robert Bowie (director, 1953–1957), Dorothy Fosdick (1948–1952), Reinhold Niebuhr (1949), Arnold Wolfers (1949), and Hans Morgenthau (1949). While out of favor after Truman, Nitze directed the Foreign Service Educational Institute, which is often referred to as the "PPS in exile." The PPS

> serves as a source of independent policy analysis and advice for the Secretary of State. The Policy Planning Staff's mission is to take a longer term, strategic view of global trends and frame recommendations for the Secretary of State to advance U.S. interests and American values. . . . In his memoirs *Present at the Creation*, former Secretary of State Dean Acheson characterized the role of Policy Planning: "To anticipate the emerging form of things to come, to reappraise policies which had acquired their own momentum and went on after the reasons for them had ceased, and to stimulate and, when necessary, to devise basic policies crucial to the conduct of our foreign affairs."[39]

Dorothy Fosdick, the first senior woman in a policy position in the State Department, was appointed to serve on the PPS in 1948. She had previously served in the State Department's Division of Special Research, the department's first attempt at long-term planning during World War II. The PPS was essentially an internal think tank composed of state intellectuals with access to external advisers as required. Of the 1954 conferees, Niebuhr, Wolfers, and Morgenthau had acted as advisers to the PPS.

In addition to enduring and qualitatively significant connections with agencies of the state, several conferees were also connected to other institutions closely linked with the foreign-policy elements of the state. For example, there were at least eight members of the bipartisan Council on Foreign Relations, the establishment's core liberal internationalist think tank (Fox, Wolfers, Nitze, Reston, Niebuhr, Thompson, Rusk, and Bowie). Lippmann had been a member during the 1930s. Fosdick would have worked with CFR members during her years at the Division of Special Research, as that was where the CFR's War and Peace Studies were conducted (Shoup and Minter 1977). Niebuhr had been a leading figure in two key CFR organizations and had led pro-war ad hoc single-issue organizations in 1940 and 1941: the Committee to Defend America by Aiding the Allies and the even more hawkish Fight for Freedom (Chadwin 1968).

Connections with philanthropic foundations were also strong. Of course, the Rockefeller Foundation organized and hosted the conference. Dorothy Fosdick was closely associated with the Rockefeller family, which supported her father's Riverside Church in New York; her uncle, Raymond B. Fosdick, was president of the foundation from 1936 to 1948. Fosdick's work in the wartime State Department was closely connected with Rockefeller Foundation–backed foreign-policy planning initiatives by the Council on Foreign Relations from 1940 to 1945 (Parmar 2004). The Ford Foundation was represented at the conference by its vice president, Don Price, and the University of Chicago's Morgenthau was a long-time adviser to what is now known as the Carnegie Council on Ethics in International Affairs but was originally known as the Church Peace Union and, later, the Council on Religion and International Affairs. Price went on to become the founding dean of the Kennedy School of Government at Harvard.

Most of the conferees may be characterized or characterized themselves as one or another form of "realist." Nine conferees may be so categorized: realists (Morgenthau, Lippmann, Bowie, Wolfers), realist hawks (Rusk, Nitze), liberal realists (Fox, Fosdick), and Christian realist (Niebuhr). Although such a categorization is open to challenge,[40] what further bound the conferees was their underlying assumption of the importance of military force in world affairs and, particularly, in postwar U.S. foreign policy. Most of the conferees had been, of course, early twentieth-century Progressives— state builders armed with a sense of the importance of state regulation, rational policy making, and even a degree of planning. Their attitude in general toward the state and their "realistic" view of the world, therefore, combined to focus on *state power*, helping cement their ties with the American state as the principal vehicle for global leadership.

Finally, the long-lasting significance of the group of 1954 conferees is underlined by the fact that many still had a future in their chosen field: most of them were to continue in active service for many decades, indicating the enduring character of the foreign-policy elite. Paul Nitze was instrumental in resurrecting the second incarnation of the Committee on the Present Danger in 1976—and the third in 2002/2003. Nitze also served as special adviser to the president and as secretary of state in the Reagan administration. Dorothy Fosdick's long association—as aide and adviser— to Henry "Scoop" Jackson continued until his death in 1983. Upon her death in 1997, Richard Perle paid a tribute to her. The names of Reinhold Niebuhr and Hans Morgenthau, both of whom opposed the Vietnam War, were invoked on opposite sides of the bitter debates over the 2003 American war of aggression against Iraq (Mearsheimer 2005; Loconte 2002).

THE 1954 CONFERENCE

The content of the conference proceedings receives appropriate attention in the rest of this volume. My own attitude toward the proceedings stems from the core concern of this chapter: to suggest that the development of academic IR (along with many other older disciplines) was part of a broader, long-term foreign-policy establishment project to promote American globalism, to expand the American imperium, to usher in "the American century." The funding over decades of academic IR, other social sciences, university area-studies programs, and the sponsorship of relevant think tanks, and so on, as exemplified but not exhausted by the discussion of the YIIS, above, constituted the construction of the intellectual infrastructure for globalism. Wedded as this development was to the conception of the American century, it would ultimately, but not exclusively, be evaluated according to its outcomes, its impacts in producing the kinds of knowledge that American globalism was thought to "require." Of course, professional academics are neither pawns on a chessboard nor the playthings of elites; that is not the argument here.[41] However, when intellectual institutions and programs are financed, when the objective structures are established at the cost of hundreds of millions of dollars, there is a high degree of "hardwiring" into their very being the assumptions underlying their formation. These assumptions are also "policed" through the annual report to the philanthropic foundations. External factors do not entirely determine the evolution of an academic discipline, but they are very important to the kinds of scholars recruited and financed, the theories and methodologies favored, the directions of empirical research fostered and conducted, the networks within which prestige is sought, and, very significantly, the lines of enquiry that become marginal or marginalized.[42] The 1954 conference, viewed as a small step along the road to American globalism, was in its *broadest* sense consistent with past Rockefeller Foundation efforts. That it was not especially successful or productive is beside the point: it was not the only foundation initiative, and other U.S. philanthropies were also funding a whole series of initiatives at the same time (a kind of "basket" of investments by "venture capitalists"; Weaver 1967). Nevertheless, the central question of the relevance of academic theory to the practitioner was a very tough test for Morgenthau, Wolfers, and Fox.

Kenneth W. Thompson (1955, 733), a conference organizer and, later, a vice president of the Rockefeller Foundation, reported that policymakers want "'an applicable body of theory in foreign policy.' Practical men with first-hand diplomatic experience point to the need for rational generalizations and intellectual structures to extract meaning from the jet stream of contemporary events."[43] In particular, Paul Nitze asked some tough questions and raised serious concerns. In his view, "the immediate object of our foreign policy must be the fostering and elaboration of an international environment in which nations organized as we are can prosper and survive. The means to this end must be the development of the influence and power of ourselves and our friends and the reduction of the power of our enemies" (cited by Thompson 1955, 744n22). The policymaker, however, in trying to do this, must deal with concrete cases, while the theoretician deals in generalizations and abstractions. Nitze argued that "a wrong theory, an oversimplified theory, or a theory applied out of context can produce disastrous results" (Thompson 1955, 738).

Conversely, William Fox and Hans Morgenthau argued that while theory could not provide a blueprint for action in most concrete circumstances, it could achieve a great deal by ordering evidence: theory "gives order and meaning to a mass of phenomena which without it would remain disconnected and unintelligible. . . . [Theory] helps us to understand and distinguish the relatively fixed, the changing but controllable, and the manipulatable aspects of world politics" (Thompson 1955, 735). Theory is the basis of policy technology, in other words.

Rusk pointed out that when the Truman administration, of which he was part as assistant secretary of state for Far Eastern affairs, among other posts, considered the U.S. response to the outbreak of the Korean War, the predominant "theory," analogy, or mental image was derived from the 1930s—that is, Manchuria in 1931, Abyssinia in 1935, and Munich in 1938—and the consequences of appeasing aggressors.[44] Thompson's conclusion was to suggest that practitioners' "judgment and wisdom" often results from "a pragmatic conception of theory" that augurs well for continued and "wider contacts between theorists and practitioners." Both theorists and practitioners, he argues, each in their own language, accept that ideas and theories must be "tested" against experience. They just needed to be more creative in their interactions (Thompson 1955, 739).

CONCLUSION

The immediate benefits of the 1954 conference probably disappointed the participants. Certainly, Paul Nitze stated that he and his colleagues in Policy Planning felt "that much of the contemporary academic work in the theory of international politics fell between two stools. It did not have sufficient depth in philosophic insight to give much light on the question of the long range content of our national purpose and on the other hand much of it failed to meet the test of being relevant to the realm of possible action."[45] Yet, benefits there were, including making practitioners and academics more aware of each others' roles and problems, dissecting theory production and possible usages, introducing the complexity and difficulties inherent in crisis decision-making into academic theorizing, and suggesting ways forward to more fruitful future dialogue. Of course, one of the by-products of the conference on its academic participants was a greater understanding of practitioners' dilemmas—in a nuclear world— and the filtering down of that understanding to colleagues, graduate students, and so on. Nitze also—understandably from his experience of selling NSC-68 through the Committee on the Present Danger—called for greater academic attention to "public opinion and [specifically] in reducing the area of conflict between public understanding on the one hand and rational consideration of the national interest on the other."[46]

More concretely, participants suggested a number of initiatives to the Rockefeller Foundation to try to improve work in the theory/practice nexus: more seminars; subsidies to retired professors to write theoretical work in IR, as doctoral candidates usually wrote empirical theses; subsidies to university presses to encourage them to publish more theoretical work despite low demand; and the possibility of month-long summer meetings between academics and foreign-policy practitioners in Washington, D.C., to continue the 1954 dialogue.[47]

In the longer term, the 1954 conference may be seen as an attempt at initiating a major boost for organized discussion of IR theory in the United States and Britain. For example, Rockefeller followed up 1954 by funding a symposium on IR theorizing in 1957, the book of which published the papers of several 1954 conference participants—Nitze, Morgenthau, Fox, Wolfers, Niebuhr—and also Kenneth N. Waltz (Swarthmore) and Charles P. Kindleberger (MIT). In addition, participants in 1957 included Bernard Barber, Arno J. Mayer, Warner Schilling, Kenneth W. Thompson, Robert W. Tucker, and Martin Wight (Fox 1959, x). In 1959, a Rockefeller grant supported the formation of the British Committee on the Theory of International Politics, and in 1961 Fox, Morgenthau, Thompson, and Quincy Wright participated in a conference at the University of Maryland entitled "The Role of Theory in International Relations."[48] In the late 1950s, the Rockefeller Foundation—prompted by its vice president, Kenneth W.

Thompson—funded the British Committee on the Theory of International Politics. Interestingly, Tim Dunne (1998, 90) suggests—citing Thompson—that the American IR-theory group largely failed to achieve much beyond a couple of meetings due to "deep divisions" between foreign-policy makers and academics.

Ultimately, the discussions between scholarly *theorists* and policymakers are likely to be frustrating due to the differing ends of each. Nitze expressed an essential belief among "practical men" about the limitations of theory.[49] As Lewis Coser (1965, 135–136) argues,

> the relationship between power and intellect usually proved to be unstable. The general tension between the intellectuals' preoccupation with general and abstract values and the routine institutions of society asserted itself. Intellectuals tended to turn in disdain from the practical concerns of decision-makers immersed in day-to-day compromise and adjustments, and men of power were wary of what they called the impracticality and the lack of realism of intellectuals. Power holders and intellectuals have [enjoyed] short periods of honeymoon, but no stable union has ever been achieved.[50]

It is unsurprising, then, that the Rockefeller Foundation's IR-theory initiative—proposed by Rusk—faded away with the escalation of the Vietnam War, which was famously opposed by the realist Hans Morgenthau. For the foundation, however, the 1930s and 1940s development of IR may have achieved at least a key part of its original purpose: to place at the very center of scholarly thinking the importance of power and violence in world affairs,[51] the centrality of the state and, specifically, of U.S. state leadership—a hegemonic power to replace Britain—and the need, therefore, for the political class and people of the United States to accept those basic facts. Thereafter, the most pressing need may have been for scholars engaged in empirical IR and, particularly, foreign-area studies, who furnished voluminous empirical studies and developed powerful knowledge networks between the United States and the world's strategic nations and regions (Parmar 2002a). As Morgenthau noted in 1952:

> practical needs . . . still provide one of the major arguments in favor of area studies; they are also apparent in the selection of the areas most frequently studied. Russia and the Far East vie with Latin America . . . with those areas that American foreign policy is primarily concerned. . . . Aside from the training of prospective government officials, area studies are frequently mo-

tivated by the recognition of America's predominant place in world affairs, which . . . entails the desire to learn all the facts about all regions of the world.

(WALLERSTEIN 1997, 207–208)

In addition, in the bid for U.S. hegemony there was great demand for *economists* to work with "developing" the economies of newly independent Third World countries such as Indonesia, India, and Pakistan in the arena of cold-war ideological competition (Rosen 1985). Olson and Groom (1991, 106) note that the postwar period witnessed the emergence of "a 'paper triangle' between academic entrepreneurs, the great foundations, and the national security establishment. The principal effect . . . was to stress regional [country and area] and strategic studies." As ever, wherever the major foundations had made the initial investment, the federal government followed: the 1958 National Defense Education Act poured millions of dollars into area studies over the next twenty years, generating impressive advances in university foreign-language teaching, new professional associations and conferences, and so on. As a Social Science Research Council survey showed in 1973, "the centers and their faculties provide a repository of expertise on which government can and does draw for research, consultants, or temporary employment. . . . The government also uses these centers for the training of current employees" (Wallerstein 1997, 209–210). The cold-war university, then, served as a vehicle for the promotion of U.S. hegemony.[52]

The 1954 conference brought together some of the most significant elites in IR, the policy world, and foreign-affairs journalism. This was no random group but a subset of the confluence of elite forces identified by Olson and Groom. As individuals, they had already made a mark in American life: most of them continued for several decades to do so. The role of the major American philanthropic foundations was to foster a fairly narrow spectrum of intellectual developments in academic empirical research, theory, and methodology, with the ultimate underlying aim of promoting American hegemony. That the IR theory program was not particularly successful shows that foundation and other elites do not always get what they want. But what the program does show are the underlying principles for funding specific IR and other similar initiatives. Foundations provide the "seed corn" for new initiatives and finance the seminars and conferences between leading scholars, policymakers, and other elites. They finance knowledge networks—the intellectual infrastructure—that might generate new and useful ideas, new information, or new perspectives that would practically benefit policymakers, as well as useful knowledge. Sometimes they fail; sometimes they produce unintended consequences. Much of the time, they succeed in generating large university programs dedicated to research, teaching, and training, with scholars fully networked with state elites, that directly and indirectly benefit American hegemony.

NOTES

1. Extracts from NSC-68, "United States Objectives and Programs for National Security," the April 1950 seminal cold-war blueprint, the main author of which was Paul Nitze.

2. NSC-68.

3. This is not to suggest that there was no such thing as a "Soviet threat" or that there is no "terrorist threat" today. It is merely to argue that the threats were and are much exaggerated for political purposes, providing profound legitimacy for America's global expansionism. For analysis of the U.S. wartime planning for global expansion *before* there was any "Soviet threat," see Shoup and Minter (1977) and Parmar (2004).

4. Indeed, the overall stated aim of NSC-68 recognizes a desire "to foster a world environment in which the American system can flourish," arguing that that would be achieved through containment of the Soviet Union but is also "a policy we would probably pursue even if there were no Soviet threat . . . [a] policy of attempting to develop a healthy international community" of U.S.-dominated organizations, such as the IMF, World Bank, NATO, the Marshall Plan, the Inter-American system, and so on. As Thomas G. Paterson (1989, 352) argues, the Truman administration exaggerated the Soviet threat to justify "its own expansionism" and desire to "practice global interventionism" for decades.

5. Henry "Scoop" Jackson was a Democratic congressman and senator from Washington State (1941–1983) and mentor to the likes of Richard Perle, Douglas Feith, and Paul Wolfowitz.

6. IR was not alone, however, as a discipline in part designed to serve elite interests: there were similar factors at work in other social sciences such as political science, area studies, and economics. See, for example, Oren (2003).

7. Of course, not all realists believed in U.S. global hegemony—and Morgenthau is an example—but a very large proportion of realism's founders did.

8. That this was part of a broader concern among American East Coast elites is evidenced by Henry Kissinger's Harvard International Seminar, designed to convince foreign elites of the depth of U.S. national culture and, thereby, the credibility of U.S. power. See Parmar (2006).

9. An excellent example of this is the Rockefeller Foundation's funding of the Council on Foreign Relations' War and Peace Studies Project (1940–1945), which helped not only increase state planning capacity but also helped develop a sense of America's postwar ambitions for global hegemony (which included international institution building, particularly the United Nations). What this shows is that Rockefeller Foundation funds were used to construct a sense of national interests that would,

in part, be realized through international organizations mistakenly often seen as the preserve of "idealist" Wilsonians. See Shoup and Minter (1977).

10. Coser (1965, 339) names Dean Rusk, Dean Acheson, and John Foster Dulles as examples of the interconnections of foundation heads and the American state.

11. Karl Marx, cited by Ralph Miliband (1984, 162–163). Marx further noted that "the class which is the ruling material force of society, is at the same time its ruling intellectual force."

12. The consent of the governed is "organized. . . . The State does have and request consent, but it also 'educates' this consent, by means of the political and syndical associations; these, however," Gramsci concludes, "are private organisms, left to . . . private initiative." Cited in Parmar (2004).

13. The eighteenth-century conservative political theorist Edmund Burke noted that a key part of the state's stability was derived from a partnership "not only between those who are living, but between those who are living, those who are dead, and those who are to be born"; see his *Reflections on the Revolution in France* (1986 [1790], 194–195).

14. It is clear, however, that YIIS was not the only IR initiative sponsored by the Rockefeller and Carnegie foundations. See Parmar (2001).

15. Yale University—International Relations, funding notes, 17 May 1935 and 16 May 1941, Folder 4941, Box 416, Series 2005, Research Group (RG) 1.1, Rockefeller Foundation Archives, Rockefeller Archive Center, Sleepy Hollow, N.Y. (hereafter designated RG).

16. Neutrality Acts were passed in 1935, 1936, 1937, and 1939. At the same time, movements to revise those laws also began. See Chadwin (1968) and Parmar (2000).

17. See Yale Institute Annual Report, 1942 in Yale University—International Relations, Folder 4957, Box 417, Series 2005, RG 1.1, Rockefeller Foundation Archives, RAC.

18. See Inter-Office memo by J. H. Willits, 29.2.40; letter, Frederick S. Dunn (Director of YIIS) to Willits, 2.6.41; letter, Dunn to Willits, 11.8.44; and YIIS annual report, 1938–1939, 3; all in Folders 4944, 4947, and 4955, Boxes 416 and 417. See also Fox (1966) for the policy-oriented character of YIIS, of which Fox was a member.

19. Memorandum, "Yale University—Research in International Relations," March 6, 1940, Folder 4944, Box 416, Series 2005, RG 1.1, Rockefeller Foundation Archives, RAC.

20. Figures compiled from annual reports and other internal Rockefeller Foundation sources.

21. Memo, 29 February 1940. Folder 4944, Box 416, Series 2005, RG 1.1, Rockefeller Foundation Archives, RAC. According to Fox, Dunn's motive, to advance practical knowledge to enhance U.S. national security, was what ensured foundation support. The foundation's director of the division of social sciences, Joseph H. Willits, wrote that Spykman's ideas showed wisdom, maturity, "hard-headedness, realism and scholarly standards"; cited in Olson and Groom (1991, 50–51).

22. YIIS *Annual Report*, 3–4, 1942.

23. YIIS *Annual Report*, 1–4, 1942 (italics mine).

24. Memorandum, "A Security Policy for Postwar America," March 8, 1945, Folder 4948, Box 417, Series 2005, RG 1.1, Rockefeller Foundation Archives, RAC.

25. See review, "The Gyroscope of Pan-Americanism," November 1943, Folder 4946. Box 416, Series 2005, RG 1.1, Rockefeller Foundation Archives, RAC. Written by the historian Samuel Flagg Bemis, it was entitled *The Latin American Policy of the United States* and published in 1943. The book, as described by a foundation re-

viewer, was "readable and provocative." Bemis claimed that U.S. policy toward Latin America was a benevolent or "protective imperialism, designed to protect, first the security of the Continental Republic . . . and the security of the entire New World, against intervention by the imperialistic powers of the Old World." It was, he continued, "an imperialism against imperialism. It did not last long and it was not really bad."

26. Dunn to Willits, August 1944, Folder 4947, Box 412, Series 2005, RG 1.1, Rockefeller Foundation Archives, RAC.

27. *Annual Report* 1941–1942, p.18–19; p. 25.

28. *Annual Report* 1945–1946.

29. RFA, *Annual Report*, 14–15, 1943.

30. Almond was a member of YIIS.

31. Lambert Davis (Harcourt, Brace) to George W. Gray (Rockefeller Foundation), Folder 4945, Box 416, Series 2005, RG 1.1, Rockefeller Foundation Archives, RAC. (So influential that it was also produced in Braille.)

32. Folder 4945, Box 416, Series 2005, RG 1.1, Rockefeller Foundation Archives, RAC.

33. Spykman cited in Ramos (2003, 242).

34. "Radio Program Notice," April 6, 1945, Folder 4948, Box 417, Series 2005, RG 1.1, Rockefeller Foundation Archive, RAC .

35. That YIIS members were so engaged with the formation of the United Nations correctly suggests that the fledgling international organization was seen, at least in part, as a potential instrument of American power. See Shoup and Minter (1977) and R. Hilderbrand (1990).

36. Olson and Groom (1991, 118) claim that the publication of this journal was "one of the most significant events in the history of the field" of international relations.

37. The move to Princeton followed the inauguration in 1950 of A. Whitney Griswold as president of Yale. Griswold was opposed to YIIS' policy-oriented work and, especially, its advocacy of globalism. Griswold also had a number of personal differences with Frederick Dunn. See Ramos (2003).

38. It is important here to recall that Morgenthau (1952, 1965) supported the view that the Soviet "threat" drove U.S. national-security policy and that it was an authentic threat requiring "containment," but he also felt that it was inappropriately and badly applied in Asia. To be sure, such sentiments placed Morgenthau close to the boundaries of "thinkable thought" but still within them. See Chomsky (1982, 74).

39. See http://www.state.gov/s/p/.

40. "Realism" is not an uncontested term or categorization: there are political realists, liberal realists, defensive realists, offensive realists, neorealists, democratic realists, and structural realists, among others. The core of realism, though, is the recognition that power is central to international affairs and that whatever our ethical position or values may be, without understanding the structure and dynamics of power in the world, a realist foreign policy or a realistic understanding of the world is impossible. On those grounds, men like Rusk and Nitze are "offensive realists" in practice, maximizers of American power attempting to ensure its global hegemony. For the most developed version of offensive realism, see Mearsheimer (2001) and Jervis (2004). For an interesting history of the misrepresentation of protagonists in the great debates of IR, see Kahler (1997, 20–53).

41. For an argument that challenges this interpretation, see the contribution by Brian C. Schmidt in this volume.

42. Coser (1965, 339) argues that foundations are "important gatekeepers of ideas. With the power of the purse, they are in positions to foster certain ideas or lines of inquiry while neglecting or de-emphasizing others."

43. This is a direct quotation from Dean Rusk's opening remarks at the 1954 conference; "Conference on International Politics," transcript, 240.

44. Rusk stated that "in the State Department with regard to the Korea situation, their general policy was based a good deal on what they had learned about aggression in the last 25 years." "Conference on International Politics," transcript, 251 (appendix 1 of this volume).

45. Paul Nitze, "The Implications of Theory for Practice in the Conduct of Foreign Affairs" (appendix 5 of this volume, 279).

46. Ibid., 5.

47. See "Conference on International Politics," transcript, 260–62; Arnold Wolfers, "Theory of International Politics: Its Merits and Advancement" (appendix 6 of this volume).

48. Schmidt, unpublished notes; see also Harrison (1964), the book of the 1961 conference.

49. The same appears to be the case today. As Stanley A. Renshon (2007, 293) argues, "there is [a] substantial gap between the contributions of professional international theory and research and the necessity of actual judgments under uncertainty."

50. The sociologist Robert Merton put it more strongly when he suggested that "the union of policy-makers and intellectuals tends to be nasty, brutish and short" (cited in Coser 1965, 140).

51. Olson and Groom (1991, 104–134) argue that "power" constituted the mainstream IR consensus by the 1950s, even if the self-same scholars backed the UN Charter.

52. This development was hardly new. See Gruber (1975).

REFERENCES

Almond, Gabriel A. 2002. Area studies and the objectivity of the social sciences. In *Ventures in political science*, ed. G. Almond, 109–130. Boulder: Lynne Rienner.

Arnove, Robert F, ed. 1980. *Philanthropy and cultural imperialism*. Boston: G. K. Hall.

Augelli, E., and C. Murphy. 1988. *America's quest for supremacy and the Third World. A Gramscian analysis*. London: Pinter.

Barnett, R. J. 1973. *Roots of war*. Baltimore, Md.: Penguin.

Barrow, C. W. 1990. *Universities and the capitalist state. Corporate liberalism and the reconstruction of American higher education, 1894–1928*. Madison: University of Wisconsin Press.

Campbell, D. 1998. *Writing security*. Manchester: Manchester University Press.

Chadwin, M. L. 1968. *The hawks of World War II*. Chapel Hill: University of North Carolina Press.

Chomsky, N. 1982. *Towards a new cold war*. New York: Pantheon.

Cohen, W. I. 1980. *Dean Rusk*. Totowa, N.J.: Cooper Square.

Coser, L. 1965. *Men of ideas*. New York: Free Press.

Dunne, T. 1998. *Inventing international society: A history of the English School*. Basingstoke: Macmillan.

Eisenach, E. J. 1994. *The lost promise of Progressivism*. Lawrence: University Press of Kansas.

Engermann, D. C. 1999. New society, new scholarship: Soviet studies programmes in interwar America. *Minerva* 37: 25–43.

Fox, W. T. R., ed. 1959. *Theoretical aspects of international relations*. Notre Dame, Ind.: University of Notre Dame Press.

Gruber, C. S. 1975. *Mars and Minerva: World War I and the uses of higher learning in America*. Baton Rouge: Louisiana State University Press.

Harrison, H. V., ed. 1964. *The role of theory in international relations*. Princeton, N.J.: D. Van Nostrand.

Hilderbrand, R. 1990. *Dumbarton Oaks: The origins of the UN and the search for postwar security*. Chapel Hill: University of North Carolina Press.

Hoare, Q., and G. Nowell-Smith, eds. 1971. *Selections from the prison notebooks of Antonio Gramsci*. London: Lawrence and Wishart.

Hodgson, G. 1972–1973. The establishment. *Foreign Policy* 9: 3–40.

Holland, M. 1991. Citizen McCloy. *Wilson Quarterly* 15: 22–42.

Jackson, R. 2005. *Writing the war on terrorism*. Manchester: Manchester University Press.

Jervis, R. L. 2004. *American foreign policy in a new era*. New York: Routledge.

Kahler, M. Inventing international relations: International relations theory after 1945. In *New thinking in international relations theory*, ed. M. W. Doyle and G. John Ikenberry, 20–53. Boulder, Colo.: Westview.

Leuchtenberg, W. E. 1952–1953. Progressivism and imperialism. *Mississippi Valley Historical Review* 39: 483–504.

Loconte, J. 2002. The war party's theologian. President Bush carries on the liberal tradition of Reinhold Niebuhr. http://www.opinionjournal.com/taste/?id=110001782.

Mearsheimer, J. J. 2001. *The tragedy of great power politics*. New York: W. W. Norton.

———. 2005. Hans Morgenthau and the Iraq war: Realism versus neo-conservatism. http://www.opendemocracy.net/democracy-americanpower/morgenthau_2522.jsp.

Melman, S. 1985. *A permanent war economy*. New York: Simon and Schuster.

Miliband, R. 1984. *The state in capitalist society*. London: Quartet Books.

Morgenthau, H. J. 1952. The national interest of the United States. *American Political Science Review* 46: 961–988.

———. 1965. We are deluding ourselves in Vietnam. *New York Times Magazine* (April 18).

Morton, L. 1963. National security and area studies. The intellectual response to the cold war. *Journal of Higher Education* 34: 142–147.

Olson, W. C., and A. J. R. Groom. 1991. *International relations then and now*. London: Routledge.

Oren, Ido. 2003. *Our enemies and US: America's rivalries and the making of political science*. Ithaca, N.Y.: Cornell University Press.

Parmar, I. 2000. Engineering consent: The Carnegie Endowment for International Peace and the mobilisation of American public opinion, 1939–1945. *Review of International Studies* 26: 35–48.

———. 2001. Edward Meade Earle and the rise of realism in the United States Academy. Manchester Papers in Politics, paper 3/01, Department of Government, University of Manchester.

———. 2002a. American foundations and the development of international knowledge networks. *Global Networks* 2: 13–30.

———. 2002b. "To relate knowledge and action": The impact of the Rockefeller Foundation on foreign policy thinking during America's rise to globalism. *Minerva* 40: 235–263.

———. 2004. *Think tanks and power in foreign policy*. Basingstoke: Palgrave.

———. 2006. Challenging elite anti-Americanism in the cold war: American foundations, Kissinger's Harvard seminar and the Salzburg seminar in American studies. *Traverse* 1: 116–129.

Paterson, T. G. 1989. *Major problems in American foreign policy.* Vol. 2: *Since 1914.* Lexington, Mass.: D. C. Heath.

Polsby, N. W. 1993. Foreign policy establishment moves to middle. *Public Affairs Report* 34, no. 1: 12–13.

Ramos, P. 2003. The role of the YIIS in the construction of United States national security ideology, 1935–1951. Ph.D. dissertation, University of Manchester.

Renshon, S. A. 2007. Premature obituary: The future of the Bush doctrine. In *Understanding the Bush doctrine,* ed. Stanley A. Renshon and Peter Suedfeld, 289–318. New York: Routledge.

Reynolds, D. 1991. *Britannia overruled: British policy and world power in the twentieth century.* London: Longman.

Roberts, P. 1992. "All the right people": The historiography of the American foreign policy establishment. *Journal of American Studies* 26: 409–434.

Rosen, G. 1985. *Western economists and Eastern societies.* Baltimore, Md.: The Johns Hopkins University Press.

Rosenberg, E. S. 1982. *Spreading the American dream.* New York: Hill and Wang.

Sanders, J. W. 1983. *Peddlers of crisis: The committee on the present danger and the politics of containment.* London: Pluto.

Shoup, L., and W. Minter. 1977. *Imperial brain trust.* New York: Monthly Review Press.

Thompson, J. A. 1992. Another look at the downfall of "fortress America." *Journal of American Studies* 26: 393–408.

Thompson, K. W. Toward a theory of international politics. *American Political Science Review* 49: 733–746.

———. 1980. *Masters of international thought.* Baton Rouge: Louisiana State University Press.

Weaver, W., ed. 1955. *U.S. philanthropic foundations.* New York: Harper and Row, 1967.

Wiebe, R. H. 1980. *The search for order, 1877–1920.* Westport, Conn.: Greenwood.

8

REALISM AND NEOLIBERALISM

From Reactionary Modernism to
Postwar Conservatism

PHILIP MIROWSKI

BRIAN LAMB: Dr. Milton Friedman, why did you choose or why did they
ask you to write the introduction to the F. A. Hayek *Road to Freedom*
fiftieth anniversary . . .

MILTON FRIEDMAN: *Road to Serfdom.*

LAMB: Yes, that's your title on your book. Why did you do it?

FRIEDMAN: The reason they asked me was very clear, because Hayek and I
had been associated for a very long time, in particular in an organization
called the Mont Pèlerin Society that he founded. The charter meeting
was in 1947 in Switzerland. Hans Morgenthau, who was a professor at
the University of Chicago when I was there, a political scientist, when I
came back from the meeting, he asked me where I had been, and I told
him that I had been to a meeting that had been called by Hayek to try to
bring together the believers in a free, open society and enable them to
have some interchange, one with another. He said, "Oh, a meeting of the
veterans of the wars of the nineteenth century!" I thought that was a
wonderful description of the Mont Pèlerin Society.[1]

The documents gathered together for the first time in this volume shed
new light on the origins of what was destined to become the discipline of
"international relations" within the postwar field of academic social sciences and on the birth of what later became designated as the "realist"
school of IR. On those grounds alone they will prove of great interest to
historians of the discipline, as well as to diplomatic historians, as ably testified by the other contributions to this volume. But there is another way in
which one can come to appreciate the implications of the documentary
evidence of this meeting in 1954, one that seeks to identify it as symptomatic of a larger political project that had begun to germinate out of the ru-
ins of World War II. This project, which was not narrowly confined within

any particular disciplinary boundaries, although it was rather overrepresented on the campus of the University of Chicago in the immediate postwar period (Gunnell 1993, 131), was built around an across-the-board critique of American liberalism as being ill prepared to meet the postwar challenges of a treacherous and temerarious world.[2] Intellectuals who had considered themselves of a principled and conservative bent, far from feeling at home in the new world order, found themselves instead appalled by the dominant politics of the land of the victors. Not surprisingly, many European scholars uprooted by the twin siroccos of the Great Depression and the Nazi accession to power who ended up in the United States circa 1950 felt oppressed (if not outright disgusted) at the upbeat triumphalism, the shallow scientism, and Lil' Bo Peep liberalism that they felt engulfing them, and they wondered what could be done to counter what they perceived as the naïveté and utter lack of sophistication of their newfound comrades. In one sense, that is the crux of the story behind the anecdote that prefaces this paper.

There, someone who would become one of the main protagonists of our 1954 meeting, the political scientist Hans Morgenthau, confronted his fellow Chicago faculty member, the economist Milton Friedman, hard upon the heels of the first meeting of the organization that would become the incubator of postwar neoliberalism. The émigré Morgenthau seems to disparage the enthusiasm for classical liberalism on the part of the native-born Friedman, who later recounted his disdain as a badge of courage. But nothing back then was actually as it first seems. For beyond the obligatory genuflections in the direction of the Scots Enlightenment, the founder and intellectual impetus behind Mont Pèlerin, Friedrich Hayek, in fact conceived of the mandate of that society as a thoroughgoing critique and reformulation of classical liberalism for a new age, a revision and recalibration of political theory, taking the lessons of the Great Depression and Nazism into account. That description could just as easily be applied to Morgenthau as well, and it comes close to the retrospective position taken by his intellectual biographer (Frei 2001), as well as others familiar with the European background (Sollner 1987, 165; Hoffmann 1981, 657). Moreover, for some contemporaries, Hayek's best-selling *Road to Serfdom* was yoked together with Morgenthau's *Scientific Man Versus Power Politics* (1946) as constituting evidence of a "chain of reaction" propagating out of the University of Chicago (Nash 2006, 60). After all, in the anecdote Friedman appeared to be on good terms with Morgenthau, which at least hints at some important commonalities. So perhaps there existed at least as many similarities as there were differences between the nascent program of "realism" in IR and the nascent political program of neoliberalism: both were concertedly transnational; both were distressed at the state of contemporary political theory; both were heavily inflected with German social thought (although prudently managing to disguise that fact in the American context); both were concerned to recast "conservatism" in a sleek, modernist, forward-looking idiom for the Sputnik Age (and *not* to pine for a return to some nineteenth-century Golden Age); and ultimately, at least within the disciplinary precincts of IR, they both apparently shared sufficient conceptual DNA to subsequently produce a "neo-neo synthesis"[3] within a generation.

Hence there is some reason to suspect that a comparison of the early histories of realism in IR and neoliberalism at Mont Pèlerin in the period surrounding the Rockefeller Conference can help us come to grips with the tortured quest for a "theory of politics" so evident in the transcripts. It might also open up the existing history of IR to larger contemporary cultural developments, which appear to have been lacking in previous accounts. We begin by briefly describing the phenomenon of German "reactionary modernism" of the 1920s and 1930s, which we will suggest were a major source of inspiration for both Morgenthau's realism and Hayek's neoliberalism. Their shared heritage lay in a parallel concern with the prospects for rational political action when faced with the breakdown of liberal politics, something that came naturally to those who had lived to see the dissolution of the Weimar Republic. We then turn to a brief summary of Hayek's trajectory, in part based upon Mirowski (2007). Finally, we return to IR in the shape of Morgenthau's early intellectual development, comparing and contrasting his position with Hayek. We shall suggest that while their respective solutions to the problem of liberal order were at loggerheads in some respects, as the Friedman-Morgenthau encounter hints, they also shared some profound common denominators, most notably dependence upon a fortified state to resist the perils of democracy. We conclude with some quick observations on how this curious consanguinal relationship then played itself out in the later history of IR after the 1954 conference.

"THE ANTI-INTELLECTUALISM OF THE INTELLECTUALS"

Jeffrey Herf (1984) has provided an intriguing characterization of a broad swathe of political thought in Germany from World War I through the

Nazi era. He identified an intellectual construct called "reactionary modernism," which he associated with figures as diverse as Hans Freyer, Ernst Jünger, Carl Schmitt, Werner Sombart, and Oswald Spengler. The key common denominator for this position was an attempt to reconcile nostalgic strains of German romanticism with modernist technological means-ends rationalism. Herf's book provides evidence of numerous cultural figures of that era taking note of what appeared to be a novel conceptual trend: Thomas Mann, for instance, is quoted as expressing his dismay toward "a highly technological romanticism." Herf was especially concerned to locate this phenomenon as an artifact of what he considered to be the odd and exceptional situation of Weimar Germany, with its uneasy combination of advanced industry and poorly developed political franchise, but on the whole, he did not directly tackle political or economic history.

Herf's focus on intellectual history sometimes left something to be desired in terms of empirical support for his broad claims, and thus other historians have taken up related lines of inquiry in examinations of debates about industrial rationalization in early twentieth-century Germany, metaphorical descriptions of the human body as a machine (Rabinbach 1992), enthusiasm for aviation and military equipment (Rennenberg and Walker 1994), and widespread demands for an ethos of *Sachlichkeit* (sobriety, or matter-of-factness; Trommler 1996) that celebrated the functionality of the machine as an exemplary model for individual conduct. Some philosophers have also taken to rounding out its metaphysical outlines (Cooper 1999). Although we cannot deal with them here, these approaches have demonstrated the pervasiveness of a particular perspective on science within German thought and culture, complementing the scholarship that emphasizes that the National Socialists strove to foster an "alternative modernity" that blended a disdain for rationalism, individualism, parliamentarianism, and feminism with a fascination for mass politics, social engineering, eugenics, productivism, and technology. These studies have greatly enhanced our knowledge of how the Nazi movement appropriated and reshaped one version of enthusiasm for twentieth-century technology as an interventionist social doctrine, so as to recast itself as an exemplary "modern" project.

For our current purposes, it will suffice to quickly sketch some of the major components of the reactionary-modernist (RM) arsenal of doctrines. On the "modernist" side of the account, these thinkers tended to exalt the free creative spirit who would leave behind the plodding bourgeois souls that constitute the masses by refusing to accept any limits to their ambitions. Although this ideology had its obvious roots in the Kantian quest for the free authentic self, it tended to then adopt the Nietzschean line of the triumph of the will over mere reason and thus elevate the spirit above the mundane constraints of the dictates of physical limitations. A fascination with the technics of power became the acceptable face of this inclination, thus avoiding the temptation to descend into utter solipsism. Interestingly enough, this tended to be propounded in the context of a critique of philosophical positivism and a defense of absolutes posited to exist beyond rational justification. Those aspects then dovetailed within RM with a political romanticism that tended to denigrate the dominance of reason in political and social affairs and, in particular, sought to expel "science" from that realm. It displayed contempt for the tawdry give and take of interest-group politics and, to some extent, for any participation in politics by the superior intellects to whom the spirit of the nation owed its ongoing metempsychosis. In RM, there always persisted a subtext of powerful forces driving events behind or beyond the realm of appearances; only the elect could handle this awareness of the true sources of dynamism propelling the nation forward through history. This ineluctably evasive doctrine has since earned the sobriquet "the anti-intellectualism of the intellectuals" for RM (Herf 1984, 28).

RM was an avowedly antiutilitarian doctrine, which went some distance in explaining its predilection to abandon much of the specific content of the nineteenth-century tradition of political liberalism and renounce the relevance of neoclassical economics. Sometimes this tended to become conflated or confused with a more aesthetic version of modernism, with its reification of the self-referential character of practice, the focus on the Promethean individual to the detriment of the collective, and the ultimate suppression of attention to the political and material conditions that serve to support and maintain everyday activity.[4] Hence there existed a tendency within RM to sporadically approach politics as a quasi-aesthetic phenomenon and to subtly shift its definition of success from the art of the attainable to the art of the spectacle or the technical management of expectations. As Walter Benjamin so astutely observed, "fascism sees its salvation in giving the masses not their rights but instead a chance to express themselves" (quoted in Herf 1984, 34).

With the defeat of the Nazis, explicit expression of RM sentiments became *verboten* pretty much everywhere, but that should not be taken to mean that strong elements of RM doctrines nevertheless did not make their way into deep into the psyche of American postwar conservative thought. Indeed, much of the infusion of continental philosophy into postwar American social science carried with it, to a greater or lesser degree, the marks of RM ideas. This admission has taken quite a while to be absorbed and digested in the late twentieth century, although the extensive literature on the influence of Carl Schmitt on legal, political, and economic thought has been one of the most prominent beachheads of this realization.[5] Less appreciated, I believe, is the notion that RM formed the necessary background conditions of existence for the early expressions of the political doctrines both of realism in IR and of neoliberalism in the context of the Mont Pèlerin Society. True, there have been a few writers who have pointed to the close proximity of Hans Morgenthau to some of the more prominent RM theorists in his early career (Sollner 1987; Gusejnova 2006; Scheuerman 1999), but on the whole they have not taken it upon themselves to further explore the ways in which Morgenthau's version of realism embodied various RM tenets.[6] Morgenthau himself notoriously accused Schmitt of stealing some of his own ideas (in Thompson and Myers 1984, 16). Historians internal to the IR profession have proven much more willing to look to Weber and Nietzsche for assistance in understanding Morgenthau than to seriously examine RM thinkers.[7] The Nietzschean doctrine of the will to power was, of course, an important precursor for RM, but the Weberian stress on means-ends rationality was something that RM tended to repudiate (Cooper 1999).

The current state of play when it comes to understanding Hayek is, if anything, even more rudimentary, given the contemporary outpouring of hagiographic literature seeking to ennoble his role as the father of modern neoliberalism. To your average denizen of the Heritage Foundation or the Manhattan Institute, it might seem the height of perversity to suggest that the writer who equated the Nazis with the communists in his best-seller *The Road to Serfdom* might have himself borne a tempered respect for RM theory, to the point of owing it some recognizable debts. Nonetheless, that is indeed one thesis that we will propound in this paper.

The reader of the transcripts herein of the May 1954 discussions cannot help but notice the way the individuals gathered there kept circling back to the vexed concepts of "theory," "rationality," and "science." I suppose the modern reader will find them dissatisfying to the point of frustration, since the principals cannot seem to arrive at sufficient common ground to erect those very platforms from which to launch the project they all clearly yearn for: that is, a dedicated discipline devoted to international politics.[8] The disconnect becomes palpable when they turn to Morgenthau, as they so frequently do, to supply them with the parameters within which a "general theory" will operate. We would suggest that much of their frustration can be traced to the fact that many of the Americans present tended to equate science and rationality with physics (as Niebuhr says, "natural science laws") and instinctively sought to appropriate it as a weapon with which to indict their enemies for "irrationality," whereas Morgenthau often was speaking an alien dialect of RM. As he says, "many possible lines of action are available for the policy-maker in determining how he can act rationally" (transcript, appendix 1 of this volume, 254). It is fascinating to contemplate the extensive work of translation required within the American context to convert this essentially decisionist RM concept of rationality into something that later became known as "realism"; in America, the "real" was recruited to stand in as the polar opposite to the "volitional." But in the interim, the slippage in idiom opened a space for Morgenthau to be regarded as an original and profound thinker, someone who was continually pulling the rug out from under those who sought to reduce international politics to a set of legalistic maxims or moralistic precepts.

Yet there was more than one way to undermine the faith in the integrity of the apparently straightforward determinate rational act; that is why it becomes enlightening to juxtapose the Hayekian neoliberals to the Morgenthau realists. It is noteworthy that Walter Lippmann was present by invitation both at the creation of neoliberalism—the forerunner of Mont Pèlerin was the "Colloque Walter Lippmann" in 1938[9]—and at the birth of realism, in the 1954 meeting documented herein. For both sets of political thinkers, Lippmann appeared to be the acceptable Western face of something very much resembling RM and hence a pretext for its pipeline into the American context. Not only had Lippmann been arguing for the doctrine, so resonant with the conservative soul, that economic planning would inevitably lead to totalitarian government but that, ironically,

> the American people as a whole have never consistently believed that all their interests could be placed unreservedly at the disposal of the people, however refined their representation. . . . They have not believed wholeheartedly that democracy was safe for the world. This unbelief is, I believe, an intuition that there is something lacking in the theory of democracy, that somewhere the doctrine of popular sovereignty as conceived by its apostles is inconsistent with essential facts of human experience.
>
> (LIPPMANN 1965, 15)

In 1932, he was already arguing that democracy and international diplomacy were incompatible bedfellows and that "there did not exist, and there does not exist, a workable system of democratic diplomacy" (Lippmann

1965, 370). Soon after the Rockefeller seminar, he would write in his *Public Philosophy*:

> Devitalization of the governing power is the malady of democratic states. As the malady grows the executives become highly susceptible to encroachment and usurpation by elected assemblies; they are pressed and harassed by the haggling of parties, by the agents of organized interests, and by the spokesmen of sectarians and ideologues. The malady can be fatal. It can be deadly to the survival of the state as a free society if, when the great issues of war and peace, of security and solvency, of revolution and order are up for decision, the executive and political departments, with their civil servants and technicians, have lost the power to decide.
>
> (LIPPMANN 1965, 465)

Here, emanating from the very citadel of liberalism, was a respected popular figure arguing that it was not possible to legislate or otherwise deploy political action in an entirely rational fashion, that liberalism and democracy might be at loggerheads, that democracy only debilitated stable international relations, and therefore one should unconditionally delegate substantial portions of political action to various elites on decisionist grounds. It is no accident the Lippmann also pioneered the terminology of the "cold war," since he could be regarded as searching for (an almost oxymoronic) double-truth doctrine—one for the masses, another for the elites—that would resonate with the predicament that some elite sectors of American society felt acutely in that era. Both the nascent neoliberals and the budding realists found this concoction irresistible, although one cannot help but notice that Lippmann himself kept his distance from both projects once they had gotten off the ground.

HAYEK AS REACTIONARY MODERNIST

We shall set out our approach to the issue of the neoliberal debt to reactionary modernism here as an exercise in synecdoche by focusing exclusively upon the work of Friedrich Hayek[10] and then strive to highlight the ways in which Hayek resembled Morgenthau in broad philosophical orientation. Clearly we cannot do justice to the whole range of Hayek's thought nor even fully take into account the distinct ways in which he changed his fundamental philosophical stance at least twice in his career.[11] Neither can we document a rich intellectual interplay between the contemporary positions of Hayek and Morgenthau, because it seems there was very little record of personal interaction. Although they did overlap on the Chicago faculty, they almost never cite each other in their writings.

Nevertheless, we shall propose that examination of Hayek's predicament helps us situate Morgenthau's role in the formation of IR (and his participation in the 1954 conference) in an entirely different light. In particular, we want to stress the way that the both of them (by different paths) came to advocate the proposition that politics was not reducible to "reason," yet, against all odds, both fostered the development of "epistemic communities" that would develop their insights. Precisely because they were both steeped in the RM tradition, it was taken as given that the masses and the intellectuals could not be trusted to act rationally, and therefore social theory had to relinquish its Pollyanna liberalism and forge special doctrines that would ensure what each considered to be rational political action. Neither ever mistook "voting" for "democracy." In the RM tradition, both were vocal antipositivists yet managed to appeal to "Nature" in the course of promoting what they insisted was "science"—after both had gone through an early phase of denouncing "scientism." Both felt that political activities of the liberal state had to be restrained by the arm's-length intervention of experts, who would themselves nonetheless maintain their disengagement from sordid politics. Both were staunchly opposed to utilitarianism, although for very different reasons. And in a quest most characteristic of RM, both sought the solution to the crises of liberalism that they saw all around them in their own particular vision of a strong state, often intimately informed by the doctrines of Carl Schmitt, although one must concede that the outlines of that ideal state subsequently diverged fairly dramatically between the realists and the neoliberals.

Perhaps the quickest way to begin to understand Hayek as an RM theorist is to comprehend how he came to believe that the intellectuals serving as high priests of reason had become a fifth column undermining freedom from within. His solution involved a species of authoritarian control over a peculiar version of irrationalism.

Hayek's began his career steeped in the positivism of Ernst Mach. Most of the positivists whom Hayek encountered in Vienna were avid socialists: As Rudolf Carnap testified, "most of us [in the Vienna Circle], myself included, were socialists. But we liked to keep our philosophical work separated from our political claims" (1963, 23). The one exception to this latter reticence was Otto Neurath, who openly championed positivism as a means to socialist (but not conventionally Marxist) ends. At the other end of the spectrum stood Ludwig Wittgenstein, with whom Hayek was acquainted. He was claimed by the Vienna Circle as one of their own but was left cold by socialism and harbored a deep streak of what Neurath disparaged as the "philosophy of the ineffable": for Wittgenstein, "a language which had not grown organically seemed to him not only useless, but despicable" (Carnap 1963, 26). This must have fostered some cognitive dissonance for Hayek, who had set out regarding himself as subscribing to the project of a scientific understanding of first, psychology, and later, society.

While in Vienna, this lurking contradiction might not chafe so insistently, but what was a minor irritation there became a debilitating syndrome once Hayek moved to London to accept a chair at the London School of Economics in 1932. There, the issue was not so much the dominance of abstract positivism as a philosophical position as it was the almost ubiquitous association of the "scientific method" with socialist ambitions. Many of Hayek's formative political activities in this period were not aimed at Marxists per se as they were at *scientists* who were promoting socialism as the logical extrapolation of a scientific worldview. Among other activities that I would cite as pivotal was Hayek's participation in the founding of the "Society for Freedom in Science" and his attempt to ally himself with Michael Polanyi to argue for an entirely different portrait of the operation of science (McGucken 1984). It was during this period that an RM-inflected hostility to positivism became characteristic of his work.

This period has been identified by Bruce Caldwell (2004) as "Hayek's Transformation" and is bookmarked by his oft-quoted Ur-text "Economics and Knowledge," which coincides with his "Abuse of Reason" project. There, Hayek had recourse to a cobbled-together "philosophy of the ineffable" to try to reconcile his ambition to be a scientist, his hostility to socialism, the ambition of many natural scientists to portray socialism as scientific, and the failure of his previous forays into "Austrian" macroeconomic theory. It was from this point forward that Hayek entertained many RM themes. He argued that the market was no longer a set of pipes channeling capital though roundabout channels but was rather an information processor, organizing and conveying the appropriate information to the relevant actors, by an instrumentality that could not be fully comprehended or manipulated by any central planner. Just as he began to assert in this period that the mind could not come to an adequate understanding of its own operations, he also wanted to assert that "Reason" could not on its own devices fully comprehend why markets are *the* superior format of social organization. This was the *fons et origo* of Hayek's own version of the "anti-intellectualism of the intellectuals."

Hayek might have appealed to the "ineffable" after the manner of Wittgenstein, but instead he opted for recourse to the long Germanic philosophical tradition that sought to differentiate the *Naturwissenschaften* from the *Geisteswissenschaften*, particularly the neo-Kantian school of Heinrich Rickert (1863–1936) and Wilhelm Windelband (1848–1915), as filtered through Dilthey, Weber, and their students. In this period, Hayek began to denounce "scientism" in terms recognizable to those steeped in neo-Kantian Germanic philosophy but rather less familiar to his new English audience. In Rickert's terminology, the natural sciences were "nomothetic" (looking for transtemporal natural laws), whereas the social sciences were intrinsically "idiographic" (treating individual phenomena in their unique aspects, especially with regard to their historical rootedness and distinctive "complexity"). Hayek, in the essays collected together in his *Counterrevolution of Science*, sought to explain the enthusiasm of the natural scientists for social planning as an illegitimate conflation of the two distinct projects.[12] Because the "engineers" were treating the economy as a natural object subject to prediction and control, they were not in any position to understand the kind of information-mediation functions that Hayek was now insisting were the mainstay of the market: since no mind could fully encompass the operations of the market, neither could the cognitive capacities of the scientists. This was a garbled reprise of the antipositivist German precept that prediction and control were inappropriate goals for the *Geisteswissenschaften*, since they would violate human freedom and epistemological novelty.

The possibilities for a misreading of these prognostications were compounded when Hayek moved to Chicago in 1950. The conviction that the social and natural sciences were unified and not distinct was almost taken as a priori truth in the America of the mid-twentieth century: this was not solely or exclusively a local doctrine of the positivists. Hence the disconnect between Hayek and his potential audience grew dauntingly huge. Therefore, as a consequence of fallout from his "Abuse of Reason" project, in this period Hayek became saddled with the reputation of being "not an economist." He persisted in this limbo until he was rehabilitated by the award of the "Nobel" Bank of Sweden Prize in 1974.

It was during this intervening period that Hayek took to denouncing "intellectuals" as political quislings in fairly familiar RM terms. For instance, he famously sneered at the "professional secondhand dealers in ideas" (1967, 178) and bemoaned that capitalist news outlets and conservative university trustees had proven unable to curb their advocacy of socialism and promotion of a hyperbolic conception of democracy (1967, 183). He echoed many of his German predecessors in suggesting, "it may be that a free society as we have known it carries in itself the forces of its own destruction . . . that the free growth of ideas which is the essence of a free society will bring about the destruction of its foundation" (1967, 193). Indeed, his disdain for freewheeling debate in the political arena was a muted echo of the same disdain found in Carl Schmitt.

I heartily endorse Bruce Caldwell's (2004) thesis that sometime after 1945 Hayek finally decided that he would employ natural science to "naturalize" the market and therefore paint socialist planning as "unnatural." This attempt to conjure a special kind of "science" more in tune with his conservative politics is a further hallmark of the RM influence on the neoliberals. Hayek's modernist reconciliation at the cognitive level comprised at least three components:

1. Hayek would now concede the portrait of a single "unified science," which he had been resisting for at least a decade or more. There was no open renunciation of his prior position; instead, he simply began to rely upon Karl Popper to inform people on what "real science" looked like (Hacohen 2000).

2. Hayek began to endorse various aspects of the "cybernetics" project, which sought to reduce thought to mechanism. This was the source of his embrace of the "sciences of complexity," which he derived from Warren Weaver (Mirowski 2002a, 175).

3. With a lag, Hayek began to appeal to "evolution" to explain how an ineffable complex order, which he simply equated with the market, could have come about. The onus for ineffability was thus shifted from Germanic philosophy to biologistic metaphor.

To put the matter with a certain crude concision: for Hayek, the proposition that "markets do the thinking that people cannot" was extricated from its relatively romantic status during World War II to assume its more concertedly naturalistic status after 1945 by means of an endorsement of the proposition that "matter can think." The ontological flattening of the "thing that thinks" allowed him to blur the level that his analysis operated upon, be it "brains" or "individuals" or "groups." "It is more than a metaphor to describe the price system as a kind of machinery for registering change, or a system of telecommunications" (1972, 87). The reason that he could imagine cognition distributed in this manner was that he was concurrently describing the individual mind equally as a machine for registering change.

The reason that Hayek felt it was so important to portray the market as doing the thinking was that he posited that all the little conventional reasons of mankind—that reward is connected to effort, that there is such a thing as commensurability of need and recompense, that justice would govern social interaction—were nothing more than the pathetic illusions of the masses. "It ought to be freely admitted that the market order does not bring about any close correspondence between subjective merit or individual needs and rewards . . . the results for each individual may be as much determined by circumstances wholly beyond his control as by skill or effort" (1967, 172). In this sense, the rationality of the market would only be apparent to a narrow elite, at best, and this was the Achilles' heel and the tragedy of democratic politics.

Here Hayek's thesis that the brain will never fully comprehend itself became wedded to the parallel thesis that science informs us that the hoi polloi will never fully comprehend the current evolved natural order. Finally we observe that Hayek sought to naturalize the market and thus refute socialists by committing something very akin to the "Naturalistic Fallacy" (Angner 2004). The family resemblance to some central RM doctrines becomes quite noticeable at this juncture.

Even though he had arrived at a modernist and organicist account of "the truth," the problem still remained that the intellectuals and the masses were stubbornly resisting capitulation to the organic wisdom of the market; at this point, Hayek shifted his efforts from what one might consider political ontology to political epistemology. Here we return to the event that opened this chapter. It was during his Chicago period that he turned his pen to explicit political theory (see Hayek 1960, 1967, 1973, 1979b) and his organizational efforts to creating a parallel epistemic community, in the format of the Mont Pèlerin Society, to counteract the pernicious influence of the intellectuals. Both offered authoritarian solutions to what Hayek believed to be the core weaknesses of classical liberalism.

Let us briefly survey the political theory first. It is a watchword among those familiar with the German literature (Christi 1984, 532) that Hayek reprises Schmitt's thesis that liberalism and democracy should be regarded as antithetical under certain circumstances:

> Liberalism and democracy, although compatible, are not the same . . . the opposite of liberalism is totalitarianism, while the opposite of democracy is authoritarianism. In consequence, it is at least possible in principle that a democratic government may be totalitarian and that an authoritarian

government may act on liberal principles . . . [in] demanding unlimited power of the majority, [democracies] become essentially anti-liberal.

(1967, 161)

Since his conception of nature informed him that the masses will never understand the true architecture of social order, and since intellectuals will continue to tempt them to futile intervention and otherwise mucking up the market, Hayek was led to propound as the central tenet of neoliberalism the standard refrain of RM: that a strong state was necessary to neutralize what he considered to be the pathologies of democracy. The notion of freedom as unhindered exercise of personal participation in political decisions was roundly denounced (1960, 13). Paraphrasing Walter Benjamin, citizens must learn to forget about their "rights" and instead be given the opportunity to express themselves through the greatest information-conveyance device known to mankind, the market.[13] This was not the night-watchman state of the classical liberals, however; rather, the neoliberals, through the instrumentality of the strong state, sought to *define and institute* the types of markets that they (and not the citizenry) were convinced were the most advanced.[14] In this, they were merely echoing Schmitt's position that "only a strong state can preserve and enhance a free-market economy" and "only a strong state can generate genuine decentralization, [and] bring about free and autonomous domains" (quoted in Christi 1998, 31, 34n7). This was echoed (without attribution) by Hayek: "If we proceeded on the assumption that only the exercises of freedom that the majority will practice are important, we would be certain to create a stagnant society with all the characteristics of unfreedom" (Hayek 1960, 32).

One can therefore only second the verdict of Christi that "in truth, Hayek owed much to Schmitt, more than he cared to recognize" (1998, 23). For Hayek and the neoliberals, the *Fuehrer* was replaced by the figure of the entrepreneur, the embodiment of the will-to-power for the community, who must be permitted to act without being brought to rational account. While he probably believed he was personally defending liberalism from Schmitt's withering critique, his political "solution" ended up resembling Schmitt's "total state" more than he could bring himself to admit. If it had been apparent that he was effectively advocating an authoritarian reactionary modernism as a replacement for classical liberalism, it would certainly have not gone down smoothly in the West right after World War II; evidently, those pesky intellectuals would need to be countered and neutralized as well. Further, there was no immediate prospect of a strong authority taking over the American university system (by contrast with Germany in the 1930s) and sweeping the stables clean. In an interesting development not anticipated by Schmitt, Hayek hit upon the brilliant notion of developing the "double-truth" doctrine of neoliberalism—namely, that an elite would be tutored to understand the deliciously transgressive Schmittian necessity of repressing democracy, while the masses would be regaled with ripping tales of "rolling back the nanny state" and being set "free to choose"—by convening a closed Leninist organization of counter-intellectuals. There would be no waiting around until some charismatic savior magically appeared to deliver the Word of Natural Order down from the Mont to the awestruck literati. Intellectual credibility would not be left to the vagaries of "spontaneous order."

The organization that Hayek conceived to address this task was first convened in Mont Pèlerin on April 1–10, 1947; it became by all accounts the effective zero point from which the "Neoliberal Thought Collective" was born.[15] In his opening address, he admitted that they would not be able to discuss the "Rule of Law," because he did not want to extend membership to lawyers (1967, 156);[16] after a decade or so, this would be reversed. The reason the Mont Pèlerin Society (MPS) should serve as a distinct exemplar of how to conjure and sustain an epistemic community is because it exists as part of a rather novel institutional structure of intellectual discourse, one we could think about as a "Russian-doll" approach to the integration of research and praxis in the modern world. The Neoliberal Thought Collective was structured very differently from the other "invisible colleges" that sought to change people's minds in the second half of the twentieth century.

Unlike most intellectuals in the 1950s, the early protagonists of the MPS did not look to the universities or the academic "professions" or to interest-group mobilizations as the appropriate primary instruments to achieve their goals. The early neoliberals felt, with some justification, that they were then excluded from most high-profile intellectual venues in the West. Hence the MPS was constituted as a private, members-only debating society whose participants were handpicked (originally by Hayek, but later through a closed nomination procedure) and that consciously sought to remain out of the public eye. The purpose was to create a special space where people of like-minded political ideals could gather together to debate the outlines of a future movement diverging from classical liberalism without having to suffer the indignities of ridicule for their often blue-sky proposals and to evade the fifth-column reputation of a society closely aligned with powerful but dubious postwar interests.[17] Even the name of the society was itself chosen to be relatively anodyne, signaling little substantive content to outsiders (Hartwell 1995, 44). Many members would indeed hold academic posts in a range of academic disciplines, but this was not a precondition of MPS membership. The MPS could thus also be expanded to encompass various powerful capitalist entrepreneurs. One then might regard specific academic departments where the neoliberals eventually came to dominate (the University of Chicago economics department,[18] the London School of Economics, L'Institut Universitaire des Hautes Etudes Internationales at Geneva, Chicago Law, Freiburg, the Virginia School) as the next outer layer of the Russian doll, one emergent public face of the thought collective—although one often never publicly linked to the MPS. Another shell of the Russian doll became the special-purpose foundations for the education and promotion of neoliberal doctrines, such as the Volker Fund and the Foundation for Economic Education. These institutions were often set up as philanthropic or charitable units, if only to protect their tax status and seeming lack of bias.[19] The next shell would consist of general-purpose "think tanks" (the Institute for Economic Affairs,[20] the American Enterprise Institute, *Schweizerisches Institut für Auslandforschung* [Swiss Institute of International Studies]) that sheltered neoliberals who themselves might or might not also be members in good standing of various academic disciplines and universities. The think tanks then developed their own next layer of protective shell, often in the guise of specialized satellite think tanks existing to get quick and timely position papers out to friendly politicians or provide talking heads for various news media and opinion periodicals. Further outer shells have been innovated as we get closer to the present—for instance, "astroturfed" organizations consisting of supposedly local grassroots members, frequently organized around religious or single-issue campaigns. Outsiders would rarely perceive the extent to which individual protagonists embedded in a particular shell served multiple roles or transubstantiated between shells; nor would they detect the strength and pervasiveness of the network's ties, since they could never see beyond the particular shell of the Russian doll before their noses.

To mount an attack against those despised "second-hand dealers in ideas," Hayek realized that he had to mobilize his own battalions of dealers and construct an ongoing internal critique, thus equipping his acolytes with some of the ideas they would retail. Hayek thus conjured a group-think congenial to what he considered to be the Truth, since it would not conjure itself. This group then conjured a state that fostered a flourishing market, since it would not conjure itself. Hayek realized that one had to

embrace and revel in the contradiction of an "organized" spontaneous order and create an *entire set of institutions* to generate and promote the sort
of social science (and even natural science!) that he felt would stand as a
bulwark against creeping totalitarianism.

There is one more aspect of the Hayekian project we need to cover for
our present purposes. If one accepts the theoretical necessity of the strong
state, as neoliberals do, then presumably it will be embedded in a world of
other states, some of them commensurate in strength and even perhaps
committed to the same set of neoliberal principles. Although this would
have seemed a rather unlikely prospect in the 1950s (since most neoliberals at that juncture were utterly transfixed by the communist threat), it
was nevertheless a possibility that Hayek had to confront, especially as he
came to become ever more embroiled in political theory. In his wartime
screed *The Road to Serfdom* (1944, 230) he merely ridiculed the "realists" as
inconsistent:

> It is curious to observe how those who pose as the most hard-boiled real-
> ists, and who lose no opportunity of casting ridicule on the "utopianism" of
> those who believe in the possibility of an international political order, yet
> regard as more practicable the much more intimate and irresponsible in-
> terference with the lives of different peoples which economic planning in-
> volves; and believe that, once hitherto undreamt-of power is given to an
> international government, which has just been represented as not even ca-
> pable of enforcing a simple Rule of Law, this greater power will be used in so
> unselfish and so obviously just a manner as to command general consent.

He clearly imagined "a superior political power which can hold the economic interests in check" (1944, 232), but he also obviously possessed no
idea what that would look like. In his *Constitution of Liberty*, he simply
gave the entire question of war and international order a pass (1960, 262).
Late in life (1979, 132–133), he vaguely imagined the existence of a supranational authority that would promulgate the rule of law he had been theorizing for two decades, but it appears he had gotten little further on specif-
ics than he had in 1944. Even though a "catallaxy"—his terminology for the
supposed spontaneous order found in markets—was coined from the Greek
word meaning "to turn from enemy into friend," apparently in the international sphere the shade of Carl Schmitt could not so easily be exorcised
with mere terminology. Schmitt, notoriously, defined the sphere of politics
as the ability to stipulate the distinction between friend and enemy (2007).
Just as the market was a scaled-up version of the individual mind for

Hayek's neoliberals, the community of nations was treated as a scaled-up version of his ideal of the individual state. Nowhere did Hayek give any credence to the argument that the legalist approach to international relations had lost much of its allure since World War II; nor did he begin to entertain the notion that the putative community that rationality embodied within the market might be no match for the rivalry of multiple strong nation states, precisely because no common rule of law could be expected to exist between them. This was all the more curious, because (for instance) he explicitly allowed in passing the necessity of national military conscription in his neoliberal utopia. Clearly Hayek was invested in the doctrine that market operations were exempt from one of the key insights of Carl Schmitt in his *Concept of the Political*: the grounding of sovereignty lies in the ability to designate the Other a friend or an enemy. Yet the denial of this exemption was the starting point for Hans Morgenthau.

MORGENTHAU AS REACTIONARY MODERNIST

While the realist movement in IR often likes to trace its prehistory back to Herbert Butterfield and E. H. Carr—due in no small measure to Morgenthau's own efforts at construction of a genealogy—it is curious that no historian has noted that as early as 1919 Carl Schmitt was proposing "research into reality" as the appropriate antidote to *Political Romanticism*. Now, what counted as "real" turned out to be tremendously variable in the twentieth century; in the American context, it was supposed to designate a certain stance of tough-mindedness shorn of all sentimentality, idealism, and moral utopias. On those grounds, there was no figure more "realist" than Carl Schmitt in the period just prior to World War II, but just mentioning that fact and provoking the inevitable outraged reaction should tell us that something rather more was going on with the appeal to "realism" as the basis for the foundation of the academic discipline of international relations in the immediate postwar period. After all, the hallmark realist critique of the League of Nations appeared as early as 1926 in Schmitt's *Der Kernfrage der Voelkerbunds*. We shall propose instead to read the realism of Hans Morgenthau as a relatively successful attempt to translate a defanged version of reactionary modernism into the American context. As Scheuerman has reminded us: "Foreshadowing post 1945 Realist theories of IR, Carl Schmitt repeatedly argued that recourse to typically liberal forms of legal conflict resolution necessarily rests on a fiction" (1999, 147).

Since the audience for the current volume will be familiar with the writings of Morgenthau, it should suffice to merely indicate the ways in which he followed the RM playbook fairly closely in his writings of the 1940s and 1950s. As expected, Morgenthau felt impelled to denounce "positivism," and not just Kelsen's legal positivism (1958, 211–213), even as logical positivism was coming to dominate analytical philosophy at Chicago in the same era. He equated utilitarianism with scientism, only to observe, "the ideal of scientism applied to politics is the disappearance of politics altogether" (1958, 242; also 1946, 75). The reason for this denunciation came straight out of Schmitt: to deny the existence of power as a separate phenomenon was to conjure away the subject matter of politics. Although he prudently played it down in the transcripts herein reproduced, he was a constructivist about truth in the RM tradition:

> A political science that is true to its moral commitment ought at the very least to be an unpopular undertaking. At its very best, it cannot help being a subversive and revolutionary force with regard to certain vested interests— intellectual, political, economic, social in general. For it must sit in continuous judgment upon political man and political society, measuring their truth, *which is in good part a social convention* [my italics] . . . social conventions about power, which political science cannot help subjecting to a critical—and often destructive—examination, are one of the main sources from which the claims to power, and hence power itself, derive.
>
> (1958, 29–30)

It took a certain fortitude, a certain steely will to power, to acknowledge that a "truthful" political theory would be wildly unpopular with the masses. It is significant that this is one of the few junctures that he explicitly signals his debt to Schmitt: "Power thus corrupts, not only the actor on the political scene, but even the observer. . . . This is the lesson taught by the fate of the political romantics of whom the outstanding representatives are Adam Muller and Carl Schmitt" (1958, 35). Like Hayek, Morgenthau was driven to analyze and neutralize the corruption that he perceived in the cognitive regularities of the intellectuals and the masses with regard to political action. What is interesting is the extent to which their diagnosis initially travels along parallel tracks only to arrive at very different destinations.

For Morgenthau, as for Hayek, prewar attempts at constructing a liberal state have proven a disaster, and not just in the international arena. He wrote: "political reality disavows, and does so continually and drastically, the postulates of liberal philosophy" (1958, 112). "In a tragic contradiction of Shakespearian dimensions, liberalism in the international field was destroyed by the very forces it had, if not created, at least helped to dominate the Western world" (1948, 67). The overall solution to the problem, as in RM and Hayek, was to vest veto power in the state, as the only agency capable of facing up to the tragedy and with the ability to transcend the debilitating dynamic: "The cure is a state strong enough to hold its own against the concentration of private power" (1958, 120). Moreover, the invocation of technology as the driving force behind the change in political realities was Morgenstern's attempt at a modernist appeal to nature within his romantic conception of conservative thought: "The escapism of free trade is not different from the escapism of world government or of the United Nations or of disarmament or of other mechanical devices whereby since the First World War men have tried to escape the domination of modern technology and the lust for power" (1958, 244).

It is striking to observe the extent to which Morgenthau keeps these reactionary modernist cards prudently close to his chest during the 1954 meeting,[21] which probably accounts to a great degree for the profoundly unsatisfying character of the attempts of all concerned to try to reach some common agreement on the outlines of a "theory" of IR. His position paper insists upon the principle that foreign policy is pursued by rational men through rational means, only to then allow that "foreign policy is deflected from its rational course by errors of judgment and emotional preferences, the latter especially where foreign policy is conducted under conditions of democratic control" (appendix 2 of this volume, 265). This is about as close as he felt he could get to the thesis that the interminable character of parliamentary/legislative debate merely reveals the crisis of the liberal state, a characteristic Schmittian theme given wide currency by the book *The Concept of the Political*, to which Morgenthau had devoted an entire manuscript of his own as critique.[22] As Schmitt wrote, "although liberalism has not radically denied the state, it has neither advanced a positive theory of the state . . . but has attempted only to tie the political to the ethical and subjugate it to economics" (2007, 61). The latter route was the path pursued by the neoliberals. But couldn't Hayek just as easily have inscribed the following sentences? "If the majority could be trusted with power, the liberal safeguards would be unnecessary. Since it cannot be so trusted, its freedom must be curtailed for the very sake of freedom" (Morgenthau 1958, 113).

It is fascinating to see how Morgenthau transmutes this critique into a badge of virtue in the American context. Instead of drawing the dire conclusions from it as Schmitt inevitably does, Morgenthau instead develops it into a justification for the existence of a separate quasi-academic profession of IR kept distinct from economics on the one hand and from the legal profession on the other. In *Scientific Man*, Morgenthau devoted an entire chapter to a refutation of the liberal notion that free trade would promote the harmony of interests in the international sphere, instead insisting, "the liaison of state power and economics in the international field, far from maintaining peace and order, is a source of conflict and war" (1946, 86). Yet when Dorothy Fosdick proposed that free trade naturally reconciles national interests in the transcripts (transcript, 245), Morgenthau fell noticeably silent. In Morgenthau's project, the line must be drawn such that economics and politics remain mutually exclusive fields of inquiry (1946, 77), and furthermore, it should be acknowledged that liberalism fails precisely because it violates that separation. In another chapter, Morgenthau rejects the claim of legal scholars to comprehend the dynamics of international affairs on essentially Schmittian grounds: "The question to be answered is not what the law is but what it ought to be, and this question cannot be answered by the lawyer, but only by the statesman" (1946, 120). Of course, the stipulation that the central theoretical term of IR is "power" and that the appropriate vehicle of analysis in IR is "the state" (Morgenthau 1954, chap. 3) is only partially refracted Schmitt and is rendered less threatening by the caveat that the political markers that Morgenthau lays down should "only" apply to the international sphere. In both instances, liberalism is disparaged for wishing away the central phenomenon of power (Scheuerman 2007).

In a move reminiscent of Hayek in the 1940s, Morgenthau attempted to demarcate his political position from its rivals by accusing them of "scientism," turning this into yet another reason why the other social sciences (and especially the "behaviorist" enthusiasms of the 1950s) must be kept well away from the study of international relations: "the conditions which make the application of scientific methods to domestic politics at least a temporary and partial success are entirely and permanently absent in the international sphere. . . . In the international sphere the reduction of political problems to scientific propositions is never possible" (1946, 103). But sentiments such as those were hardly welcome in Sputnik-era America, as the other participants at the conference demonstrated by whiling away their time discussing quantitative measurement, falsification, empiricism, and other euphemisms for physics envy. This put Morgenthau in a singularly awkward position of insisting that "the greatest present pitfall is the general social science tendency toward a particular conception of what is scientific" (transcript, 257), without being predisposed to explain to the gathered faithful what that precise particular conception was, and expressing skepticism that IR theory could even be taught systematically at the doctoral level (260). Indeed, the academic scientist would only gesture ineffectually at political phenomena because "the supreme value for him is not power but truth" (1946, 101). We hear nothing about the constructivist character of truth in that context.

To those blissfully innocent of the whole neo-Kantian problematic of the *Natur/ Geisteswissenschaft* and the concomitant disparagement of prediction in the human sciences, these sentiments must have seemed perverse if not darkly oracular. "Scientism is unable to visualize the problems, fields of knowledge, and modes of insight to which science has no access" (Morgenthau 1946, 124). Why then would the Rockefeller Foundation want to support such a countercultural phenomenon as this RM-inspired IR? In part, it seems that some segments of the postwar policy elite, plus a few rogue intellectuals, were willing to entertain these seemingly perverse doctrines *as long as they were quarantined to a delimited sphere of international politics.* In other words, in American culture it would be permissible to foster and inculcate these beliefs in a small circle of diplomats and scholars prepared to live outside the domestic boundaries of standard liberal political life and sheltered from the demands of quotidian economic endeavor and the imperatives of democratic politics. "Morgenthau quarantined the agency of *Bildung* to a policy elite institutionally buffered from direct political responsibility to follow the will of the masses. And here we arrive at Morgenthau's 'conservative liberalism'" (Shillam 2007, 316). The Schmittian doctrine of "the exception" had become domesticated into another cold-war "double-truth" doctrine in postwar realism. It was implicated in the very conditions that midwifed the "birth of IR."

The similarities and differences with the neoliberals are telling. First off, while both RM-inflected doctrines began with the premise that existing liberal conceptions of the state were hopeless and that the corruption of the state could be traced to the pathologies of parliamentary democracy, the neoliberals eventually worked their way toward a position that suggested that the solution was the infiltration and takeover of the state apparatus by an elite cadre to recreate and restructure a market society. The early realists had no need for such drastic measures; they could imagine a "separate peace" wherein a diplomatic elite untethered from the fetters of democracy could ply their trade in the transnational sphere, deploying the constrained logic of the balance of power. Yet strangely, just like the neo-liberals, they eventually encountered great difficulties in conceptualizing the map coordinates of this arena of activity poised "outside the state." Toward the end of his textbook, Morgenthau wrote: "There is no shirking the conclusion that international peace cannot be permanent without a world state, and that a world state cannot be established under the present moral, social, and political conditions of the world" (1954a, 481). Yet some-how the cadre of diplomats were destined to be lumbered with the seem-ingly impossible task of bringing about the conditions that would eventu-ally permit the possibility of conjuring the world state into existence. The realist contradiction between elite cosmopolitan values and mass politics was not really addressed. As Scheuerman argues, "Morgenthau was never able to think creatively enough about the possibility of a novel global order because he carried too much Schmittian intellectual baggage" (2007, 79). The same might be said of Hayek.

The similarities and differences between respective conceptions of epis-temic communities also turned out to be significant. The neoliberals had to conjure a whole complement of counteracademic institutional struc-tures, from the semi-secret Mont Pèlerin to the phalanx of think tanks, as described in the previous section. By sharp contrast with the neoliberals, the realist version of RM was both more quickly assimilated and more readily welcomed into the existing elite academic environment, and room was even cleared for it with alacrity to join the postwar American social sciences, even in the face of Morgenthau's hesitations. The role of the Rock-efeller Foundation in convening this conference illustrates the potential acceptance of this insider strategy. Partly the RM themes were used as a pretext to renounce earlier commitments to an internationalist peace studies rooted in international law, thus conforming to the new darker vi-sion of cold-war rivalry, which had taken hold since 1946. Hence an aca-demic realignment was an a priori presumption of the exercise. Partly the domestication was achieved by erasing all visible traces of Schmitt while preserving his central doctrine that politics was not reducible to reason and that liberalism was incapable of underpinning a stable global political order. One possible explanation for the presence of such figures as Rein-hold Niebuhr and Walter Lippmann at the 1954 conference lies at that nexus; they provided the domestic cover for what would otherwise have been tagged an alien doctrine rapidly rejected by American body politic: "Butterfield, Reinhold Niebuhr and myself have tried to show how much more ambiguous and involved the relations between reason and politics are than is suggested by [Laski's] simple rationalistic faith. . . . Reason in the abstract has nothing to say about the solution of social conflicts" (Morgenthau 1958, 380, 346). As Niebuhr says in the transcript, "statesmen are not as rational as sometimes maintained" (241). This, too, was a form of anti-intellectualism for the intellectuals.

The neoliberals posited a general prevalence of irrationality as the innate predicament of mankind in order to justify their own grab for power; Morgenthau attempted to square the circle of a sheltered elite preempting a democratic electorate by blaming science itself—another common RM theme: "Science has already destroyed that realm of inner freedom through which the individual could experience his autonomy. . . . Science has created the technological instruments for the effective exercise of totalitarian control" (1972, 5). Here, Morgenthau prudently waited until the end of his career to echo Schmitt: "Mankind has waited two centuries for the triumph of scientific reason in the affairs of man. It has waited in vain" (1972, 12).[23] Earlier, around the time of the conference, he was instead proclaiming: "Foreign policy is pursued by rational men who pursue certain rational interests with rational means. . . . This rationality . . . makes a theory of international relations possible" (appendix 2 of this volume, 265). Yet this rationality was a delicate flower, neither resembling the mechanical means-ends rationality of the behaviorists nor the ineffable market rationality of the neoliberals. It was something that almost had to be passed down from master to apprentice in the company of a small handpicked elite: "in this inescapable tension between reason and experience, between theoretical and practical knowledge, between the light of political philosophy and the twilight of political action, is indeed the ultimate dilemma of politics" (Morgenthau 1958, 381). In this respect, Morgenthau's regimen for elite training more closely resembled Michael Polanyi's description of mystic monastic science than the organized surrender to the marketplace of ideas of Friedrich Hayek. It may be no accident that Polanyi was another displaced *Mitteleuropa* conservative philosopher (and briefly a member of Mont Pèlerin) stranded late in life on the south side of Chicago.

THE AFTERMATH

Jan-Werner Müller is right to insist that those who sought to learn something from Carl Schmitt after 1945 were mostly concerned to critique and recast liberalism as a flawed and crippled ideology, but it is hard to agree that "Schmitt immunized his adversarial successors against liberal triumphalism once and for all" (2003, 246). It would have been almost impossible to attract any sort of audience in postwar America without coming to terms with the upbeat optimism, the bottomless faith in science, and the conviction that the United States would serve as a shining beacon of hope for the world's dispossessed. The neoliberals managed to endow reactionary modernism with a happy ending that it lacked in 1945 by a renewed appeal to science, in the guise of a cybernetic model of information processing appended to some dubious theses about the necessary directionality of the arrow of time in societal evolution. Morgenthau certainly was never tempted by their cybernetic theory of markets, but he also found he had to couch his own reactionary modernism in some version of nature that vaguely resembled the American scientism so contrary to his own inclinations: "Conservatism holds—as we saw the realist philosophy of international relations to hold—that the world, imperfect as it is from the rational point of view, is the result of forces inherent in human nature. To improve the world one must work with these forces, not against them" (1958, 285).

I think it is fair to say that even this level of accommodation was not sufficient to render RM palatable in the American context. Over time, the neoliberal project was brought ever closer to established American notions of science and nature in their juxtaposition with the social by continually straining to reconcile the Schmittian decisionist definition of politics at its heart with the economic notion of "rational choice": indeed, this is the best way to understand both the rise of public-choice theory (Amadae 2003) and the subsequent evolution of the Chicago School of economics. Politics was thereby collapsed back into economics, after RM had precipitated their divorce. The field of international relations accomplished something similar by the "realists" sloughing off what was regarded as Morgenthau's excessively tragic vision of the world, reinstating the optimism behind Pax Americana by fiat, and slowly combining whatever was left with "science" in the format of neoclassical rational-choice theory,[24] and then later, a more direct merger of realism with the IR variant of neoliberalism itself. Although not often discussed in these terms, one might thus regard the trajectory of the post-Morgenthau history of IR as two postwar tributaries of the river of reactionary modernism finally reconverging under the hydraulic pressure of events, plus some heavy-duty reengineering of the global international landscape. Thus Müller is once again correct to observe: "Modernity, as an age of neutralizations and depoliticizations, was at least partially endorsed, rather than deplored" (2003, 247).

NOTES

I would like to thank Nicolas Guilhot for numerous conversations on these issues. Nevertheless, he should not be held to account for anything found herein.

1. Transcript of C-Span program "Booknotes," November 20, 1994.

2. Recent attempts to explore this argument include Raynor (2000), Mirowski and Plehwe (2009), and Guilhot (2008).

3. This is the terminology of Ole Wæver; see Smith (2000). While we briefly return to this reunion in the conclusion, we shall unfortunately have to leave any serious consideration of that latter phenomenon to a subsequent paper.

4. This last aspect of RM is still a favorite of historians who seek to account for the breakdown of the Nazi war machine in World War II.

5. See, for instance Scheuerman (1999, 2007), Christi (1998), Horton (2006), Caldwell (2005), and Sollner (1987).

6. At a late stage of the composition of this paper, I encountered the one exception to this generalization: Scheuerman (2007).

7. For some examples, see Frei (2001), Williams (2004), Pichler (1998), and Shillam (2007).

8. The fact that they succeeded in an institutional sense despite the lack of common ground is the topic of many of the other essays in this volume.

9. For a description, see the paper by Denord in Mirowski and Plehwe (2009) and Steel (1980, 368).

10. We bypass Milton Friedman here because he actually read very little political theory and picked up many of his neoliberal notions secondhand at meetings of the Mont Pèlerin Society. But for further insights, see Klein (2007).

11. On this, see Mirowski (2007).

12. See, for instance, Hayek (1979a, 170–171).

13. Interestingly, here is where Hayek rejected the maximization of utility as the standard equilibrium concept in neoclassical economic theory. "Markets don't maximize happiness, rather, the use of the market mechanism brings more of the dispersed knowledge of society into play than by any other [method]" (1967, 174).

14. Hayek's frequent appeals to a "spontaneous order" often masked the fact that it was neoliberal theorists who were claiming the power to exercise the Schmittian "exception" (and hence constitute the sovereignty of the state) by defining things like property rights, the extent of the franchise, constitutional provisions that limit citizen initiatives, and the like. As Scheuerman (1999, 216) writes about the comparison to Hayek, "For Carl Schmitt, the real question is *who* intervenes, and *whose* interests are to be served by intervention."

15. This set of events have been described by many historians: Cockett (1995), Hartwell (1995), Plehwe and Walpen (2004), and Mirowski and Plehwe (2009).

16. Here in particular we see a curious parallel with the later realist movement in international relations.

17. Interestingly enough, Carl Schmitt convened his own semiclandestine invisible college, which his followers called the "Academia Moralis," at roughly the same time (Muller 2003, 53).

18. Elsewhere I have made the historical case that it was Hayek, and not any of the usual suspects, who was most directly responsible for the founding of the Chicago School of Economics. See Mirowski and van Horn (2009).

19. See the letter from Smedley to Anthony Fisher dated June 25, 1956, quoted in Cockett (1995, 131): "It is imperative we should give no indication in our literature that we are working to educate the Public along certain lines which might be interpreted as having political bias . . . it might enable our enemies to question the charitableness of our motives."

20. Hayek's crucial role in the formation of the IEA is discussed in Cockett (1995, chap. 5).

21. Scheuerman (2007) reports that not only was Morgenthau familiar with the Weimar-era Schmitt but seems to have followed his publications well after World War II.

22. Scheuerman (1999, 227) claims there was a "hidden dialogue" between Morgenthau and Schmitt in the period 1927–1932, although Morgenthau's published volume *La Notion du Politique* (1933) is rather direct evidence of influence. Scheuerman calls *Scientific Man Versus Power Politics* "a popularized version of Schmitt" (1999, 244).

23. Schmitt explicitly dealt with the "scientific as the antithesis of the political" in his *Concept of the Political* (2007, 23).

24. We refer here to the work of Kenneth Waltz, often dubbed "neorealism" in IR (Guzzini 1998; Baldwin 1993). Interestingly enough, it was the Chicago economist Hugo Sonnenschein who is quoted in Frei's biography of Morgenthau as opining he needed a good dose of optimism (2001, 203).

REFERENCES

Amadae, Sonja. 2003. *Rationalizing capitalist democracy.* Chicago: University of Chicago Press.

Angner, Erik. 2004. Did Hayek commit the naturalistic fallacy? *Journal of the History of Economic Thought* 26: 349–361.

Baldwin, David, ed. 1993. *Neorealism and neoliberalism.* New York: Columbia University Press.

Caldwell, Bruce. 2004. *Hayek's challenge.* Chicago: University of Chicago Press.

Caldwell, Peter. 2005. Controversies over Carl Schmitt: A review of recent literature. *Journal of Modern History* 77: 357–387.

Carnap, Rudolf. 1963. Intellectual autobiography. In *The philosophy of Rudolf Carnap*, ed. Paul Schlipp, 3–84. La Salle: Open Court.

Christi, F. R. 1984. Hayek and Schmitt on the rule of law. *Canadian Journal of Political Science* 17: 521–535.

Christi, Renato. 1998. *Carl Schmitt and authoritarian liberalism.* Cardiff: University of Wales Press.

Cockett, Richard. 1995. *Thinking the unthinkable: Think tanks and the economic counter-revolution, 1931–83.* London: Fontana.

Cooper, David. 1999. Reactionary modernism. In *German philosophy since Kant*, ed. Anthony O'Hear, 291–304. Cambridge: Cambridge University Press.

Frei, Christoph. 2001. *Hans J. Morgenthau: An intellectual biography.* Baton Rouge: Louisiana State University Press.

Friedrich, Carl. 1955. The political thought of neo-liberalism. *American Political Science Review* 49: 509–525.

Fritzsche, Peter. 1990. *Rehearsals for fascism: Populism and political mobilization in Weimar Germany.* Oxford: Oxford University Press.

Guilhot, Nicolas. 2008. The realist gambit: Postwar American political science and the birth of IR theory. *International Political Sociology* 2: 281–304.

Gunnell, John. 1993. *The descent of political theory.* Chicago: University of Chicago Press.

Gusejnova, Dina. 2006. Concepts of culture and technology in Germany, 1916–1933. *Journal of European Studies* 36: 5–30.

Guzzini, Stephano. 1998. *Realism in international relations and international political economy: Continuing story of a death foretold.* London: Routledge.

Hacohen, Malachi. 2000. *Karl Popper: The formative years, 1902–45.* New York: Cambridge University Press.

Hartwell, R. Max. 1995. *A history of the Mont Pèlerin Society.* Indianapolis, Ind.: Liberty Fund.

Harvey, David. 2005. *A brief history of neoliberalism.* New York: Oxford University Press.

Hayek, Friedrich. 1944. *The road to serfdom.* Chicago: University of Chicago Press.

——. 1960. *Constitution of liberty.* Chicago: University of Chicago Press.

——. 1967. *Studies in philosophy, politics, and economics.* New York: Simon & Schuster.

——. 1972. *Individualism and economic order.* Chicago: Gateway.

——. 1973. *Law, legislation, and liberty.* Vol. 1. London: Routledge and Kegan Paul.

——. 1979a [1952]. *The counter-revolution of science.* Indianapolis: Liberty Press.

——. 1979b. *Law, legislation, and liberty.* Vol. 3. Chicago: University of Chicago Press.

Herf, Jeffrey. 1984. *Reactionary modernism.* New York: Cambridge University Press.

Hoffmann, Stanley. 1981. Notes on the limits of realism. *Social Research* 48: 653–659.

Horton, Scott. 2006. Carl Schmitt and the Military Commissions Act of 2006. Blog post. http://balkin.blogspot.com/2006/10/carl-schmitt-and-military-commissions_16.html.

Klein, Naomi. 2007. *The shock doctrine.* New York: Morrow.

Knorr, Klaus. 1947. Economics and international relations: A problem in teaching. *Political Science Quarterly* 62: 552–568.

Knorr, Klaus, and Sidney Verba, eds. 1961. *The international system: Theoretical essays.* Princeton, N.J.: Princeton University Press.

Lippmann, Walter. 1965. *The essential Lippmann.* New York: Vintage.

McGucken, William. 1984. *Scientists, society, and the state.* Columbus: Ohio State University Press.

Mirowski, Philip. 2002. *Machine dreams.* New York: Cambridge University Press.

——. 2007. Naturalizing the market on the road to revisionism: Caldwell on Hayek's challenge. *Journal of Institutional Economics* 3: 351–372.

Mirowski, Philip, and Dieter Plehwe, eds. 2009. *The road from Mont Pèlerin: The making of the neoliberal thought collective.* Cambridge, Mass.: Harvard University Press.

Mirowski, Philip, and Rob van Horn. 2009. The rise of the Chicago School of Economics and the birth of neoliberalism. In *The road from Mont Pèlerin: The making of the neoliberal thought collective,* ed. P. Mirowski and D. Plehwe, 139–179. Cambridge, Mass.: Harvard University Press.

Morgenthau, Hans. 1946. *Scientific man versus power politics.* Chicago: University of Chicago Press.

———. 1954. *Politics among nations.* New York: Knopf.

———. 1958. *Dilemmas of politics.* Chicago: University of Chicago Press.

———. 1972. *Science: Servant or master?* New York: New American Library.

Muller, Jan-Werner. 2003. *A dangerous mind: Carl Schmitt in postwar European thought.* New Haven, Conn.: Yale University Press.

Nash, George. 2006. *The conservative intellectual movement in America since 1945.* Wilmington, Del.: ISI Books.

Pichler, Hans-Karl. 1998. The godfathers of truth: Max Weber and Carl Schmitt in Morgenthau's theory of power politics. *Review of International Studies* 24: 185–200.

Rabinbach, Anson. 1992. *The human motor: Energy, fatigue, and the origins of modernity.* Berkeley: University of California Press.

Raynor, Gregory. 2000. Engineering social reform: The rise of the Ford Foundation and cold war liberalism 1908–59. Ph.D. thesis. New York: New York University.

Renneberg, Monica, and Mark Walker, eds. 1994. *Science, technology, and national socialism.* Cambridge: Cambridge University Press.

Scheuerman, William. 1999. *Carl Schmitt: The end of law.* Lanham, Md.: Rowman & Littlefield.

———. 2007. Carl Schmitt and Hans Morgenthau: Realism and beyond. In *Realism reconsidered: Hans Morgenthau and international relations*, ed. M. Williams, 62–92. Oxford: Oxford University Press.

Schmitt, Carl. 2007. *The concept of the political.* Trans. George Schwab. Chicago: University of Chicago Press.

Shillam, Robbie. 2007. Morgenthau in context: The rise and fall of a liberal project. *European Journal of International Relations* 13: 299–327.

Smith, Steve. 2000. The discipline of international relations: Still an American social science? *British Journal of Politics and International Relations* 2: 374–402.

Sollner, Alfons. 1987. German conservatism in America. *Telos* 72: 161–172.

Steel, Ronald. 1980. *Walter Lippmann and the American century.* Boston: Little Brown.

Thompson, Kenneth, and Robert Myers, eds. 1984. *Truth and tragedy: A tribute to Hans J. Morgenthau.* New Brunswick, N.J.: Transaction Press.

Trommler, Frank. 1996. The creation of a culture of *Sachlichkeit*. In *Society, culture, and the state in Germany, 1870–1930*, ed. G. Eley, 465–485. Ann Arbor: University of Michigan Press.

Williams, Michael. 2004. Why ideas matter in international relations: Hans Morgenthau, classical realism, and the moral construction of power politics. *International Organization* 58: 633–665.

APPENDIX 1

CONFERENCE ON INTERNATIONAL POLITICS, MAY 7–8, 1954

LIST OF PARTICIPANTS

Robert Bowie	Policy Planning Staff, Department of State, Washington, D.C.
Dorothy Fosdick	2718 N. Street, N.W., Washington, D.C.
William T. R. Fox	Institute of War and Peace Studies, Columbia University, 429 West 117th Street, New York 27, New York
Walter Lippmann	New York Herald Tribune, 3525 Woodley Road, N.W., Washington, D.C.
Hans J. Morgenthau	Center for the Study of American Foreign Policy, University of Chicago, 1126 East 59th Street, Chicago 37, Illinois
Reinhold Niebuhr	Dean of the Faculties, Union Theological Seminary, Broadway at 120th Street, New York 27, New York
Paul H. Nitze	President, Foreign Service Educational Foundation, 1839 19th Street, N.W., Washington, D.C.
Don K. Price	Associate Director, The Ford Foundation 644 Madison Avenue, New York 21, New York
James B. Reston	The New York Times, Washington Bureau, 1701 K. Street, N.W., Washington, D.C.
Dean Rusk	President, The Rockefeller Foundation, 49 West 49th Street, New York 20, New York
Kenneth W. Thompson	Consultant in International Relations The Rockefeller Foundation, 49 West 49th Street, New York 20, New York
Arnold Wolfers	Sterling Professor of International Relations, Hall of Graduate Studies 214, Yale University, New Haven, Connecticut

GENERAL OUTLINE

  I.   Theory and Practice
 II.   Types of Theory
       A.   Normative Theory
       B.   General Theory of International Politics
       C.   Theory as the Basis of Action
III.   The Future for Theoretical Research

The meeting convened at 3:00 P.M., Friday, May 7, 1954. with Dean Rusk presiding.

DEAN RUSK welcomed the conferees and expressed his personal and Foundation appreciation for their attendance at the conference. We are here to try and find out something about the state of theory in international politics. What kinds of things are missing from the field? What might be done to improve it? The meeting is essentially in the hands of the conferees as there is no formal agenda. We do not intend to do any Foundation business in the short time that we have to deal with these problems.

There currently tends to be a trend toward a more lively interest in theoretical and conceptual problems illustrated in the study of international politics and emerging in theories of politics, economics, law and human behavior. We need to go back to undertake an assessment of where we are in the basic philosophic aspects of the problem of the theory of international politics. We need some generalizations and structure in order to make some sense out of the jet stream of the factual situation. We need some knowledge of the intellectual process by which practical judgments on factual situations come about, the purpose of leadership in a world society, and the situation of conflict in opposing ideologies. We need more serious attention to a sorting out of intellectual factors in our foreign policy. As far as RF is concerned, we are not interested in this matter for immediate procedural results. We have instead a dual interest. We are anxious to learn what the state of the field is intellectually and if we can do anything about it. The suggestion for this meeting came from several of the participants and is not an idea that came from RF. We should not look at this meeting in too systematic a fashion nor go away from it completely exhausted. Dean Rusk then opened the floor for questions.

I. THEORY AND PRACTICE

ARNOLD WOLFERS felt that it was very encouraging for the field as a whole that the papers which were prepared for the conference had come in. He himself is working almost exclusively in the theoretical field. The climate of opinion in universities at present is not much in favor of theory. Many think that theory is pure verbiage and forces situations into rigid theoretical patterns. They ask what we are trying to cover. What is the relationship between theory and practice? What function does theory serve? There are questions within theory of actual speculation and the ethical problem. This worries practitioners, too. AW would like the conferees first to tackle the moral problem.

REINHOLD NIEBUHR is thrilled by the fact that almost all the papers deal with the relationship of theory to practice. This is the great issue for the group. The relationship in the past between specialists in these two areas of international politics has not been too creative. Perhaps we can deal with this more specifically than the practitioners are able to do. When we speak of theory, we speak of general laws. Morgenthau's theory also deals with general laws. It is true that you don't have theory unless you know what the constants are, but there can be a creative relationship between theory and practice only if there is a theory which understands that, in practical terms, there are no general laws.

The reasons for this are not hard to discover. Theory is not essentially metaphysical; it is dramatic. To understand it we must have an intuitive understanding of the contingent factors in concrete situations. Historians and statesmen are not as rational as it is sometimes maintained; they are dealing with the trends of historical events. We need a specific knowledge of contingent factors. In modern politics there are many important examples of this. We must have theorists who understand not only that tyrannies are irrational but that there is a vast difference between Marxism and conservatism and liberalism and Communism. There is a difference between the general laws of the anatomy of tyranny and particular political ideologies and tyrannies. A general law of tyranny obscures the differences while stressing the similarities between a nihilistic philosophy, like Nazism, and one based on utopianism, like Communism. Both Nazis and Communists are in one sense irrational. However, Communists try to make political practice coincide with their theories, while Nazism took theory less seriously than action. Communism has a different irrationality than Nazism. The communists are militaristic when they have to be, but they have vast confidence in the self-fulfillment of their revolutionary theory. In some cases, if one looks for general laws, he will mess up the situation.

In general one can state the problem of theory and practice in these terms: History, if it has some uniformities, is full of contingencies and unique events. Practitioners must have some knowledge of the constants. Theorists must have knowledge of the contingent factors in history. When Chamberlain made his statement that we must have "peace in our time" he showed that he had no knowledge of the constants. He did not correctly appraise the objective political situation. Churchill today, by contrast, is maybe not making a mistake in trying to get "Peace in our Time." He may have a clearer view of both the constants and variables on the present scene. Practitioners must be aware of the constants and aware of the unpredictables and contingent factors. The Nazi will to power was a form of the general will to power, and yet it was also unique in its fanaticism. Wisdom develops when one is aware of the constants over against the unique events on the historical scene. Practitioners must often play by ear. The intuition of the practitioner is vital; it is a deductive intuition. The theorist's contribution would be very irrelevant if he thought that the only rational theory was one based on constants and general laws. Theory must be built into the knowledge of what the statesman faces.

WILLIAM T. R. FOX is impelled to associate himself with RN's point of view. He would add only one footnote. Alongside the unpredictable there must be evolved a concept of the malleable. We can't have the world just the way we want it. But in some degree we must be masters of our fate. We must learn what things can be altered. This is essential to a development of political science.

REINHOLD NIEBUHR agrees in general but stresses that the malleable and the unpredictable are actually in two different categories as generally used. The malleable must be subordinate to the unpredictable in a complete theory of politics, for we cannot predict with precision what can and cannot be controlled.

DEAN RUSK raises the question of the content and meaning of theory. He asks whether Nitze is content to have this discussion now—that is, the "Nature and Role of Theory." The issue presented in the papers by Nitze and Morgenthau is whether one or the other has preempted the word theory.

PAUL NITZE: In a rough way, one can say that practitioners make little theories out of big theories. As a policy maker, you must sort out the parts of a major generalization and reduce it to something more simple and precise. That is the important thing. The papers revolve around all aspects of theory. When I was writing the paper, it seemed to me that the important point for the practitioner was to break theory down to a manageable size. What your objectives ought to be in any given case is important, not all kinds of theoretical approaches. In the final analysis, of course, theory is essentially one. The papers on national interests, the relationship of morality to specific problems, etc., should be viewed together. In theory we look at the effectiveness of given techniques to certain specified or differentiated ends.

WILLIAM T. R. FOX: There should be an appraisal of the effectiveness of a given means to accomplish some given end.

II. TYPES OF THEORY

DEAN RUSK: Question to Walter Lippmann. He has said there isn't a policy in this situation. He seems to place objectives at one end of a spectrum, policies at the other and between them, at various intervals, the implementation of policies. Would he distinguish between objectives, policies and modes of implementation of policies? Would he differentiate between types of theory?

WALTER LIPPMANN: WTRF writes that we better come to some clearer view of what we mean by theory. The normative use is the standard by which you judge action. This is one form of theory. Another form could be a general theory of politics. There might or might not be a general theory that will tell you how the world will behave whether you like it or not. And another use of the word theory concerns the theory, conscious or unconscious, on which a man, nation, or government is acting. That to my mind is extremely useful and important. Behind almost every act is an implicit theory. This is a plural world and, therefore, one which will have conflicting theories.

REINHOLD NIEBUHR: We should bring together the various concepts of theory. There is a theory of ends but also a comprehensive theory for which you work. For the realist, theory is something that describes reality; both for the realist and the idealist, theory may also consider what should be. What are the realities? The power drives of nations, etc.? What should they be?

ARNOLD WOLFERS: The two are interlocking. We should try to focus more on one than on the other. What do nations pretend they're after? What are their real objectives? The realist says that nations are after power. The idealist says they are worried about moral ends. This is the constant debate and the lesson of mankind. The realities of the world are the main topics of scientific theory. What happens if democratic nations really want democracy and other nations don't? This does not tie the moral or immoral ends together, which we are trying to explain.

A. Normative Theory

DEAN RUSK: We are talking about three kinds of theory: 1) normative theory; 2) general behavioral theory; and 3) theory which forms the basis of action in concrete cases. Perhaps we might discuss each of them in turn. Normative theory outlines the aims and objective of states and society or the purpose of values.

PAUL NITZE: Normative theory is concerned with the selection of means as well as ends. There are practical and relative judgments in every day choices which are made on normative grounds.

DOROTHY FOSDICK: It is wrong to assume that practical choices such as those which confront policy makers are not moral choices.

PAUL NITZE: An important question is what are the processes by which you can make moral discriminations? It is possible to make moral discriminations. But then you have to go deeply into the matter of how you are going to discriminate.

DEAN RUSK: In Articles 1 and 2 of the United Nations Charter, the aims and purposes are set out. In all the debates of the last nine years no delegation has spoken against the Charter. On one occasion Mrs. Pandit said the Charter was just a bunch of words and then felt constrained to take it back. Certain practical matters are related to purpose and ethics—these things do mean something. If you will look at the action, you will find this to be so. Is it possible to have common objectives acknowledged? Yes. They are acted upon and furnish a basis for action in the lower organizations. Perhaps we should work toward the development of a more adequate normative theory inclusive of each activity. Common values play a practical role not as regards the Soviet leaders perhaps, but in the acting organizations. We might discuss some of the questions raised in Mr. Niebuhr's paper. We have a list of questions on each of the papers.

REINHOLD NIEBUHR (First question on Niebuhr's paper, page 3): "What are the standards for determining 'Justice' in a concrete situation in international politics?" They are, in philosophic terms, giving each man his due. But how do you arrive at each man's due? Via the regulative principles of equality and liberty. This at least is true in western civilization. Liberty is a proposition which arises in western cultures because of the Christian and Hebraic traditions. And theory that is true transcends its presuppositions. Nehru does not accept our presuppositions, but demands liberty for Indians. When liberty is suppressed in a nation, the vitality of the nations is suppressed. Liberty is a very inevitable norm, but is not sufficient as a principle alone—for example, national self-determination alone as a guide to politics. Why was it wrong that we attempted to do this after World War I? Because Woodrow Wilson made of self-determination an absolute coextensive with justice. But it is only one of the norms and cannot be absolute. In actuality, however, there are only two basic regulative norms—liberty and equality. These two are regulative principles. We cannot have complete equality especially in international relations. Too much equality might sometimes be an evil. Nations are against us because we have too much power in the United States, yet, without our power, western civilization might be destroyed. Power carries special responsibilities. Liberty and equality are regulative principles of justice and validate themselves in national and international experience. The concept of the vitality and liberty of the parts in the international community requires the self-determination of nations. We must have the parts in harmony with the whole. Harmony of the whole is not good if it does not include the parts, i.e., liberty and equality, and yet, liberty and equality are not good if they destroy the harmony of the whole.

ARNOLD WOLFERS: What about the whole—this is a regulative principle, too, isn't it?

REINHOLD NIEBUHR: The harmony of the whole is not good if it does not include liberty and equality.

ARNOLD WOLFERS: And liberty and equality are not good if they destroy the good of the whole.

PAUL NITZE: Tyranny is preferable to chaos.

REINHOLD NIEBUHR: Yes, it is true that Lincoln's primary purpose was to save the nation. Ethically, that is right. Good is some kind of harmony, but we must be clear that it is *some kind* of harmony; specifically it must be a particular kind of harmony which includes equality and liberty.

ARNOLD WOLFERS: Are we faced with this problem in the question "Should nations limit or allow their self interest to dominate?" It would seem in international relations there should be a sense of what the whole is.

REINHOLD NIEBUHR: It is true there should be a concern for something larger than self-interest. There should be a concern for what is behind a nation's self-interest—the principles and purpose by which the people are nourished. Nations cannot do this as such if they do not use regulative principles of liberty and equality. They cannot afford to be as altruistic as individuals.

PAUL NITZE: But in Korea the alternative to chaos was Rhee.

REINHOLD NIEBUHR: Any nation will choose tyranny rather than chaos. If a nation thinks that it is threatened with chaos, it will choose tyranny.

DEAN RUSK: What about a traditional society—a nation which is neither in a state of tyranny or chaos?

REINHOLD NIEBUHR: We in the democratic world are too prone to name as the alternatives only tyranny and chaos. There is such a thing as legitimate government and order which is neither. We have to recognize more than we have legitimate order which is neither tyrannical nor democratic. This distinguishes itself by the fact that it is not ruled by pure force or characterized by pure order. Such a society may be governed by pure force of myth, tradition or theory. There is a special form of legitimacy and beauty in traditional order.

DON K. PRICE: The Indian Constitution includes the regulatives of Justice, Liberty, Equality, and Fraternity.

DEAN RUSK: These words may be altering the Indian order.

ARNOLD WOLFERS: We think that chaos is so terrible that wherever we see it we are on the side of order. This may leave western states in an opposite camp from those who are demanding change.

REINHOLD NIEBUHR: History's contingent elements make it necessary to have regulative principles. In some cases we are forced to choose between liberty and order. How are you going to prefer one to the other? When Wilson demanded that the Austro-Hungarian Empire be split up according to the principles of self-determination, he contributed to the establishment of a resentful and impractical order. In the situation presented by the problem of self-determination vs. order, the statesman has to play by ear. He has to know what the values are and how they are related to such a situation. The Austro-Hungarian Empire was a viable economic order but not a viable political order. A balkanized Europe might have been viable politically but could it be economically viable?

DEAN RUSK: What is the nature and role of theory in this business? How does theory help us to make such discriminations?

ARNOLD WOLFERS (Question directed to RN): RN has said that nations should, in the interest of order, transcend their self-interest, although he claims that there is validity in their self-interest. He also says that their liberty has a way of producing their vitality against tyranny. They even claim to transcend their self-interest, but this is hypocrisy. We might discuss the question of hypocrisy as described in RN's paper. Where does hypocrisy end? Kennan says let's forget about morality, but the fact that nations run the risk of hypocrisy shows this is not possible.

REINHOLD NIEBUHR: Nations are moral. They are following something more than just what they like. But nations always pretend to have a purer devotion to morality than they actually have. They are not as pure in their actions as in their intentions. We may compare to our profit English vs. German politics. The Germans said that they were not going to follow moral principle if it did not serve their own interest. The English appealed to moral purpose sometimes to the point of hypocrisy, yet it has given them something that Germany has lacked. (See RN's paper for further elaboration.)

PAUL NITZE: What is this interest? In part, interest would seem to me to involve a number of considerations which fall clearly in the moral field. Certainly for the United

States it would seem to me that the national interest includes not only specific geographical power and objectives, but also certain standards of behavior of importance for others. It involves the system within which we can act most effectively.

REINHOLD NIEBUHR: It is certainly to our interests as a nation to preserve principles of justice for ourselves and to transcend our national interests.

PAUL NITZE: What is the definition of national interest? In what breadth of talents does one view the national interests? A large portion of mankind's interests are in fact a portion of the United States' interests.

REINHOLD NIEBUHR: Nations are not often subject to the idea that "He that loseth his life shall find it." Yet we must be careful defining the national interest too narrowly. Some portions within the nation do concern themselves with principles behind and above their interest. There is a utilitarian concept which says "Can't a wise man determine his interest so broadly that it will include everybody's?" There is some general impulse behind your self-interest. Sometimes self-interest by its purpose shows breadth and wisdom.

PAUL NITZE: Here again the expedient and the moral merge.

DOROTHY FOSDICK: Free trade is purely for our national interest, and yet it is to the interest of our allies. In this case, we are promoting the national interest of both. The very nature of interest will take you to a position of broader scope. In certain policy questions, issues of both common and national interest prevail. (Discussion of Marshall Plan)

ARNOLD WOLFERS: We are discussing interest from its egocentric outlook. One's own interest should transcend itself to include the harmony and justice of the whole.

DOROTHY FOSDICK: Is there a third alternative to self-interest and self-sacrifice? Neither may be realistic. There are many things in our interest which also unite.

REINHOLD NIEBUHR: An assessment of international morality is on a different level; it is necessary to find the point where the general good and the national interest come together. The individual may look beyond himself but any statesman who sacrifices the nation for a larger good is a traitor. It is necessary to see that national morality is on a different level than individual morality. Perhaps the best we can do in international society is to find the point of concurrence between national and common interests.

DOROTHY FOSDICK: If a nation acts on the basis of self-sacrifice, it brings another factor of unpredictability into the international affairs world.

HANS MORGENTHAU: This has HM's approval on a descriptive level but not on a theoretical level. You cannot reconcile foreign policy, determined by national interest, and foreign policy determined by principles, which transcend national interest. No single nation is powerful enough to pursue its own ends without including the interests of others, i.e., national interests of other nations. This is not really saying that a nation, defining its national interests in such broad terms, substitutes moral principles for self-interests. But a nation acting first in accord with its strategic interests is intelligent enough to say that a rationally defined national interest is self-demanding and self-defining. Moral considerations enter into a formulation of the national interest. Moral principles substantiate national interest. There is no clear-cut choice between following international morality and a morality dictated by the national interest.

REINHOLD NIEBUHR: The United States is a nation of very virtuous people. It therefore assumes that its actions in the world are virtuous. This is a pretense. Where is the line to be drawn between emphasizing the moral factor and overemphasizing it? Our national morality is often overemphasized. In foreign policy our virtues are ambiguous. Our leadership itself shows this when it is faced with two very concrete issues in succession. We lose by our moral pretenses. We have too narrow a statement of our moral principles.

In this sense, moral pretense is a self-defeating thing. Yet it is a necessary part of social, moral, and political cohesion.

WILLIAM T. R. FOX: Assertion of a moral purpose is a necessary thing with or without pretense. Policy is justified by recognizing implicitly or explicitly its moral rationalization. Other nations are morally justified in doing the same thing.

HANS MORGENTHAU: The denial of the statement that politics requires a choice is misleading as various examples will show. Indo-China involved a choice between our strategic aims and the moral principle of the rights of the local people.

PAUL NITZE: Indo-China is not a moral choice. There was a hierarchy of moral value there.

JAMES RESTON: There is an element of time change in this question of morality. You have a different problem in Korea and Indo-China when it comes to the moral issue. The timing is what makes the problem different. There is also duality in the situation. In the beginning of the Indo-China problem, FDR saw very clear moral purposes. This was a nation that, according to him, was entitled to freedom at the end of the war. But since then the U.S. has not always operated on the principle that the Indo-Chinese were entitled to freedom. We needed the cooperation of France in Europe while keeping their interest in the problem of Asia. We subordinated the moral rights of the people to the new value of preserving Franco-American unity.

WALTER LIPPMANN: If a normative theory exists or could exist, then our dilemma could be resolved. We would save ourselves a lot of talk if we thought such a principle for international relations were possible.

DEAN RUSK: Can we put the question in terms of Mr. Niebuhr's three principles: justice, liberty and equality? Is it possible to construct a theory which has more content than that which would be of general application? Where do we find it?

JAMES RESTON: We would have to find it in a general normative concept or theory.

REINHOLD NEIBUHR: In view of the infinitive contingencies in the historical situation, you cannot give more body to normative theory than justice, liberty and equality. An historical situation cannot produce a theory which can tell you how much you should trust the future against the present nor the past against the present or future.

ARNOLD WOLFERS: If we say the moral issue in our time is unique, then we open the door to unique problems of intuition and arbitrariness, of putting the values one prefers higher than those of someone else. You then rationalize every choice you make. If you have a hierarchy of values with stability at the top, then you have the impossible dilemma of sacrificing the national interest. We know of the Catholic set of absolutes. We have seen morally creative acts which others could only judge after the act.

WALTER LIPPMANN: The theorist is in the position of the guide to the statesman. The theorist can go further than the practitioner. Theory is not now normative, but it could become more so. It is capable of development. It is an hypocrisy to say that the study of ends is not a field for theory, but it should not be assumed that it has been accomplished. There is a field for theory here, but it has not been accomplished.

REINHOLD NIEBUHR: A good theory should have to provide the recognition of the existential fact of the difference between interests and ideals. No side can have complete victory. Britain allowed theory to have more and more differences, i.e., between Churchill and Attlee. We cannot follow this in purely theoretical terms.

WALTER LIPPMANN: Theories are capable of being modified by a process. This is what brings Britain greatness. We need a theory for the evaluation of norms as they are evolving in society.

ARNOLD WOLFERS: We might then be able to ask if equality is preferable to liberty.

WILLIAM T. R. FOX: Even if you could get a consensus of different cultures, the battle would go on. Immediate and specific evils would still be present. What kinds of theory promote a consensus about immediate and specific goods and evils?

DON K. PRICE: It is Kennan's idea that one gets into a lot of trouble by being moralistic and legalistic, but the nature of our political society demands that we do this. The United States cannot follow national interest in any calculating way. The Utopian has done more to alter our democratic institutions by choosing what he can do in our foreign policy.

KENNETH W. THOMPSON: This is the tragic conflict of politics. The fact that the people have national loyalties which transcend the national interest presents a problem and is not wholly an advantage. RN might comment on his claim that the people can conceive of our international responsibilities in broader terms than the government. Is this always good? Or are the national ideals and loyalties of the people something which can be an obstacle to the conduct of foreign policy if they too greatly exceed the limits of statesmanship?

REINHOLD NIEBUHR: You cannot let go of the problem of establishing norms. You have got to have a full statement of the norms. You must have as adequate a description of the norms as possible, but you must include the realization that normative theory cannot be universally accepted. However, theory can be changed and we get whatever peace and justice we have because there is change.

WILLIAM T. R. FOX does not believe the conflict, say between values like justice and peace, can be resolved.

REINHOLD NIEBUHR: There was a Jewish socialist who was a very religious person and when Israel was formed there was a great struggle about the constitution. This particular man said that Israel should not have a constitution because the religious people would try to guarantee their rights against the irreligious people. So an unwritten constitution was the solution. In a written constitution we are trying to provide ourselves against all eventualities and this cannot be done. The Jew thought that with a very general constitution life would be tolerable but not with an intolerable constitution. Therefore he urged that they broadly define the issues that they should definitely adopt for the unwritten constitution.

ARNOLD WOLFERS: A lot of people think we have made progress on moral issues. I think that moral theory can do a great deal to clarify the assumption of the immorality of the resort to violence. Moral theory can clarify this. There is an assumption that the *status quo* is better than the resort to violence. Theory breaks down because of an oversimplification of problems of force, ideologies, etc. Where is change better and where is it justified so that it in turn justifies violence? We need a hierarchy of values to tell us what is worth a world war. Certain cases may justify violence. Are these policies arbitrary choices? In the instances of Hitler and Danzig, the American colonies and freedom, one can make a strong case for violence.

KENNETH W. THOMPSON: Kennan makes one point about our national interest which might be mentioned here. Because of our emerging power position, we try to state our interests as if they were universal moral principles for all nations. We have concepts of justice for our own national society. How do you avoid a normative approach to international relations which imposes national morality on to the international scene? How do you escape the tendency of past great powers in the formalization of national principles into the contractual principles of international relations? It does seem to me that this at least raises serious questions regarding the ability to give content to justice or regulative principles. The British are dualistic. They have a theory of justice at home with which their operating theory of justice in their colonial empire has not always accorded.

REINHOLD NIEBUHR: The British colonial problem is varied. Your own ideological taint is what you must be careful of here. Sometimes one must settle for general regulative principles. The genesis of the common law and the unwritten constitution is better than what you can spell out. What kind of a theory would tell you whether an atomic war is preferable to yielding to the U.S.S.R.? These are choices which you cannot make in theory.

PAUL NITZE: We have made that choice. When the choice was made, we also took the risk of subjugation by the U.S.S.R. There are things that are worse than Atomic War. Under certain circumstances we would go to war atomically.

WILLIAM T. R. FOX: There is a considerable distinction between constructing a normative theory and the kinds of intellectual activity that apply to taking the next steps in foreign policy. What are the norms to be put into a normative value theory? What is the cost of one set of values as against another? What is the efficiency of a given set of means to achieve an end? What is the relevance of a particular prescription to the world as it exists, and a whole host of other activities which would clarify one's values?

B. A General Theory of International Politics

DEAN RUSK: Our second task is to consider theory in relation to the uniformities and similarities in international politics. We might ask Hans Morgenthau to review his major points regarding such a theory.

HANS MORGENTHAU: The problem of a general theory of international politics is similar to that of normative theory. We are faced with the ambiguity of historical experience. On the one hand events are unique. On the other hand, political experience contains an element of normality, regularity and rationality, and insofar as it does this it is susceptible to theoretical understanding. It is only because historical experience contains that latter element that it is possible to understand history as a continuum in the first place. The pitfall, of course, with a theory which tries to establish certain general laws out of the regularities and uniformities of historical experience is the difficulty in determining the relevance of a particular historical experience which, on the one hand, is similar to others, and on the other, is different. All philosophies of history have suffered shipwreck in the face of this contingency. I think a theory of international politics which must be political history is faced with this general problem. I think it is a problem which is essentially the same as that of a strictly normative theory. If you try to become too specific, you are bound to be confronted with experiences which lend themselves to certain deductions or misunderstandings. In actuality such experiences may not be examples of general laws. You have the summary of this thought in the adage that, "History teaches only one thing: it teaches nothing."

REINHOLD NIEBUHR: Why does Hans Morgenthau equate only rationality with the making of general laws? Such a concept does not appear to recognize the unique and dramatic in history, nor does it tell us what is unique and what is general.

HANS MORGENTHAU: Unique occurrences in history are accidental. They have no element of rationality in them. There are in history events which show a rational sequence and causal relation which makes observation possible. This is what makes it possible for us to understand them rationally.

WILLIAM T. R. FOX: Why are unique occurrences more accidental than others?

DEAN RUSK: Give us a generalized proposition, Mr. Morgenthau.

HANS MORGENTHAU: Take the principle of Machiavelli, "You should never make an alliance with a stronger nation." There were calamitous effects in Italian City States and Greek City States when they made an alliance with a stronger nation. The principle is sensible as far as it goes. But how far does it go? What are you going to do if you are a weak nation and the only nation that can promote your interest is a stronger nation? What are France and Great Britain going to do without the United States? There are disabilities because of this. There are circumstances where a weak nation ought to make an alliance with a stronger nation, even though there is a uniformity between its case and other cases, where it would not be desirable to make such an alliance. There are many circumstances which would invalidate at least for practice Machiavelli's principle.

DEAN RUSK: I am not convinced. Because there are some uniform elements, I would have supposed that you would state a proposition such as, "When weak states make alliances with more powerful states, they suffer thereby." This would be subject to testing by the study of a number of cases where this has happened. If there are cases where this has not happened, then the principle breaks down.

WALTER LIPPMANN: We need an operating rule based on theory.

REINHOLD NIEBUHR: Can we say there are unique versus general laws? History is more difficult than mere generalizations. The U.S.S.R. was and is a power state. Therefore, we know that this is a recurrence of what we have had before. This leads to a certain understanding, but it contributes as well to misunderstanding because there is also another pattern. Nationality is so difficult a proposition that we must relate unique events to it. Many patterns make up historical destiny. Rationality as it has been presented is equated with general laws. The most rational approach is highly discriminatory in relation to the real situation that we can know.

HANS MORGENTHAU: I agree insofar as the practical question is concerned.

REINHOLD NIEBUHR: A theory must do justice to the complexities of change.

HANS MORGENTHAU: Such a principle would in its generality look something like the regulative principles of normative theory.

ARNOLD WOLFERS: The choice for historians between a general law versus an historical guide confuses them. Since, as political historians, we are in history, we deal with this general theory. History has certain common elements. We possess a certain knowledge of elements in common. What we have lacked is the predictability and variability of concepts and thinking. Today we know something about behavior. We have achieved some success in the classification of behavior. There are a great number of variables. Theory is just as rational with a very high level of variables as it was with single variables. The statesman has to make choices on this level. It is a too simple abstraction to speak of Britain. It is nearer to reality to come down to more specific problems. We have to know many, many things depending on the context and on the questions that you wish currently to answer. Chances are that such a theory won't complete itself. For a complete theory we have to stay on a relatively high level of abstraction. It seems to me that we ought to try in theory, however, to get down from the highest levels of abstraction which are of no use to the concrete. We must get down, for example, to far more complex models. These must include the irrationality of many actors. If we introduce the notion that totalitarian governments in reality overestimate their own power and underestimate others, we are dealing with a specific theoretical problem. Democratic governments may accept the concept that peace is much better than violence. This may be only partly rational. Our minds in the present state of thinking cannot handle such a complex body of variables; we are simply up against something that you cannot handle.

PAUL NITZE: Is there utility in making over-abstractions? If you assume that what the U.S.S.R. wants to do is to maximize power and then trace down from there all individual variables, do you not get a logical approach to the problem? What is the maximizing procedure? What would it lead one to expect if one assumed that the purpose of the Kremlin was to maximize its power?

KENNETH W. THOMPSON: Is what you do when you talk about an abstraction like the state to proceed from some base founded on certain observations checked against history and experience? There are invariably complex elements in a foreign policy, but it is important to start from a fixed point or common denominator. You can of course start with the idea of the elite or any other individual group and use its philosophy as a clue to foreign policy. This will eventually break down into the idea that a foreign policy is nothing more than the expression of an individual's thought. When individuals with quite different political philosophies, e.g. Bevin and Churchill, or Acheson and Dulles conduct foreign policies which are similar and even identical in basic objectives, the limitations of this approach become quite obvious. Knowledge about the philosophies, motivation or irrationality of actors may not be the best starting point.

There is another approach that contends that foreign policy is incarnate in the national objectives of a particular state. This approach is not oblivious of changing or unique factors. For example, it recognizes communism as a unique element which influences historical Russian policies. But communism is not disembodied and a purely independent ideology but is expressed through the form and machinery of Soviet policy. We have now considerable literature that deals with the transformation of Marxist dogma when confronted with the imperatives of Russian national interest. With this second approach instead of starting with the actors, you start with general propositions concerning the historic interests of states. You seek to understand the reality on which those propositions are based. Then you apply or test the general principles of, say, Russian policy as it confronts a present concrete case. If you start the other way, with the actors and their biases and preferences, you have no fixed base. It is perhaps more important today to know something about the imperatives of our national security than to dissect the elements in Mr. Dulles' political and religious background. You start with the behavior of states and progress from there. At some point you will, of course, have to consider the individual actors. What interests you in a given situation is not a theory so much as an application of theory to a practical situation and at this point variable and changing factors admittedly are introduced.

ARNOLD WOLFERS: You start with a general hypothesis which you have gained from observation. If you come to the conclusion that the main center is the nation state, then you come to the conclusion that this is the most interesting subject, and this is the most vital center of the situation. But what is the primary loyalty of the people? People and individuals have definitely developed loyalties. The main center of action is states. We cannot now look at the essence of statehood and deduct anything from that. All we can see is what states want to pursue; they always need power. We cannot know the behavior pattern of states until we understand the human element. We are analyzing phenomena which we know empirically, and it depends upon the question we are asking which approach is the most fruitful one.

HANS MORGENTHAU: Arnold, are you saying that a theory of international relations ought to be strictly empirical and should make no general a priori assumptions to be defined by experience? As, for example, that the struggle for power is the essence of international affairs?

PAUL NITZE: Nations seek power—there is a second hypothesis. Nations want power in different degrees and under different circumstances.

WALTER LIPPMANN: Machiavelli was always within a situation and the facts rearranged themselves around that fact. I thought Arnold Wolfers' statement was admirable. Where, however, were you standing when you made this hypothesis? The importance of this is that great political theories are designed as advice to someone as to how to act. They are always within a system and are arranged around the facts of the situation. If you were a Guatemalan, you would construct a different political theory.

ARNOLD WOLFERS: Yes, I probably would. The right and correct theory would have to be a theory of God.

WILLIAM T. R. FOX: This would not be a theory of action.

PAUL NITZE: Confronted with the facts, how should you behave?

WALTER LIPPMANN: I feel that theory would have helped us in the three choices we faced in Korea. The decision could have been based on more than information.

DEAN RUSK: In Korea we were confronted with three choices: 1) to get out; 2) to stay at the 38th parallel; 3) or to cross the Yalu.

ARNOLD WOLFERS: In the Korean problem, the military made the decision; the people did not make this decision. We had to operate on the idea of what was likely to happen if we crossed the Yalu.

WALTER LIPPMANN: We had to consider what a power like China would allow.

ARNOLD WOLFERS: But didn't we have sufficient information to answer this question? It is not just information, it is some general hunch about how states behave that creates theory.

JAMES RESTON: In this case, though, the personality of MacArthur was involved.

DEAN RUSK: In this situation there was a very high element of risk. Some of us in the State Department thought that on balance they would not come in. The thinking was that the Chinese would never let the Russians cross their soil, so whereas the Chinese might fight, the Russians would not be able to come in without crossing Chinese soil.

JAMES RESTON: Can we deduce from British history that she would allow Malaya to go? If we say "no," this is a point at which theory can be useful.

DEAN RUSK: In the State Department with regard to the Korean situation, their general policy was based a good deal on what they had learned about aggression in the last 25 years. The decision to go into Korea was based on a theory. Also the influence upon our allies was part of the reason and this, too, was based on theory.

HANS MORGENTHAU: What are the elements of that theory? Is it applicable to Indo-China?

PAUL NITZE: Can the Korean situation apply to Indo-China, though? There is a difference in time and in location. At that time we would have risked general war. Now we do not know. We are not alone in having thermonuclear weapons. There is the H-bomb.

The meeting was adjourned at 6:00 P.M.

The meeting reconvened at 9:00 P.M., Friday, May 7, 1954.

C. Theory as the Basis for Action

DEAN RUSK: Could we now see whether we are capable of working out a generalized picture of the international scene? Mr. Nitze, you have mentioned a wartime experience in which you had a responsibility of doing something like that.

PAUL NITZE: We had experts at the end of the war looking into the experience of the Germans, Japanese, and British concerning war mobilization, and we found that each country went through exactly the same kind of experience in the same sequence of time. In the mobilization of the steel industry, of example, they were found to have operated under a similar mobilization sequence. This was found to be true in five different countries, all of which had quite dissimilar economic starting points. The facts of the situation forced people into the same solution. Do not many of these things hold for the political field as well? Malenkov's speech is an example. Anyone in this country would have written his speech if they had known all the facts. There is a core of stuff that can be generalized upon and then superimposed upon other ideas. It is useful to try to abstract.

HANS MORGENTHAU: This is a demonstration of the possibility of theory in international relations. How is it that an Indian philosopher, living 2,000 years ago, developed a theory of foreign policy, which is not only knowledgeable now, but also practical?

REINHOLD NIEBUHR: Good theory estimates the convergent factors in history. Laws in American culture tend to be too much like natural science laws. Rationality does not depend ultimately upon the conclusions to general laws. Overt law cannot be the sole source of authority. There must be justice, etc.

PAUL NITZE: Political considerations are of importance as are military considerations. They interrelate one with another. This interrelation should be more precise. For example, a great military success in Indo-China would have had bearing on political fields.

REINHOLD NIEBUHR: Could you not put it down as a law that any new weapon that is supposed to invalidate others has never succeeded in doing so?

PAUL NITZE: Isn't the difficulty when someone tries to make these principles absolute? They seldom are absolute.

ARNOLD WOLFERS: I am skeptical of this form of generalization. One has to look for much broader fields. One has to look for the rational way of doing a certain thing. A rational solution may be the moral solution. Why are there time lags between pronouncements and responses? Is it true that statements concluded in moral terms are provocative of resentment? If one has enough experience to draw up a whole series of propositions on how things appear to people, then one can transfer this to the international scene and say where this is likely to happen again. We have the rise and fall of Empires, for example. Power constellations can be studied on every level of historical relations. Personal, historical observations will give us the information from which to generalize. An example—nations which best fit the type of pattern of countries that are likely to go neutral.

REINHOLD NIEBUHR: Why is France neutral? How would you get that into a general principle?

KENNETH W. THOMPSON: The problem of European unification can be studied historically to see, for instance, why France opposes unification that would permit Germany to dominate. The chief historical objective in contemporary French foreign policy has been to safeguard her northeast frontier. One of the main British objectives has been to keep her commitments to the Commonwealth. These objectives account for policies toward Europe even in the face of Russian power.

ARNOLD WOLFERS: One can analyze situations to see what kinds of sequence of events one should look for. Certain concepts make for static situations and others make for change. What tends to make for the persistence of an image?

WILLIAM T. R. FOX: What do we know that leads us to believe that it is likely that France will behave in the way that we want her to behave?

KENNETH W. THOMPSON: Only if you study France's foreign policy, can you admit that recent French behavior has its peculiar rationality. The element of uniformity in such cases is well worth noting, even though in France's case fear of Germany if it is greater than fear of the Soviet Union is probably based on a faulty picture of the international scene.

ROBERT BOWIE: There is ambiguity in this whole concept of national interest. Terms like power and national do not convey anything to RB. The picture is so big, i.e., national interest, that anything can go under that heading.

HANS MORGENTHAU: They are vital to the understanding of foreign policy, not because they convey a fixed standard. There must be a certain point of view, a certain standard of evaluation, that must be applied to all kinds of situations and contents. What remains is a series of regulative principles which give one a standard of action. You cannot expect concepts such as national interest to have fixed concrete content, but you can expect from them certain principles of thought and action which are valid regardless of time and place.

DEAN RUSK: This question is directed to the policy planning staff conferees. Were there any generalizations that you could take as being given within which your policy considerations could go forward?

PAUL NITZE: Yes, we came up with many things that we thought were useful. But none of these were general things such as, it is a bad thing to appease.

ROBERT BOWIE: What would it include?

DEAN RUSK: Give us a sample, please.

PAUL NITZE: There are two different categories involving the things you do with respect to allies and on the other hand with the U.S.S.R. itself. (Three samples of analysis.) What do you conceive the national purpose to be? What are your intentions after you have found and stated them? Where does the question of degree enter in?

JAMES RESTON: The Truman Doctrine stated that we thought the U.S.S.R. to be our enemy. It also virtually stated that we would assist *any* state which is under attack from without or within. What general principles are involved here?

ARNOLD WOLFERS: The Truman Doctrine was supposed to be directed against any communist or any other kind of totalitarian form of government bent on imperialism. It stated that we would help any government against military attack.

KENNETH W. THOMPSON: Isn't it true that the Truman Doctrine was formulated in highly moralistic terms in order to gain Congressional approval?

PAUL NITZE: Yes it is true there was a better chance of the Truman Doctrine being approved by the Senate if one brought it up and identified it with some moral principle. I objected at the time to its over-abstract terminology. After all you were at that time dealing with concrete problems such as Greece. I thought it unwise to make it so general.

JAMES RESTON: Our definition of this is different. The Truman Doctrine related specifically to the fact that England was pulling out of Greece.

KENNETH W. THOMPSON: Can we answer further DR's question about a general proposition that would be acceptable to any group? Is a basic principle Walter Lippmann's notion that commitments and power must be kept in balance? Have we tested this in the controversy about policies of containment or liberation?

PAUL NITZE: Look at this business of commitments. First it is contractual, but you can't look at it from this point. Your interests may be different from your commitments.

WILLIAM T. R. FOX: Your propositions themselves are one of the elements that go into your capabilities.

KENNETH W. THOMPSON: Yet, if commitments exceed power, you have to increase your capabilities or abandon those commitments. In foreign policy how do you balance your interests with your commitments? You have to do something about it.

ROBERT BOWIE: Commitments and capabilities sound absolute, but actually you always have contingent elements.

REINHOLD NIEBUHR: No general proposition on this point is valid as Americans have so often assumed.

ROBERT BOWIE: We need other kinds of general propositions which limit conditions which may channel the range of choice. Within the limiting conditions you have room to make a few things work. There are intermediate stages which channel. If you push outside of these channels you will fall over the cliff, but within the channel you have a place for general propositions.

KENNETH W. THOMPSON: No one has claimed that general principles were strait jackets or comparable to laws of nature. They do, however, set limits to what states can do.

WILLIAM T. R. FOX: Meeting conditions is one of the reasons that theory of international politics does not seem to be relevant at the point of decision-making.

HANS MORGENTHAU: It is implicitly relevant to the decision. If you did not have theory, you would not have any decision at all.

WILLIAM T. R. FOX: But how is theory relevant to what American decision-makers do in Europe?

KENNETH W. THOMPSON: If all of Germany fell to the U.S.S.R., the whole balance of power would shift to the East. This is a basic political conception.

JAMES RESTON: Would it be useful to say that we went wrong in the postwar period because we were willing to follow theories that were false rather than having any great theory or for that matter any theory at all? Have we tried to take theory too far?

KENNETH W. THOMPSON: Herbert Butterfield argues strongly along these lines. The theory which guided us before World War II was that we had not appeased enough. Then came Munich and following World War II we say appeasement is the avenue to all disaster. After the war we have followed just the opposite theory, one of minimizing appeasement and emphasizing coercion and collective action.

REINHOLD NIEBUHR: Action after the war came on the basis of a wrong theory. The United Nations was based on an illusion that the big powers could work together.

ARNOLD WOLFERS: This country has swung from one extreme theory to another. It did operate on a very definite theory of how nations behave. From this we swung to a balance of power theory or containment. This particular enemy, the U.S.S.R., understands nothing but power. It is not that we should give up theory, but that we should revise it. We have to start analyzing the factors in international policy. What are the factors which make for reconciliation?

DEAN RUSK: How is this applied to China and Formosa? Serious limitations were put upon the policy itself. We stated our policy and then denied ourselves the means to carry it out.

PAUL NITZE: A theory isn't important until it becomes an intention.

JAMES RESTON: There is a certain element of bluff and hypocrisy in foreign policy.

ARNOLD WOLFERS: It is not a question of "we all want security," but what price are we willing to pay for it? What price glory?

WILLIAM T. R. FOX: Price means the sacrifice of some value. The concept of means in foreign policy implies some social value as does end.

ROBERT BOWIE: Not everything is for sale.

HANS MORGENTHAU: Many possible lines of action are available for the policy-maker in determining how he can act rationally. You can to a limited extent overcome those limitations of theory by successive definitions or refinements. However in reality you can only rely on a series of informed hunches. You are not going to overcome it by conceptualizing or other refinements.

PAUL NITZE: This depends upon what your assumptions are. You cannot put yourself in the place of Hitler's advisors.

ROBERT BOWIE: Hitler did rationally those things which ultimately defeated him.

PAUL NITZE: This introduces something more than just rationality.

KENNETH W. THOMPSON: But what is the rational element? Any look at the choice Germany made, namely to fight on two fronts, shows that Hitler departed from a rational standard for Germany policy.

WILLIAM T. R. FOX: The job is to think of all the reasonable courses of action and take care of them as they follow in sequence.

HANS MORGENTHAU: You cannot operate under two or three policies at the same time. One must adapt his policies to what he decides rationally is the most likely policy for the opposition to follow and then make his own policy, at the same time being prepared to follow the second and third policies.

DEAN RUSK: You don't want to be a prisoner of the worst possible choice.

ARNOLD WOLFERS: One can also deal with opponents who one knows are not rational. One can study their madness, etc.

ROBERT BOWIE: We are mixing up three kinds of thinking. 1) We need an hypothesis which is specific, i.e., something concrete, a hypothetical situation. 2) We need a process of reasoning or analysis. 3) We need a theory of international relations which seems to be more abstract than these things.

HANS MORGENTHAU: A rational hypothesis is the expectation of the likely action on your side or on the other side. You ask yourself how a rational man acts under such circumstances, given the particular personality of the man. How is he likely to act if he is rational? How do all or any rational men act given the typical conditions with which statesmen are confronted when they make or deal with foreign policy? Any rational statesman, being confronted with certain contingencies, will apply the principle of balance of power, alliances, armaments, spheres of influence. This you can postulate and prove by a multitude of historical examples.

ROBERT BOWIE: Where does that kind of generalization get you? RB doesn't see that it gets you any further forward.

ARNOLD WOLFERS: Other governments to the extent to which they have not gone over to the Communist camp will become more concerned with their security. There is always also the possibility of revising one's position to jump to the other side. Whether the loyalty to the nation state will recede, there may be a willingness to give up national independence for the sake of becoming part of the whole. With a proper theoretical background, attention will be drawn to individual and national peculiarities. What is the psychological factor in political realities, etc.?

HANS MORGENTHAU: You can contemplate elements in the equation. You can determine how India is going to act. India has a perennial problem of foreign policy to which she will react in three possible ways. A statesman functions here intuitively.

ARNOLD WOLFERS: This theory is not hypothetical. It is categorical. We have no absolute certainty about this; it is just common sense. As soon as you begin to talk about behavior, however, you are pretty safe.

HANS MORGENTHAU: Then it becomes meaningless.

ARNOLD WOLFERS: Physicists have a statement—wherever you have particles, it is impossible to predict.

WILLIAM T. R. FOX: If we assume that increased knowledge gives increased insights, it is quite possible that two increases of insights would be running along parallel lines, so that your over-all capability to predict might not be so inadequate.

ROBERT BOWIE: The more you enlarge our insights, the more you acknowledge your range of insights.

HANS MORGENTHAU believes that there is a clear division as to what can and cannot be theoretically known.

ARNOLD WOLFERS thinks in terms of spectrum—that which can be known, that which can be known fairly well and that which can't be known.

DEAN RUSK: Is it not possible that there may be some proposition of theory that may be valid now which would not be valid in connection with future history, i.e., atoms, etc.?

PAUL NITZE: We face our problems along a moving front.

JAMES RESTON: It seems to me that we need the old look. We have been perhaps over-concentrating on new weapons. Perhaps what we need is a turning back to commandoes and rangers. Go back to the old ways. It has been talked about, but no decisive action has been taken.

KENNETH W. THOMPSON: Is there often a lag between reality and theory? For example, at present we assume there is a bi-polar world, but this may already have disappeared. The centers of authority are perhaps no longer solely in Moscow and Washington. They may be in Tokyo, Berlin, Geneva, Seoul, etc. We cannot make everyone's decisions for them as we might have in 1947.

The meeting was adjourned at 11:30 P.M.

The meeting reconvened at 9:30 A.M. Saturday, May 8, 1954.

III. The Future for Theoretical Research

DEAN RUSK: Could we now discuss ways or means of strengthening the field? Let us put this question both to the teachers and practitioners. 1) What is the state of research on the campuses? 2) And what would you, the practitioners, like to see done?

ARNOLD WOLFERS: I think we should perhaps start by answering the question how much is being done. On the undergraduate level, courses are given which proceed on a topical basis. Those using Hans Morgenthau's textbook stress a theoretical approach. This type of approach has spread throughout the country. Many of the courses concentrate on international politics. Partly due to the Sprout book and the initiative of the Navy, much work on the undergraduate level is centered on the foundations of power. At the graduate level, international politics is taught on a rather high level, and new teachers are being produced who have been trained at this level. I think that the result has been that quite a group of sophisticated teachers are emerging who are showing great interest in the field. However, the newness of the field is illustrated by the fabulous lack of literature. One cannot find a monograph or study which is an attempt to bring present knowledge together.

WILLIAM T. R. FOX: Are you implying that what is missing is theoretical treatment of middle-sized problems?

ARNOLD WOLFERS: I would say that is so. One question we have not resolved is should one multiply general works in this field or find little problems to work on, aiming toward an eventual over-all study? For instance, students and scholars have become interested in image studies. A few have been published, but nobody has investigated them as to their value, so that you cannot put students on this type of work because they are really on their own with very little to guide them. There are some image studies currently underway, such as studies of Taft, Churchill, etc., which may lead to a series of implicit or explicit theories. When these are completed, somebody ought then to analyze them for clarification, interrelation, etc.

REINHOLD NIEBUHR: Should we think of what kinds of theory studies would be most helpful to the American scene? All of us have our opinions. First, I would think that any theoretical studies solving some of the vacillation between idealism and realism would be of value. The typical realist does not recognize many of the intractable and novel elements in any situation. Analyzing the constants would frustrate both the idealists and the realists. The idealist does not recognize the constants. Any significant theory would be one that cut both ways against the American tendency to think that history is more malleable than it is, or that it is characterized by universal laws.

The second set of studies would be rather appealing to the empiricists, and we do have the empirical tradition as well as the theoretical one. Empirical studies would be to analyze component parts, national security, power, etc. A detailed analysis of concepts into their component parts shows that this is a more complex thing than either the theorist or empiricist imagines. Historical studies of American foreign policy can be empirical in this sense. They will dramatize the oscillation between idealism and realism.

HANS MORGENTHAU: To continue Dr. Niebuhr's line of thought, one could demonstrate the convergence of those trends and the complexity of the problems to which they give rise by analyzing American statesmen. This is the general intellectual trend that we are parading at Chicago in order to show not by explicit theories but by theoretical treatment of historical personalities and policies what their theoretical approaches to foreign policy are and were. We can study idealism and realism. What is the relationship between them and what are the decisive elements which make them different. What were the tragic choices in Lincoln's political life? Or John Adams or John Q. Adams? What are the influences of theory today on the American scene? I would guess that one can influence American thinking better by applying theory to the study of history than by pure theory.

However, there are three main obstacles to the development of academic interest in a theoretical treatment of international politics. They are: 1) The current events approach to international relations which, of course, is intellectually the easiest approach. 2) The greatest present pitfall is the general social science tendency toward a particular conception of what is scientific. Everything qualifies as scientific that can be described in a particular social science jargon or pressed into a social science conceptual framework. Everything that cannot is not scientific and hence inferior. This tendency to identify theory with a particular type of social science has inhibited progress in the development of theory and general interest in a theory of international relations. 3) You have the tendency toward eclecticism which is the exact opposite of theory. You regard as belonging to international relations everything that transcends national boundaries. You then put everything into a bag and shake well and the only common requirement is that a thing transcend national boundaries. This becomes disconnected material. There is no conceptual framework. You have first to realize what particular trends oppose theory before you can start making theoretical concerns more fruitful and generally acceptable in the academic field.

DEAN RUSK: Does all this mean that a theorist is more or less indifferent to the work of the social scientist? What standards would theory have to use?

HANS MORGENTHAU: He does not need to be. The social scientist should be able to help the theorist to a very large extent. The scientific approach, however, must be contained within very narrow limits, e.g., where you can measure voting behavior, opinion polls, etc., where you have clearly established mechanical patterns.

REINHOLD NIEBUHR: The social scientists have been clearly influenced by Freudianism, e.g., in UNESCO a study of human aggressiveness. Basically this is one of the crucial problems in international relations and in social sciences, namely, the dominant approach which stands for reducing historical realities to a biological level, as against pure natural realities.

DEAN RUSK recalls in the State Department reading theoretical statements coming in from outside and thinking that the statements might be all very well, but they did not seem to have much to do with the kinds of things that he had to deal with. Somewhere between Hans Morgenthau's theory and Reinhold Niebuhr's there must be some kind of middle ground.

ARNOLD WOLFERS: I take my hat off to American social scientists as opposed to European social scientists. (That is, with respect to the kind of studies they turn out.) Europeans generalize about the nature and dignity of man and how man is being treated. In this country they set out to see whether this is so. With regard to the problems of wages, etc., in plants, the social scientists in the U.S.A. take the time to go out and get the workers' opinions and therefore they get results. People in Asia are in revolt because of something. Some people in America say let's go out and see what it is. What they often find is a minority in charge. In international relations we cannot go out into the field, but when you study individual statesmen, you have verification. Lasswell made some interesting studies about the symbols within a nation. Are people becoming more or less nationalistic?

WILLIAM T. R. FOX: We can point to qualitative content analysis, when there is no point or chance of being quantitative, e.g., Berelson.

HANS MORGENTHAU: There is the problem of what words mean and what they represent. There is a real question of what you can draw from qualitative word meaning. We are faced with the frequency with which certain words are used. You might well find, for example, that the use in society of certain words with religious connotation does not at all indicate any amount of religious devotion, but exactly the opposite. It may indicate a once devout religious society whose religion is in decline. This kind of efficiency in the counting of words is useless if there is no theory behind it. It is more than a mere technical question as to whether much useful knowledge can come out of counting words, because behind these technical procedures there is a theory as to what words mean and what conclusions you can draw by the quantitative examination of words and what is meant by the words. Theory without verification is metaphysics, but empiricism without theory is aimless.

ARNOLD WOLFERS agrees 100 percent with Hans Morgenthau, that good theory is served by good verification.

HANS MORGENTHAU: The breakdown of words does not tell you anything.

WILLIAM T. R. FOX: I would be a little bearish about the argument that a certain type of data collection is necessarily useless or meaningless. No method all by itself will give you anything. Having some system for collecting data, could give you organized data in semi-statistical form with a meaning that could then be argued about. It probably would mean something.

HANS MORGENTHAU: Data collecting is meaningless if there is no theory behind it to give it meaning.

REINHOLD NIEBUHR: The theory behind data collecting may be the wrong theory. You need more and more empiricism to break down propositions which are not true. Yet some American social scientists deny they have any theory at all.

KENNETH W. THOMPSON: An invalid theory coupled with the concealment of its assumptions makes the problem more difficult. Some students claim there are no assumptions.

PAUL NITZE: Suppose the presupposition guiding a project assumes that you are dealing with individuals who are biological. The implicitness of this presupposition is the more dangerous because it is never advanced as a presupposition, but is advanced as a guide for study. Current threads in theory began with Descartes; we have had a dogma that poses for a description of empiricism. If literature is historical, this forces it out of the realm of historical empiricism.

ARNOLD WOLFERS: You have to presuppose the rational man.

REINHOLD NIEBUHR: You have to presuppose the individual man who is preconditioned by his historical conditions. You can verify it as exactly as a social scientists does and as clearly as a natural scientist can.

KENNETH W. THOMPSON: The inhibition to theory has something to do with the great respect of social scientists for the man who has no theory. If you say you want to begin examining a particular problem like power, it is oftentimes said that your answers and conclusions are prejudged by the fact that you want to study something in particular. Some people hold that one group of students begin with a blank slate and another group starting with a theory or general interest is dogma bound.

REINHOLD NIEBUHR: If you say metaphysics, then you are assuming that history moves by actualizing facts. Metaphysics raises the whole specter of Toynbee. Metaphysics bedevils the historical scene. History is a realm of drama.

PAUL NITZE: People shy away from the metaphysical. Urge that they don't. Dulles' January 12th speech is a good example.

HANS MORGENTHAU: Dulles' January 12th speech is a classic example of the enormous difficulties you have in understanding international relations because you do not know what the speech means.

PAUL NITZE: This is not so. Anybody could see what Dulles' speech meant.

ARNOLD WOLFERS: It is important that we realize that evaluating theoretical propositions is in itself a very difficult task. In a way they are drawn out of impressionistic verification. Can we gain more by knowing more about it? We play hunches. It is not always necessary to go into tremendous field studies.

HANS MORGENTHAU: The trouble with such a field study as one might do in France is that the ambiguities you find on the theoretical level are bound to reappear when you try to interpret the empirical material. For example, today there are always doubts about the way the French people are going to go. You may refine and quantify the results, but I am afraid you can never resolve them.

PAUL NITZE: In finding out what fields are profitable to explore and bringing together hypothetical propositions that would really test your theoretical structure, you have not got a theoretical structure or several structures which are reasonable. They will break down. The great lack today is in a theoretical development which is adequately complex for the study of today's knowledge, so that it can be tested with whatever techniques are available and relevant.

WILLIAM T. R. FOX: There are among us several different kinds of theory. When the foundations decided to encourage area studies, this did not represent the acceptance of a theoretical proposition of a rather high order. For the student of international relations, the information was collected area by area and the job of the student of international relations comes in coordinating it. The principal approach, in contrast to area approach, was to find out how states behave. All by itself, however, it may overstress the uniformities and some of the significant uniquenesses will slip by (cf. pattern approach). Data have been collected whose object is to illuminate uniquenesses rather than the uniformities. How are we going to reduce the frequency of war in our state system? How can we predict in order to confound our predictions?

REINHOLD NIEBUHR thinks what Mr. Fox is saying about international relations is what anyone would say about any kind of historical studies. The framework of inquiry determines to a certain degree what you will find. This poses very great problems of verifications of complexities.

DON K. PRICE: All sciences proceed by testing their collection of specific data. It is not by this that you distinguish the social sciences from natural sciences.

ARNOLD WOLFERS: In a sense one can say you are always guessing. We never have absolute knowledge of anything. A hypothesis means that there is an element of guessing in everything. We can improve the guesses, and we can get some verifications.

WILLIAM T. R. FOX: In the short-run the practitioner today is superior. The academician in the middle or long-run may have something more to say, however.

DEAN RUSK: Maybe many of these empirical studies we have been talking about are historical studies. How many governments instruct their delegates at the United Nations?

HANS MORGENTHAU: It is important to know what the relation between the government and its representatives in the United Nations is. It is important from the theoretical point of view in that it throws light on the United Nations. From a practical standpoint you can learn which delegate to collar the morning of the vote.

DON K. PRICE: The Stein Group at Princeton is working with problems such as this.

ARNOLD WOLFERS: In what way have we decided that the theory, which we have now, is important?

DEAN RUSK: Is the field of theory suitable for the type of training by the Ph.D. route?

ARNOLD WOLFERS: Economists do this.

HANS MORGENTHAU: A number of my students are working on Ph.D. theses dealing with the theory of international relations, with regard to certain statesmen, but I am skeptical about pure theoretical studies on the Ph.D. level.

DEAN RUSK: If a person wants to work in international relations on a totally creative level on his Ph.D., can he?

REINHOLD NIEBUHR: As long as you work over a body of historical material and come to grips with other peoples' ideas, you can produce your own theory, although the intervention of verification is evident in all the humanities. I get so many questionnaires that I throw most of them out.

ARNOLD WOLFERS: Some of the Yale students feel that they cannot devote their thesis to creative theory work, but should choose something which can be marketed.

DEAN RUSK: What about theory produced by senior men with long public or private careers? Learned Hand quit being a judge and became a philosopher.

ARNOLD WOLFERS: Everybody really has something that he wants to produce. There is the problem of men who are about to retire. Teaching on the whole depreciates after a certain age. There should be more opportunity for research after retirement. Most of AW's colleagues do not feel that they can afford to retire to pure scholarship.

REINHOLD NIEBUHR: There would only be a small number to whom you would want to give this kind of aid and there would only be a small amount of creative work resulting. John Hay Whitney and Guggenheim offer something along this line.

ARNOLD WOLFERS: Universities appoint research professors; you should perhaps give funds to the university.

REINHOLD NIEBUHR suggests help to young men at the assistant professor level. This is a very productive level at which to work.

DEAN RUSK: Publications. To what extent do you have the impression that there are notable contributions that do not get published?

ARNOLD WOLFERS: Surely all dissertations do not get published. Only in history do they get published.

DEAN RUSK: Is there a series of volumes where articles or monographs could be published?

HANS MORGENTHAU: Commercial publishing houses do not like to take the risk.

DEAK RUSK: Do you have to go out and get articles to fill up *World Politics?*

WILLIAM T. R. FOX: It is dangerous to do so. The answer to the question is, I think, "No."

HANS MORGENTHAU: Articles represent an area where it is difficult. An article which is not on the highest level of theory but on a lower level is difficult to publish. On the popular level, it is possible to get a slightly lower level of theory published, e.g., *New Republic.*

REINHOLD NIEBUHR: I would like to say something about the baneful effects of the fact that university presses have ceased to be university presses and have become commercial houses. University presses want to know what the possibility of making money on the project is. It is now more difficult to publish really learned works here than in any other country in the world. Due to the rise in prices these presses must have a guarantee of 5,000 copies to make it economically feasible. Would the undergirding of publications be a worthwhile project for foundations?

ARNOLD WOLFERS: The same problem applies to translations; e.g., translation and publication of Meinecke would be invaluable but the only publishing house that would undertake it is a British house.

KENNETH W. THOMPSON: We have talked about four kinds of theory: 1) normative theory—here well-known people can publish, but young men would not have the same chance; 2) the general type of theory—here the market is better; 3) descriptive theory or theory as a basis for action—there is not much outlet for this anywhere; 4) more rigorous empirical scientific theory—I think *World Politics* has done a great service for this type of writing.

DEAN RUSK: The potential costs in this field are very great. We have kept publishing subsidies down to cases where the Foundation is supporting an ongoing research program. We would like to raise the question of the usefulness of seminars, meetings, etc., among scholars. We have felt in the past that in order to be a success, the participants in such meetings must be dedicated to the topic of the meeting. If it is vital that a certain group get together, then it becomes more interesting as far as the Foundation is concerned.

ARNOLD WOLFERS: Many people who are out in the woods, particularly those not on the east coast would be keen on an idea that would bring them together.

WILLIAM T. R. FOX: Meetings without an agenda—do you need a frame of reference for a continuation of meetings? Or is the work so primitive that we might well have a series of meetings to be defined?

REINHOLD NIEBUHR: You need a rather specific topic and specific topics for papers. You should not bring people together without having them contribute papers, etc.

WILLIAM T. R. FOX: What about communication among scholars? If you had six or eight people with sufficient common interest and if they were at the seminar stage in preparation of research, perhaps this type of meeting might be a constructive way to get them together. There must be a focus to such meetings. Submitting their own work for discussion and possible revision would be very creative.

DEAN RUSK: Should we gather people together for a month in the summer?

HANS MORGENTHAU: Such a meeting should have a focus.

DEAN RUSK: Is there any point in having facilities in Washington where scholars could come any time they wished for study and discussion?

ARNOLD WOLFERS: This might create demands on the people's time here in Washington.

PAUL NITZE: I think you have to refine your work down to specific material before you can get people interested.

The meeting was adjourned at 12:00 noon.

Folder 70, Box 8, Series 910, Research Group 3.1, Rockefeller Foundation Archives, Rockefeller Archive Center, Sleepy Hollow, N.Y.
Reproduced with the permission of the Rockefeller Archive Center.

APPENDIX 2

THE THEORETICAL AND PRACTICAL IMPORTANCE OF A THEORY OF INTERNATIONAL RELATIONS

HANS J. MORGENTHAU

T HE CASE for a theory of international relations must be made on three grounds: its justification as such, its uses, and its content. In other words, three questions must be answered: Is a theory of international relations possible? Is it useful? And what ought its content to be?

I.

That men throughout the ages have thought little of a theory of international relations is borne out by the fact that but rarely an attempt to develop such a theory has been made; as rare instances of such attempts, Kautilya and Machiavelli come to mind. Men have generally dealt with international relations on one of three levels, all alien to theory: history, reform, or pragmatic manipulation. That is to say, they have endeavored to detect the facts and meaning of international relations through the knowledge of the past; or they have tried to devise a pattern of international relations more in keeping with an abstract ideal than the empirical one; or they have sought to meet the day-to-day issues of international relations by trial and error.

Yet each of these approaches presupposes, and in actuality reveals, a theoretical conception of what international relations are all about, however fragmentary, implicit, and unavowed such a theoretical conception may be. In historians with a philosophic bent, such as Thucydides and Ranke, the history of foreign policy appears as a mere demonstration of certain theoretical assumptions which are always present beneath the surface of historic events to provide the standards for their selection and to give them meaning. In such historians of international relations, theory is like the skeleton which, invisible to the naked eye, gives form and function to the body. What distinguishes such a history of international relations from a theory is not so much its substance as its form. The historian presents his theory in the form of a historical recital, using the historic sequence of events as demonstration of his theory. The theoretician, dispensing with the historical recital, makes the theory explicit and uses historic facts in bits and pieces to demonstrate his theory.

What holds true of the historian of international relations applies also to the reformer. He is, as it were, a "forward-looking" theoretician. His scheme of reform provides an explicit theory of what international relations ought to be, derived from an explicit or implicit theory of what international relations actually are. What has prevented William Penn, the Abbé de St. Pierre, or contemporary World Federalists from developing a complete theory of international relations is their primary concern with practical reform rather than the absence of theoretical elements in their thinking.

It is this same practical concern which has prevented the practitioners of international relations from developing an explicit theory of what they are doing. Even a perfunctory perusal of the speeches, state papers, and memoirs of such divers types of statesmen as Bismarck, Churchill, Stalin, and Wilson shows that their relationship to theory is even closer than we found that of the historian to be. For the great statesman differs from the run-of-the-mill diplomatist and politician exactly in that he is able to see the issues confronting him as special cases of general—that is, theoretical—propositions. Here again it is not the substance of his thinking but the form in which it manifests itself which distinguishes the statesman from the theoretician of international relations. Here again it is his practical concerns, not his alienation from theory as such which prevents him from becoming a theoretician. Yet it illuminates the theoretical essence of the statesman's thinking that whenever practical concerns receded into the background or seemed best to be served by theoretical considerations, the four great statesmen mentioned above naturally transformed themselves from practitioners into theoreticians, making explicit in systematic or aphoristic form the theoretical foundations of their statecraft.

While these considerations establish the case for the possibility and even the necessity of theoretical understanding of international relations, they do not establish the case for an explicit systematic theory of international relations. What has stood in the way of the development of such a theory in the past is the same formidable difficulty which has frustrated the attempts to develop a theory of history and of politics in general: the ambiguity of the material with which the theoretician must deal. This material consists of events which are, on the one hand, unique occurrences that happened in this way only once and never before or since. As such, they are beyond the grasp of theory. On the other hand, these same events are also specific instances of general propositions, and it is only as such that they are susceptible to theoretical understanding. It is the task of theory to detect in the welter of the unique facts of experiences that which is uniform, similar, and typical. It is its task to reduce the facts of experience to more specific instances of general propositions, to detect behind them the general laws to which they owe their existence and which determine their development.

Yet where is the line to be drawn between the unique and the general in that sphere of experience which we call international relations? Two events in this sphere may be alike in certain respects; they will never be alike in all respects. How do the differences between the two situations influence the validity of the theoretical proposition which we might have developed from one of them? We might have learned from one situation that it is wrong to make concessions to an imperialistic nation or to intervene in a war between two other nations. Obviously, it cannot follow that one ought never to make concessions to an imperialistic nation nor intervene in a war between two other nations. A theoretical proposition is correct only under the assumption that all the relevant elements in the situation which have given rise to it are present in another situation and that no new circumstances are intervening, modifying their relevance. But how do we know with any degree of certainty which elements in the first situation are relevant to the theoretical proposition, whether these elements are present in the second situation, and what new elements in the second situation counteract the others? Here we can only play by ear, and must be satisfied with a series of hunches which may or may not turn out to be correct.

A theory of international relations must, then, guard against the temptation to take itself too seriously and to neglect the ambiguities which call it into question at every turn. A theory of international relations which yielded to that temptation would become a metaphysics, superimposing a logically coherent intellectual scheme upon a reality which falls far short of such coherence. A theory of international relations, to be theoretically valid, must build into its theoretical structure, as it were, those very qualifications which limit its theoretical validity and practical usefulness.

II.

What makes a theory of international relations possible in spite of the ambiguities of its subject matter is the rationality in which both the mind of the observer and the object of observation, that is, international relations partake. Foreign policy is pursued by rational men who pursue certain rational interests with rational means. The observer, however handicapped by the ambiguities referred to above, is able, by virtue of his own rationality, to retrace the steps which foreign policy has taken in the past and to anticipate those it will take in the future. Knowing that behind these steps there is a rational mind like his own, the observer can put himself into the place of the statesman—past, present, or future—and think as he had thought or is likely to think. This rationality, which the observer of the international scene and that scene have in common, makes both the history and practice of foreign policy possible. It also makes a theory of international relations possible.

A theory of international relations is a rationally ordered summary of all the rational elements which the observer has found in the subject matter. Such a theory is a kind of rational outline of international relations, a map of the international scene. Such a map does not give us a complete description of the landscape as it is at a particular historic moment. It rather gives us the main features of its geography which are not affected by historic change. Such a map then will tell us what are the rational possibilities for travel from one spot on the map to another, and which road is most likely to be taken by certain travelers under certain conditions. Thus it imparts a measure of rational order to the observing mind and, by doing so, establishes one condition for successful action.

A theory of international relations must be conscious of the fact that foreign policy is deflected from its rational course by errors of judgment and emotional preferences, the latter especially where foreign policy is conducted under the conditions of democratic control. A theory of international relations, by the very fact of painting a rational picture of the international scene, points to the contrast between what the international scene actually is and what it tends to be, but can never completely become. The differences between the empirical reality of international relations and a theory of international relations is like the difference between a photograph and a painted portrait. The photograph shows everything that can be seen by the naked eye. The painted portrait does not show everything that can be seen by the naked eye, but it shows one thing that the naked eye cannot see: the human essence of the person portrayed. Thus a theory of international relations must seek to depict the rational essence of its subject matter.

By doing so, a theory of international relations cannot help implying that the rational elements of international relations are superior in value to the contingent ones and that they are so in two respects. They are so in view of the theoretical understanding which the theory seeks; for its very possibility and the extent to which it is possible depends upon the rationality of its subject matter. A theory of international relations must value that rational nature of its subject matter also for practical reasons. It must assume that a rational foreign policy is of necessity a good foreign policy; for only such a policy minimizes risks and maximizes benefits and, hence, complies both with the moral precept of prudence and the political requirement of success. A theory of international relations must want the photographic picture of the international scene to resemble as much as possible its painted portrait.

Hence a theory of international relations presents not only a guide to understanding, but also an idea for action. It presents a map of the international scene not only in order to understand what that scene is like, but also in order to show the shortest and safest road to a given objective. The use of theory, then, is not limited to rational explanation and anticipation. A theory of international relations also contains a normative element.

III.

The content of such a theory of international relations is not to be determined a priori and in the abstract. A theory is a tool for understanding. Its purpose is to bring order and meaning to a mass of phenomena which without it would remain disconnected and unintelligible. Its content, then, must be determined by the intellectual interest of the observer. What is it we want to know about international relations? What concerns us most about them? What questions do we want a theory of international relations to answer? The replies to these three questions determine the content of theory, and the replies may well differ not only from one period of history to another, but also from one contemporaneous group of observers to the other.

Hypothetically one can imagine as many theories of international relations as there are legitimate intellectual perspectives from which to approach the international scene. But in a particular culture and a particular period of history there is likely to be one perspective which for theoretical and practical reasons takes precedence over the others. In the culture and period of history in which we are living, the focus of intellectual interest is obviously directed towards the political aspects of international relations. This being so, a theory of international relations must focus upon these political elements, and its organizing principle ought to be that social configuration which constitutes the distinctive characteristic of the political sphere: the struggle for power.

This is not the place to develop a systematic outline of a theory of international relations built around this concept. It is only by way of example that attention is called to a number of issues with which such a theory must come to terms.

1. The nature, purposes, and limits of a theory of international relations.
2. The nature of man.
3. The nature of power, its constant and changing elements.
4. The manifestations of the struggle for power on the international scene.
5. The problem and elements of national power.
6. The concept of the national interest, its constant and changing elements.
7. The problem of nationalism and national sovereignty.
8. The problem of balance of power, its constant and changing aspects.
9. The limitations on the struggle for power, actual and potential.
10. The problem of international morality.
11. The influence of the modern technology of warfare upon international relations.

12. The struggle for the minds of men as a new dimension of international politics.
13. The relations between international politics and military strategy.
14. Foreign policy and domestic politics.
15. The democratic control of foreign policy.
16. The problem of diplomacy.

APPENDIX 3

THE MORAL ISSUE IN
INTERNATIONAL RELATIONS

REINHOLD NIEBUHR

T HE MORAL issue is so persistently raised, both in the theory and in the practical conduct of international affairs, not only because men honestly seek to do the right in their collective, as well as in their individual, life; but because they cannot follow their interest without claiming to do so in obedience to some general scheme of values. Since they are more inclined to follow their own interests in collective than in individual behavior, the moral pretension plays a very large part in politics, particularly in international politics. This is why the alleged father of modern political realism and cynicism, Machiavelli, made the pretension of moral aims a part of the science of politics even though he officially disavowed the reality of genuine moral motives in the life of the nation.

Moral questions assume moral criteria, by which we measure good and evil. Despite the perennial debate upon the question of the source and content of moral standards, we need not be detained too long on this question, because only the strictest Aristotelians will define the good as conformity to a pre-established ontological pattern of being. In social ethics at least, the freedom of man and the consequently wide variety of historic and dramatic patterns and configurations which he is able to elaborate, makes it necessary to have a more flexible definition of the good. It is usually defined tentatively in the phrase of Santayana as "the harmony of the whole which does not destroy the vitality of the parts." This definition excludes all tyrannically enforced harmonies and makes freedom to assert the unique vitality of each part, the criterion of moral value. It does not however, provide for discrimination between the interests of various members or parts of the whole, so that one member be not unduly sacrificed for another in the inevitable subordination of one to another, which is a necessity of the organization of any community, national or international. We thus arrive at a definition of the good for man's togetherness which makes justice, informed by the transcendent principles of liberty and equality, the criterion of morality. It is the practically unanimously accepted criterion, at least in the Western world, as informed by Hebraic and classical standards. It must be added that equality and liberty are only regulative principles of justice; community is not possible without a certain degree of subordination of one member to another, and without a modicum of coercion. Therefore liberty and equality are not simple possibilities but only regulative principles. Naturally the debate on how much or how little of either subordination or coercion is necessary or desirable is endless.

Political morality contains an inevitable ambiguity because the factors of interest and power, which are regarded as an irrelevance in pure morality, must be at least tentatively admitted to the realm of social morality. Self-interest may be a source of discord ultimately;

but it is tentatively necessary to prevent the harmony of the whole from destroying the vitality of the parts. In similar fashion, granted the persistence of individual and collective interest, power, despite its dangers, must be admitted tentatively both to assure a proper counterweight against power in the interest of justice; and to provide for the coercion which is necessary for the order of the community. This moral ambiguity is raised to a special height in the morality of international relations because the rational community is so large and imposing, from the viewpoint of the individual, that it constantly makes claims upon his conscience, according to which its good is the end of the moral question. In the words of Hegel, the nation represents "concrete universality" for the individual. It is however more obvious in this day of international interdependence than ever before, that this is not so, for both the individual and the nation must face the more ultimate question, how the good of the nation may fit into a more general and universal scheme of value.

The force of "alter-egoism" is however so strong on the national level that it is almost universally recognized that a nation cannot simply espouse a more universal value at the expense of its interests. The highest morality possible for nations seems to be, not a sacrifice of its interests, but a prudent self-interest, which knows how to find the point of concurrence between its interests and the more universal interest.

This proposition is generally recognized by all sophisticated observers of national behavior. The moral problem in international relations would thus seem to be above debate. But a closer analysis of the facts reveals two very grave moral questions even if these facts be accepted:

A) Is not a consistent emphasis upon the national interest as self-defeating in national, as in individual life? Does not a nation, concerned too much with its own interests define those interests so narrowly and so immediately (as for instance in terms of military security) that the interests and securities which depend upon common devotion to principles of justice and upon established mutualities in a community of nations, are sacrificed? To obviate this peril we may have to make more rigorous distinctions between what is possible for governments and what is possible for nations. Perhaps the situation is that a government cannot morally transcend what the nation regards as its interests. But it would be fatal for the security of the nation if some loyalties beyond its interests were not operative in its moral life to prevent the national interest from being conceived in too narrow and self-defeating terms.

B) The second question arises from the fact of moral pretension which plays an even larger part in the life of nations than in the life of individuals. The same nation which insists on the one hand that it cannot act beyond its interests, claims, as soon as it acts, that it has acted, not out of self-interest but in obedience to some higher claim of "civilization" or "justice." How shall we deal with these claims? We had an amusing illustration of the problem at the beginning of the war. A British minister, seeking to honor us, declared upon our entry into the war that we had never been neutral since our loyalty to the principles of a democratic civilization had thrown the weight of our sympathies on the anti-Nazi side. This compliment was embarrassing since the Administration was under criticism by our isolationists and nationalists for having dragged us into the war against our interests. Secretary Hull therefore demanded and received an apology from the bewildered British minister.

The problem comes to us in another form in the operations of the Marshall Plan, as indeed in the whole exercise of our hegemony in an impoverished world. Despite the strong emphasis upon national interest we have been inclined to claim more benevolence for our policies than they deserve. We have thus aroused the resentments of people already inclined to criticism by their envy of our power and wealth. Particularly in France, we have been accused of compounding the sin of imperialism with the sin of hypocrisy. Though the exercise of our hegemony is a splendid example of the application of a wise self-interest when informed by loyalty to principles, transcending national interests, it is important not to claim too much for the moral quality of our policies. This is the more true since some of our "benevolence" is prompted, not so much by concern for the health of the free world but by reluctance to open American markets to a genuinely reciprocal trade.

This issue proves that the problem of moral pretension is a very basic one in international relations. We will be accused of hypocrisy by the world as the British were before us. We will resent this charge. But it will be at least partly true. We must learn how to moderate our moral pretensions. But those who criticize us must learn that hypocrisy is an inevitable byproduct in the life of any nation which has some loyalty to moral principles, but whose actions do not fully conform to those principles. The price of eliminating these hypocrisies entirely is to sink into a consistent cynicism in which moral principles are not operative at all. On this point the contrast between the British and the Germans is instructive. The British could crown their hypocrisies by Lionel Curtis's book *Civitas Dei*, in which the British Empire is absurdly equated with the kingdom of God. The Germans were naturally scornful of the pretensions but they ended by trying to build an empire which was clearly of the devil. One could make similar comparisons between the inevitable pretensions involved in our failure to realize the "American dream" in our race relations, so poignantly described in Myrdal's *American Dilemma*, and the consistent realism and unhypocritical cruelty of the South African approach to this problem.

These considerations must persuade one that the moral issue in international relations consists as much in moderating moral pretensions as in establishing moral norms for man's collective life. The continued ambivalence of all men toward these two issues, claiming in one moment that a nation has no obligation beyond its interests and in the next moment that it is loyal to obligations without consideration for its interests. This ambivalence is very revealing about the moral anguish of modern man amidst the political issues of his collective life.

Recently the distinguished Cambridge historian, Herbert Butterfield, has analyzed the moral issue in international relations in such a way in his *Christianity, Diplomacy and War* as to regard the element of moral pretension as a more persistent cause of conflict between nations than the competition between frankly avowed national interests. It is Butterfield's thesis that in the absence of an authentic religion, which regards all men and nations as falling short before an ultimate divine judgment, political causes have generated moral pretensions of religious proportions. These self-righteous claims make for unlimited and irreconcilable wars. Butterfield describes the present "cold war" as a tension between "two organized systems of self-righteousness." Thus he accuses a "Christian" and "democratic" civilization of the same monstrous pretensions as a system informed by an idolatrous religion. The point is worth making provisionally because it calls attention to the peril of pretentious claims and the tendency toward unlimited wars in the modern period, precisely because the moral claims are made too unqualifiedly on each side. The argument rather supports George Kennan's thesis that regard for the national interest can be more wise, because more moderate, than modern moralism in democratic policies.

But Butterfield betrays the animus of European neutralism and incidentally the failing of all religious humility, which is too intent on proving all causes to be equally dubious in the ultimate instance. He makes the embattled causes equally ambiguous in the immediate instance by the doubtful expedient of defining the cruelty of communism as nothing but the extremism of all revolutionary movements, which will abate as the revolution spends itself. Thus he obscures the permanent source of cruelty in a false religious political totalitarianism and effaces a very valid distinction between a free or open society and a tyrannical one. This proves that it is as necessary to make moral distinctions in political issues as it is to moderate the moral pretensions of each contestant.

It is significant that the moral issue in international relations should reveal itself in the two dimensions. The two questions: A) should the nation be bound by moral principles?; and B) how can the nation be prevented from claiming too much moral virtue for its actions? prove the ambiguity in which the actions of nations are enveloped. It must be observed in conclusion that a full consideration of the problem which is exhibited in the moral pretensions of nations leads us beyond the moral issues, and raises wider questions about the relation of political theory in the practice of statesmen in contemporary America. For moral pretension is but one aspect of the general inclination of modern men, who are undoubtedly agents in history, to forget that they are also creatures in the very historical process in which they must take responsible action.

Refusal to admit the moral ambiguity, and the very tentative character of any nation's virtue is one form of this blindness. The realistic statesman, intent upon the national security who advises his nation that "there is nothing which America cannot do if we approach our problem with sufficient vigor," exhibits another form of this blindness, particularly dangerous to a nation which faces the paradox that it is less master of its own fate in the day of its supreme power than in the day of its impotence.

But the statesmen are relatively free of this blindness, compared with the prevailing social science of our day, which insists that the historical realm is analogous to the realm of nature; and that the proper "scientific technics" can assure men mastery over their historical fate, as complete as their previous mastery over nature. Fortunately, the political sciences are less infected by this illusion than sociology, for instance. But they are sufficiently infected to make many of their studies irrelevant to the practice of statecraft in a day, in which the watchword must be "sufficient unto the day is the evil thereof." In other words the paramount problem for contemporary study of international relations is to supplant the illusions which we have inherited from the French Enlightenment and which are most characteristically expressed in the influence of Auguste Comte upon our social thought, with the wisdom of an Edmund Burke (and, one might add, of a Winston Churchill). This basic problem of political philosophy must be solved before political theory can become relevant to the issues which the statesmen of our nation face.

Folder 69, Box 8, Series 910, Research Group 3.1, Rockefeller Foundation Archives, Rockefeller Archive Center, Sleepy Hollow, N.Y.
Reproduced with the permission of the Rockefeller Archive Center.

APPENDIX 4

INTERNATIONAL RELATIONS THEORY AND AREAS OF CHOICE IN FOREIGN POLICY

WILLIAM T. R. FOX

THE APPARENT chaos of interstate relations in a multiple-sovereignty system can be "ordered" in a variety of ways by disciplined and disinterested observers. Some observers see regularities in the behavior of the states they are observing which permit them to theorize about the behavior of states in general, e.g., "All states seek to maximize their power positions." Others are able to explain the cycles of victory and defeat which various states have experienced in terms of key relationships, e.g., that between the "haves" and the "have nots" or that between "land power" and "sea power" or the struggle over some key area, the "Rimland," for example. Others leave questions of state motivation to one side and concern themselves solely with explanations for power differentials between states. No one of these approaches is more theoretical than another. None of them is necessarily incompatible with any other. What kind of abstraction is useful depends on the intellectual operation in which one is engaged.

Cartographers understand that no one flat map can be accurate as to more than one of the following: areas, directions, shapes. A globe sacrifices no two of these to the third, but it is incapable of showing detail and is of little use for navigation or geological surveys, for example. The analogy to international relations theory here suggested by cartography may be pertinent and exact.

No one theory may be equally accurate in explaining the cycle of peace and war, the rise and fall of great states, the extent to which the future is already implicit in the past, why certain states are "great powers," and so forth. A "globe" theory which comprehended all these might not be of very much use in understanding, for example, how Western diplomacy has in our century sought to avoid having to deal with a Russo-German coalition. Theories of less architectonic proportions might be more useful in explaining this particular uniformity of state behavior, although of little use in some other context.

A theory which explains why States A, B, C . . . were strong and J, K, L . . . were not has its role, particularly if strength and/or weakness is really explained. While useful, it would have the same limited usefulness as the anthropologist's conception of a "pecking order" in indigenous cultures. It explains who has what—e.g., "status is measured by the number of cattle one owns"—but not who gets what, i.e., what qualities cause one's herd of cattle to grow and his fellow's to shrink. A conception of a pecking order in our state system is useful if one is seeking to explain the behavior of states in a state system at any given time or within a time period too short for the pecking order to be modified. It is useless to explain why the family of great powers changes, sometimes even without inter–great power war. It is equally useless in explaining how a policy-maker can achieve for his state optimum security in an insecure world or how states generally can achieve an all-round increase in security.

The future is not *tabula rasa* on which we are free to write what we choose. But neither are we puppets dancing on the stage of history in response to "first causes," "basic factors," or, for that matter, inevitable progress toward bringing the Kingdom of God down on God's earth. National political action consists in achieving the best possible reconciliation of the desirable and the possible.

We ought therefore to attempt to order the blooming, buzzing confusion of world politics by collecting and arranging our data so that it helps us to understand the relatively fixed, the changing but uncontrollable, and the manipulatable aspects of world politics. Within the range of the changeable we need to collect data which helps us to predict ever more accurately the consequences of particular courses of action.

If man is to have the opportunity to exercise some measure of rational control over his destiny, the limits of the possible and the consequences of the desirable have both to be investigated. A theory of international relations is thus needed which distinguishes

a)   the "givens" in the world political equation—resources, shapes of continents, conception of politics as an unending process (however its form may change), etc.

b)   long-run basic changes—rise of nationalism, spread of coal-and-iron technology, the demographic revolution, etc.

c)   consequences of state policy—the policies of other states over which one's own state has relatively slight control and the policies of one's own state which are not chosen primarily in a foreign policy context,

d)   the remaining area of choice—levels of preparedness; patterns of alliance; use of organization to adjust conflict or facilitate peaceful change, etc.

Although I would not have chosen to submit a paper of my own as an example of theoretical activity in international relations, Mr. Thompson believes the accompanying paper, "The Integration of Civilian and Military Considerations in the Making of National Policy," may serve some purpose in advancing our discussion of what "theory" is or ought to be. This paper is undoubtedly theoretical if one means only that it smells of the lamp and that its writer could prepare it simply by sitting and cogitating. But when one asks how it happens that one has selected this particular problem as being in some context or other "important," he realizes that there must have been some theory, implicit or explicit, underlying his choice. In this case, there was a theory of world politics in which the relationship of force to policy was regarded as crucial and in which the relation of potential to available power was determined by choice rather than by history or geography. There have, however, been studies of civil-military relations based on quite different theories, e.g., that standing armies are an important threat to democratic institutions, that wars are caused by munitions-makers, or that the real sinews of war are to be found in a strong economy rather than a fully-cocked military machine. And the data selected for analysis were consequently quite different. It is the function of theory to make fully explicit some of the implicit criteria of selection of problems for intensive analysis. The use of theory may bring out some dimensions of the problem that may otherwise be overlooked and may help the analyst to discover some implications of his analysis that will in turn lead to a modest reformulation of the theory.

Theory in the large then provides the frame in which systematic and imaginative hypothesizing can most readily occur. These hypotheses still need to be tested empirically and reformulated to take account of observed data. "Theorizing" is to be distinguished from "research"—and the distinction is undoubtedly artificial—only by the degree of generality or speciality of the propositions being examined. The more general, the more purely speculative; the more specific, the more dependent on actually observed data.

Analytical propositions, whatever the theoretical framework in which they are placed, which purport to "explain" have first to be subjected to empirical testing and then reformulated to take account of the difference between the theoretical model and the actual observations. Let us assume, however, that the analytical statements in the paper on integration of civilian and military considerations are borne out. In what way would they then contribute to our theory of international relations and how does the international relations theory aid in formulating the further testable hypotheses?

1) While basic factors such as resources, location, population, skills, etc. may determine power potential, actual power depends on the level of sacrifice which a society imposes on itself and in the efficiency of the organization which expends that portion of the national income.

2) The range of choice open to the artificers of state policy depends upon decisions made as to the degree to which power potential is transformed into readily available power and as to the form in which that power shall be mobilized.

3) World politics can hardly be understood, and certainly cannot be rationally guided, unless account is taken of existing and possible civilian-military relationships. Americans can hardly exercise rational control over their own destiny unless there is the most complete possible understanding of the presently existing civil-military relationships in this country and of the advantages and disadvantages of possible modifications in the present relationship.

Folder 69, Box 8, Series 910, Research Group 3.1, Rockefeller Foundation Archives, Rockefeller Archive Center, Sleepy Hollow, N.Y.
Reproduced with the permission of the Rockefeller Archive Center.

APPENDIX 5

THE IMPLICATIONS OF THEORY FOR PRACTICE IN THE CONDUCT OF FOREIGN AFFAIRS

PAUL NITZE

I N A short paper it may be helpful to give a particular focus to the subject. I propose therefore to address the impact of theory on practice from the standpoint of the State Department Policy Planning Staff (S/P).

That political theory and political philosophy have a direct bearing on practice is hardly debatable. The principal problems presenting themselves to a body such as S/P are of such a degree of complexity that they cannot be intelligently discussed, even among the members of the staff, without simplifications, abstractions, and assumptions. Facts must be ordered to bring out significant generalizations; assumptions have to be made as to the probably causal interrelations between diverse factors; judgments must be made as to the hierarchy of values and of objectives. Without the tools of theory and political philosophy (whether their use is implicit or explicit), it would be impossible to proceed in any rational manner. To deal with such problems as present themselves to S/P in the full richness of their reality would require methods analogous to the simultaneous solution of an almost infinite series of equations in the higher calculus. Many of the problems are without clear precedent; they cannot be resolved solely on the basis of tradition or of historical experience. The question is not whether to use the tools of political theory and political philosophy. The question is rather what tools are applicable to what situations and to what end.

Some have suggested that the freedom of action of those conducting our foreign policy is so restricted by the pressures of public opinion, special interest groups, and political factions in the Congress that there is little point to broader considerations of political theory or philosophy. This I do not believe to be true. Under Mr. Acheson a serious effort was made to separate consideration of the national interest in a given context from consideration of the probable domestic popularity or the domestic political feasibility of a given course of action. Resolution of conflicts between the two sets of consideration was considered to be the responsibility of the resident and his senior advisors. Certainly many sources of action which appeared to be in the national interest from S/P's viewpoint were either deemed to be politically infeasible or became feasible only after considerable delay. But on many of the most important issues we in S/P were more troubled by the difficulties of clearly thinking through the merits of the problem ourselves than in consideration of the domestic feasibility of the various possible courses of action. As an example, after the initial defeat on the Yalu, should the war be extended to Manchuria, should Korea be evacuated, should an attempt be made to secure a settlement within Korea? As far as domestic public opinion was concerned either of the first two courses seemed most likely to achieve domestic support. After the most painful analysis and soul searching the third course was judged to be the wisest and was carried through to decision almost solely by Mr. Acheson's personal will and determination.

Many who have had the responsibility of dealing with important practical decisions are distrustful of formal theory. A wrong theory, an oversimplified theory, or a theory applied out of context can produce disastrous results. Most people dealing with practice are properly skeptical about carrying any theory too far. Some go so far as to completely condemn theories which, as stated, are oversimplified even though they may in fact contain some partial element of wisdom and helpfulness. They prefer to prick out a policy by the case method. One relies on what seems to have worked in the past or, if there is no good precedent, one tries something attempting to avoid getting so deeply committed as not to be able to try something else if the first decision doesn't work. This would be fine if one could always do it. Some decisions just aren't reversible. Having built a hydrogen bomb we have built one. Having not bombed beyond the Yalu in 1950 the identical circumstances will never reoccur. Before the results of the application of wrong theory become so obvious that the theory is forced out of circulation by the consequences of their deficiencies, incalculable disasters and many years may flow by. Furthermore, the deficiencies of one body of theory having become explicit, there is a general tendency to overcompensate in the opposite direction.

In this context Keynes's comment would seem to be applicable to a broader field than the economic field which he was discussing.

> But apart from this contemporary mood, the ideas of economists and political philosophers, both when they are right and when they are wrong, are more powerful than is commonly understood. Indeed the world is ruled by little else. Practical men, who believe themselves to be quite exempt from any intellectual influences, are usually the slaves of some defunct economist. Madmen in authority, who hear voices in the air, are distilling their frenzy from some academic scribbler of a few years back. I am sure that the power of vested interests is greatly exaggerated compared with the gradual encroachments of ideas. Not, indeed, immediately, but after a certain interval; for in the field of economic and political philosophy there are not many who are influenced by new theories after they are twenty-five or thirty years of age, so that the ideas which civil servants and politicians and even agitators apply to current events are not likely to be the newest. But, soon or late, it is ideas, not vested interests, which are dangerous for good or evil.

Keynes's quotation, however, implies that those who are engaged in practice do not themselves have original and valid insights in their subject. I believe this to be incorrect. Many of those who were actively engaged in finance saw much of what Keynes had to say about economics, and to some extent with greater clarity, long before Keynes had published his theory. The point is that in the realm of practice thought focuses on the concrete series of actions which it appears important and possible to undertake. Theory attempts to deal with the full continuum of the subject. Even for those in Wall Street, for instance, who in their daily actions had been operating on insights fully consistent with Keynes's "General Theory of Employment, Interest and Money" a clear and lucid statement of the theory gave additional elucidation and clarity to something they understood well enough in detail but had not put together in its full generality.

Similarly in the field of foreign affairs, policy tends to focus on certain modes in the continuum where action appears both possible and significant. But a host of influences from the full reality of the situation keep flowing in to modify or confound the best thought through plans of those who worked out the policy.

Two points would seem to flow from this analysis. The first one is that broad theories can serve a function in elucidating the nature of the continuum. The second is that those engaged in practice may have insights derived from concentrated experience and thought on the particular nodes where action was significant and possible which can both assist the theoretician and serve to test checks on his theories.

At the outset of this paper it was suggested that simplifications, abstractions, and assumptions were necessary in any attempt to reason about foreign affairs. There is the opposing consideration, however, that over simplification presents great dangers. Any set of theories which does not deal at least with the minimum necessary and sufficient elements of a situation is of little help to the practitioner.

I have little patience with those behaviorist theories which maintain that there is no such thing as a better or worse decision in foreign affairs and that the proper subject for the student of international affairs is merely what decisions were in fact made and why. Almost invariably value judgments remain in this type of analysis but in implicit rather than explicit form. It would seem much better to get necessary value judgments out into the open where they can be looked at than to have them obscured in a pseudo-scientific approach.

We found in S/P that many of the important questions forced us back to deeper questions of the ontological and moral order. The question as to whether to proceed with the construction of a hydrogen bomb was in part a question of economies in scarce neutrons, in scarce scientific talent, and in scarce dollars and the resources the dollars represented. This part of the analysis presented certain technical difficulties but merely technical difficulties. The other part of the analysis dealing with the moral and political considerations presented difficulties of a wholly different order.

At the moment there appears to be less conscious effort to apply the tools of political theory and political philosophy explicitly in the process of policy decision than in the last administration. Perhaps the greatest contributions of theory today can be in the general area of public opinion and in reducing the area of conflict between public understanding on the one hand and rational consideration of the national interest on the other. In any event, however, the prior question would seem to be that of gaining greater clarity and precision as to where the national interest lies and what can be done about it.

The concept "national interest" seemed to us in S/P to be useful shorthand as implying something broader than the narrow interests of one or another domestic group. It was not considered useful as implying anything further as to content. The long range interest of the United States may very well correspond with the major interests of a much larger group than the citizens of the United States. It may in fact necessarily correspond with the basic interests of the vast majority of mankind while being in conflict with certain short range and partial interests of the United States. The essence of the problem seemed to us not to be whether to follow the national interest but what the national interest in a given context was and what in the realm of the possible, could be done to promote it.

From such considerations we in S/P were led on the one hand toward the more philosophical considerations which seemed to be necessary for clarity as to the basic content of the national interest and on the other hand to attempts at greater precision as to what was in the realm of the possible. Frankly, it was our opinion that much of the contemporary academic work in the theory of international politics fell between two stools. It did not have sufficient depth in philosophic insight to give much light on the question of the long range content of our national purpose and on the other hand much of it failed to meet the test of being relevant to the realm of possible action. We rather felt that the band of what might be within the realm of the possible, either for good or evil, was quite broad and expanded the further one chose to look forward into the future but that effective action addressed to the real situation would be required to keep it moving in the right direction.

Folder 69, Box 8, Series 910, Research Group 3.1, Rockefeller Foundation Archives, Rockefeller Archive Center, Sleepy Hollow, N.Y.

APPENDIX 6

THEORY OF INTERNATIONAL POLITICS:
ITS MERITS AND ADVANCEMENT

ARNOLD WOLFERS

WHILE IT may be difficult to agree and perhaps premature to seek agreement on the content and scope of a theory of international politics, one which would bear comparison with economic theory, the purpose of theory can be defined. It is not to provide a substitute for the art of decision-making in foreign affairs, which in view of the infinite number of combinations of multitudes of variables that form any concrete solution, must always remain in part a matter of risky choices based on more or less rational hunches. Positively, however, by producing generalized knowledge about the way significant factors operate in the international arena, theory serves a) to satisfy man's need for intellectual orientation in one of the most vital sectors of his existence and b) to help policy makers enhance the rationality of their choices.

The relationship between theory and practice closely resembles that which exists in medicine. The medicine man of an earlier age was turned into a physician as philosophical and scientific inquiry clarified the values of health, sanity, and happiness which he serves, enlightened him on the way blood cells, viruses and other abundantly observable elements behave under identifiable and varying circumstances and suggested carefully tested ways in which undesired events like convulsions or abscesses could be cured or minimized. If, for lack of such guidance, the practitioner of policy must usually rely on what he believes to be his intuition and common sense, it is not hard to discover that in fact he is applying rough generalizations which he has picked up or frequently deduced from a single experience. Thus, policies are chosen today because "we dare not repeat the error of Versailles, Ethiopia, or Munich" as if the causal nexus between these complex events and the outbreak of World War II had been determined without ambiguity on the basis of careful analysis. The chances are that all of the available theoretical thought on peace treaty making, deterrence of aggressors or appeasement would not fill the pages of more than a single sizeable publication. Despite the forbidding difficulties, then, which stand in the way of respectable theoretical insight in this field—as they must have done, e.g. in psychiatry—there is no excuse for scholarly resignation to ignorance and fumbling in the dark.

Some theoretical effort has been going on for a long time. In the English-speaking world it was for centuries left to the moral philosopher who was chiefly concerned, of course, with a critical appraisal of the values toward which policy was being or should be directed and of the means that should or should not be employed. The need for such awareness and critical appraisal of the value judgments underlying both policy and scholarly inquiry into policy is generally conceded today. While the scientist in his theoretical work is primarily concerned with the "is" rather than the "ought," he has learnt from experience how much error can arise from naïve unawareness of one's own value preferences.

In the twenties it was assumed that all peoples wanted peace and justice in just the way Americans supposedly did and that these two values moreover were always compatible. When in the thirties, scholars set out to attack these assumptions as naïve, unrealistic and in fact hypocritical, they in turn, with little more realism, took it for granted that power and national survival were the values to which all states were unalterably dedicated. Much work, then, is still to be done by the philosopher of values if only for the sake of scientific discipline.

To accept this does not mean believing that such philosophical investigation could arrive at knowledge of a pattern of values which is absolutely valid and could guide policy makers absolutely. It may be wiser to expect and desire no more than clarification of the values of one's own culture and that of other peoples and convincing arguments to back the validity of one's own. This is a task, then, which calls for the disciplined use of the skills of meditation, speculation and evaluation most developed among philosophers and theologians, though not for the dogmatism of those who for lack of observable evidence appeal to faith in authority or uncommunicable revelation. Assertions like that of George Kennan that "state behavior is not fit for moral judgment" can, I believe, be disproved by means of evidence as valid as any accepted in the sciences.

The task of developing theory falls predominantly to the political scientist whose specialty are those types of social relations in which power is an important, if not the most essential condition. This does not preclude the likelihood that much of the generalized knowledge will have to be borrowed and adapted from men in the other social sciences and history. Political Science turned to this task in the thirties in sharp reaction to the prevailing "ought"-centered approach of the idealist scholar. While the working model of the realist school, a system of power-seeking nation-states, was closer to reality than the one which unconsciously had guided the thought of its predecessors, the inclination of many "realists" to mistake their highly abstract conceptual model for the living reality of the contemporary world—an error not unknown to economists—led to another wholesome reaction.

In a country blessed with a climate of empiricism, it is hardly surprising that two questions were asked:

1. Were these "states" with their dogmatically alleged uniformities myth or reality?
2. Were the assertions concerning their behavior and relations based on empirically verifiable evidence or were they derived from some alleged metaphysical insight into the nature of man and things?

As a result, behavioral or psychological aspects centering on the unmistakable existence of individual persons and methodological problems were pushed to the fore.

While the swing of the pendulum toward the behavioral elements led to a neglect of the no less real situational components—power configurations, institutional, or geographical setting, e.g.—the benefits of the new outlook for theory proved invaluable. The "fire and water" stage as Kurt Lewin called a similar stage in physics came to an end when generalizations no longer had to be drawn from the behavior of small numbers of highly complex entities such as great powers or empires but could be derived from the study of such abundant simple elements as human demands, expectations, choices, ambitions, fears, and reactions to environmental factors, the atoms, ions, and velocities of international politics.

The concern for empirical verification proved hardly less fruitful, particularly when it became clear that the alternative to unverifiable dogma comprised far more than quantitative measurement. There was danger that the quest for maximum reliability and communicability such as only quantification can provide, would discourage studies on phenomena which were not amenable to such measurement and on the other hand lead to the exertion of effort on the quantitative verification of hypotheses so trivial that they deserved no interest. Today it is agreed that verification can take many forms of observation and introspection and that qualitative difference moreover can in some instances best be expressed by mathematical symbols.

Despite the importance of empirical verification, so often contemptuously neglected in Europe, the main job of the theorist *qua* theorist is not verification but the creative elaboration of fruitful hypotheses which bear on the relationship between specified variables. This in turn calls for much preliminary effort of classification, semantic clarification, detection of critical and identifiable variables, and development of useful concepts. The recent discussion of that elusive and ambiguous concept, the "national interest" has shown to what lengths the theorist must go before he can extricate himself from the verbal trickeries of the political marketplace and come to grips with the underlying problems.

The kinds of topics to which theory will have to address itself, if the ground is to be covered in time, are not hard to find. In fact so much has been left undone that the following represents but a random collection of examples:

1. What types of actors, individual and corporative, national, sub-, trans-, and supranational affect the course of world events and what, e.g., are the factors which give them their position and tend to change their position in the hierarchy of actors? What specifically is the impact of present-day ideological and revolutionary forces on the respective position of major powers and how does it operate?

2. What are objectives of the actors and what, e.g., are the factors which affect the place of an actor on a continuum from unlimited expansionism to self-denying retreat?

3. What are the means at the disposal of the actors and what, e.g., accounts for different degrees of willingness to resort to and to initiate violence or to make specific sacrifices for the sake of increments of power or security?

4. What are the chief determinants of foreign policy and what, e.g., are the relationships between a determinant such as a specified geographical setting and specific policies?

5. What are the chief configurations of power (such as bipolarity or balance) and what, e.g., accounts for identifiable variations of national attitude (such as quest for dominance or indifference) in the response to these configurations?

6. What are the uniformities, varieties and changes of national interpretation of the national interest and what influence, e.g., do class structure, national traditions, myths, and culture or external danger, respectively, tend to have on such interpretation?

7. What types of policy for the promotion of peace or the solution of conflict are there, on what assumptions do the expectations of their efficacy rest and what, e.g., are the factors upon which the chances of success of mediation, deterrence through power, punitive peacemaking, peace propaganda, or enunciation of moral principles depend?

In view of so much need for theoretical investigation, the question arises whether steps can be taken to stimulate and facilitate research in this field. The answer must come for the most part out of the discussion because it can only arise from the experience of those engaged in work of this kind. The following is said in the way of tentative suggestions:

1. Students writing Ph.D. dissertations in international relations tend to shy away from the theoretical problems or have to be dissuaded from tackling them. The risk is often too great that work undertaken here may turn out to be too difficult, too time-consuming, or too inconclusive and that, even if successful, no group of readers will agree on its merits. It would be well worthwhile for a group of interested instructors in the field to get together in conference to work out suggestions of manageable types of theoretical dissertations (image studies have recently proved workable and attractive to students, though some get bogged down in a word counting type of content analysis which, compared with the effort, adds little to the results).

2. If theoretical work is little suited for dissertations, it is an ideal field for particularly gifted and sophisticated young men, rapidly growing in number, who would be prepared to devote one or two years to post-doctoral research under the guidance of older scholars. Such opportunity exists at Princeton but might usefully be extended in a way which would permit promising candidates to work at places and under theorists of their choice.

3. Mature scholars are being discouraged from extensive theoretical work in this field because the chances of publication of works on a high level of abstraction are slim, if they exceed the length of an article. *World Politics* has been a relief to many, but a book series or books put out by a group of collaborating scholars would be worth considering.

4. "Elder statesmen" in the field of theory frequently lack the time for research because of the increasing burden of other activities. Periods of leave from teaching and administration, more ample research assistance, opportunity to continue research under favorable conditions after retirement come to mind as possible solutions.

5. Personal contact among theorists is infrequent, though, sporadically, series of conferences on international relations have been held. The need for closer contact is likely to be felt most by those who work on isolated posts, with few or no advanced graduate students or in a climate unhospitable to theoretical effort. It has been suggested, therefore, that some form of regular get-togethers for discussion and exploration of problems (a seminar?) deserves attention. While most work in theory must necessarily be carried on by scholars working individually, help, criticism, and encouragement on the part of competent colleagues is invaluable, often indispensable. Many of the most promising young scholars of recent vintage, too, are scattered over the country in colleges where they lack the stimulation which they received as graduate students in seminars dealing with relatively advanced theoretical problems.

It is to be hoped that the discussion will uncover many other means of promoting any or all of the types of effort upon which progress in theoretical knowledge depends. There is no need to fear that such promotion will cut in on the practical application of theory to concrete and pressing problems of the times; the appeal which policy advice exerts on the scholar can be relied upon to be sufficient if it is not excessive.

Folder 69, Box 8, Series 910, Research Group 3.1, Rockefeller Foundation Archives, Rockefeller Archive Center, Sleepy Hollow, N.Y.

CONTRIBUTORS

NICOLAS GUILHOT is a senior researcher at the CNRS (Centre National de la Recherche Scientifique) and visiting scholar at NYU. He has previously taught at the London School of Economics and Columbia University. His work focuses on the history of the social sciences, international relations, democracy, and human rights. His publications include *The Democracy Makers: Human Rights and the Politics of Global Order* (New York: Columbia University Press, 2005) and numerous articles in *Actes de la recherche en sciences sociales, Minerva, International Political Sociology*, and *Constellations*, among other journals. He is currently working on a history of IR theory entitled *Morgenthau's Flight: International Relations from Decisionism to Rational Choice*.

ROBERT JERVIS is Adlai E. Stevenson Professor of International Politics at Columbia University. His *Why Intelligence Fails: Lessons from the Iranian Revolution and the Iraq War* will be published by Cornell University Press in early 2010. His *System Effects: Complexity in Political Life* (Princeton University Press, 1997) was a co-winner of the APSA's Psychology Section Best Book Award, and *The Meaning of the Nuclear Revolution* (Cornell University Press, 1989) won the Grawemeyer Award for Ideas Improving World Order. He is also the author of *Perception and Misperception in International Politics* (Princeton University Press, 1976), *The Logic of Images in International Relations* (Princeton University Press, 1970; 2nd ed., Columbia University Press, 1989), and *The Illogic of American Nuclear Strategy* (Cornell University Press, 1984). His most recent book is *American Foreign Policy in a New Era* (Routledge, 2005). He was president of the American Political Science Association in 2000–2001 and has received career-achievement awards from the International Society of Political Psychology and ISA's Security Studies Section. In 2006, he received the National Academy of Science's triannual award for behavioral science's contributions to avoiding nuclear war. He was a Guggenheim Fellow in 1978–1979 and is a Fellow of the American Association for the Advancement of Science and the American Academy of Arts and Sciences. He chairs the Historical Review Panel for the CIA and is a National Intelligence Council associate. His current research problems include the nature of beliefs, IR theory and the cold war, and the links between signaling and perception.

PHILIP E. MIROWSKI is Carl E. Koch Professor of Economics and the History of Science and Fellow of the Reilly Center for Science, Technology, and Values at the

University of Notre Dame. His areas of specialization are in the history and philosophy of economics and the politics and economics of knowledge, with subsidiary areas in evolutionary computational economics, the economics of science and technological change, science studies, and the history of the natural sciences. His most recent books are *The Effortless Economy of Science* (Duke University Press, 2004; winner of the Ludwig Fleck Prize from the Society for the Social Studies of Science), *Machine Dreams* (Cambridge University Press, 2001), *ScienceMart™* (Harvard University Press, 2010), and the edited volumes *Agreement on Demand* (Duke University Press, 2006), *Science Bought and Sold* (University of Chicago Press, 2001), and *The Road from Mont Pèlerin* (Harvard University Press, 2009). His work has previously been the subject of a conference at Duke University (proceedings published as *Non-Natural Economics*, ed. Neil de Marchi) and one of the profiles in Michael Szenberg, ed., *Passion and Craft*. His book *More Heat Than Light* (Cambridge University Press, 1989) has been translated into French (2001). He has been the recipient of fellowships from Fulbright, the Santa Fe Institute, and NYU, and was elected visiting fellow at All Souls' College Oxford. He has received grants from the NSF, NEH, and the Seng Foundation, and was elected president of the History of Economics Society for 2011.

INDERJEET PARMAR is a professor of government at the University of Manchester. His research interests focus on the history, ideology, and politics of the U.S. foreign-policy establishment and Anglo-American foreign-policy elites. He is the author of several books, including *Think Tanks and Power in Foreign Policy* (Palgrave, 2004), and journal articles. He is currently writing a research monograph entitled *Foundations of the American Century: Ford, Carnegie, and Rockefeller Foundations and U.S. Foreign Affairs, 1920s to the Present* (Columbia University Press, 2011). He is vice chair of the British International Studies Association.

BRIAN C. SCHMIDT is an associate professor of political science at Carleton University, Ottawa. He is the author of *The Political Discourse of Anarchy: A Disciplinary History of International Relations* (SUNY Press, 1998) and *Imperialism and Internationalism in the Discipline of International Relations*, co-edited with David Long (SUNY Press, 2005). His articles have appeared in *International Studies Quarterly*, *The Review of International Studies*, *Millennium: Journal of International Relations*, and others.

JACK SNYDER is the Robert and Renée Belfer Professor of International Relations in the department of political science and at the Saltzman Institute of War and Peace Studies at Columbia University. His books include *Electing to Fight: Why Emerging Democracies Go to War* (MIT Press, 2005), co-authored with Edward D. Mansfield; *From Voting to Violence: Democratization and Nationalist Conflict* (Norton, 2000); and *Myths of Empire: Domestic Politics and International Ambition.* (Cornell University Press, 1991).

ANDERS STEPHANSON is the Andrew and Virginia Rudd Professor of History at Columbia University, where he teaches the history of U.S. foreign relations along with historiography and other matters. He is forever trying to write a conceptual history of the U.S. project known as the cold war.

OLE WÆVER is professor of international relations at the University of Copenhagen and director of CAST, Centre for Advanced Security Theory. Among his books are *Regions and Powers: The Structure of International Security* (with Barry Buzan, 2003) and *International Relations Scholarship Around the World* (ed. with Arlene B. Tickner, 2009). Recent articles include "Macrosecuritisation and Security Constellations: Reconsidering Scale in Securitisation Theory" (with Barry Buzan) in the *Review of International Studies* (2009); "Peace and Security: Two Evolving Concepts and Their Changing Relationship," in *Globalization and Environmental Challenges: Reconceptualizing Security in the Twenty-First Century* (Springer, 2009); and "Waltz's Theory of Theory" in *International Relations* (2009). He is coauthor (with Katherine Richardson et al.) of "Climate Change: Global Risks, Challenges, and Decisions: A Synthesis Report" (http://www.climatecongress.ku.dk; June 2009). Ole Wæver was elected to the Royal Danish Academy of Sciences and Letters in 2007.

INDEX